Applied Social Science Methodology

An Introductory Guide

JOHN GERRING
University of Texas at Austin

DINO CHRISTENSON
Boston University

CAMBRIDGE
UNIVERSITY PRESS

CAMBRIDGE
UNIVERSITY PRESS

University Printing House, Cambridge CB2 8BS, United Kingdom

One Liberty Plaza, 20th Floor, New York, NY 10006, USA

477 Williamstown Road, Port Melbourne, VIC 3207, Australia

4843/24, 2nd Floor, Ansari Road, Daryaganj, Delhi – 110002, India

79 Anson Road, #06–04/06, Singapore 079906

Cambridge University Press is part of the University of Cambridge.

It furthers the University's mission by disseminating knowledge in the pursuit of education, learning, and research at the highest international levels of excellence.

www.cambridge.org
Information on this title: www.cambridge.org/9781107071476
10.1017/9781107775558

First published 2017

Printed in the United States of America by Sheridan Books, Inc.

A catalogue record for this publication is available from the British Library.

Library of Congress Cataloging-in-Publication Data
Names: Gerring, John, 1962– author. | Christenson, Dino, author.
Title: Applied social science methodology : an introductory guide / John Gerring,
University of Texas, Austin, Dino Christenson, Boston University.
Description: Cambridge, United Kingdom ; New York, NY : Cambridge University Press,
2017. | Includes bibliographical references and index.
Identifiers: LCCN 2016044617| ISBN 9781107071476 (Hardback : alk. paper) |
ISBN 9781107416819 (pbk. : alk. paper)
Subjects: LCSH: Social sciences–Methodology.
Classification: LCC H61 .G4659 2017 | DDC 300–dc23 LC record available
at https://lccn.loc.gov/2016044617

ISBN 978-1-107-07147-6 Hardback
ISBN 978-1-107-41681-9 Paperback

Applied Social Science Methodology
An Introductory Guide

This textbook provides a clear, concise, and comprehensive introduction to methodological issues encountered by the various social science disciplines. It emphasizes applications, with detailed examples, so that readers can put these methods to work in their research. Within a unified framework, John Gerring and Dino Christenson integrate a variety of methods – descriptive and causal, observational and experimental, qualitative and quantitative. The text covers a wide range of topics including research design, data-gathering techniques, statistics, theoretical frameworks, and social science writing. It is designed both for those attempting to make sense of social science, as well as those aiming to conduct original research. The text is complemented by practice questions, exercises, examples, key term highlighting, and additional resources, including related readings and websites. An essential resource for undergraduate and postgraduate programs in communications, criminal justice, economics, business, finance, management, education, environmental policy, international development, law, political science, public health, public policy, social work, sociology, and urban planning.

JOHN GERRING is Professor of Government at University of Texas at Austin. He is the author of many books including *Social Science Methodology: A Unified Framework*, second edition (Cambridge, 2012) and *Case Study Research: Principles and Practices*, second edition (Cambridge, 2017). He is also co-editor of the Cambridge series, 'Strategies for Social Inquiry'.

DINO P. CHRISTENSON is Associate Professor of Political Science at Boston University and a Faculty Affiliate at the Hariri Institute for Computational Science & Engineering. His articles have appeared in *American Political Science Review*, *American Journal of Political Science*, *Political Behavior*, and *Social Networks*, among others.

Contents

Contents

Detailed Contents

Detailed Contents

Figures

Tables

Abbreviations and Notation

Symbol	Description
A	Event or option
a	Y-intercept or constant of a regression equation
α	Significance level (read as "alpha")
$\lvert\rvert$	Absolute value operator
ATE	Average treatment effect
ATT	Average treatment effect on the treated
B	Event or option
b	Slope coefficient for independent variable (read as "beta")
$\vert$	Expression of conditionality
CI	Confidence interval
Cov	Covariance
D_{ij}	Distance from observation i to j
D_{Greedy}	Distance from a greedy algorithm
$D_{Optimal}$	Distance from an optimal algorithm
ΔX	Change in values of X (read as "delta X")
Δ_i	Causal treatment effect for individual i
df	Degrees of freedom
$\ldots$	Expression of omission of values in a repeated operation (read as "ellipsis")
e	Error term or random component, usually of a regression equation
E	Expectation or expected value
ESS_Y	Explained sum of squares for Y
exp	Natural exponential function
H_X	Hypothesis about the effect of X on Y
i	Individual or unit in the sample of observations, not j
$\perp\!\!\!\perp$	Expression of independence
j	Individual or unit in the sample of observations, not i
k	Maximum number in a series of variables or coefficients
M	Mechanism or pathway connecting X to Y
MOE	Margin of error
MS_e	Mean squared errors
μ	Mean of a population or probability distribution (read as "mu")
N	Sample size or number of observations, but occasionally units or cases
N_{Col}	Number of cases in a column

(cont.)

Symbol	Description
N_{Row}	Number of cases in a row
NA	Expression that value is not available, unknown or missing
$1 - \alpha$	Confidence level
P	Probability
p	P-value
Pct_{Col}	Column percents
Pct_{Row}	Row percents
π	Constant value, approximately 3.14 (read as "pi")
$Prop$	Proportion
Q	Variable; the antecedent cause (to X) that may be used as an instrumental variable
r	Pearson's correlation coefficient
r^2	Coefficient of determination
RSS_e	Residual sum of squared errors
$s_{\overline{X}_1 - \overline{X}_2}$	Standard error of difference between means
s_b	Standard error of b
s^2	Variance of a sample
s	Standard deviation of a sample
SE_e	Standard error of the estimate
Σ	Summation operator
σ	Standard deviation of a population or probability distribution
$\sigma_{\overline{X}}$	Standard error of the mean
σ^2	Variance of a population or probability distribution
SP	Sum of products
SS_X	Sum of squares for X
SS_Y	Sum of squares for Y
T_i	Treatment condition for individual i
$Time_{1-N}$	Time-periods, usually referring to occasions when key variables are measured
t	T-ratio
X	Variable; usually an independent variable of causal interest
$\overline{X}$	Mean of X (read as "X-bar")
X_C	Control group condition, $X = 0$ when binary
X_T	Treatment group condition, $X = 1$ when binary
$X \leftrightarrow Y$	Expression that X causes Y and Y causes X
$X \rightarrow Y$	Expression that X causes Y
$X - Y$	Expression that X covaries with Y
Y	Variable; usually the dependent variable or outcome
$\overline{Y}$	Mean of Y (read as "Y-bar")
$\hat{Y}$	Predicted, fitted or estimated values of Y (read as "Y-hat")
Y_i	Outcome or effect for individual i

Abbreviations and Notation

(cont.)

Symbol	Description
Y_{iC}	Potential outcome if i does not receive treatment (i.e., in control group)
Y_{iT}	Potential outcome if i receives treatment (i.e., in treatment group)
Z	Background factor(s) that affect Y and may also affect X, and thus may serve as confounder(s)
z	Z-score

Acknowledgments

We are grateful for comments and suggestions received from Joe Bizup (Chapter 14), Taylor Boas (Part IV), Colin Elman (Chapter 13), Diana Kapiszewski (Chapter 13), Ryan Moore (Chapter 23), Max Palmer (Chapter 17), Laurel Smith-Doerr (Chapter 16), Peter Spiegler (Chapter 5), Arun Swamy (Chapter 5), and Susan Wishinsky (Chapter 11), as well as reviewers for Cambridge University Press. We are also grateful for our students, Christina Jarymowycz, Joshua Yesnowitz, Matthew Maguire, Sahar Abi-Hassan, and Cantay Caliskan, who worked on various aspects of the manuscript and related materials. Finally, we want to thank our editor at the Press, John Haslam, who shepherded this book along the path to publication, rendering wise counsel and keeping our noses to the proverbial grindstone.

Chapters 1–4, 6–8, 10, 12, and 17 draw on material published originally in Gerring's *Social Science Methodology: A Unified Framework* (Cambridge University Press, 2012). Chapter 9 is based loosely on Gerring's "Selecting Cases for Intensive Analysis: A Diversity of Goals and Methods" (*Sociological Methods & Research*, 2016, joint with Lee Cojocaru) and *Case Study Research: Principles and Practices*, 2nd edn. (Cambridge University Press, 2017). Readers may refer to these works for a more detailed treatment of these subjects.

Preface

Once upon a time, the practice of social science could be understood as the application of commonsense and intuition – something you might develop in the course of growing up. This is no longer true, or only partly true. Although commonsense and intuition are still useful, the social science disciplines have moved well beyond what can be understood without specialized training.

If you want to become an artist, musician, engineer – or pretty much anything, these days – developing your technique in these highly specialized areas is essential. It takes great dedication, countless hours of concentrated work, and professional guidance. The same may be said for social science in the contemporary era. One may mourn the death of the amateur social scientist. But one might as well reconcile oneself to the fact.

In response, methods courses have proliferated at both the undergraduate and graduate level. Likewise, methodological skills are in high demand in the social sciences and their cognate professions. Successful careers in government, communications, education, social work, business, law, and all of the policy fields require a solid grounding in methodology. Whether one is applying for graduate programs or for a job, the material covered in this book should stand one in good stead.

Indeed, a working knowledge of social science tools of analysis may prove more crucial for one's career than whatever substantive knowledge one acquires in the course of a college education. What one knows is less important than what one can *do*, and what one can do depends on a working knowledge of methodology.

These developments may be viewed as part of a broader sea-change, driven by the rise of computers and the Internet. With sophisticated IT tools at our disposal, factual knowledge about a subject is no longer at a premium and can usually be obtained from a Google search or from a specially designed database in milliseconds. Likewise, any repetitive procedure can be programmed as a set of algorithms on a computer. This means that the value of an education is no longer in the facts or established protocols you might learn. This sort of knowledge can be produced by machines in a more timely and accurate fashion than by the human brain. Our value-added, as humans, stems from our capacity to identify important questions and think through practical solutions to those questions in a creative fashion. This is the function of a broadly pitched course on methodology and it is what this text is designed to convey.

The present text is appropriate for use in introductory or intermediate methods courses at the undergraduate, master's, or doctoral level. It is designed to assist those who are attempting to make sense of social science as well as those who are conducting original research. We assume no prior methodological knowledge, though we do presume that the reader has some background in at least one field of social science, e.g., anthropology, communications, criminal justice, economics (including business, finance, and management), education, environmental policy, international development, law, political science, psychology, public health, public policy, social work, sociology, or urban planning.[1]

We try to address key points of social science methodology in an applied fashion – so that readers can put these methods to work. Note that insofar as we can impact the societies we live in (in a conscious fashion) social science is indispensable. We can't enhance economic growth, health, and education – or reduce poverty, crime, conflict, inequality, and global warming – without consulting the work of social scientists. To understand that work, and to conduct original research on these topics, an understanding of the methodological principles underlying this set of practices is indispensable. We hope that you will approach social science methodology not simply as a means for self-advancement (though there is surely nothing wrong with that!) but also as a set of tools for changing – and preserving – the world.

A Wide-Ranging Approach

In many textbook markets the offerings are fairly similar. A standard format has been developed over the years that everyone adheres to (more or less), and the courses that utilize these texts bear a strong resemblance to each other. There is scholarly consensus in the field about how to teach a subject.

This does not describe the topic at hand. Gazing out across the social science disciplines one finds a wide range of methodological approaches, reflected in a wide range of textbooks. As a service to the prospective reader (and instructor) it may be helpful to indicate how this volume differs from other textbooks in this crowded field – and why.

Some methods texts limit their purview to a specific discipline, e.g., political science, sociology, or economics. This may seem reasonable, and it allows one to focus on a set of substantive problems that orient a field. However, few substantive problems are confined to a single discipline. In order to learn about crime, for example, you will probably need to read across the fields of sociology, psychology, law, political science, economics, and criminology. The same is true for most other problems, which do not observe neat disciplinary boundaries.

Of course, important differences in theory and method characterize the disciplines. But it does not follow that one is well-served by a text that offers only one view of how to conduct social science. A narrow methodological training does not prepare one to integrate knowledge from other disciplines. To understand the range of literature on a topic and to think creatively about methods that might be applied to that topic it makes sense to adopt an ecumenical approach. Hence, this book focuses broadly on the methodological principles of *social science* rather than on methods practiced within a single discipline.

Some texts are focused primarily on quantitative methods, i.e., statistics or econometrics. While these are important skills, this approach has a tendency to reduce methodology to mathematics. And this, in turn, presents a narrow and technical vision of social science that is not faithful to the way in which social science is practiced (or, at any rate, to the way it should be practiced). Statistics are the handmaiden of methodology, not the other way around.

Some texts are focused exclusively on qualitative methods. This is a hard topic to define, and these books are varied in their content and approach. A few are strongly anti-positivist, meaning that they reject the scientific ideal as it has been understood in the natural sciences. While we agree with the standard critique of a narrowly positivist approach to social science we also think the natural sciences and social sciences share a good deal in common. In any case, a book that treats only qualitative components of social science is missing a good deal of the action. Both qualitative and quantitative approaches are required as part of everyone's social science education. Certainly, they are both required in order to make sense of the social science literature on a subject.

One way to handle this problem is to include both qualitative and quantitative methods within a single text but to keep them separate, with the idea that the tools are distinct and each draws on a different epistemology (theory of knowledge). In our opinion, this claim is difficult to sustain: "qualitative" and "quantitative" tools tend to blend together and their epistemological traditions are not as far apart as they might seem. More important, a segregated approach to knowledge is not helpful to the advancement of social science. If knowledge on a topic is to grow it must be based on a unified epistemology that encompasses both qualitative and quantitative methods. This is the approach taken in the present text.

The most distinctive feature of this book is its wide-ranging approach to the subject. The text is intended to encompass all of the social science disciplines, qualitative and quantitative methods, descriptive and causal knowledge, and experimental and observational research designs. We also address the nuts and bolts of how to conduct research, as laid out below.

Naturally, there are some topics that we do not have time or space to engage.[2] However, relative to most methods texts this one qualifies as highly inclusive, offering an entrée to myriad aspects of social science methodology. To our way of thinking, these topics are all essential. And they are also closely linked. While there are many ways to do good social science these diverse approaches also share certain common elements. Only by grasping the full extent of social science's diversity can we glimpse its underlying unity.

Outline and Features

With a text of this size the reader may want to read strategically, focusing on chapters that are most relevant to your current work and interests, skipping or skimming chapters that cover topics about which you are already well-informed. A good textbook need not be read cover-to-cover.

However, readers should also be aware that the book is organized in a cumulative fashion, with later sections building on previous sections. Something may be lost if you peruse the text in a scattershot fashion.

Part I sets forth the basic *building blocks* of social science methodology. Chapter 1 introduces our topic, social science methodology, expanding on themes in the Preface and introducing several specific examples that will be referred to throughout the book. Subsequent chapters within this section focus on (2) arguments (including theories and hypotheses), (3) concepts and measures, and (4) analyses.

Part II focuses on *causal* arguments and analysis. This topic is broken down into chapters dealing with (5) causal frameworks, (6) causal hypotheses and analyses, (7) experimental research designs, (8) non-experimental research designs, (9) case study research designs, and (10) diverse tools of causal inference.

Part III deals with the process of research and the presentation of results. This includes (11) reading and reviewing the literature on a subject, (12) brainstorming (finding a research topic and a specific hypothesis), (13) data gathering, (14) writing, (15) public speaking, and (16) ethics.

Part IV deals with statistics. This is divided into several topics: (17) data management, (18) univariate statistics, (19) probability distributions, (20) statistical inference, (21) bivariate statistics, (22) regression, and (23) causal inference.

Every effort has been made to divide up these subjects in a way that makes logical sense and to avoid unnecessary redundancies. Of course, topics do not always neatly divide into separate chapters and sections. There is a holistic quality to social science methodology; diverse topics invariably bleed into one another. To assist the reader, we indicate where the reader might look for further elaboration of an issue. You may also consult the Detailed Table of Contents or the Index.

An objective of the book is to introduce readers to *key terms* of social science methodology. When a term is first introduced, or when it is formally defined, it is printed in bold. At the end of each chapter the reader will find a list of these bolded terms, which may be useful for purposes of review. In the Index, we indicate the page on which a term is defined by printing that number in bold.

The online materials for this book include series of questions and exercises for each chapter under the heading Inquiries. These inquiries serve a review function, summarizing the main points of the chapter. Some questions are speculative, building on the material presented but also moving beyond it. Instructors may draw on these inquiries to structure class discussion, to construct quizzes or exams, or for assignments.

In posing questions and constructing exercises we are sensitive to the fact that readers of the book have diverse disciplinary backgrounds. Consequently, many of the inquiries are presented in a manner that allows for tailoring the questions to the reader's particular field of expertise. Rather than imposing a particular concept or theory on a methodological issue we might ask readers to choose a concept or theory with which they are familiar and employ it to address a question in their course of study.

An introductory textbook of modest length must deal with topics in an expeditious fashion. Accordingly, we have omitted many qualifications, caveats, and citations to the literature in favor of a streamlined approach. Although the treatment in this text is somewhat more detailed than that found in many textbooks it is still highly selective when placed within the context of scholarly work on these subjects. This is the cost of writing a short book on a long subject. Readers who choose to continue in some branch of social science should view this book as a point of departure on their methodological journey. The online materials include lists of suggested readings and web sites related to topics broached in each chapter, under the heading Resources. Consider these references as an invitation to further study.

Building Blocks

This part of the book is focused on fundamental elements of social science, elements that form building blocks for everything else. In Chapter 1, we lay out the rationale for a unified approach to our subject, social science methodology. In Chapter 2, we discuss social science arguments, with primary attention to descriptive and causal arguments. In Chapter 3, we turn to the topic of conceptualization and measurement. In Chapter 4, we discuss the generic features of empirical analysis.

1 A Unified Framework

The purpose of social science is to make a difference in the world by applying reason and evidence to problems of general concern. Every question of social science relates (or *ought* to relate) to normative concepts such as justice, democracy, human rights, prosperity, happiness, or equality.

What distinguishes **social science** from casual conversation, journalism, or political rhetoric may be summarized as follows. First, social science involves the systematic application of reason and evidence to problems with explicit attention to method and to possible sources of error. Second, social science is accompanied by realistic estimates of uncertainty with respect to whatever conclusions are drawn from the evidence. Third, social science attempts to provide a comprehensive treatment of a subject within whatever scope-conditions are defined by the study. All relevant information should be included; none should be arbitrarily excluded. Finally, social science adopts a disinterested posture with respect to all goals except the truth. Its purpose is to get as close to the truth as possible, in all its complexity, rather than to provoke, entertain, elucidate moral truths, or advance polemical claims.

These features render social science less stimulating than other media, where there is generally a premium on brevity, accessibility, provocation, righteousness, or humor. Social science is a sober profession. However, for those excited by the prospect of getting it right, and willing to expend some energy to get there, the practice of social science may be highly rewarding.

Consider the problem of *crime*, a topic that often evokes hot rhetoric and strong opinions. Most media reports and political speeches offer little useful information about the prevalence of crime, its sources, and its potential solutions. Instead, they exploit the public's fascination with gruesome events and, in the process, provoke fear. From this perspective, the cold gaze of social science offers some relief.

Researchers have spent a good deal of time studying the rise and fall of violent crime in the United States and elsewhere. In the early 1960s, the United States enjoyed a low homicide rate of 5 murders per 100,000 inhabitants. Over the next two decades this rate doubled – to 10 per 100,000 inhabitants – peaking in the late 1970s or early 1980s, at which point the United States could claim the highest rate of violent crime of any advanced industrial country. Subsequently, the crime wave began to fall, and it now rests approximately where it was in 1960.[3] What factors might explain this extraordinary rise and subsequent decline?[4] What impact did the rise-and-fall of crime have on attitudes (e.g., toward immigrants and minorities) and on behavior (e.g., voting turnout and party affiliation)?

Those who study crime cross-nationally also rely on murder rates to measure overall crime. Although cross-national statistics are prone to error, the greatest over-performers and under-performers are evident. At present, the highest violent crime rates in the world are found in Belize, Côte d'Ivoire, El Salvador, Guatemala, Honduras, Jamaica, and Venezuela – where there are 38–96 murder victims per 100,000 inhabitants every year. By contrast, murder rates in 25 countries are equal to, or less than, one per 100,000. This is an extraordinary range of variation, and it is only partly a product of economic development. Note that the murder capitals identified above are by no means the poorest countries in the world, and many relatively poor countries have murder rates of less than three per 100,000 – including Algeria, Armenia, Azerbaijan, Bangladesh, Bhutan, China, Egypt, Fiji, Iran, Jordan, Maldives, Micronesia, Nepal, São Tomé, Tajikistan, Tonga, and Vanuatu.[5] Another fascinating puzzle.

These questions are causal. But if we probe a bit we will quickly encounter issues of conceptualization and measurement. How shall we define criminal activity? Is murder a useful proxy for crime in general? What distinguishes murder from politically motivated acts of violence such as those accompanying terrorism or civil insurrection? (Is the Oklahoma City bombing, which claimed the lives of 168 Americans in 1995, a multiple homicide, or an act of domestic terrorism?) How has the definition of crime changed over time? How does it differ across countries or across regions within a country? How is crime understood within different communities?

These are the sorts of questions social science aims to address, and they are highly consequential. Improvements in our understanding of crime should help us to design better criminal justice policies. Does community policing work? Does cleaning up visible manifestations of lawlessness in a neighborhood (e.g., fixing broken windows) affect the crime rate in that neighborhood? How effective are deterrents such as harsh jail sentences or capital punishment? How effective is the alternative approach based on rehabilitation of convicted criminals? Do features of our educational system affect the propensity of children to engage in criminal activity? Is crime rooted in socioeconomic deprivation? How is it affected by different social policies? Do different policy solutions work in different contexts, or for different sorts of criminal activity?

Those interested in questions like these should also be interested in social science **methodology**. The reason is that complex questions elicit debate among scholars. To understand this debate – to see why researchers agree and disagree and to make a determination about which is most believable – one needs to understand the nature of the theories and the evidence employed to evaluate theories and test related hypotheses.

Of course, most citizens and policymakers do not spend a great deal of time reading social science. Instead, they read journalistic accounts of social science research. There is surely nothing wrong with this. At the same time, one must bear in mind that newspaper articles and blog postings rarely explain the sort of background considerations that would allow one to informatively choose among rival conclusions about the same subject. This is not their fault; it is a limitation of the genre. The attraction of journalism is that it offers a brief account of a complex subject, suitable for consumption over breakfast, in the car, or on the train. If one wishes to go deeper – to read the reports upon which journalistic accounts are based – one must have a passing knowledge of social science methodology. (One would hope that journalists who offer pithy summaries of social science work also possess that deeper knowledge.)

Methodology should not be confused with a mastery of facts. While the latter is important, it is by no means sufficient to a determination of truth. Indeed, when experts disagree it is rarely over the facts of a case. It is, rather, over how those facts should be interpreted. An understanding of methodology involves an understanding of the logic of inquiry, i.e., the way in which one reaches conclusions from a body of evidence. This is what an informed consumer of social science must have if she is to decipher social science work on a subject.

For those who aim to become *producers* of social science the importance of methodology is even more apparent. Anyone who is dissatisfied with the field of criminology as it now stands would do well to design their own study. And designing such a study will require considerable training in the wiles of methodology if the result is to add anything to our knowledge of this complex subject. Methodology thus lies at the heart of contemporary political debates, providing the set of tools by which we might tackle social problems in a rational fashion.

The Purpose of Unity

This book embraces a broad view of social science. It encompasses work that is primarily descriptive as well as work that is primarily causal. It encompasses work that is experimental (involving a randomized treatment) and observational (i.e., non-experimental). It encompasses quantitative and qualitative research. It encompasses a range of strategies of data collection, from standardized surveys to ethnography.

The book is also intended to encompass a wide range of disciplines, including anthropology, communications, criminal justice, economics (and subfields such as business, finance, and management), education, environmental policy, international development, law, political science, psychology, public health, public policy, social work, sociology, and urban planning. Although these fields focus on different substantive problems, the methods they employ – and the methodological obstacles they encounter – are quite similar. Indeed, there is almost as much methodological diversity *within* a single discipline such as anthropology, sociology, or political science as there is *across* these disciplines.

Of course, there are many ways to do good social science. Sometimes, it makes sense to combine diverse methods in a single study – a **multi-method** approach to research (see Chapter 10). In any case, much depends on the nature of the evidence available and the nature of the question under investigation. It would be folly to propose a uniform method or theoretical framework for all of social science, or even for a single discipline. Methods pluralism is easy to justify. Indeed, it is impossible to avoid.

However, beneath the diversity of methods there is (or at least ought to be) a degree of methodological consensus.[6] Note that if standards of truth are understandable only within the context of specific fields or theoretical traditions there is no way to adjudicate among contending views. Each truth becomes entirely self-reflective. Thus, while it is reasonable to cultivate a diversity of tools, it is unreasonable to cultivate a diversity of methodological standards. A discovery in sociology ought to be understandable, and appraisable, by those who are not sociologists; otherwise, it cannot claim the status of truth. Nor will it be of much use to anyone outside of sociology.

Moreover, as a matter of good scholarship, writers in the social sciences ought to be able to converse with one another. Economists interested in political economy should be cognizant of – and should seek to incorporate, wherever possible – work in political science. And vice versa. Even arguments demand a common frame of reference. Without such shared ground they are merely statements of position. Here, science degenerates into a chorus of yeas and nays reminiscent of *Monty Python*'s "Argument Clinic" sketch.[7]

This is why the natural scope for the present volume is social science writ-large rather than a single field or subfield. Thinking about methodological topics in diverse settings forces us to think in new ways, to justify our choices on methodological grounds rather than on grounds of convenience or familiarity. It is not sufficient for sociologists to say that they do things in a certain way because that's what they have always done. Likewise for economists, political scientists, and the rest of our quarrelsome band.

Accordingly, this book aims to provide a framework that reaches across the social sciences, providing common ground for those engaged in diverse topics and diverse research methods. We have looked to uncover the shared norms that govern activity – implicitly or explicitly – in the community of social scientists. What makes a work of social science true, useful, or convincing ("scientific")? Why do we prefer one treatment of a subject over another? These are the sorts of ground-level judgments that define the activity of methodology. With these judgments, we hope to identify the threads that tie our methodological intuitions together into a relatively unified framework across the disciplines of social science.

Our approach centers on the identification of basic *tasks* of social science, *strategies* enlisted to achieve those tasks, and *criteria* associated with each task and strategy. These are laid out schematically in tables throughout the book.

Note that each task and criterion is viewed as a *matter of degree*. Achieving precision, for example, is not an either/or proposition. One tries to obtain as precise an estimate as possible, in full knowledge that there will always be some element of imprecision (variability). The same goes for other tasks and criteria.

Note also that the tasks, strategies, and criteria laid out in the subsequent pages are sometimes in conflict with one another. For example, theories aim for both precision and breadth; however, achieving one may involve sacrifices for the other. Methodological *tradeoffs* of this sort are ubiquitous. This means that every task, strategy, or criterion must be understood with a ceteris paribus caveat. Precision is desirable, all other things being equal.

Although a relative and multidimensional standard may seem rather open-ended, this does not imply that anything goes. It means that the researcher must search for the theory and research design that maximizes goodness along a set of (relatively fixed) dimensions, reconciling divergent demands wherever possible. The goodness of a theory or research design is therefore judged only by reference to all possible theories or research designs that have been devised, or might be devised, to address the same research question. Best means *best possible*.[8]

This allows for all sorts of theories and research designs to enter the social science pantheon without shame or disparagement – but only if no better expedient can be found. It supposes that studies with weak theories or evidence answer a very difficult question: could an argument or research design be improved upon? What is achievable, *under the circumstances*?

If a research ideal is entirely out of reach – by virtue of lack of data, lack of funding sources, lack of cooperation on the part of relevant authorities, or ethical considerations – it is pointless to admonish an author for failing to achieve it. Perfection becomes the enemy of scientific progress. We must guard against the possibility that work adding value to what we know about a subject might be rejected even when no better approach is forthcoming. Standards must be realistic.

If, on the other hand, a better approach to a given subject can be envisioned and the costs of implementation are not too great, a study that chooses not to utilize that demonstrably better approach is rightly criticized. We must guard against the possibility that second-best approaches will drive out first-best approaches simply because the former adopt easier or more familiar methods. Mediocrity should not be the enemy of excellence. This is what we mean by *best-possible, under the circumstances*.

Equally important is to embrace the uncertainty of our enterprise, honestly and forthrightly. Weaknesses in design and analysis should be openly acknowledged rather than hidden in footnotes or obscured in jargon and endless statistical tests. This is important not just as a matter of intellectual honesty but also for the long-run development of the social sciences. The cumulation of knowledge in a field depends more on methodological transparency than on "statistically significant" results.

Examples

The following chapters intersperse abstract methodological points with specific examples. While these examples vary, we draw repeatedly on three subjects that have played a key role in contemporary social science and in recent methodological debates: **worker-training programs**, **social capital**, and **democracy**. Readers who are unfamiliar with this terrain may use the following sections to acquaint themselves with these subject areas – though we do not pretend to offer anything like a comprehensive review.

While each has its disciplinary home turf – economics, sociology, and political science, respectively – it should be appreciated that these disciplinary categories are increasingly fluid. Economists, sociologists, and political scientists have worked on all three issue-areas. And these subjects are also important for cognate fields such as business, education, public policy, and social work. In this sense, our exemplars encompass the far reaches of social science.

Readers should also be aware that the three topics exemplify very different kinds of social science work. The first embodies a specific causal intervention – participation in a worker-training program – that operates on an individual level. We utilize this example frequently because many methodological principles are easier to discuss at the individual level. The other two topics embrace broader and more diffuse social and political institutions that are usually understood to operate at a societal level.

Worker-Training Programs

Unemployment is a problem not only for those who find themselves without a job but also for society at large, which must bear the costs of supporting the unemployed (provided there are systems of relief, either private or public) and must bear the negative externalities brought on by unemployment (e.g., an increased tendency for criminal activity). The public policy question is how governments can best deal with this byproduct of capitalism.

One approach centers on worker-training programs. These programs enroll unemployed, or under-employed, persons with an attempt to boost their job-relevant skills. Programs may also seek to enhance morale and to educate participants in job-search strategies and workplace norms. Programs may be short in duration, or longer-term. They may be administered in conjunction with an apprenticeship. They may be accompanied by incentives for employers to participate. In short, there is great variety in the implementation of this category of social program directed at the unemployed.

The key question of interest is whether participation in such a program enhances a person's probability of finding a job or enhances their long-term earnings. Insofar as there may be such an effect, we wish to know why – that is, the mechanisms through which the causal effect operates. Is it because participants are more persistent in their search for work? Is it because they have better skills, better morale, or better workplace behavior? Is it because employers view participation in a program as a sign of motivation? Many explanations might be offered.

For present purposes, what bears emphasis are the methodological properties of this field of research. There is, first of all, a key concept – the worker-training program, which seems fairly clear in most settings but is actually rather blurry around the edges. Does a one-day program focusing on advice for job-hunting qualify? How about a person who enlists government support to take classes at a community college? How about a program that emphasizes job placement with relatively little emphasis on training? There is, second, the hypothesis – that participation in such a program enhances employment and salary. There is, third, the theory, which concerns all the reasons that the hypothesis might be true (if indeed it is true).

Social Capital

Our second example, centering on the concept of social capital, is considerably more complex. We shall define social capital as the benefits that derive from social networks that extend beyond family and clan. Where networks are intensive and extensive, societies should experience higher trust, lower crime, better public health, better governance, and as a result of these first-stage benefits, stronger growth. Likewise, individuals with more extensive networks should experience greater benefits (e.g., more economic opportunities) than individuals with circumscribed networks.

Indicators of social capital include membership in voluntary associations (e.g., unions, fraternal and sororal organizations, neighborhood associations, and clubs) and political engagement (e.g., voter turnout). These may be explored separately or combined in a single index.

Some years ago, Robert Putnam discovered that many indicators of social capital in the United States showed a marked downturn beginning in the 1950s, suggesting a deep and far-reaching decline in social capital.[9] (Similar patterns were found in some other advanced industrial countries, though not quite to the same degree.[10]) This spurred a good deal of hand-wringing about the state of the union, along with many social science studies. Some of these studies showed a mixed picture – decline in some areas but not in others, or a redirection of activity from some areas to other areas.[11] Another interpretation is that the decline is real but largely a function of the extraordinary high level of social capital found among members of the "greatest generation" – those who came of age in the 1930s and 1940s. From this perspective, the postwar decline represents a return to a normal level of social capital. The controversy has been difficult to resolve because most of the available measures of social capital stretch back only to the mid-twentieth century; thus, we have only a vague sense of the level of social capital existing in the United States prior to the 1940s.

Another set of controversies concern the *causes* of this decline. Are they the product of a general disenchantment during the turbulent 1960s, the entry of women into the labor force (pulling them away from social networking activities), migration, suburbanization, increasing diversity, or changing technologies (especially television and the Internet)?

Still another set of controversies concern the possible *effects* of this decline. At first, the decline of social capital was linked to a rise in the crime rate. The rate of violent crime began to decline in the 1990s, however, casting doubt on a possible link between social capital and crime. The decline of social capital may also be linked to social and political instability, though evidence of such effects is thin. A third sort of effect may be decreasing concern for others, as manifested in lower public support for welfare programs intended to help less privileged members of society. Finally, one may conjecture that declining social capital imperils the willingness of citizens to support government, as manifested in anti-tax crusades and declining faith in political institutions.

Leaving aside various controversies that attend the "decline of social capital" thesis, let us take a moment to consider the possible impact of social capital on governance and economic development more generally. Putnam's first book on the subject argued that differences in social capital between the northern and southern regions of Italy could account for differences in the quality of governance across the (well-governed) north and the (poorly-governed) south.[12] Specifically, where reciprocity-relationships were extensive and social trust was high this boosted the quality of government. Where social networks were limited to the extended family and social trust was low, as it seemed to be in the southern regions of Italy, it was difficult to establish effective government. This had repercussions for growth and that is why, Putnam reasoned, we see a prosperous north and a much less prosperous south. One can also hypothesize that there might be direct effects from social capital to growth.[13] For example, where networks are limited and trust is low, markets are more difficult to maintain, competition is likely to be limited, and transaction costs will be high. Indeed, scholars have argued that the strength or weakness of social capital is a key to long-term patterns of development around the world.[14]

In recent years, proponents of social capital have confronted the apparent fact that there are "good" and "bad" sorts of social capital. It is often noted that gangs are a voluntary network of individuals who prey on society. Likewise, neighborhood associations sometimes form in order to exclude social groups deemed threatening to the community. At the extreme, race riots may be understood as an expression of social capital. Indeed, Weimar Germany, which spawned the xenophobic ideology of Nazism, was a society rich in extra-familial social networks.[15] In response, theorists now distinguish between "bonding" and "bridging" social capital. The first relates to social networks among people who are similar to each other – ethnically, socioeconomically, and so forth. The second refers to social networks that reach across social divides. The claim is that these two types of social capital have divergent effects on a variety of outcomes. In this fashion, a significant modification of the original theory is introduced.

Of course, these matters are complicated. What we have offered above is a brief review of a large and complex literature. Our purpose is not to represent the entirety of these debates but merely to illustrate several key elements of social science argumentation. Note, first, the key concept, social capital, and various indicators that have been used to measure it. Note, second, the descriptive hypothesis that social capital has declined in recent decades in the United States (and perhaps elsewhere). Note, finally, various hypotheses about the causes and effects of that decline and theoretical expectations about why (i.e., the mechanisms by which) social capital might lead to enhanced governance and economic development.

Democracy

Democracy refers generally to rule by the people. Below this level of abstraction, there is great debate about how to best define this key concept. Most definitions include the idea of electoral contestation. That is, in order to be considered democratic a polity must allow free and fair elections with a broad electorate; those elected must be allowed to take office; and elective bodies must not be constrained by unelective bodies such as a military tribunal or monarch. Additional attributes such as constraints on the exercise of power, civil liberty, political equality, deliberation, and full participation might also be included in a definition of this key concept.

There are a variety of cross-national indicators of democracy. However, most of these empirical measures focus on the electoral component of the concept, as set forth above. Most also regard democracy as a matter of degrees, stretching from autocracy (i.e., dictatorship, authoritarian rule) to full democracy. This includes the widely-used indices produced by Polity ("Polity2," a 21-point scale) and Freedom House ("Political Rights," a 7-point scale).[16]

Sometimes, however, it is important to divide up the world of polities into those that are (predominantly) autocratic and those that are (predominantly) democratic. The most widely employed binary indicator (0 = autocracy, 1 = democracy) is the Democracy–Dictatorship (DD) index developed by Adam Przeworski and colleagues.[17] Accordingly, a regime is a democracy if leaders are selected through contested elections. To operationalize this conception of democracy the authors identify four criteria:

1 The chief executive must be chosen by popular election or by a body that was itself popularly elected.
2 The legislature must be popularly elected.
3 There must be more than one party competing in the elections.
4 An alternation in power under electoral rules identical to the ones that brought the incumbent to office must have taken place.[18]

All four conditions must be satisfied in order for a polity to be considered democratic.

With respect to democracy, it is helpful to distinguish several sorts of research questions. First, what is the empirical pattern of democratization throughout the world? Samuel Huntington discerns three democratic "waves" in the contemporary era – the first beginning in the early nineteenth century, the second after the conclusion of World War II, and the third beginning in the 1970s.[19] Criticism of this account centers, first of all, on Huntington's definition of democracy. If it is broadened to include female suffrage and informal impediments to suffrage for males (e.g., "Jim Crow" laws in the American South), historical patterns of democratization look rather different.[20] A second issue concerns the denominator – the total number of countries under examination. Conventionally, these are defined as sovereign nation-states. However, it will be noticed that the number of sovereign states expands rapidly over the observed period, especially in the 1960s when most of Africa was liberated from colonial rule. This means that an apparent downturn in the rate of democracy may be due to a statistical artifact: the momentary increase in the number of countries considered as part of a global sample.[21] A final issue concerns how to regard the concept of a "wave." Does it refer to changes in the global level of democracy (as measured by Polity, for example), to net-transitions to democracy, or to linkages among cases of democratization (diffusion)?[22]

Causal questions begin with democracy's rise. What might account for the pattern of democratization that we see across the world over the past two centuries? Structural (distal) explanations are grounded variously in geography, colonial history, religion, ethnicity, modernization, and particular types of authoritarian rule. Proximate causes include features of the transition itself such as whether liberalization (civil liberties, constraints on executive power) occurred prior to an electoral opening or whether a pact was established among important political players. None has been conclusively established.[23]

A separate set of causal questions concern democracy's causal effects. Does a transition (or improvement in the quality of democracy) bring with it improvements in the quality of governance (e.g., less corruption, more provision of public goods)? Does it foster higher levels of education, health, and infrastructure, or greater equality across the sexes and across ethnic groups within a society? These outcomes might be summarized in the phrase, does democracy bring development? Again, we find vast disagreement.[24]

A somewhat separate question concerns whether regime-type influences the conduct of foreign policy. According to the well-known theory of the democratic peace two countries that are democratic should never fight wars with one another.[25] A softer version of this thesis interprets the matter probabilistically: two countries that are democratic are less likely to fight wars with each other than any other pairing of countries.

Again, it must be stressed that our purpose is not to offer a comprehensive overview of this immense subject but simply to display some of the methodological properties of the debates that occur around the subject. In particular, we have outlined debates over the key concept (democracy), various indicators for that concept (including Polity, Freedom House, and DD), an influential descriptive account (Huntington's three waves of democratization), and two general causal questions, one pertaining to the causes of democratization and the other to its effects.

CONCLUSIONS

The examples introduced above were chosen because they are prominent and also highly contentious. Scholars have differing views of the definition and measurement of key concepts, the descriptive features pertaining to the phenomenon, and/ or the causes or effects of that phenomenon. This is especially the case for social capital and democracy, and somewhat less so for worker-training programs.

Some may feel that these ongoing debates are an indication of the weakness of social science – its failure to reach closure, even with questions as old as democracy. While this is certainly an abiding characteristic of social science one must also bear in mind that our difficulties in reaching consensus arise primarily from the nature of the problems themselves. If we were to choose simpler problems we would no doubt arrive at greater consensus with respect to their answers. Indeed, the simplest problem among our three examples – worker-training programs – is also the one that has garnered the greatest scholarly consensus.

It is not clear that society would be better served if social science narrowed its focus to tractable questions, ignoring the macro-level features that – presumably – operate over long periods, at macro levels, and sometimes beneath the surface of social life. This includes social capital and democracy, along with other similarly diffuse topics.

In any case, we hope that these examples serve as an invitation to our topic – social science methodology. For, it is only by understanding the methodological properties of these topics that we can hope to understand these debates – and, perhaps, over time, to attain greater consensus.

KEY TERMS

- Social science
- Methodology
- Multi-method
- Worker-training programs
- Social capital
- Democracy

Arguments

Social science is organized around arguments. This is what we hope to prove, or disprove, by an empirical analysis. Science proceeds as arguments are advanced, revised, and proven or disproven.

A **theory** is the reasoning behind an argument. It explains a relationship, its mechanisms (if the relationship is causal), scope-conditions, background conditions, and any additional information needed to interpret the argument. One might theorize that democratization enhances economic growth because it holds leaders accountable, and accountable leaders are more likely to adopt policies that serve the public good.

If a theory is presented in a formal manner, perhaps with a set of mathematical expressions, it may be referred to as a **model**. At present, however, we do not distinguish between an argument, theory, or model; these terms will be used more or less synonymously.

A **hypothesis** is the specific, testable element(s) of any argument. One might hypothesize that as a country becomes more democratic its GDP (gross domestic product) growth increases. Our use of the term "argument" is thus meant to encompass both theory and hypothesis.

This chapter begins by distinguishing various types of social science argumentation. Arguments central to social science are generally classifiable as either descriptive or causal, so we spend considerable time on these genres. Next, we contrast these genres with other sorts of arguments such as those that are predictive, normative, or prescriptive. Finally, we lay out the characteristics of a good descriptive or causal argument. (Additional criteria specific to causal arguments are postponed until Part II of the book.)

Descriptive Arguments

A **descriptive argument** describes some aspect of the world. In doing so, it aims to answer *what* questions (e.g., *when, whom, out of what, in what manner*) about a phenomenon. Descriptive arguments are about what is or what was.

Note that many features of the world are intrinsically important. We want to know which countries are democratic and which are not, and in what ways they are democratic or undemocratic. We want to know how many Jews, gypsies, gays, and socialists were killed in the European Holocaust. We want to know the

Descriptive Arguments

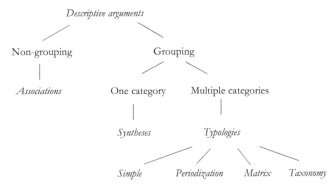

Figure 2.1 Taxonomy of descriptive arguments

intellectual origins of individualism, and how it evolved through time and across cultures. We want to know whether the media in a country presents a biased view of news events, and in what direction that bias runs.

Descriptive arguments that are general in nature (they apply to a large number of events) may be classified as *associations*, *syntheses*, or *typologies*. Typologies, in turn, may be understood as *simple, periodization, matrix, or taxonomy*. This is how social scientists carve up nature. These are the patterns that we look for when attempting to describe events in the social world.

These various genres may be arranged within a taxonomy, as shown in Figure 2.1. However, the taxonomy probably won't make much sense until after these concepts have been explained, so the reader is advised to return to this figure when she or he has finished this section of the chapter.

Associations

A descriptive argument that involves a relationship among several factors is **associational**. Many studies have focused, for example, on the degree to which involvement in politics is skewed toward the middle and upper classes. That is, they are focused on the association between social class and political engagement.[26]

We might hypothesize that where the value of one factor, X, is high, the value of another factor, Y, is high and correspondingly where X is low, Y is low, as depicted in panel (a) of Figure 2.2. Or we might claim that they are inversely related – where X is high, Y is low, as depicted in panel (b). We might also hypothesize that X and Y are related in a curvilinear (nonlinear) pattern such as an inverted U, as illustrated in panel (c). There are an infinite number of ways in which two factors may be related, and things naturally become more complicated if additional factors (beyond X and Y) are integrated into the argument.

Trend analysis seeks to discover a relationship between a phenomenon and the passage of time. For example, Robert Putnam finds that social capital in the United States has declined precipitously since the 1930s and 1940s. This is demonstrated by examining patterns in political engagement (turnout and other forms

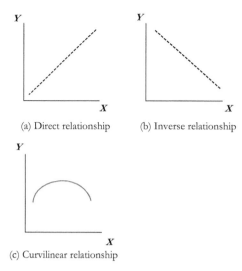

Figure 2.2 Possible relationships among two factors

(a) Direct relationship   (b) Inverse relationship

(c) Curvilinear relationship

of political activity) and membership in unions, fraternal and sororal organizations, churches, and neighborhood associations such as bowling leagues, school associations, and clubs. Many of these indices show a marked downturn since the mid-twentieth century, suggesting a widespread decline in social capital.[27]

Network analysis focuses on interrelationships among many units (which may be understood in spatial, temporal, or functional ways). Researchers have studied political networks, corporate networks, networks extending across business and politics, terrorist networks, transportation networks, interest group networks, as well as social networks, including those built around websites such as Facebook (see Chapter 5). A common focus of network analysis is the centrality of various nodes, i.e., the extent to which an individual (or group) serves as a communicative hub within a network of individuals (or groups). Scholars also attempt to determine what factors predict an individual's position within that network, and what implications the structure of a network might have on various outcomes (e.g., the probability of finding a marriage partner or influencing a collective decision).[28]

Syntheses

Some multidimensional arguments attempt to group together diverse dimensions into distinct categories. If there is only one category of interest (others are not well-defined), this style of argument may be called **synthetic**. The claim here is that diverse attributes of a topic revolve around a central theme that unifies the attributes, lending coherence to an otherwise disparate set of phenomena. Synthetic arguments are therefore holistic endeavors, emphasizing similarities rather than differences among the chosen sample of cases.

This type of argument is often applied to cultural analysis. For example, Louis Hartz (building upon Tocqueville) argues that American political culture is "liberal" – a term he understood as an amalgam of individualism and antistatism. This large-order concept helps to organize many features of American politics and society going back (he argues) to the Revolution, including the absence of redistributive measures, the weakness of labor and socialism, the minimal presence of the national state, and the contrasting robustness of civil society. It is also consistent with a longstanding narrative about American life, visible in political speech and in other popular media, that praises individual freedom and equal opportunity while decrying the corruption of politics.[29] Whether this ideology explains political outcomes such as the failure of socialism is, for present purposes, not important. It is sufficient to note that a large number of relatively distinctive features of American history fall into place when placed within the rubric of the liberal tradition.

A second example of social-scientific synthesis is provided by Orlando Patterson's acclaimed study of slavery. Patterson begins by showing that through history slaves have occupied diverse roles in society. They have been entrusted with the management of large commercial enterprises and the leadership of empires, though they are routinely allocated to menial tasks. Accordingly, slaves have been rich and they have been poor. What all of these experiences have in common – indeed, about all they have in common, according to Patterson – is that slaves are deprived of a social identity distinct from their owners. As property, their identity is not unique to them. It is this feature of "social death" that constitutes the distinctive (and therefore defining) feature of slavery throughout history.[30]

These are very different sorts of descriptive syntheses. But they both aim to satisfy the same methodological goal, i.e., to summarize many attributes and many phenomena in a single concept or phrase. Of course, the attempt to synthesize is also, at the same time, an attempt to differentiate. For example, the liberalism of American culture is contrasted with the non-liberal cultures of Europe. The social death of slaves is contrasted with the social life enjoyed by free people. Insofar as these distinctions are explicit and insofar as they provide the grist for extensive empirical analysis a synthesis begins to look more like a typology – our next topic.[31]

Simple Typologies

Where multiple discrete categories are defined, the result is a **typology**. Here, the goal is to sort phenomena into categories that are mutually exclusive and exhaustive on the basis of a consistent categorization principle (or principles).[32] Let us begin with some examples.

Max Weber argues that political authority draws upon three alternate forms of legitimacy: traditional, charismatic, or rational-legal. Traditional authority derives from conformance with established custom. Thus, a king in a country with a longstanding monarchy is regarded as legitimate because his position accords with the accepted practice of rulership (assuming, that is, that he is the legitimate heir to the throne). Charismatic authority derives from a leader's personal attributes, which may be imbued with special and perhaps supernatural powers. Leaders who elicit extraordinary devotion and whose position stems not from birth or from their position within a hierarchy are often regarded as charismatic. Rational-legal authority is derived from a leader's position within a constitutional (rule-of-law) system. The leader's power is contingent upon the office that she or he holds, and is bound by the strictures pertaining to that office. Once she or he steps outside the office, or steps beyond the legal bounds of the office, she or he loses authority. In contrast to charismatic authority, rational-legal authority is impersonal. In contrast to traditional authority, it is rational in the sense of being constituted within a web of rules that are logically consistent rather than arbitrary or ad hoc.[33]

Simple typologies of this nature are ubiquitous. Aristotle classifies polities as monarchies (rule of one), oligarchies (rule of a few), or democracies (rule of many). Samuel Finer, working over the same subject many years later, organizes polities according to the nature of their rulers: Palace, Church, Nobility, or Forum.[34] Albert Hirschman argues that the influence of constituents on organizations may be felt through exit and/or voice.[35] Gosta Esping-Andersen divides the world of welfare regimes into those that are liberal, corporatist, or social democratic.[36]

More complex typologies may be understood as periodizations, matrix typologies, or taxonomies.

Periodization

A typology that is temporally ordered may be understood as a **periodization**. For example, it is argued that several waves of democratization have advanced across the world over the past two centuries, each with distinctive features.[37] The first wave began in the early nineteenth century in the United States, where white males were granted the right to vote in the first mass-suffrage elections. This wave crested after World War I, when the rise of fascism in Europe temporarily beat back the tide of democracy. The second wave began after World War II with the defeat of fascism and the rise of many newly independent nations – some of which were (at least briefly) democratic. The third wave began with the overthrow of dictatorship in Portugal in 1974, extending to Latin America and the Asia-Pacific in the 1980s, and Eastern Europe and Africa in the 1990s.

Grand periodization schemes have absorbed many thinkers. Tocqueville proclaimed the beginning of a democratic age sometime in the late eighteenth century, which may be compared with the previous feudal or aristocratic ages. Along these lines, Marx proposed to typologize recorded human history into feudal, capitalist, and communist stages.

Other periodization schemes focus on a single country. For example, many students of American political history are convinced that fundamental political changes have occurred only episodically, during "realignment" periods.[38] Others defend an older tradition, dividing American political history into "eras" (Revolutionary, Jacksonian, Civil War, Reconstruction, et al.). Still others argue that the topic is best approached through an even more differentiated periodization defined by presidencies.[39]

Each attempt to establish a periodization appeals to the same general desiderata, i.e., to identify key points of change within a historical topic such that the resulting periods are mutually exclusive and exhaustive (along whatever dimensions are of interest to the study).

Matrix Typologies

When a typology is formed by the intersection of several categorical variables the result is a **matrix typology**. Following Robert Dahl, we can posit that there are two core components of democracy, *contestation* and *participation*. The intersection of these two factors produces four types, which Dahl labeled (a) *closed hegemony*, (b) *inclusive hegemony*, (c) *competitive oligarchy*, and (d) *polyarchy*, as illustrated in Table 2.1.[40]

Table 2.1 A matrix typology: regime-types

		Participation	
		Low	*High*
Contestation	*Low*	Closed Hegemony	Inclusive Hegemony
	High	Competitive Oligarchy	Polyarchy

Matrix typologies may contain any number of factors, resulting in any number of compound types (cells). However, the two-by-two matrix is still the most common – presumably because adding a third (or fourth) dimension does not usually result in discrete and recognizable types.

Taxonomies

A typology that stretches in a hierarchical fashion across several levels of analysis may be referred to as a **taxonomy**. For example, one might stipulate that there are two basic polity types: autocracy and democracy. Among democracies, some are direct and others representative. Among representative democracies, one finds electoral, liberal, majoritarian, participatory, and egalitarian varieties. The nested quality of this family of terms may be illustrated in tabular format (see Table 2.2) or in a tree diagram (see Figure 2.3).[41]

Note that each subordinate level of the taxonomy possesses all the attributes of the superordinate category, plus one (or several). Each concept within a taxonomy may therefore be defined by specifying its superordinate category plus its differentiating attribute or attributes – its *genus et differentium*. (Concepts so defined are

Table 2.2 Regime taxonomy in tabular format

ATTRIBUTES

TERMS	Gov. form	Rule by few	Rule by people	Direct	Indirect	Elections	Rule of law	Majority rule	Popular partic.	Consult- ation	Equality	Total
I. Polity	•											1
A. Autocracy	•	•										2
B. Democracy	•		•									2
1. Direct	•		•	•								3
2. Representative	•		•		•							3
a. Electoral	•		•		•	•						4
b. Liberal	•		•		•		•					4
c. Majoritarian	•		•		•			•				4
d. Participatory	•		•		•				•			4
e. Deliberative	•		•		•					•		4
f. Egalitarian	•		•		•						•	4

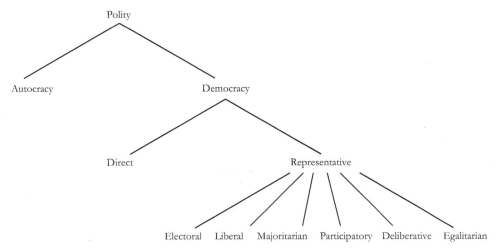

Figure 2.3 Regime taxonomy in tree-diagram format

sometimes described as "classical" in reference to their Aristotelian lineage and their venerable place within the field of logic.)

Causal Arguments

The reader may have noticed that many of the descriptive relationships introduced in the previous section could be reformulated as **causal arguments**. Instead of saying that X and Y are associated (correlated) with each other, for example, we might claim that X causes Y. While the shift may appear subtle, this is more than a minor change of terminology. It is a fundamentally different argument.

A causal argument (or theory) involves at least two elements: a *cause* and an *outcome*. To say that a factor, X, is a cause of an outcome, Y, is to say that a change in X generates a change in Y relative to what Y would otherwise be (the counterfactual condition), given certain background conditions (ceteris paribus assumptions) and scope-conditions (the population of the inference).

As an example, let us focus on the causal role of a worker-training program (as introduced in Chapter 1). A reasonable hypothesis is that participation in the program (X) will enhance a participant's earnings (Y). If the relationship is causal, the participant's earnings should be higher than they would be if she had never participated in the program, all other things being equal.

A causal argument implies a *counterfactual*. The counterfactual in this example is that the worker does *not* participate in the worker-training program. The counterfactual outcome is that she does not realize a gain in earnings (or experiences less of an increase than she would have gained had she participated in the program).

Importantly, when one asserts that X causes Y one is asserting that the actual (ontological) probability of an event is increased by X, not simply a theory's fit with the available data. This is what distinguishes a causal argument from description or prediction. To be causal, the factor in question must *generate*, *create*, or *produce* an effect.

Of course, it is not always possible to specify precisely why X generates a change in Y. Yet, in identifying X as a cause of Y one is presuming the existence of a causal *mechanism* – understood here as the pathway or process or chain of intermediary variables by which X affects Y. In our example, the mechanism might be the factual information about a particular occupation that is imparted in the worker-training program. Or it could be the imparting of job search skills such as how to construct a resume. Or it could be general workplace comportment (how to relate to one's boss and co-workers). Lots of potential mechanisms might be identified, and any combination of them may be at work if the relationship is causal.

Causal relationships occur against a *background* of other factors. These are conditions that make any causal relationship possible. One would not expect worker-training programs to have any causal impact in a country where jobs (and promotions) are allocated by clientelistic networks or political patronage. Likewise, one would not expect a worker-training program to affect earnings in a collapsing economy. So we might stipulate that the background conditions of the argument include an intact economy and meritocratic appointment and promotion practices. Unless otherwise specified, these background conditions are presumed to hold constant: they do not vary. This is known as the ceteris paribus (all else equal) assumption, and is implicit in all causal arguments. Often, the ceteris paribus conditions of an argument are obvious enough. But when they are not, the writer should spell things out.

Other Arguments

Description and causation are the dominant modalities of social science argumentation. However, they do not exhaust the universe of arguments. Since other styles of argument occasionally enter into social science (and always inform the work of social science in a tacit fashion) it is important that we survey this field, even if only very briefly. Our survey includes arguments that are *predictive*, *normative*, and *prescriptive*.

Predictive arguments (forecasts) attempt to tell us something about the future. That is, a factor, X, is thought to help predict an outcome, Y. This looks a lot like a causal argument; indeed, most causal arguments serve a predictive function. However, in saying that X predicts Y we do not presume that X causes Y. For example, it has been argued that a rise in infant mortality is a strong predictor of state failure.[42] This does not imply that killing babies will bring down a state – a rather absurd, not to mention gruesome, idea. It seems more likely that some other factor is causing both X and Y. Infant mortality rates thus serve a useful predictive function without possessing causal attributes.

Normative arguments are about the moral goodness/badness of a phenomenon. For example, studies of foreign aid might be couched in positive or negative terms, implying that development assistance granted by developed countries to less developed countries is a good or bad thing. Frequently, the normative freight of an argument is fairly subtle, as revealed in an author's choice of topic and his or her choice of words. But even when an author is careful not to tip her hat, it may be impossible to avoid certain normative preferences because they are embedded in our language. Imagine discussing topics such as human rights or fascism in a neutral fashion.

Prescriptive arguments enjoin us to take, or to refrain from taking, certain actions. They are often wedded to normative arguments. For example, a normative argument might be that foreign aid is benevolent. The implicit prescriptive argument is that we ought to increase development assistance.

We have now surveyed five types of arguments, as summarized in Table 2.3. The question naturally arises why we give preference in this book to description and causation. A first point to note is that normative and prescriptive arguments are not empirical in the usual sense of the term. One cannot prove or disprove a statement like *Foreign aid is good*, or *We ought to be more generous in our assistance to the developing world*, by appealing to facts. Of course, one could build a case for such arguments by appealing to facts. This, one might say, is the job of social science. But the case itself would be constructed with descriptive and causal arguments – and perhaps with predictive arguments as well. Thus, we might count up the amount of money devoted to foreign aid and to which countries, and which goals, it is allotted – a descriptive account. We might try to determine whether this assistance fostered stronger economic performance in the countries in which it was distributed – a causal account. And we might try to ascertain what effects additional aid will have in the future – a predictive account. Each of these arguments might be summarized in a few key hypotheses, and these hypotheses could be subjected to empirical proof, on the basis of which they could be proven right or wrong. (Of course, things are rarely so simple; but this is the general goal, at any rate, of an empirical approach to science.)

The result of this extensive empirical investigation might influence our views of the normative and prescriptive aspects of foreign aid. But the latter are not empirical matters in the same way as descriptive, causal, and predictive arguments.

Table 2.3 Typology of arguments

- **Descriptive**. An argument about patterns in the world. ←
- **Causal**. An argument about what generates change in an outcome. ←
- **Predictive**. An argument about what predicts future variation in an outcome. ←
- **Normative**. An argument about what is right or wrong, good or bad. ←
- **Prescriptive**. An argument about what actions one should take. ←

Because normative and prescriptive arguments are nonempirical they are generally downplayed in the work of social science.

In this light, one might wonder about our choice to omit a detailed consideration of predictive arguments from the remainder of this book. Predictions of course can be empirically verified and are a bona fide part of the arsenal of social science. Our reason for excluding them from the book is more pragmatic than principled. At this point in time, models whose primary goal is predictive have not played a large role in most of the social science disciplines. (Prediction: this may change.)

In any case, it is useful to be able to parse arguments, i.e., to distinguish elements of an argument that are descriptive, causal, predictive, normative, prescriptive, or some combination thereof. This is important as a matter of clear expression and logical argumentation. For example, if normative arguments are disguised as description it will be difficult to figure out what an author is arguing – not to mention if she or he is right or wrong. Likewise, one must be careful when inferring prescriptive conclusions from a causal argument. The causal argument that foreign aid contributes to higher rates of child vaccination is consistent with a prescriptive argument that we should (nonetheless) curtail foreign aid. Only in parsing these arguments will you be able to tease these things apart. Thinking logically means, in the first place, distinguishing among different styles of argumentation.

Because social science is grounded in empirical arguments (descriptive, causal, predictive) it often assumes a rather austere tone. Consider the prospect of military intervention in order to support democracy abroad. An editorial or political speech on this topic is likely to foreground the normative and prescriptive elements of the subject. The writer or speaker who supports intervention is likely to dwell on the evils of autocracy in that country, on how many people have suffered and how they have suffered. She or he will advocate a course of action, and will prognosticate about what is likely to happen if we refuse to intervene. A social science study, by contrast, will likely highlight descriptive and causal aspects of the topic. What is the history and the current situation? What causes are at work? What is the general relationship between intervention and democratic transition? These are things that can be empirically verified, even if they are somewhat less exciting. The mark of a good social scientist is an ability to hold normative and prescriptive passions in check – harnessing them to the wheel of science.

Good Arguments

Having outlined different sorts of arguments we turn to the qualities of a good argument – descriptive and causal arguments, that is. What makes a theory (and its associated hypotheses) satisfactory?

Social science arguments strive to achieve a number of virtues, including *precision, generality, boundedness, parsimony, logical coherence, commensurability,*

Table 2.4 Theorizing: general criteria

Precision (specificity)
- Is it precise?

Generality (breadth, domain, population, range, scope)
- How broad is the scope? How many phenomena does a theory describe/explain?

Boundedness (scope-conditions)
- How well-bounded is it?

Parsimony (concision, economy, Occam's razor, reduction, simplicity)
- How parsimonious is it? How many assumptions are required?

Logical coherence (clarity, consistency; *antonym:* ambiguity)
- How logically coherent is it?

Commensurability (consilience, harmony, logical economy, theoretical utility; *antonym:* adhocery)
- How well does it cumulate with other inferences? Does it advance logical economy in a field?

Innovation (novelty)
- How new is it?

Relevance (everyday importance, significance)
- How relevant is it to issues of concern to citizens and policymakers?

innovation, and *relevance*, summarized in Table 2.4. Whatever the topic might be, a social science theory is more useful if it is precise, general, well-bounded, parsimonious, coherent, commensurable, innovative, and relevant. Now, let us clarify these key objectives.

Precision

Theories strive for **precision**. The more precise a claim, the more useful it is, in the sense of providing more information about a putative phenomenon.

It also makes the argument more amenable to testing. If you are unconvinced by this, consider the opposite: a perfectly imprecise statement about the world, e.g., "Municipal governments in Africa are democratic, autocratic, or somewhere in between." This sort of statement includes all possibilities since all polities must be classifiable somewhere on this spectrum. At the limit, a statement of no precision whatsoever says absolutely nothing about the world, and therefore is completely unfalsifiable.

Generality

If the fundamental purpose of social science is to tell us about the world then it stands to reason that a theory informing us about many phenomena is, by virtue of this fact, more useful than a theory pursuant to only a few phenomena. We will refer to this goal as **generality**, though it might also be called generalizability, breadth, or scope.

One wishes for a theory to encompass as many phenomena as possible. The more one can explain with a given argument the more powerful that argument is. Theories of great breadth tell us more about the world by explaining larger portions of that world. Thus, a theory of democracy that satisfactorily describes or explains regime-types across all nation-states is superior to one that applies to only a single region of the world or a single historical epoch. And a theory or theoretical framework describing or explaining different types of phenomena, such as evolution, is more useful than one pertaining to only a single outcome.

Boundedness

A theory should be *well-bounded*. That is, the boundaries of the theory – where it holds true (or is thought to hold true) and where it does not – should be clarified. These boundaries in time and space are sometimes referred to as the *scope-conditions* of a theory. Thus, if a theory about worker-training programs applies only to unemployed workers (and not to the under-employed), this is important to clarify. Theorizing on this subject is incomplete unless boundary conditions are established. Note that even "universal" theories have some boundary conditions, implicit in the concepts with which they have been articulated.

Boundedness is not established simply by carefully articulating boundaries. It is essential that those boundaries make sense – that they be true, or at least plausibly true (for they are not always easy to test). In framing an argument the researcher's objective is to identify those phenomena that properly belong within the scope of a theory, excluding those that do not. Inferences should be *appropriately* bounded – neither too big nor too small. An *arbitrarily* bounded inference, one that follows no apparent logic, is not convincing.

For example, if we stipulate that our theory of democratization applies to Sweden but not to Norway the reader would probably not be convinced. This scope-condition seems highly arbitrary, since these countries are very similar to each other. However, we may be able to justify this distinction with a more general scope-condition. For example, we might argue that our theory of democratization applies only to non-oil producing countries, i.e., to countries that are not subject to a "resource curse." Since Norway is a large oil producer it might make sense to exclude it from the boundaries of the inference.

Parsimony

A fourth general goal of science is reduction, i.e., reducing the infinite plenitude of reality into a carefully framed argument from which unnecessary dross is removed. To the extent that a theory achieves this goal it is *parsimonious*. Like a lever, it lifts heavy weights with a moderate application of force. It is efficient, and its efficiency derives from its capacity to explain a lot with a minimal expenditure of energy.

The goal of **parsimony**, sometimes expressed as *Occam's razor*, is not assessable by the length of a study. Indeed, lengthy analyses may be required to provide evidence for a pithy argument. But it does call for a summary statement of key propositions.

Note that when a theory is parsimonious it is easier to test because there are fewer moving parts. More importantly, there are probably fewer assumptions necessary in order to sustain the argument. This latter point deserves some discussion.

Theories build upon what we know already – or think we know – about the world. Nothing starts entirely from scratch. A good theory requires fewer departures from common sense, fewer leaps of faith, fewer a priori assumptions. A poorly constructed theory, by contrast, asks the reader to accept a great deal about the world upon the authority of the author. This sort of inference does not build on solid foundations. It is stipulative. The point, then, is not to do away with assumptions but to limit them – or at least the most questionable of them – as much as possible. This is perhaps the most important implication of parsimony as a criterion of good theorizing. The best sort of theory has only one empirical question at issue – the main hypothesis – all else is already firmly established and likely to be accepted by the reader.

Logical Coherence

In order to be meaningful an argument must demonstrate some degree of **logical coherence**. If there are many moving parts, as in a broad and abstract theory, they ought to hold together. A complex theory should revolve around a single core and the precepts should be logically linked. One facet should imply the others. Indeed, if the parts of an argument are inconsistent, the argument itself is virtually meaningless, and surely untestable.

Examples of logical inconsistency are not hard to find. While Marxist theory is premised on the idea that social classes advance their self-interest, the final stage of socialism seems to take as its premise that people are no longer motivated by self-interest – or have a very different idea of what that is.

Commensurability

Theories assume meaning within a field of pre-existing concepts and theories, typically a field or subfield of study. If a theory fits comfortably within a body of work we shall say that it possesses **commensurability**. This might be achieved by subsuming other theories within a new theoretical framework, or by offering a clarification or refinement of an existing theory. In any case, the theory advances logical economy in the field, thereby assisting the cumulation of knowledge about a subject.

If it does not – if it sits by itself in a corner and does not relate productively to other theories – then it is likely to be dismissed as "ad hoc," or "idiosyncratic."

It does not fit with present understandings of the world. It has little theoretical or conceptual utility.

Of course, deviant theories and neologisms (novel concepts) may be extremely useful in the long run. Indeed, the first sign of breakdown in a broad theory or paradigm is the existence of findings that cannot easily be made sense of. Yet, until such time as a new theory or paradigm can be constructed (one that would gather the new findings together with the old in a single overarching framework) the wayward proposition is ad hoc, idiosyncratic, and apt to be ignored.

Innovation

A novel theory presents a new way of thinking about some arena of activity. This, by itself, may constitute a significant contribution to our knowledge of the world, even if it cannot easily be demonstrated or proven (though it must at some point be falsifiable). It might mean the discovery of a new topic, never previously described or conceptualized. (Recall that all topics familiar today were once brand spanking new.) It might mean a new explanation for an outcome of general concern. Or it might mean the reformulation of an existing theory. There are many ways to achieve theoretical **innovation**.

A recent example of theoretical innovation is the theory of social capital – the idea that social networks have far-reaching consequences for governance and for economic performance (see Chapter 1). This idea is a relative newcomer to the theoretical toolkit of social science, having been developed over the last several decades. Note, however, that it was not launched all at once. Social capital theory was the work of many scholars across the fields of economics, political science, and sociology. And it continues to evolve. Arguably, any influential work on a subject alters the general theory on that subject in some fashion and can therefore claim the mantle of innovation.

Relevance

A theory, finally, should be *relevant* to things that matter to non-social scientists ("real people"). **Relevance** does not mean that lay citizens need to understand its intricacies (for some theories can be quite technical). But they should care about what it describes or explains. It is worth reminding ourselves that social science is not a disembodied body of knowledge – the way pure mathematics is sometimes described. It emanates from the needs and concerns of human beings. It is for, and about, society.

Indeed, most social scientists aim to affect public opinion and/or the course of public policy with their work, in some fashion. And it seems fair to judge the theories that possesses a strong claim to relevance as superior (ceteris paribus) to those that do not. And it seems fair to ask writers to justify the reader's potential expenditure of time, effort, and money with some sort of payoff. Readers are not likely to be carried very far on the strength of a writer's method or prose if they do not feel that there is something important at stake in the investigation. They must care about the outcome.

Arguably, truth-claims are enhanced when a writer frankly proclaims her preferences at the outset of the work. This way, possible inaccuracies in evidence or presentation are easier to detect, and to evaluate. Hidden prejudices probably do more harm than those that are openly avowed. Yet, it must be stressed that the value of a work of social science derives from its value-added as descriptive or causal propositions about the world, not its normative point of view or prescriptions for action. To say, "Y is good" or "We should do Y" is to say very little.

Social science is most powerful when the normative and prescriptive angles of a work are handled delicately. The most compelling arguments for increased spending on social welfare programs, for example, are those that demonstrate causal relationships, e.g., that particular programs aid in alleviating conditions of poverty and do not have negative externalities. Such studies do not proclaim baldly "Poverty is bad," or "We should increase social welfare spending," although there is no question that these views undergird a good deal of research on poverty and social policy. So long as the author's research is sound, one need not concern oneself with her normative position on the matter.

Finally, it seems appropriate to observe that the vast majority of social science analysis has little to do with what is good or bad. No one – or virtually no one – argues against the virtues of peace, prosperity, democracy, and self-fulfillment. What is relevant (in the larger sense of the word), is any knowledge that might help us to achieve these desiderata. Here is where social science matters, or ought to matter.

CONCLUSIONS

This chapter began by distinguishing various types of social science argumentation. The most important of these are descriptive and causal, each of which has many subtypes. These dominant forms of argument were then contrasted with predictive, normative, and prescriptive arguments. In the final section, we set forth the characteristics of a good descriptive or causal argument, namely *precision*, *generality*, *boundedness*, *parsimony*, *logical coherence*, *commensurability*, *innovation*, and *relevance* (see Table 2.4).

A number of these goals relate to a theory's testability, or **falsifiability**. Karl Popper, who invented the term, pointed out that in order to be true, a theory must also have the potential to be false. Unless a theory admits this possibility it has no empirical content; it is neither true nor false. Of course, some very general theories do not translate easily into testable hypotheses. Nonetheless, the process of empirical testing must occur *at some point*, and in this sense every theory embraces Popper's project.[43]

It should be acknowledged that the eight criteria in Table 2.4 are by no means easy to satisfy. Indeed, there are many situations in which one or more of these demands are not met, or are only partially met. There are also plenty of situations in which attaining one objective entails sacrificing another. The more precise a theory, the less general it may be. The more commensurable an argument the less innovative it may be. And so forth. Thus, when we say that it is important to strive for a goal we do not mean to imply that other goals should be neglected. We mean, rather, that the researcher should attempt to balance these divergent goals in a satisfactory manner, achieving the best possible compromise among various criteria – or, at the least, acknowledging the sacrifices made on one or more dimensions in order to achieve success along other dimensions.

In the following chapter we proceed to the components of an argument, namely its key *concepts* and the *indicators* chosen to measure those concepts.

KEY TERMS

- Theory
- Model
- Hypothesis
- Descriptive argument (association, synthesis, typology)
- Trend analysis
- Network analysis
- Periodization
- Matrix typology
- Taxonomy
- Causal argument
- Predictive argument
- Normative argument
- Prescriptive argument
- Precision
- Generality
- Boundedness
- Parsimony
- Logical coherence
- Commensurability
- Innovation
- Relevance
- Falsifiability

3 Concepts and Measures

Arguments are articulated with the use of key concepts. Indeed, the argument of a study is inseparable from its key concepts since the latter are the linguistic tools with which an argument is formulated. Any study of democracy, for example, must wrestle with the problem of how to define this key term – which will guide our discussion in this chapter.

Concepts, in turn, receive empirical meaning through the indicators chosen to measure them. Any study of democracy must be concerned not only with how to define democracy but also with how to **operationalize** (measure) this abstract concept.

Conceptualization and measurement are thus closely linked. This is why we have chosen to present them together in this chapter, which begins with concept formation and proceeds to measurement.

Concepts

The key concepts of social science are never fixed and, regrettably, not always clear. Many abstract concepts – such as *democracy* or *social capital* – are employed in a variety of ways and thus mean different things in different contexts. This is true even of more specific concepts such as *worker-training programs*. (Does a one-day program focusing on advice for job-hunting qualify? How about a person who enlists government support to take classes at a community college, or an apprenticeship program?)

The persistent ambiguity of key concepts makes it difficult for the reader, who may struggle to figure out what a term means in a given context and how it connects with other work (using the same or similar terms). It also makes it difficult for writers, who must identify which of several terms they should adopt in their own work and how they should define the chosen term.

Sometimes, the task of forming concepts seems highly arbitrary. And this, in turn, may prompt readers to adopt a skeptical attitude toward the subject. At the same time, the choice of concepts is never entirely arbitrary. Some choices are usually better than others, and a few are patently absurd.

In this spirit, we offer the following criteria, intended to guide the process of concept formation in the social sciences. A good concept, we shall argue, is

Table 3.1   Criteria of concept formation

Resonance (familiarity, normal usage; *antonyms:* idiosyncrasy, neologism, stipulation)
- How faithful is the concept to extant definitions and established usage?

Internal coherence (depth, essence, fecundity, fruitfulness, natural kinds, power, real, thickness)
- How many attributes do referents of a concept share?

External differentiation (context, contrast-space, perspective, reference-point, semantic field)
- How differentiated is a concept from neighboring concepts? What is the contrast-space against which a concept defines itself?

Theoretical utility
- What utility does a concept have within a larger theory and research design?

Consistency (*antonym:* slippage)
- Is the meaning of a concept consistent throughout a work?

resonant, internally coherent, externally differentiated, theoretically useful, and *consistent* in meaning, as summarized in Table 3.1.

Resonance

Consider the following definition of "democracy": *a furry animal with four legs.* This is nonsense, of course. And it is nonsense precisely because it breaks radically with common usage. This is not what anyone thinks of when they hear the word democracy and it doesn't share any elements of prevailing definitions of the term.

Forming a concept involves choosing a term, and a definition for that term, that **resonates** with standard usage in ordinary speech or in a specialized language region (i.e., a field of inquiry). Idiosyncratic concepts (such as the foregoing example) should be avoided, wherever possible.

Of course, sometimes there is no concept that defines a topic in precisely the way that you wish to define it. In this case, some departure from ordinary usage is required. But this neologism should deviate from ordinary usage as little as possible. Otherwise, a term loses touch with its semantic roots.

Internal Coherence

Concepts strive to identify those things that are alike, grouping them together, and contrasting them with things that are different. Apples with apples, and oranges with oranges, as the phrase goes. A concept that accomplishes this possesses **internal coherence**. It may also be described as fecund, fruitful, illuminating, informative, or insightful.

Consider three conceptualizations of regime-type. One differentiates between democracies and autocracies;[44] another distinguishes pure democracies, competitive authoritarian states, and pure autocracies;[45] and a third establishes a 21-point index that is intended to function as an interval scale.[46] Which of these is most satisfactory? Evidently, each may be satisfactory for different purposes. However, for descriptive purposes the utility of a schema hinges largely upon its fecundity. In the present instance, this means: which schema best describes the subject matter? More specifically, which schema most successfully bundles regime characteristics together, differentiating them from other bundles? Is the natural break-point among regimes to be found between autocracies and democracies (a two-part classification), among pure democracies, competitive autocracies, and pure autocracies, or is there instead a continuum of characteristics with no clear "bundles," justifying a continuous dimensional space?

Naturally, many other options might also be considered. Some might argue that regime-types are multidimensional, and therefore inappropriate for a unidimensional scale (see discussion below).[47] But all such arguments appeal to the ideal of internal coherence.

External Differentiation

A concept cannot be internally coherent unless it is distinguishable from other concepts. If apples are indistinguishable from oranges, the coherence of "apple" is called into question.[48] **External differentiation** is thus implied by internal coherence. Coherence refers to how similar a set of phenomena are to each other while differentiation refers to how different they are from surrounding phenomena. Concepts that possess both attributes may be described as "carving nature at the joints" (to use the Platonic metaphor) or identifying "natural kinds" (in Aristotelian language).

How, then, does a concept establish clearly demarcated borders? A key element is to specify carefully how a concept fits within a larger semantic field composed of neighboring concepts and referents. We shall refer to this as the background context or *contrast-space* of a concept.

Concepts are defined in terms of other concepts – boys in terms of girls, nation-states in terms of empires, parties in terms of interest groups. These neighboring terms (synonyms, near-synonyms, antonyms, and superordinate/subordinate concepts) give meaning to a concept. Precisely because of the interconnectedness of language, the redefinition of a term necessarily involves some resettling of its semantic field. It is impossible to redefine one term without also, at least by implication, redefining others. Any redefinition of democracy changes our understanding of authoritarianism.

It follows that a new concept should unsettle the semantic field as little as possible, leaving other concepts as they were (more or less).[49] Indeed, a new term or redefinition that poaches attributes from neighboring concepts is laying the ground for future conceptual anarchy. It may resonate on first reading, but is likely to foster confusion in that field or subfield over the longer-term. "Crowded" semantic fields are an example of this. Consider the many terms that have been developed over the past several decades to refer to citizen-based groups – civic association, voluntary association, civil society organization, citizen sector organization, non-governmental organization (NGO), interest group, and grassroots organization. While subtle differences may be established among these terms, one must also recognize that the endless propagation of terms is not productive for this field of study. Often, neologisms are a sign of conceptual disarray rather than of theoretical fecundity.

In any case, it is incumbent upon writers to clarify how their chosen concept(s) differ from neighboring concepts sharing the same semantic and phenomenal space. This requires establishing clear contrasts with what lies *outside* the boundaries of a concept. It should be clear how democracies differ from dictatorships, and how social capital differs from ordinary networks.

Theoretical Utility

We have said that concepts play a key role within a theory (or theories). So it stands to reason that we should think about their function within that theory – its **theoretical utility** – when choosing terms and definitions.

One important function of a concept is to help define the limits of a theory, its **scope-conditions**. If one is arguing that a theory of electoral politics operates only within democracies, one must define what a democracy is – and this definition will be partly driven by what one perceive as the key elements of the theory. Perhaps the theory of electoral politics requires multi-party competition but not equal access to media and campaign finance. The definition of "democracy" should reflect that.

Within a causal theory, key concepts define the causal factor(s) and the outcome. Typically, concepts designed for use as **dependent variables** group together many attributes. Here, a diffuse definition may be fruitful. By contrast, concepts designed for use as **independent variables** are generally smaller, more parsimonious. Additionally, concept formation in the context of causal models must be careful to employ concepts that differentiate a cause from its effect, so that circularity in the argument is avoided. (These points will become clearer after a reading of Part II, focused on causality.)

Consistency

Having formed a concept, one should employ it with **consistency** throughout a study. And it should mean the same thing in all contexts that are relevant to a study. If not, the concept will generate unwanted ambiguity.

Inconsistency – where a term means something different in different contexts – creates a problem of conceptual stretching.[50] Suppose, for example, that democracy is initially defined as the existence of multi-party elections. Later on, the author uses the term in a way that suggests that civil liberties are essential to the achievement of democracy. Clearly, the term is being used inconsistently, and this cannot help but generate confusion.

One way to avoid this sort of inconsistency is to distinguish among several key terms that share common attributes by the addition of a qualifier. In this example, one might want to distinguish *electoral democracy* from *liberal democracy*.

Consistency does not imply that all users of a concept should understand it in the same way. With multivalent concepts such as democracy this is clearly impossible. Regardless of how "democracy" is defined by an author, some people will continue to use the term in different ways. There is no harm in this (so long as the chosen term resonates with at least one common meaning of the term). Indeed, the progress of social science depends upon the development of specialized terms, which coexist with a variety of everyday or specialized meanings. The criterion of consistency imposes restrictions only on the author of a study (who must use terms in a consistent fashion), not on other authors or speakers.

Strategies of Concept Formation

Having surveyed general criteria pertaining to concepts, we turn to strategies that may help to achieve these goals.

Concept formation generally begins with a survey of potential concepts. As one is formulating a theory, it is important to gather together the various terms that might be used to describe this phenomenon and commonly used definitions of these terms. Thus, if you are contemplating *social capital* you might also want to think about related terms such as *civic engagement*, *civic associations*, *civil society*, *social networks*, *participation*, and *voluntary associations*. Which of these terms expresses most accurately and precisely what you are trying to say? Which encompasses your subject, but does not extend beyond it? A well-chosen concept helps to establish the boundaries around an argument, as discussed above.

Once you have settled on a key term, begin to consider various ways of defining that term. This may be done by consulting scholarly books, dictionaries, and usage patterns. Think to yourself, what do people mean when they say "*X*"?

If there are a number of plausible definitions it may be worthwhile to break these down into their component parts. This approach is usually more useful than a listing of definitions. For example, there are an infinite number of definitions of *democracy*. However, these definitions tend to repeat standard elements, which can be organized into a single table, as shown in Table 3.2.[51]

Table 3.2 provides a fairly encompassing set of traits associated with democracy. Yet, because of the number and diversity of these attributes, this table of attributes does not take us very far toward a final definition. In order to create a more tractable – and internally coherent – empirical concept, one must go further. This next step – toward a specialized definition – is crucial. To achieve it, two approaches will be reviewed: *minimal* and *maximal*.

Minimal

One strategy seeks to identify the bare essentials of a concept, sufficient to differentiate it from neighboring concepts without excluding any of the phenomena generally understood as part of the concept. The resulting definition should be

Concepts and Measures

Table 3.2 Democracy: fundamental attributes

Electoral (elite, minimal, realist, Schumpeterian)
- *Ideals:* contestation, competition.
- *Question:* Are important government offices filled by free and fair multi-party elections?
- *Institutions:* elections, political parties, competitiveness, turnover.

Liberal
- *Ideals:* limited government, horizontal accountability, individual rights, civil liberties, transparency.
- *Question:* Is power constrained and individual rights guaranteed?
- *Institutions:* independent media, interest groups, judiciary; written constitution with explicit guarantees.

Majoritarian (responsible party government)
- *Ideals:* majority rule, centralization, vertical accountability.
- *Question:* Does the majority (or plurality) rule?
- *Institutions:* consolidated and centralized, with special focus on the role of political parties.

Consensual
- *Ideals:* power sharing, multiple veto-points.
- *Question:* How numerous, independent, and diverse are the groups and institutions that participate in policymaking?
- *Institutions:* multi-party system, proportional electoral laws, supermajorities, oversized cabinets, federalism.

Participatory
- *Ideal:* government by the people.
- *Question:* Do ordinary citizens participate in politics?
- *Institutions:* election law, civil society, local government, direct democracy.

Deliberative
- *Ideal:* government by reason.
- *Question:* Are political decisions the product of public deliberation?
- *Institutions:* media, hearings, panels, other deliberative bodies.

Egalitarian (social)
- *Ideal:* political equality.
- *Question:* Are all citizens equally empowered?
- *Institutions:* socioeconomic and political factors that generate conditions for political equality.

capable of substituting for all (non-idiosyncratic) uses of the term without too much loss of meaning. This means of course that it should not conflict with any (non-idiosyncratic) usages.

You might try this out by substituting various definitions of democracy for the term "democracy" in a sentence. That is, think of a sentence including the word "democracy." Now substitute the term for one of its definitions, as summarized in Table 3.2 or elsewhere. Does it make sense? Or does it seem strained, partial?

Each attribute that defines a concept minimally is regarded as a necessary condition; all entities must possess this attribute to be considered a member of the set. Collectively, these attributes are jointly sufficient to bound the concept. **Minimal definitions** thus aim for crisp borders, allowing for the classification of entities as "in" or "out."

Sometimes, minimal concepts are crafted around an abstract core principle such as "rule by the people." In this instance, the core meaning satisfies the criterion of resonance, for all invocations of democracy revolve in some way around this idea. However, such an abstract definition does not achieve crisp borders for the concept; indeed, it scarcely identifies borders. In this respect, it is problematic. (The rulers of North Korea would probably claim that their system of government enshrines rule by the people.)

A more common approach is to identify a specific component of the term that nearly everyone agrees upon. If we are limiting ourselves to representative democracies (excluding direct democracies), one might argue that free and fair elections constitutes a necessary condition of democracy. This attribute suffices as a minimal definition for it is sufficient to bound the entity empirically. That is, having free and fair elections makes a polity a democracy; no other attributes are necessary. And this definition is sufficient to distinguish democracy from neighboring concepts such as dictatorship.

The caveat, of course, is that we are defining democracy in a very minimal fashion, leaving other attributes often associated with the concept in abeyance. This imposes some costs in resonance. The stripped down meaning of democracy sounds hollow to those attuned to the concept's many nuances. It ignores a lot.

Maximal

Maximal definitions aim for the inclusion of all (non-idiosyncratic) attributes, thereby defining a concept in its purest, most "ideal" form. This would of course include the attribute(s) that defines the concept minimally – its necessary condition(s). As Weber describes it, "an ideal-type is formed ... by the synthesis of a great many diffuse, discrete, more or less present and occasionally absent *concrete individual* phenomena, which are arranged according to those one-sidedly emphasized viewpoints into a unified *analytical* construct."[52]

Following this recipe, one might create an ideal-type definition of democracy that includes most or all of the dimensions listed in Table 3.2. Of course, some might be excluded if it could be argued that they detract significantly from the coherence of the overall concept. Blatantly contradictory elements – such as the majoritarian and consensus components of democracy in Table 3.2 – should be avoided.

Ideal-types, as the term suggests, need not have a specific real-life empirical referent. Perhaps no extant polity achieves democracy in its purest form. To be of service, however, an ideal-type must approximate real, existing entities so that the latter can be scored according to how closely they resemble the ideal. Ideal-types are always matters of degree.

Coda

Not all definitions follow a minimal or maximal logic. Others are shaped primarily by theoretical utility, i.e., by the functions the concept is expected to perform within a larger argument and an associated research design. All definitions should, in any case, respect the general criteria of *resonance, internal coherence, external differentiation, theoretical utility*, and *consistency*, as summarized in Table 3.1.

Remember that the overarching goal of a concept is to help an argument along, to clarify what the author is trying to articulate. A key concept should not overshadow an argument. Although it is important to be self-conscious about the terms and definitions you choose, it is also important not to spend too much time defining terms; otherwise, the conceptual discussion will detract from the main point. So, define your terms carefully, making as few departures from everyday usage as possible. And then move on.

Measures

Having defined a concept, the critical issue is how to recognize it when we see it. Can democracy be distinguished from autocracy? Can a situation of high social capital be distinguished from a situation of low social capital? What do these concepts mean *empirically*?

Operationalizing a concept involves choosing an **indicator** to represent that concept empirically. This may also be referred to as a *dimension, measure*, or *variable*. Whatever the terminology, an indicator is the primitive empirical proposition underlying all other generalizing arguments about the world. An indicator of democracy might be the existence of multi-party competition. An indicator of human development might be the infant mortality rate (the rate of deaths between the ages of 0 and 1 as a share of 1,000 live births). Alternatively, a number of indicators may be combined into a single *index* in order to better represent a concept.

The problem of measurement stems from the fact that most (and perhaps all) important social science concepts are not directly observable. They are *latent*. All abstract concepts fall into this category. We cannot "see" democracy or social capital. Many terms in the social science lexicon suffer this shortcoming. Alienation, anomie, charisma, civil society, collective conscience, crisis, culture, democracy, dogmatism, equality, false consciousness, hegemony, ideology, legitimacy, mass society, national character, petty bourgeois, rationalization, sovereignty, state, and status anxiety are all "fuzzy" concepts. We may be able to define them in a general way, but we have immense difficulty locating their referents in empirical space. These are the sorts of measurement problems that social science is at pains to resolve.

In the following sections we review various strategies of measurement, along with the challenges that each strategy entails. These strategies involve: (a) levels of

Table 3.3 Measurement strategies

Levels of abstraction
- High
- Medium
- Low

Scales
- Categorical (Nominal, Ordinal)
- Numeric (Interval, Ratio)

Aggregation
- Boolean
- Additive
- Multiplicative
- Factor-analytic

Objectives
- Discrimination
- Grouping

abstraction, (b) scales, (c) aggregation techniques, and (d) basic objectives, as summarized in Table 3.3.

Levels of Abstraction

All empirical concepts of interest to social science encompass multiple **levels of abstraction**. At the very least, one can distinguish between the attributes that define a concept and the indicators that operationalize it, generating two tiers: (a) **conceptualization** and (b) **measurement**. This is probably sufficient for a small-order concept like *political parties* or *elections*.

For more abstract concepts like *democracy* multiple tiers may be required to adequately represent all the levels of analysis implicit in the concept, and to fully operationalize it – to bring it down to earth, so to speak. Consider the following hierarchy:

1. *Democracy* (the latent concept of theoretical interest)
   2. *Electoral* (a conception of democracy)
      3. *Free and fair elections* (a key component of electoral democracy)
         4. *Validation of an election by international election observers* (an indicator of free/fair elections)

Here, four tiers of a concept are illustrated. Naturally, one might add levels at the bottom of the hierarchy (e.g., a more specific and operational definition of international election observers to determine the freeness and fairness of elections and how disagreements among them should be resolved), at the top (e.g., a superordinate category that subsumes democracy such as *governance*), or somewhere in the middle. The tiers on a ladder of abstraction are in some sense arbitrary and can be expanded or contracted like an accordion.

Sometimes, problems of measurement can be resolved, or at least mitigated, by moving down the ladder of abstraction, e.g., from #1 (Democracy) to #2 (Electoral) to #3 (Free and fair elections) to #4 (Validation of an election by international election observers). Small, concrete things are often easier to measure than large, abstract things.

Naturally, at a certain point micro-level phenomena become less observable, and more difficult to measure. This is the situation faced in fields like biology and physics, where molecules and subatomic particles are at the frontiers of measurement. In the social sciences, however, the individual (i.e., the whole human being) is usually regarded as the most disaggregated unit of analysis. In these fields, problems of measurement are generally the product of abstraction, not of specificity.

At the same time, as one scopes down from "democracy" to low-level indicators one may find that the connection between the concept and the phenomena becomes highly attenuated. A chosen indicator may be highly precise but of questionable validity with respect to a high-order concept of theoretical interest. For example, if one attempts to measure the existence of democracy solely by looking at the decisions of international election observers one may feel that important elements of the concept are being ignored. This is the tradeoff encountered when moving along a ladder of abstraction: precision is usually enhanced as one moves down while conceptual validity is enhanced as one moves up. (These terms are formally defined in Chapter 4.)

Scales

Measurement is an inherently comparative venture. It presumes a **scale** – i.e., a standard metric by which heterogeneous things can be systematically and precisely compared. Hence, all attempts at measurement face a problem of equivalence or consistency across contexts. A chosen measure must mean the same thing, and must adequately represent the concept of theoretical interest, across all contexts to which it is being applied. The challenge is therefore to find a way to compare things across diverse contexts without too much loss of meaning or distortion.

Some scales are **categorical** (qualitative), by virtue of the fact that the distance between categories is undefined. Other scales are **numeric** (quantitative) by virtue of the fact that the distance between categories is defined and measured along a numeric scale. Within this two-part classification other subtypes fall, as indicated in Table 3.4.

Among categorical scales, those that are **nominal** define members of the same class (they are examples of something) but are unranked. For example, apples, oranges, and grapes are all correctly classified as fruit; but they are not more or less of anything relative to each other.

Table 3.4   Typology of scales

		Different categories	Ranked categories	Distance between categories measured	True zero
Categorical	Nominal	x			
	Ordinal	x	x		
Numeric	Interval	x	x	x	
	Ratio	x	x	x	x

Ordinal scales are members of the same class and also ranked: very sweet is sweeter than sweet. But one does not know the true distance separating each level in the scale. It is unclear, for example, how much sweeter "very sweet" is relative to "sweet."

Among numeric scales, those that are **interval** are characterized by a consistent measure of distance between categories. For example, the distance between 3 and 4 on a temperature scale (Celsius or Fahrenheit) is the same as the distance between 25 and 26, and is defined by a formal rule, consistently applied across the scale.

Ratio scales are interval scales with a true zero, indicating the absence of whatever quantity is being measured (a null set). In the case of money, 0 signals no money. In the case of temperature on the Kelvin scale, 0 indicates the absence of all thermal energy.

Frequently, interval and ratio scales fulfill the requirements of a numeric scale only within certain bounds. For example, life-span is bounded on the lower end at zero (arguably, it is also bounded at the upper end, though this boundary is more difficult to define).

Because scales are defined for specific purposes the same phenomena may be differently classified. For some purposes, it may be sensible to consider varieties of fruit as nominal categories. For other purposes, it may be sensible to consider them as part of an ordinal scale (more or less acidic) or a ratio scale (using a ratio measure of acidity).

For many topics, it is correct to regard higher-level scales as more informative. Thus, we would ordinarily interpret an ordinal scale for temperature ("hot," "medium," "cold") as less precise (and therefore less informative) than an interval scale (e.g., Celsius) or ratio scale (e.g., Kelvin). However, this is true only with reference to that particular phenomenon. It would not be true for sex, for example, since this dimension admits of only two categories – male and female (as usually understood). Here, an interval scale reduces to a nominal scale.

Note also that while more precise indicators promise more, they also demand more. Specifically, they require a greater number of assumptions about the nature of the underlying data. If any of these assumptions are false, or only partially true, any inference building upon that indicator will be cast in doubt.

Table 3.5 A single index with multiple interpretations

Key concept: *Electoral contestation*[53]

Authoritarianism: No elections or elections with only one party or candidate.

Semi-authoritarianism: Elections in which more than one party or candidate runs but not all parties and candidates face the possibility of losing.

Semi-democracy: Elections in which more than one party or candidate run and all parties and candidates face the possibility of losing but not all parties or candidates are allowed to participate.

Democracy: Elections in which only anti-system extremist groups are banned and all parties and candidates face the possibility of losing.

Let us explore some examples.

For many purposes, it is essential to distinguish polities in a dichotomous fashion, as democratic or authoritarian (autocratic).[54] This produces a nominal scale with two categories, also known as a **binary** scale or dummy variable. These categories might be Yes/No, Present/Absent, High/Low, Male/Female, or, in our example, Democratic/Autocratic.

For other purposes, one may require a more finely graded indicator of democracy. Gerardo Munck defines a four-level ordinal index of electoral contestation including categories for authoritarianism, semi-authoritarianism, semi-democracy, and democracy.[55] Here, each category is distinguishable and clearly ranked relative to the concept of theoretical interest. Defining attributes for each category are elaborated in Table 3.5. If one is willing to accept the additional assumption that categories in the four-point scale are equidistant, one may regard this index as an interval scale. And insofar as the first category comprises a true zero – no contestation whatsoever – the index may also be understood as a ratio scale.

This example nicely illustrates the fact that the same set of categories may be differently interpreted, according to different assumptions about the underlying empirical phenomena and different uses for which the same indicator may be enlisted.

Choices among scales are often driven by their relative tractability. For some purposes, binary scales are more useful than interval scales, and vice versa. The point to keep in mind is that these decisions, while analytically convenient, often involve either a loss of information and/or the introduction of bias in the variable of interest. Although there are no "natural" scales, some interpretations of reality are more plausible than others.

Aggregation

While concrete concepts such as infant mortality may be measurable with a single indicator, more complex concepts such as democracy usually require the inclusion of several elements into a single index. In these settings, researchers must grapple with the problem of **aggregation**.

Perhaps the simplest way to construct an index is with the deterministic conditions prescribed by **Boolean** (set theory) logic. In this setting, all indicators must be coded in a binary (0/1) fashion. For purposes of illustration, let us return to the attribute of democracy known as "free and fair elections." This attribute may be understood in one of three ways.

1   As a *necessary* condition of democracy, a polity must embody this attribute, though there may be other membership conditions as well. A polity must have free and fair elections in order to qualify as democratic, but having free and fair elections is not sufficient to qualify as democratic.

2   As a *sufficient* condition, this feature is sufficient by itself to qualify a polity as democratic, though there are understood to be other conditions that would also qualify a polity as democratic. For example, one might take the position that democracy can be achieved either through free and fair elections or through deliberative decisionmaking. In one version of democracy people rule through chosen representatives and in another version of democracy the people rule directly (on the model of the Athenian polis). In this situation, two attributes are substitutable for the other. The possession of either attribute is sufficient to define a concept.

3   As a *necessary-and-sufficient* condition of democracy, this is the only characteristic that matters. A polity with free and fair elections is a democracy; one without is an autocracy. That is all there is to it.

Boolean conditions aggregate in an explicit and clear-cut fashion. For example, if democracy is operationalized with three necessary conditions, all must be satisfied in order to code a case as democratic. If democracy is operationalized with three sufficient conditions, one or more conditions must be satisfied in order to code a case as democratic. If democracy is operationalized with a single necessary-and-sufficient condition, this condition must be satisfied in order to code a case as democratic; no other conditions are relevant.

Set-theoretic conditions may be combined in various ways to form a single aggregation formula (so long as they don't contradict each other). In principle, there is no limit to the number of necessary or sufficient conditions that can be accommodated.[56] Set-theoretic conditions are thus easy to aggregate.

Unfortunately, it is often difficult to reduce the complexities of social life to traits that can be coded in a binary fashion without losing important information or making arbitrary judgments. Likewise, attributes do not always combine in a crisp, Boolean fashion to capture the concept of interest. Thus, we are led to consider a variety of alternatives.

An **additive** index combines indicators by addition, with the assumption that each component is equal (in importance) and independent (its contribution to the concept of interest is independent of the values of other indicators). Suppose four attributes – X_1, X_2, X_3, X_4 – are considered relevant to measuring democracy. An additive index could be constructed in two steps. First, one would need to adjust the scales of these variables so that they align with one another. Note that if one indicator is scored from 0 to 1 and another from 0 to 100 the latter will carry 100 times the weight of the former in an additive index. Interval scales may be aligned by finding a common denominator (e.g., 100) or by converting each variable to standardized ("Z") scores, as explained in Chapter 17. The second and final step is to add each indicator together $(X_1 + X_2 + X_3 + X_4)$.

A **multiplicative** index combines indicators by multiplication, with the assumption that each component is equal but not independent (its contribution to the concept of interest depends on the values of other indicators). Here, too, it is important to examine the impact of diverse scales – although the correct solution is not always to align them to a common scale. For example, it may be important to maintain a binary scale (0/1) rather than to convert it to an interval scale.

Zero plays an especially important part in multiplicative indices. Note that if any indicator is equal to zero the resulting index will take on the value of zero, regardless of the value of other indicators. An example of this can be found in Tatu Vanhanen's index of democracy, which combines two factors: (a) the competitiveness of an election (100 minus the share of the vote garnered by the largest party) and (b) the rate of participation in that election (turnout, understood as a ratio of the total population, from 0 to 100%). These are multiplied together and divided by 100 to form an index of democracy.[57] Note that if only one party is allowed to compete in elections, factor (a) will take the value of zero. When multiplying this with (b) the participation rate, the result will also be zero – regardless of how many people show up to vote. This underscores an assumption, namely that participation does not count for democracy unless some degree of multi-party competition is allowed. North Korea is not more democratic than Cuba even if it has higher turnout elections.

A **factor-analytic** index is generated by factor analysis, with the assumption that each component is equal and independent. This approach uses an algorithm – usually *principal components* – to find the common dimension(s) among a number of indicators. Typically, researchers are only interested in the first dimension, the one that explains the most variance across the chosen indicators. But sometimes, they will retain other dimensions to be used as indices for concepts of theoretical interest.

In this fashion, Michael Coppedge, Angel Alvarez, and Claudia Maldonado explore empirical patterns across 15 measures of democracy, including the well-known Freedom House and Polity indices.[58] They discover that about 75% of the variance in these measures is reducible to two relatively distinct components: *contestation* (competitive elections and associated institutions) and *inclusiveness* (e.g., broad suffrage and high turnout). Since these components have strong grounding in democratic theory,[59] there are good reasons to regard them as more than empirical artifacts.

Having surveyed a few of the most common methods of aggregation it is important to point out that approaches to aggregation are much more variegated than is suggested by this short list. Researchers may combine different approaches. They may weight some factors more than others, with the notion that certain factors are a priori more important. Or they may construct aggregation approaches that bear little resemblance to any of the foregoing approaches.

By way of conclusion, we note that aggregation matters. The same indicators, put together in very different ways, may produce very different indices. Whatever solution to aggregation is chosen, the researcher should be sure that it is *clear*, *explicit*, and *replicable*. That is, it should be possible for another researcher to follow the choices made by the original researcher, thereby reconstructing the index.

Objectives

The construction of an indicator may aim to achieve maximum *discrimination* among entities or optimal *grouping* among entities. The first will likely utilize numeric scales and the second will likely enlist categorical scales, as discussed above. One or the other of these fundamental objectives governs all measurement instruments. Needless to say, a single instrument is unlikely to serve both goals at once.

Discrimination refers to the ability of an instrument to reveal finely graded differences of degree – usually unidimensional but occasionally multidimensional – in some latent trait possessed by a sample of people, objects, or events. Accordingly, a test of educational achievement should provide the basis for a maximally sensitive scale (measuring differences in knowledge or ability in a subject among test-takers) with a minimal number of standardized questions. This requires that each question on the test be independent of all others and that each reflect different levels of the latent trait of interest (knowledge/ability in some subject area), thus adding to the information provided by the other questions. If two individuals with different levels of knowledge/ability give the same answer to the same question that question is not helping to discriminate between them (i.e., it is redundant). Likewise, if two questions are interdependent – such that an answer to question #2 depends (in some logical fashion) upon the answer given to question #1 – then no new information is learned from question #2. The result of a well-crafted measurement tool (constructed for the purpose of maximum discrimination) is a finely graded scale with no bunching, that is, scores are evenly distributed across the sample of respondents.

Grouping, on the other hand, refers to the ability of an instrument to sort items into discrete categories on the basis of similarities and differences in some latent trait(s). Common techniques include factor analysis, principal component analysis, cluster analysis, and Q-sort analysis. Note that the goal of crisp categories may not always be fully achievable. But it is the guiding objective. The success of a technique is its ability to sort items into discrete categories, apples with apples, oranges with oranges. If phenomena are not grouped naturally into categories ("apples," "oranges," . . .), then the job of the measurement instrument is to discern break-points in numeric scales. This may be accomplished in an inductive or deductive manner – which brings us to our next topic.

CONCLUSIONS

Arguments take shape with concepts, and concepts take empirical shape through indicators. This is the succession of topics we have followed through Chapters 2 and 3. It is worth remembering that these topics are interwoven. Concepts are built for use in arguments; they don't always make sense outside of that particular context. Indicators are inextricably linked to the concept they are intended to measure. They have no intrinsic meaning.

Nonetheless, in order to understand each component of social science methodology we need to take these components apart. That is what the foregoing chapters have attempted to do. In the next chapter, we look at the task of empirical analysis, i.e., how arguments are tested.

KEY TERMS

- Operationalization
- Resonance
- Internal coherence
- External differentiation
- Theoretical utility
- Scope-condition
- Dependent variable
- Independent variable
- Consistency
- Minimal definition
- Maximal definition
- Indicator
- Level/ladder of abstraction
- Conceptualization
- Measurement
- Scale (categorical, numeric, nominal, ordinal, interval, ratio)
- Binary
- Aggregation
- Boolean
- Necessary and sufficient conditions
- Additive
- Multiplicative
- Factor-analytic

4 Analyses

We began (in Chapter 2) with arguments and proceeded (in Chapter 3) to conceptualization and measurement. In this chapter, we turn to the problem of how to analyze an argument empirically. This may be referred to variously as *appraisal, assessment, corroboration, demonstration, empirics, evaluation, methods, proof,* or *testing*. Pursued in a self-conscious fashion, this stage of research involves a **research design**, i.e., an explicit method of selecting and analyzing data.

We begin by introducing a set of key terms that are necessary to understand the construction of a research design. We proceed to a discussion of the general issues that all analyses encounter. This includes precision and validity, internal and external validity, sample representativeness, sample size, probability and non-probability sampling, and missing-ness. The terms and topics introduced in this chapter will enter the narrative in later chapters repeatedly. This chapter therefore plays a foundational role in the book.

Definitions

A standard empirical analysis involves a number of components, which must be clarified before we continue. Much of this vocabulary is borrowed from survey research. Nonetheless, the concepts are helpful in all styles of research, whether quantitative or qualitative, and are illustrated in Figure 4.1.

The most basic unit in any analysis is an **observation**. Observations are the pieces of evidence deemed relevant for demonstrating an argument. In a standard matrix (rectangular) dataset, an observation is usually represented as a row. Each row in Figure 4.1 represents a single observation.

Each observation should record values for all relevant **variables**. In causal analysis, this includes X (the causal factor of theoretical interest) and Y (the outcome of interest), along with any other variables deemed essential for the analysis. In a rectangular dataset, variables are usually represented with vertical lines. There are three variables in Figure 4.1: X, Z, and Y.

An observation is drawn from a **unit** or **case** – bounded entities such as individuals, organizations, communities, or nation-states, which may be observed spatially and/or temporally (through time). The terms *unit* and *case* are more or less equivalent. (While a unit is bounded spatially, a case may also have implicit or explicit temporal boundaries.)

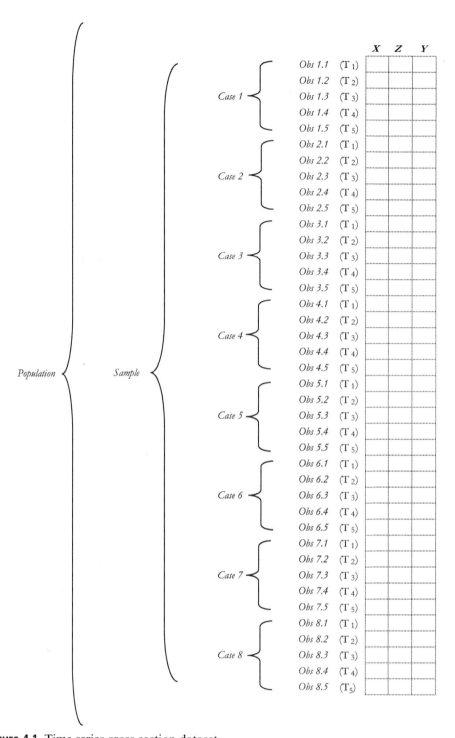

Figure 4.1 Time-series cross-section dataset
Population = Indeterminate. Cases/Units = 8. Sample/Observations (N) = 40. Cells = 120.
Time-periods (T) = 5. Variables (X, Z, Y) = 3.

Collectively, the observations in a study comprise a study's **sample**. The size of a sample is the total number of observations, often denoted as "N." (N may also refer to the number of units or cases, which may be considerably less than the number of observations. This should be clear from context.)

A **population** is the universe of phenomena that a hypothesis seeks to describe or explain. It usually remains unstudied, or is studied only in a very informal manner, e.g., through the secondary literature.

The sample (the observations that are actually studied) is drawn from the population, and is usually much smaller. Hence, the notion of *sampling* from a population. Note, however, that the term sample, as used here, does not imply that the studied observations have been chosen randomly from a population. This ideal is rarely followed in practice, as discussed below.

Occasionally, a set of observations includes the entire population of interest. This is known as a **census**. A population census includes all persons residing within a country (though of course coverage is never entirely comprehensive). Likewise, a census study of nation-states would include all nation-states. Since census studies (where $N_{sample} = N_{population}$) are rare, we leave them aside in the following discussion.

These interrelated concepts are illustrated in Figure 4.1, where we can see a fairly typical time-series cross-section research design in a rectangular dataset format. Recall, observations are represented as rows, variables as columns, and cells as their intersection. Note that cells are nested within observations, observations are nested within units (aka cases), units are nested within the sample, and the sample is nested within the population.

Hypothetically, let us imagine that the population of the inference includes all worker-training programs in the United States and the sample consists of eight programs, observed annually for five years, yielding a sample of forty observations ($N = 40$). The **units of analysis** (the type of phenomena treated as observations in an analysis) in this hypothetical example are program-years.

All these terms are slippery insofar as they depend for their meaning on a particular proposition and a corresponding research design. Any changes in that proposition may affect the sorts of phenomena that are classified as observations and units, not to mention the composition of the sample and the population. Thus, an investigation of worker-training programs might begin by identifying *programs* as the principal unit of analysis but then shift to a lower **level of analysis** (e.g., *participants*) or a higher level of analysis (e.g., *states*) at different points in the study. Sometimes, different levels of analysis are combined in a single study. This is common in *case study* work (see Chapter 9) and is the defining feature of *hierarchical (multi-level)* statistical models.

Before leaving this discussion of basic terms we must address the important distinction between *quantitative* and *qualitative* analysis. This contrast is ubiquitous, and will no doubt be familiar to the reader. But it is also ambiguous since these terms can be defined in many different ways, and sometimes they are not defined at all. In this text, we adopt the following definitions.

Quantitative analysis is a formal analysis of matrix-based observations. A matrix observation is the conventional sort, represented as a row in a rectangular dataset (illustrated in Figure 4.1). Each observation is coded along a number of dimensions understood as columns in the matrix and as variables in an analysis. All observations are regarded as examples of the same general phenomenon and are presumed to have been drawn from the same population. Each is regarded as comparable to all the others (with some degree of error) with respect to whatever analysis is undertaken. The analysis is "formal" insofar as it rests on an explicit framework of inference such as logic/set theory, Bayesian statistics, frequentist statistics, or randomization inference.

By contrast, **qualitative** analysis refers to an informal analysis of non-comparable observations. Non-comparable observations cannot be arrayed in a matrix format because they are examples of different things, drawn from different populations. The analysis is "informal" insofar as it is articulated with natural language and is unconnected to an explicit and general framework of inference. When applied in the context of causal inference this sort of evidence may be referred to as *causal-process observations, clues, colligation, congruence, genetic explanation, narrative analysis*, or *process tracing*.[60]

There is a strong elective affinity between quantitative analysis and large samples, as well as between qualitative analysis and small samples. One would be hard-pressed to apply informal styles of analysis to a sample of 1,000. Likewise, one would be hard-pressed to apply a formal analysis to a sample of two. The size of a sample thus influences the style of analysis. However, it does not determine it. This is apparent in the middle range. A sample of 20 may be analyzed formally or informally (or both). Thus, when we use the terms quantitative and qualitative the reader should understand that the former usually (but not always) corresponds to large samples and the latter usually (but not always) corresponds to small samples. The qual/quant distinction is not solely a matter of N.

So defined, there is no epistemological gulf separating quantitative and qualitative analysis. Indeed, any qualitative analysis can be quantified – with the cost of reducing complex, multifaceted data into matrix observations. Many quantitative datasets began life, one might say, as a series of qualitative observations. These were then coded in a systematic fashion to generate a set of observations that could be arrayed in a dataset. Often, this is useful. But not always; nor is it always possible. That is why qualitative analysis continues to play an important role in social science research – and especially in case study research, as discussed in Chapter 9.

That said, quantitative analysis is dominant in many fields and also has a more developed methodology. Consequently, when we use the term "observation" or "analysis" in this book the reader can assume that we are talking about the quantitative variety, unless stated otherwise.[61]

Precision and Validity

Social science analyses strive for *precision* (aka *reliability*) and *validity* (aka the absence of *bias*). **Precision** refers to the closeness of repeated estimates of the

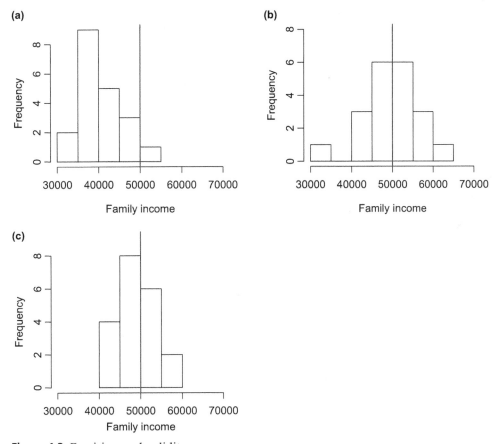

Figure 4.2 Precision and validity
Methods of sampling: (a) hardline telephones, (b) hardline phones and cell phones, (c) door-to-door canvassing. Vertical line: true value, according to US census.

phenomenon of interest when using the same measurement instrument or causal model. **Validity** refers to the closeness of an estimate to the true (often unknown) value. To explore these concepts we employ a hypothetical example.

In recent years, survey researchers have employed a number of techniques to obtain representative samples of the general public. These include (a) hardline telephones, (b) hardline phones and cell phones, and (c) door-to-door canvassing.

In order to evaluate their precision and validity, we shall imagine employing each of these recruitment techniques to conduct 20 surveys of the general public in the United States. Each survey includes 2,000 participants, who are chosen in whatever fashion the pollster believes will result in the most representative sample. There is only one question on the survey: What is your family income? For each sample, we calculate the **median** (that value for which there are equal numbers of values above and below). These results are plotted on the graphs in Figure 4.2.

We shall assume that census results represent the true value of household income in the country. In 2006, the United States Census Bureau reported that the median annual household income was roughly $50,000. This value is represented by a vertical line in Figure 4.2, and is the quantity of theoretical interest.

Results for the first recruitment technique – hardline telephones – are presented in panel (a) of Figure 4.2. They suggest that this method is fairly precise, as the estimates cluster tightly around the sample median. However, the sample median falls far from the true value (the median value for the population, as revealed by census data), suggesting that the method is not valid.

Results for the second recruitment technique – hardline phones and cell phones – are presented in panel (b). They suggest that the method is imprecise, as estimates vary widely around the sample median. However, the sample median falls close to the true value, so the technique may be regarded as valid (in repeated sampling).

Results for the third recruitment technique – door-to-door canvassing – presented in panel (c), is both precise (tightly clustered) and valid (close to the population value of interest). Thus, on the basis of this set of tests, door-to-door canvassing is superior to the other sampling techniques. Of course, these results are entirely hypothetical. You should also note that many other factors – including cost – may figure into a pollster's decision to employ a method of sampling. Nonetheless, the illustration is effective in demonstrating a crucial distinction between precision and validity.

Let us now elaborate a bit on these concepts and their employment in social science research.

Precision, or reliability, refers to level of stochastic (random) error, or **noise**, encountered in measurement or some other feature of estimation. Precision in measurement is often assessable through **reliability tests**, where the same technique of data gathering is employed multiple times in order to ascertain its reliability. Reliability tests might focus on a survey technique, as in our example, on experts who code data from a primary or secondary source, or on any aspect of data collection. If multiple applications of the measurement instrument reveal a high level of consistency one may regard the chosen instrument or model as reliable (precise). This is typically calculated as the inverse of the **variance** (i.e., dispersion around the mean). Greater variance means less reliability. The same logic applies to precision in causal inference, i.e., when one is comparing models employed to assess a causal relationship between X and Y.

If the opportunity to test multiple iterations of an indicator or model is not present then the issue of reliability remains at the level of an assumption. But it is nonetheless crucial. A high probability of random error may doom even the simplest generalization about the world.

Validity, by contrast, refers to *systematic* measurement error, error that – by definition – introduces bias into the resulting analysis. One often finds, for example, that the level of accuracy with which an indicator is measured varies directly with some factor of theoretical interest. For example, in constructing international indicators for human development (e.g., life expectancy, literacy) and economic performance (e.g., inflation, GDP) we rely on surveys conducted in countries throughout the world. Sometimes, these surveys present a more favorable picture of the quality of life or the strength of the economy than is warranted. And there is some reason to imagine that autocratic governments engage in this practice to a greater extent than democratic governments. If so, these indicators suffer from systematic bias. However, because we cannot be sure of this bias, and have no estimate of its extent, we have no easy means to correct it.

While we can usually assess reliability we rarely have a fix on the problem of validity. Note that our hypothetical example is highly unusual in one important respect: we know the true value of the measure of interest – $50,000. In the world of social science it is rare to possess a definitive measure of anything of great substantive importance. Indeed, our hypothetical example might be challenged on the ground that population censuses are never entirely comprehensive; some citizens escape the prying eyes of government surveyors. In the 2000 US Census, for example, despite elaborate advertising and outreach, the overall mail response rate was only 64%.[62] Worryingly, these non-respondents may be quite different than respondents, leading to systematic bias, a problem the Census Bureau is aware of and attempts to evaluate.[63] For example, homeless people are less likely to be contacted in a census and since homeless people have much lower family income than people with stable addresses it is reasonable to suppose that all census-based data (unless adjusted to correct for this deficiency) is biased to some extent. Various sociodemographic groups and geographic areas have been shown to be underrepresented, especially Blacks and Hispanics.[64]

All of this is to say that validity, unlike reliability, is very difficult to test in a definitive fashion. Even our toy example is open to dispute. And with more complex concepts such as democracy or GDP the points of potential dispute are multiplied. For causal inferences, which build on descriptive inferences, the problem is magnified even further.

Internal and External Validity

Typically, researchers examine only a small number of instances of a phenomenon of interest. If one is trying to ascertain the median income within a large population, as in the example explored above, one might sample only 2,000 respondents. On this basis one would hope to infer median income across 320 million people. Even more striking is the attempt to learn something about human nature from experiments conducted on a sample of college students drawn from a single classroom, a common practice in psychology. Here, a sample of several hundred may be the basis for generalizations about the entire human race.

In either case, social science must grapple with a crucial question: how to relate findings drawn from a sample to a larger population of interest.

This problem engages researchers in a two-level game. The first part of the game concerns reaching conclusions about the sample. The second part of the game is about extrapolating those conclusions to a larger population, sometimes referred to as a problem of **inference**.

To distinguish these two spheres of truth social scientists invoke a distinction between **internal** and **external validity**. The first refers to the validity of a hypothesis with respect to the studied sample. In our previous example, a problem of internal validity may arise if respondents lie about their family income, perhaps in response to perceived norms. If so, a calculation of mean family income for a single sample – or a group of samples – may be too high or too low.

The second issue arises when we try to extend sample-based results to a larger population. Naturally, if there are problems of internal validity there are likely to be problems of external validity. But even if our analyses of the sample are correct they may not be correct across a larger population. This is the problem of external validity, toward which the rest of the chapter is directed.

With respect to external validity, two characteristics of a sample are especially relevant: *sample representativeness* and *sample size*.

Sample Representativeness

The external validity of a study is grounded largely on the **representativeness** of a chosen sample. Is the sample similar to the population with respect to the hypothesis that is being tested? Are we entitled to generalize from a given sample to a larger universe of cases?

In the case of research into income one must consider whether the sample exhibits the same income distribution as the general population. In the case of research into cognitive properties of human nature one must consider whether college students are similar in these respects to other humans (and how far back in time a result might be generalizable). And with respect to studies of worker-training programs one must consider whether the chosen program sites are representative of a larger population of programs that one wishes to understand.

Note that questions about representativeness are also questions about how to *define* the population. Consider the study of worker-training programs that focuses on programs in the state of New York. It could be that results from this study are generalizable (a) to that state (only), (b) to the United States, (c) to advanced industrial societies, or (d) to all societies in the contemporary era. Likewise, it could be that the results are generalizable (a) to native-born unemployed persons between the ages of 20 and 50 without disabilities, (b) to unemployed people between the ages of 20 and 50 without disabilities, (c) to people between the ages of 20 and 50 without disabilities, (d) to people without disabilities, or (e) to all people.

The point is that any consideration of external validity forces one to be very specific about the population and the scope-conditions of an inference. What is the population, exactly? What is it, exactly, that is generalizable to that population?

Unfortunately, these questions are often difficult to answer in a definitive fashion, for reasons already discussed (see *Boundedness* in Chapter 2). However, they must be addressed, even if only in a speculative fashion.

Sample Size (*N*)

The second characteristic that impacts a study's external validity is the size of the sample upon which the study is based. More observations are better than fewer because they provide a more precise estimate of the quantity of interest.

Suppose one is trying to figure out the effect of a worker-training program on employment prospects or earnings but one has available information for only one program. Under the circumstances, it will probably be difficult to reach any firm conclusions about the matter. Of course, one case is a lot better than none. Indeed, it is a quantum leap. Yet, empirical research with only one case is also highly indeterminate, and apt to be consistent with a wide variety of competing hypotheses. Conclusions about a broader population are hazardous when one considers the many opportunities for error and the highly stochastic nature of most social phenomena.

One sort of problem stems from problems of sampling error encountered when the sample is very small. Note in order to make accurate inferences about a larger population one must have a sample that is similar to that population in relevant respects. The chances of finding such a sample when the sample is small are considerably reduced. One's chances of achieving a representative sample increase with sample size – if the sample is chosen randomly from the population. We provide a more detailed look at the importance of sample size in probability sampling in Chapter 21.

Uncertainty associated with sampling variability is captured in a statistic known as a **confidence interval**. A confidence interval indicates the bounds within which a true value is likely to fall at a chosen level of probability. A 95% confidence interval means that our confidence interval captures the true value 95% of the time. A 90% confidence interval means that our confidence interval captures the true value 90% of the time. We describe how to calculate confidence intervals and provide a more precise treatment of their interpretation in Chapter 21.

A larger sample is advisable if everything else is equal. Of course, this is sometimes not the case. For example, sometimes increasing the size of a sample decreases its representativeness. Consider a sample that is representative. Now add cases non-randomly. Chances are, the larger sample is less representative than the smaller sample. Likewise, sometimes one can gain greater leverage on a question with a carefully chosen small sample than with a large sample; this is the justification for purposive case selection procedures, discussed in the context of case study research (Chapter 9). In particular, an empirical study whose sole purpose is to disprove an invariant causal or descriptive law can achieve this purpose with a single observation – so long as it contradicts the hypothesis.

The point remains, obtaining a large sample is a noble objective so long as it doesn't interfere with other goals. When it does, the researcher needs to decide which goals to prioritize – or, alternatively, adopt a multi-method research design that incorporates large- and small-*N* components.

How large is large enough? What is an appropriate size for a sample? There is no easy answer to this question. It is not the case that sample size should be proportional to the size of the population. Sampling error rests primarily on the size of the sample not the sample/population ratio. Following precedent, i.e., what other scholars have done, may be appropriate – but only if the goals of your analysis are similar to theirs. Occasionally, one may calculate an appropriate sample size by stipulating the goals of the analysis and an acceptable confidence interval for the variable of theoretical interest. However, this only works if there is a single hypothesis (not a multitude of hypotheses) and if it is possible to identify a benchmark confidence interval (which is not always possible).

Requisite sample size depends, in general, on the relative strength of the "signal" (the variable of theoretical interest) relative to background "noise" (factors that might muffle the signal). Let us say that instead of seeking to estimate the height of individuals within a population we were interested in estimating the impact of a day-long worker-training program on subsequent earnings over the succeeding two years. As one might imagine, the impact of a single day's training on subsequent earnings is likely to be fairly minimal, and many factors other than training affect earnings. In this setting, one would presume that the ratio of signal to noise is pretty low, requiring a great many observations in order to discern a causal effect (if indeed there is one).

Probability Sampling

The preferred approach to sampling is to choose cases *randomly* from the population. Because cases are chosen randomly, one knows the probability that any given case will be chosen as a member of the sample. This approach to sampling is therefore referred to as **probability sampling**.

In **simple random sampling**, each case within the population has an equal chance of being selected for the sample. (This is sometimes referred to as an *equal probability sample*.) The mechanism of selection might be drawing balls from an urn, as in raffles. More commonly, random selection is achieved with a random-number generator from a computer program. (These may be found online or as part of a software package.) The statistics we introduce in subsequent discussion assume random sampling.

In **systematic sampling**, members of a population are chosen at equal intervals, e.g., every 10th or every 1,000th. This assures equal probability sampling *if* the chosen interval is not associated with any particular feature of the population, a matter that may be difficult to discern.

In **cluster sampling**, members of a population are divided into clusters (groups), clusters are chosen randomly (using some random-selection mechanism), and then each member of the cluster is automatically included in the sample. This approach is usually taken for logistical reasons, i.e., when it is easy to include all members of a naturally occurring cluster such as a school, neighborhood, census tract, or family.

In **stratified sampling**, each member of the population is assigned to a stratum and cases are chosen randomly from within each stratum. If the number chosen from each stratum does not reflect the proportional size of that stratum within the population, cases will need to be re-weighted so that the resulting sample is representative of the population. For example, in a sample of 2,000 individuals drawn from the United States it may be important for theoretical reasons to identify strata composed of various minority groups. While some minorities like Hispanics and African-Americans are quite large, others such as Jewish-Americans are quite small (roughly 3% of the general population). A stratum composed of 3% of 2,000 yields a sub-sample of only 60 individuals – too small to allow for precise estimates of the actual population of Jews in the United States. Under the circumstances, it probably makes sense to *over-sample* among Jews, granting Jews a greater probability of entering the sample than members of other social groups. Let us say that the researcher decides to select twice as many Jews as their share of the population would allow, raising their share of the sample to 6%. Representativeness can then be restored to the sample by down-weighting Jews in the sample – in this case, granting half the weight to Jewish respondents as to other respondents. This approach is generally cheaper to implement than the alternative approach – doubling the size of the entire sample (e.g., from 2,000 to 4,000) – and achieves the same results. Naturally, it requires that one identify those strata which are of theoretical interest prior to drawing the sample.

Various approaches – simple, systematic, cluster, stratified – may be combined in *multi-stage sampling*. For example, one might begin with clusters, stratify within clusters, and then sample randomly within each cluster/stratum. The key point is that whatever system of probability sampling is employed, disproportionalities should be corrected (by weighting) so that the sample is representative of the population of interest.

A key advantage of probability sampling is that one can estimate sampling variability (from sample to sample), thus providing estimates of precision to accompany whatever inferences one wishes to draw. It is not enough to say that a sample is "large" and therefore "precise." One wishes, as well, to know *how* precise a given sample estimate is, that is, how close it is likely to be to the population parameter.

Non-Probability Sampling

A very different approach to sampling is to select cases *non-randomly* from a population. A small number of cases may be selected with specific purposes in mind, as in case study designs (see Chapter 9). Cases may be chosen in a **snowball** fashion. This approach is common in interview-based research, when one relies on each respondent to suggest other possible respondents – creating a snowball effect (the ball of respondents gets larger as each new snowflake joins the ball). Cases may also be chosen for logistical reasons, e.g., because they are accessible, cheap, or for some other reason easy to study. This is sometimes known as **convenience sampling**.

In all of these approaches the researcher has no way of assessing the probability, for each case in the population, of being selected into the sample. Accordingly, these approaches are sometimes referred to as *non-probability samples*. Such approaches produce samples of uncertain representativeness. We don't know how similar they are to the population of interest; likewise, we may be uncertain about what that population is. If the sample is small, as it is with case study designs, then the study also faces a problem of reliability (imprecision).

From the perspective of external validity there is little to be said in favor of non-probability sampling. However, external validity is not the only goal of social science research, and other goals sometimes require non-probability approaches to sampling.

At an early stage of investigation, when not much is known about the phenomenon of interest and before one has identified a specific hypothesis, it is common to focus on a small number of cases so that one may observe those cases in an intensive fashion. Likewise, if one already has a clear sense of a relationship but one does not know why it obtains, one might prefer to focus on a small number of cases, intensively observed. These are classic justifications for a case study research design.

While it may be feasible to select a single case, or several cases, randomly from a population, our earlier discussion – of sample size – shows how unreliable such tiny samples can be. For this reason, one is generally advised not to use a probability-based method for choosing a very small sample. The exception would be a situation in which cases found within the same stratum are all equally informative. Here, one may elect to choose cases within that stratum randomly. While this introduces an element of randomness, it applies only to the chosen stratum or strata. Presumably, not all strata would be included so that the resulting sample remains unrepresentative of the population.

Even where studies incorporate a large sample it still may be undesirable, or impossible, to implement probability-based sampling procedures. Worker-training programs cannot draw randomly from the universe of unemployed people because many people will refuse to participate. As such, the sample of subjects analyzed in such a study are not likely to be representative of the larger population of unemployed – though they might be considered representative of a smaller population vaguely defined as "those who are willing to participate in a worker-training program."

Wherever random sampling techniques are inapplicable researchers must struggle to define the representativeness of a sample, and hence the plausible generalizability of results based on that sample. This is true regardless of whether the sample is very small (i.e., a case study format) or very large.

Missing-ness

In the discussion so far we have assumed that all cases in the population can be accessed through probability sampling procedures and that the chosen cases can be included in the sample, i.e., they can be studied. Unfortunately, this does not always hold.

There may be slippage between the population and the **sampling frame**, those members of the population who are accessible to the probability sampling procedure. For example, if a survey is conducted by telephone the only persons who can become members of the sample are those who have telephones. Thus, if one has access to all telephones – through random-digit dialing – one can obtain a representative sample of telephone owners.

Another source of bias occurs when a chosen case cannot be studied, or can be studied only partially. This might be because a respondent refuses to participate in a study (*non-response*). It might be because the respondent completes only part of a survey or does not adhere to the protocol of an experiment (*non-compliance*). It might be because a chosen case is especially sensitive, for political or ethical reasons, and therefore cannot be included in the sample. In a historical study, it might be that a chosen case does not offer the archival records that would be required in order to conduct the study. Lots of things may intervene to thwart the goals of a sampling procedure.

We shall refer to these problems generically as **missing-ness**, that is *missing data*. What is meant by missing data is that a sample lacks observations for some units that should (by some probability-based principle of selection) be included.

If the pattern of missing data is random it causes little harm. Suppose that those who own phones and agree to conduct a survey are no different (in relevant respects) to those who do not. The survey researcher need only increase the number of calls in order to obtain the desired sample size, which will in any case be representative.

If, however, the pattern of missing-ness is systematic then the sample will be biased. For example, if telephone owners are different from those who don't own telephones in ways that are relevant to the analysis, estimates will be biased away from the (true) population parameters. (A good deal of research has gone into this question, with inconclusive results.)

A potential solution is to fill in missing data, creating a full sample that is larger and – one hopes – more representative than the truncated sample. If one has a good guess about the nature of the missing data one may develop a simple decision rule for filling in missing observations. For example, if one knows (from other sources) the mean income of persons without telephones, and their share of the general population, one might use this value for all such phantom respondents, thus rectifying the non-representativeness of the sampling frame.

Another approach is to employ a statistical model (an algorithm) to estimate missing values based on patterns in the data that have been gathered. This requires knowing something about the cases that have missing values. Let us say that we know their telephone prefix, and that we can safely assume people with the same prefixes share certain characteristics (because they live in the same area or were assigned their cell phone number at the same time). On this basis, we might estimate the income of these non-respondents based on information that we have already collected from respondents with the same prefix who answered their phones and completed the survey.[65]

CONCLUSIONS

In this chapter, we have introduced the core elements of empirical analysis in social science, applicable to both descriptive and causal analyses. After reviewing key terms, we discussed the twin goals of precision and validity. Next, we distinguished between internal and external validity. The final sections of the chapter dealt with the attempt to achieve external validity. This quest involves sample representativeness and sample size. Specific techniques include probability sampling, missing-ness, and **non-probability sampling**.

By way of conclusion, it is worth pointing out the obvious: all empirical knowledge is to some extent uncertain. This stems, arguably, from stochastic features of the world at a subatomic level – a matter debated by scholars of philosophy of science and physics. It stems, in any case, from our inability to attain perfect understanding of the complex world around us. Consequently, there is always a degree of uncertainty about any statement we might make about the world, even if the degree of uncertainty is judged to be quite small. Note that as the topic increases in importance the level of uncertainty usually rises in tandem. We can make mundane statements about the world with a high level of certainty, but we cannot pronounce upon the causes of democratization, or the causes of war and peace, with such assurance. It follows that the most relevant work in social science – in the sense of addressing issues that ordinary people care deeply about – is often accompanied by a high degree of uncertainty.

One of the features that distinguish science from other modes of apprehending the world – for which "journalism" is our convenient foil – is the attempt to represent uncertainty in a forthright and realistic manner (rather than sweeping it under the rug, so to speak). To that end, we must address a common misunderstanding.

Measures of precision, as discussed in this chapter, usually encompass only one source of uncertainty – that associated with sampling from a population. Other sources of uncertainty such as that associated with measurement (discussed in Chapter 3) or causal inference (discussed in Part II) are not generally incorporated into sampling-based statistics. Thus, when you encounter terms that purport to measure uncertainty – e.g., *variance, standard error, t statistic, confidence interval* – it is important to bear in mind that these statistics are probably taking account of only one threat to inference. Other threats to inference, although more common and more problematic, are harder to measure in an objective fashion, and hence go unreported or are dealt with in prose. This is another reminder that methodological adequacy is often not summarizable in handy statistical formats. You have to slog through the details of a research design to see its strengths and weaknesses.

KEY TERMS

- Research design
- Observation

Key Terms

- Variable
- Unit/case
- Sample
- Population
- Census
- Unit of analysis
- Level of analysis
- Quantitative
- Qualitative
- Precision
- Validity
- Median
- Noise
- Reliability tests
- Variance
- Inference
- Internal/external validity
- Representativeness
- Sample size
- Confidence interval
- Probability sampling
- Simple random sampling
- Systematic sampling
- Cluster sampling
- Stratified sampling
- Snowball sampling
- Convenience sampling
- Sampling frame
- Missing-ness
- Non-probability sampling

II Causality

Causation is the central explanatory trope by which relationships among persons and things are established – the cement of the universe, in Hume's words.[66] Without some understanding of who is doing what to whom we cannot make sense of the world that we live in, we cannot hold people and institutions accountable for their actions, and we cannot act efficaciously in the world. Without a causal understanding of the world it is unlikely that we could navigate even the most mundane details of our lives, much less plan for the future. This is obvious in the policy world, where causal understanding undergirds any rational intervention. One must have some sense of what impact a policy is likely to have in order to support its adoption.

Even where causal understanding does not relate to future changes in the status quo we are likely to be reassured when we can order events around us into cause-and-effect relationships. "When we have such understanding," notes Judea Pearl, "we feel 'in control' even if we have no practical way of controlling things."[67] Causality is not just a methodological preoccupation. It is also a way of relating to the world. That said, there are important differences between causal inference in everyday contexts and in social-scientific contexts.

Chapter 5 introduces a variety of causal frameworks that are widely employed in social science today. They may be viewed as the building blocks of a causal explanation. Chapter 6 defines the topic of causality, and lays out the attributes of a good causal hypothesis and the core components of causal analysis. Chapter 7 discusses experimental research designs, where the causal factor of interest is randomized across groups. Chapter 8 discusses large-N observational designs (i.e., non-experimental designs). Chapter 9 deals with case study designs, where the number of units is limited to one or several. Chapter 10 reviews and reflects on various aspects of causal inference, serving as a coda for this part of the book.

5 Causal Frameworks

There are many sorts of causal factors and many sorts of causal mechanisms. Indeed, the variety of causal frameworks is so great that no overview can hope to be comprehensive. Even so, certain explanations are common enough across the social sciences to deserve our attention.

Three general causal frameworks are ubiquitous. *Motivational* frameworks include interests, norms, and psychology. *Structural* frameworks include material factors, human capital/demography, and institutions. *Interactive* frameworks include explanations grounded in adaptation, coordination, diffusion, networks, and path dependence. These varied approaches to explanation are summarized in Table 5.1.

In this chapter, we lay out each framework along with a few illustrative examples. The final section of the chapter adds important clarifications to this scaffolding and discusses how the various frameworks might be put together to provide a coherent overall explanation.

By providing an overview of these frameworks we are providing an overview of the theories that inform the social science disciplines, as well as an entrée to the

Table 5.1 Causal frameworks

Motivational frameworks
- **Interests** (that which benefits an actor)
- **Norms** (values, beliefs, ideology, culture, identity)
- **Psychology** (cognition, emotion, personality, genetics)

Structural frameworks
- **Material factors** (financial resources, geography, technology)
- **Human capital/demography** (health, education, skills, migration, life-cycle events)
- **Institutions** (formal rules and organizations)

Interactive frameworks
- **Adaptation** (feedback, competition, selection, evolution, efficiency, functionalism)
- **Coordination** (collective action, externalities, credible commitment, transaction costs)
- **Diffusion** (demonstration effect, exposure, ideas, information, knowledge, exposure)
- **Networks** (informal associational structures, social capital)
- **Path dependence** (contingent moments [critical junctures] leading to fixed trajectories)

topic of causality. Although this chapter is not essential to those that follow, it will help you to have a sense for the substantive theories that inform later discussions of causal inference.

Motivational Frameworks

One set of explanations center on motivations, i.e., what impels people to behave in certain ways or to think about things in certain ways. Three **motivational frameworks** predominate in the work of social science: *interests*, *norms*, and *psychology*.

One need not worry about which of these frameworks is "rational" or "irrational." (Whatever conclusions one might draw would depend upon how one chooses to define that complex term.) The point is that they motivate, and thereby help to explain, human attitudes and behavior.

Interests

Attitudes, preferences, and behavior are often the product of **interests**, i.e., what it is in the interest of a person or group to think or to do. That includes material factors (e.g., money), power, or status.[68]

Interest-based explanations play a key role in Aristotle's *Politics* and are also a hallmark of Marxist theory and of studies that adopt an economic interpretation of human behavior, including work by Charles Beard, Gary Becker, and the collaborative team of Daron Acemoglu and James Robinson.[69] Accordingly, if one wishes to explain why elites generally resist revolutionary change, and why members of the landless proletariat occasionally support fundamental change, one might begin with the notion that each group has something to gain by the positions they take in this struggle. Likewise, if one wishes to explain why rich people generally support conservative parties and poor people generally support liberal or left-wing parties, one might suppose that these well-established partisan preferences are grounded in the divergent interests of these social classes – in the one case for property rights and limited taxes and in the other case for redistribution of wealth. By the same token, a reasonable starting point for any analysis of inter-state relations is that each state has a set of interests – e.g., land, resources, power – that it wishes to protect, and if possible expand. This is the foundation of the *realist* paradigm of international relations. And finally, in understanding the behavior of politicians a reasonable starting point is the assumption that politicians desire to attain public office and, once in office, desire to maintain their position.

Interest-based explanations are often self-evident, a primal explanatory trope. When we are asked to explain a phenomenon we are apt to look first to self-interest as an explanation. However, this sort of explanation is not always as clear-cut as it may seem.

First, the various goals assembled under the rubric of interests – money, power, and status – are not always in sync. For a politician, staying in office may maximize her power while leaving office may enhance her pocketbook (if more remunerative jobs are available in the private sector). Here, two interest-based explanations collide.

Second, short- and long-run interests may conflict. For example, it may be in one's short-term interest to purchase consumption goods and in one's long-term interest to invest. To take another example, one may maximize short-term gain by stealing; but long-term financial gain is probably maximized by working hard and following prevailing rules and norms. Different temporal frames thus suggest different courses of action, and the choice between the two will depend upon other (non-interest-based) factors.

Third, actors often find themselves with conflicting interests based on different social identities. To simplify, let's think of interests as referring solely to money. If a person sacrifices to pay for her child's education she is sacrificing her interest as an individual but satisfying her interest as a parent. Likewise, one's financial interest as a member of one group (say, an ethnic group) may conflict with one's financial interest as a member of another group (say, a social class).

Fourth, since interests are often unclear, actors in the same objective position may nonetheless have different ideas about their (true) interests. For example, some members of the working class may believe their interests are best served by a socialist program while others believe their interests are best served by a conservative or liberal program. Karl Marx regarded members of the working class as victims of "false consciousness" if they did not support the communist cause. Others might argue that working classes rarely stand to benefit from communist revolutions, and thus their true interests lie with capitalism.

To sum up, it is often possible to infer attitudes and behavior from an individual's (or group's) position by assuming that people are acting to maximize their perquisites, power, or status (according to some definition of what that is). There is almost always a self-interest explanation for a persistent pattern of behavior. However, the plasticity of the concept of self-interest – the multitude of things that seem to satisfy this explanatory framework – should give one pause. There is a sense in which self-interest explains everything, and nothing.

Norms

Interest-based explanations are often contrasted with those based on **norms**. By this, we mean to include values, ideologies, beliefs, belief-systems, philosophies, worldviews, religions, cultures, identities, and other related concepts. When we use these terms we suppose that the norm in question is not simply a reflection of interests (as described above) or of factual information about the world (as described under the rubric of diffusion below). We also suppose that a norm carries special force. It is what we *ought* to do, i.e., what is expected of us (by some reference group whose opinions we value). Norms follow a logic of *appropriateness*.

Norms may be regarded as specific to a particular action such as the norm against incest. They may also be understood as part of a broader ideational *system* – an ideology, culture, belief-system, or value-system. For those who define themselves in religious terms the norm against incest would be understood as an element of their (Christian, Muslim, Buddhist, et al.) belief-system rather than as an isolated proscription. Identification with a social group (e.g., an ethnic group, national group, professional group, or college cohort) entails sharing the beliefs and values of that group. It is this set of norms that helps to define the collectivity.

Norms may be set out in a formal manner, e.g., the Old Testament's Ten Commandments, or they may take the form of informal understandings. The point is that they are shared and that they command obedience for reasons that reach beyond the interests of the actor. One feels a sense of obligation to a norm; if there is no such obligation then it is not a norm.

However, our use of the term presupposes that there is no explicit sanction for misbehavior or organization charged with maintaining that sanction. This is what distinguishes a norm from an *institution* (discussed below). For example, an electoral norm discourages politicians from lying to constituents in order to get elected. An electoral rule forbids politicians who are not citizens of a country from running for office. Infringement of the first brings no specific sanctions. Infringement of the second brings disqualification. This, in a nutshell, is the difference between a norm and a rule or institution, as we use these terms.

Psychology

In addition to interests, norms, and information, a person's attitudes and behavior may be affected by the way in which stimuli are processed. We shall refer to this set of explanatory factors as the realm of **psychology**.

Arguably, all individual-level behavior rests on some sort of psychological explanation. Sometimes, this explanation is so simple that we don't bother to delve into "psychology." When a consumer purchases a product after the latter is discounted this sort of behavior is consistent with an interest-based explanation and requires little comment. However, we could imagine a psychological explanation that would construct a micro-level foundation for this behavior. Someday, it may be possible to trace these micro-foundations with indicators of brain activity, as we can already do in a crude fashion with some emotions and cognitive faculties.

When writers invoke psychology it is usually to explain behavior that doesn't seem to be based solely on a calculation of self-interest, the logic of appropriateness, or the inherent truth of an idea (as revealed by some diffusion process). For example, in understanding conflict of a violent nature it may be important to understand the emotions of the actors in that conflict, emotions such as hatred, fear, or resentment. In understanding the role of information it may be important to understand how individuals calculate uncertainty. Research has shown, for example, that most people count losses more than gains, that they discount the future heavily, and that information is more believable if it is propounded by someone from their own social or political group or from a trusted authority.

Some psychological factors are widely shared among members of the species; they are universal, or nearly so. Other psychological factors may be specific to men or women or to persons of a specific age group. Others may be specific to individuals who occupy certain roles (e.g., leaders), inherit specific cultural traits (e.g., individualism), or have cognitive predispositions that set them apart from others (e.g., risk aversion). The notion of a *personality type* is intended to distinguish categories of people according to their way of processing information and reacting to the world.

Psychological characteristics may be hard-wired in a person's genetic makeup. These features are often referred to as *cognitive* or *innate.* A lively research agenda within the social sciences focuses on cognitive features that influence attitudes, preferences, and behavior that we observe in the world today. Other psychological features are the product of a person's culture, family, neighborhood, or some other aspect of their lived experience (perhaps in interaction with their genetic endowments). This is *learned.*

The *nature/nurture* distinction is an important one. However, we should be wary of treating it as a dichotomy. Research suggests that our genetic makeup is not entirely fixed at conception, and may evolve over time through lived experiences. In some respects, our nature is nurtured.

Structural Frameworks

A second set of explanations center on structural features that condition the perceptions, motivations, and capacity of actors. Three **structural frameworks** are common in the work of social science: *material factors, human capital/demography*, and *institutions*.

Material Factors

Material factors enable and constrain what humans can do. They include financial resources (e.g., income or capital), geography, and technology. An explanation based on material factors may be described as *materialist.* While materialist structures often work in tandem with interest-based motivations, as discussed above, they are not identical, as will become clear.

Individuals with lots of financial resources have the capacity to attain many goals that are beyond the reach of those without such resources. Moreover, those with and without money may see things differently, and behave differently, by virtue of their social class position. The poor usually vote differently from the rich; they are more likely to support redistributive policies; and they are more likely to commit violent crimes. Social class matters, as researchers since Karl Marx have reminded us. The primordial question of social science, Marxists would argue, is *who has what?*

Material explanations may also hinge upon the *distribution* of a good within a population, i.e., who has *more*. Sometimes, the distribution of a good matters more than its absolute level. For example, happiness may depend more upon one's standing relative to others than one's actual (absolute) income. Here, income becomes a marker for success and thus determines one's social status. It is not having a car that matters but rather whether others in the neighborhood also possess cars, or whether they possess fancier cars than you do.

Just as rich people are different from poor people, rich societies are different from poor societies. Work in the **modernization** paradigm may be understood as an exploration of all the ways in which the advance of material development affects society, culture, and politics. An intriguing (but also controversial) example is "mother love" – the bond of attachment between a mother and child. Nancy Scheper-Hughes argues that the strength of this bond is to some extent determined by infant mortality rates within a society. As rates fall and infants are expected to survive through the perilous period of childhood, parents begin to invest emotional energy in their children at an earlier age.[70] If so, mother love – seemingly, the most natural emotion of all – is explained as a product of material conditions.

Geography provides another type of material explanation. If one lives in a mountainous or heavily forested area that is distant from the sea or a navigable river one is likely to be relatively isolated. Over time, such isolation may prevent development and preserve long-established cultural practices. Marvin Harris's book, *Cows, Pigs, Wars, and Witches*, explores the role of geography and other material factors in the development of cultural practices around the world.[71] Jared Diamond's more recent synthesis, *Guns, Germs, and Steel*, explores the ramifications of geography for long-run development.[72]

Technology is a third type of material factor, referring to tools that help produce or achieve an outcome. A generous reading of "tool" includes everything from the invention of writing to biogenetic compounds and prophylactics (birth control). As such, technology represents a key factor in the arts, in the economy, and in all aspects of human life. Some technological factors operate over long periods of time and in ways that are scarcely apparent to those of us who inherit their historical effects. Alberto Alesina, Paola Giuliano, and Nathan Nunn argue that "the descendants of societies that traditionally practiced plough agriculture today have lower rates of female participation in the workplace, in politics, and in entrepreneurial activities, as well as a greater prevalence of attitudes favoring gender inequality."[73] If the authors are correct, the timing of a technological advance in agriculture – namely, the plow – has an impact on gender roles many centuries later.

Human Capital/Demography

Human capital and **demographic** explanations focus attention on individual attributes such as education, skills, health, migration, age, and life-cycle events such as birth, marriage, and death. These attributes may also be aggregated up to describe a population. For example, one can speak of the educational attainment of an individual or the (average) educational attainment of a population.

Education is generally acknowledged to be a strong predictor of success, at all levels. Individuals with more education earn more than individuals with less education. Businesses with a lot of smart, well-trained people are likely to out-perform businesses with weaker employees. Countries with high human capital are thought to enjoy a significant advantage over countries with high illiteracy. Economists have also found that measures of health show a strong relationship to individual- and country-level achievement. Demographers have explored the various causes of high and low fertility across societies, and the impact of fertility on gender roles, infant survival, and cultural attributes such as individualism. The so-called **demographic transition** – a point in time when mortality rates fall and birth rates fall – is thought to have vast implications for society and is widely regarded as a key element of economic and social development.

It seems clear that human capital/demography explains a lot about human attitudes and behavior, at individual, group, and societal levels.

Institutions

Institutions refer to humanly created rules and the organizations that establish and maintain those rules. Together, they create incentives that condition preferences and behavior – and may, over time, affect the construction of norms.

A *rule* is understood as formal, explicit, and (usually) written, and is connected to sanctions or rewards for good/bad behavior. For example, electoral law establishes the context for elections, affecting the behavior of candidates, parties, and voters. Property law establishes the context for the operation of markets, affecting the behavior of investors, producers, and consumers. Those who do not abide by these rules are subject to prosecution.

Rules are enforced by *organizations*, which is why we incorporate both elements into our definition of an institution. An organization might be religious (e.g., the Catholic church), economic (e.g., a firm), political (e.g., a government), or social (e.g., a kin-group). In order to qualify as an organization, a group must have relatively clear boundaries, explicit criteria for membership, a set of rules, and officials who make and enforce the rules. A nation-state is an organization because it possesses all of these attributes. A nation without a state, by contrast, is less organizational. It is not clear for example who is a member of the Kurdish nation, how one gains or loses membership in this body, or who is responsible for making and enforcing the rules.

Our definition of institutions is a fairly narrow one, intended to help distinguish among rival explanatory frameworks. A broader definition of the subject would encompass many of the other explanatory frameworks explored in this chapter. ("Institutions" is one of the more malleable words in the social science lexicon.) However, for present purposes a narrow definition is more useful.

However defined, social science work often focuses on the role of institutions – so much so that we are at a loss to provide specific examples for this section of the chapter, as they would encompass a majority of work in economics, political science, sociology, and related fields.

The popularity of institutions is not because institutions are necessarily more important than other explanatory factors. It is, rather, because institutions are the one explanatory factor that is solidly within our power – collectively – to change. Insofar as we want to improve society, we are likely to focus on institutional theories about how society works, for they are more relevant than factors over which we have little direct influence. When societies seek to change factors like resources, human capital, or motivational features of human existence, they do so by changing institutions that structure these outcomes. To change the distribution of resources we might propose a change in the tax code, for example. To improve the quality of human capital we might propose an increase in spending on educational programs. In this respect, institutional factors can claim primacy over other explanatory frameworks.

Interactive Frameworks

Sometimes, human attitudes and behavior are best explained as a dynamic interactive process rather than as the product of a single factor. **Interactive frameworks** include *adaptation*, *coordination*, *diffusion*, *networks*, and *path dependence*. Here, outcomes are understood as the product of interactions among people over time. Interactive factors thus combine elements already introduced as motivational or structural, building upon previous sections.

Adaptation

Adaptation focuses on the way in which individuals and groups adapt to a given environment. The notion is that, over time, the most efficient (fully adaptive) form will be achieved, with *efficiency* understood according to the preferences of the actors or by measuring success or survival.

Likewise, the attitudes and behavior of individuals and groups within a society may be understood according to the roles they play, i.e., the functions they perform within that larger society. This *functionalist* view of social relations has a long history in anthropology and sociology stretching back to Emile Durkheim.

Sometimes, the adaptive (efficient) result is obtained through a process of *feedback*. When an individual pursues a strategy (e.g., to get elected or to sell a product) she receives feedback (from voters or from consumers). Based on this feedback she may decide to change her strategy.

Sometimes, the adaptive result is obtained through a process of *competition*. In a market economy, firms compete with one another for profits and market share. Competitive pressures – Adam Smith's *invisible hand* – may prompt firms to lower costs, improve their product, or adjust their sales strategy. Likewise, in a political market, parties (and politicians) compete for votes. Competitive pressures may prompt parties to alter their platforms, change their behavior, or adopt different campaign strategies. At a national level, one might regard nation-states as engaged in a similar battle for survival, prompting adaptive changes in organization. The implicit selection mechanism at work here – with firms, parties, or states – is survival. Organizations that do not adapt may disappear. This explanatory trope is modeled on Charles Darwin's theory of *evolution*, in which a process of natural selection rewards species that successfully adapt to their environment and punishes (by extinction) species that do not.

Sometimes, adaptation happens because individuals choose outcomes that benefit them. Here, adaptation maximizes utility. Efficient outcomes might take the form of a formal contract (e.g., between a buyer and a seller) or an informal understanding (e.g., between a patron and a client). One may also regard larger societal outcomes as efficient if they maximize the preferences of members in that society. For example, it might be argued that the spread of the nation-state throughout the world in the past several centuries is due to the fact that this particular form of political organization is the most efficient way to resolve conflict and provide public goods (though not everyone agrees with this premise). In any case, adaptive explanations presume a group – which may be as small as a family or as large as a country – for whom the arrangement is efficient.

Coordination

Coordination explanations focus on the failure to achieve efficient outcomes. Specifically, they focus on situations where the pursuit of individual preferences leads to suboptimal outcomes for those concerned. In this sense, all coordination problems may be described as *collective action* dilemmas.

One common coordination problem occurs when individuals find it in their interest to *free-ride* on others. For example, citizens may prefer not to pay taxes even though they benefit from the services that government provides. Likewise, states may prefer not to lower tariffs on foreign goods even though they benefit from global free trade.

Another sort of coordination failure is the *prisoner's dilemma* – where the payoffs from a situation give each player an incentive to defect from a cooperative outcome that would benefit both parties. Consider the following stylized scenario. Two prisoners arrested for the same crime are placed in separate cells and offered the same choice by the district attorney: confess (and implicate the other defendant) or remain silent. The payoffs for each set of decisions (length of sentence in prison), as stipulated by the district attorney, are listed in Figure 5.1. Note that the optimal outcome for both prisoners – considered collectively – is to stay silent, which will mean they serve only a short, one-year term in prison. However, each prisoner is better off confessing than remaining silent, regardless of what the other prisoner decides. Defecting (confessing) is therefore the rational choice in a situation where prisoners are unable to coordinate with each other.

This hypothetical game has spawned a thousand others, each with modifications to the payoff structure, the number of players, the degree of communication

	Prisoner B	
	Remain silent	*Confess*
Remain silent	A: 1 year B: 1 year	A: 3 years B: 0 years
Confess	A: 0 years B: 3 years	A: 2 years B: 2 years

(Prisoner A — row labels; Prisoner B — column labels)

Figure 5.1 Prisoner's dilemma
Years: sentence to be served in prison.

allowed, the sort of rewards or punishments offered, and so forth. For our purposes, the key insight is that many social settings seem to exhibit coordination failures – where a suboptimal outcome is achieved because individuals (or groups) cannot successfully coordinate their activities.

A third sort of failure involves inter-temporal coordination failures such as those arising from the inability to make a *credible commitment* to a policy. Here, one party wishes to make a promise to another party but has no means of convincing the other party that the commitment will be upheld. An oft-cited example is the dictator who promises to respect property rights. In this scenario, investors have no assurance that the dictator will remain true to his/her promise in the future because a dictator – by definition – can change the rules whenever it suits him or her to do so.

A fourth sort of coordination failure (or impediment) involves *transaction costs* among individuals seeking to reach an agreement (or contract). These refer to any sort of barrier that increases the costs (on either party) of exchanging a good or service. This might involve information costs (relative to the substance of the agreement or the product being purchased), bargaining costs, or enforcement costs. While the transaction-cost framework was originally developed to understand the behavior of markets it has also been applied to politics, social institutions, and other venues.

Problems of coordination bedevil all social settings, and are especially valuable in explaining the formation of institutions and in designing new institutions. Indeed, for some writers the concept of an institution is inseparable from the coordination problem it is designed to solve. It is often argued, for example, that the primary function of government is to solve collective action problems, e.g., by internalizing costs and benefits and preventing free-riding. Likewise, some state structures may enjoy an advantage because they solve a particular coordination problem. For example, since democratically elected rulers are constrained by a constitution and an independent judiciary, as well as by an electorate (who can vote out the incumbent), democracies may be better situated to solve problems of credible commitment – assuring investors that their property will be respected in the future.

Diffusion

Some phenomena are so irresistible that their spread can be explained simply by exposure. This process is often labeled **diffusion**. It might apply to especially appealing ideas, new information that affects the way we think about a topic, or new technologies that promise great returns. Here, a *demonstration effect* of prowess is sufficient. Since information expands knowledge and facilitates learning, *knowledge*- and *learning*-based explanations are integrated into this discussion.

Consider the choice between dropping out of school and remaining in school. This choice is presumably affected by one's understanding of the payoffs to each course of action. One might know with a high degree of certainty that one can get a job and the wages that job would bring, and one might be highly uncertain about whether one could get a higher-paying job if one continued one's education. Changes in this information – gained, say, by talking to recent graduates or reading a study following the fortunes of recent graduates – are likely to affect one's decision. The same is true for other decisions, e.g., purchasing a good, casting a ballot, joining an insurrection, committing a crime, or procreating.

Not surprisingly, attempts to change behavior often take the form of information campaigns. To combat the spread of HIV/AIDS, people are informed about how the disease is spread, the consequences of contracting the disease, and methods of protecting themselves. To combat the use of tobacco and other drugs (especially among youth), people are informed of their highly addictive qualities and the consequences of long-term use. To promote a candidate, voters are informed of the candidate's background, her achievements to date, and her proposed program of action, which may be directly contrasted with her opponents' qualifications and policy commitments. Likewise, a promotional campaign for a new product may convey important information about that product.

Granted, information campaigns are generally not limited to information. There may also be a good deal of extraneous material, some normative appeals, and perhaps some downright falsehoods. Moreover, discerning information (truth) from lies is not always easy. This is why writers sometimes prefer to speak of *ideas* rather than information. In any case, the point remains that information (or ideas) about a subject often affects what an actor thinks and does.

The diffusion framework is so simple that it requires little elaboration. Suffice to say that causal explanations usually have a second focus – on the factors that encourage or discourage exposure. For example, diffusion of an idea might be enhanced by a network of communications, which in turn may be affected by communications technology (e.g., the availability of phone, email, or web-based connections). This leads to our next topic.

Networks

Wherever a stable pattern of communication among individuals (or groups) exists the resulting **network** may be mapped, i.e., drawn in a diagram or represented in a matrix. The network configuration may include additional information concerning the frequency of contact within a dyad, the duration of the event or the interconnection, the direction of the relationship, the substance of the communication, or attitudes toward others (inside and outside the network). Armed with this information, it may be possible to characterize ties as strong or weak and nodes in the network as central or peripheral. Figure 5.2 shows a typical social network (using data from Facebook), consisting of individuals and the ties between them.

The premise is that one can explain individual-level outcomes by examining their network position. For example, those with greater centrality may be more likely to receive information, to influence the behavior of others, or to fall victim of a communicable disease. At a system level, it may be possible to explain the

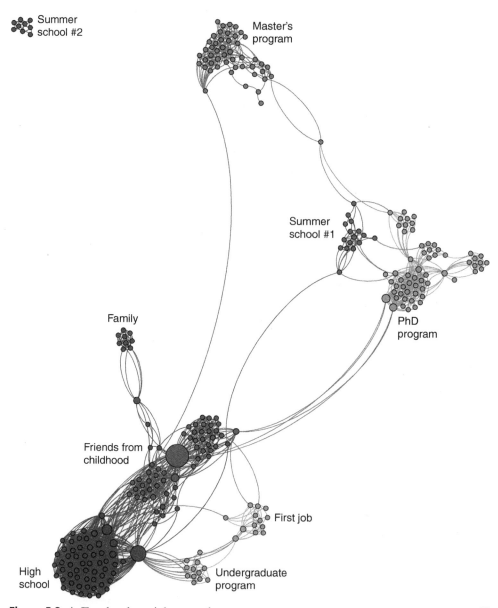

Figure 5.2 A Facebook social network

relative speed or extent by which ideas, institutions, germs, technology, or some other factor of interest diffuses through a network.

Social capital explanations focus on the relative density of social networks. In a community where individuals have lots of interconnections that extend beyond their immediate family and workplace, there is high social capital. This sort of interaction is thought to foster social trust (and is in turn the product of social trust), political engagement, and employment opportunities. At an aggregate level, social capital is often seen as a key feature in economic development and good governance. Since these arguments were already introduced at some length in Chapter 1 we shall not expatiate further.

Path Dependence

A **critical juncture** is an event that is in some respect stochastic (random), i.e., it could have been otherwise and cannot easily be explained by some other factor. Sometimes, an event of this sort has enduring consequences that flow in a structured way from the event. Here, we may refer to the resulting trajectory as path-dependent. This is the loose sense in which the terms critical juncture and path dependence are usually employed.

A narrower definition of **path dependence** refers to a situation in which an initial event is followed by a positive feedback loop ("increasing returns" or "lock-in") that works to entrench the original event. Unfortunately, it is often difficult to tell when a weak or strong version of the framework applies. And many writers do not have this more restrictive condition in mind when they use the term. Thus, we adopt the looser, more encompassing definition.

An instance of critical juncture/path dependence (by any definition) is the location of the keys on a standard English keyboard, which spell out the sequence QWERTY. The reason for this arrangement is largely accidental. An early typewriter assumed this format and later keyboards followed suit, for the simple reason that consumers (it was assumed) would not wish to learn a new system. It is, however, not highly adaptive (see discussion above), as typing speed would increase if the keys were arranged in a different fashion (once people learned the new system). But we are unlikely ever to realize that new arrangement because of sunk costs, i.e., path dependence.

Institutions usually involve a degree of path dependence. Consider that every public policy involves a set of beneficiaries and a larger set of actors whose incentives are affected by the law. For example, the passage of the Social Security Act in 1935 established a new class of government beneficiaries (old people) and a larger class of individuals (including Americans of all ages) who base their retirement and investment decisions on the existence of this policy. Once a society has adjusted to this reality it becomes very difficult to change. Other policy solutions become less feasible.[74]

Large and abstract institutions are also heavily path-dependent. Once democracy has become established in a country people accustom themselves to this form of government. Leaders gain material stakes in the system. Everyone's behavior and norms change. Consequently, democracy develops staying-power. This is one way to explain the fact that few countries revert to autocracy once they have experienced several decades of democratic rule.

Importantly, path-dependent explanations are not always efficient (in the sense of maximizing the long-run preferences or interests of all concerned). Sometimes, a low-equilibrium outcome will persist even though it is not serving anyone very well. An example would be the QWERTY keyboard. Some might argue that in the context of an aging society the shape of social security policies also qualifies as an example of a non-efficient outcome.

Building a Theory

Having introduced a typology of explanatory frameworks, summarized in Table 5.1, we need to clarify several points that have been left dangling.

First, the typology is not intended to be exhaustive. Indeed, the notion of a comprehensive set of explanatory frameworks would presume a comprehensive typology of human behavior – an unlikely prospect.

Second, each of the frameworks listed in Table 5.1 is broadly defined so as to encompass a wide variety of specific theories. Readers should not suppose that there is only one sort of materialist framework or that writers invoking material explanations agree with one another about the way the world works. There is a good deal of diversity within each framework, as we have sought to demonstrate.

Third, most of the frameworks listed in Table 5.1 can be applied at the individual or group level. For example, a person may be subject to material constraints as well as a social group, organization, or an entire nation. A group, after all, is a collection of individuals. Likewise, different explanations may apply at different levels. For example, individual behavior may respond to material incentives while group behavior is best explained by institutions.

Fourth, the outcomes of a causal theory – the phenomena one is ultimately concerned to explain – may be variously defined. Specifically, a theory may be designed to explain *attitudes* (what people think or feel), *preferences* (how people prioritize across options), *behavior* (what people do), or *conditions* (how people live or die).

Fifth, any number of possible interrelationships may be envisioned among the various frameworks. For example, a materialist theory may be enlisted to explain an institutional outcome. In this case, one framework serves as the cause and another serves as the outcome.

Finally, these frameworks often play complementary roles. Indeed, a complete causal explanation for any social phenomenon generally incorporates more than one of the frameworks listed in Table 5.1. An explanation might enlist coordination logic to explain a set of institutions; these institutions might establish material incentives; and these incentives, in turn, may serve to motivate behavior. Here, diverse frameworks are woven together into a single narrative. So, causal frameworks are not always rivals. Sometimes, they are building blocks that combine to form a coherent causal explanation.

An Example: *Birth*

As an example of how different explanatory frameworks interweave let us consider the decision to have a child, which we have classified under the rubric of demography in Table 5.1. At group levels, this decision is typically measured as the total *fertility rate*, the average number of children born to each woman within a group or society during her childbearing years.

Some societies have high fertility rates. In sub-Saharan Africa, several countries have fertility rates of 7 or more. Advanced industrial societies generally have fertility rates of 2 or less, below the rate at which a population can sustain its current level (without in-migration). Fertility rates in Hong Kong and Macao are now at about 1 child per woman, an astounding fact in light of human history. Only a century ago, fertility rates in most countries were close to those found today in the developing world. Indeed, fertility is an area where enormous change has occurred over a relatively small period of time, with immense consequences for humankind and for the natural environment.

A range of theoretical frameworks have been enlisted to explain fertility. Interest-based explanations regard procreation as a choice based on a calculation of costs and benefits. Fertility goes down when the costs of bearing a child go up relative to the associated benefits. This, in turn, is affected by the material situation in which adults find themselves, calling forth materialist explanations. Urban dwellers are less likely to need the labor provided by their children than those living in the countryside; likewise, space is scarcer and more expensive. Both of these factors alter the calculus of childrearing as the process of urbanization moves forward. Likewise, social insurance policies designed to care for adults in their old age lessen the need for children to serve as caretakers; in this fashion, the long-term payoff provided by children is lowered. Finally, as child mortality rates fall (as they have virtually everywhere in the world), the number of births required to achieve a given family size also declines. Here, mortality alters fertility.

However, varying fertility rates around the world do not seem to be solely the product of material considerations. Indeed, families are much larger in some parts of the world – especially in sub-Saharan Africa – than would be explainable on the basis of a narrow conception of self-interest. One possibility is that people are not correctly calculating the costs and benefits of having a child under current conditions; instead, they may be following norms of behavior that were established some time ago, under very different conditions (e.g., when child mortality was high). Perhaps norms lag behind objective circumstances. If so, we may think of material factors as the ultimate cause and norms as the proximate cause of behavior. If so, a change of norms may be required to affect fertility rates in a society. Another possibility is that adults are not thinking about procreation in a cost–benefit framework at all; choices about when to marry, when to engage in sex, and whether to use birth control are instead based on deeply rooted cultural norms (including religious prescriptions) about what is expected, i.e., a logic of appropriateness.

A third approach to fertility focuses on institutions. Public policies may prohibit or encourage the use of contraception and abortion. Policies may explicitly discourage large families in countries where the government wishes to depress the birth rate (e.g., the one-child policy in China) or encourage larger families in countries where depopulation is regarded as a problem (e.g., child allotments, offered in many advanced industrial countries).

A fourth approach focuses on psychological factors affecting the decision to have intercourse, utilize contraception, nurture a fetus to term, and seek appropriate medical assistance. A fifth approach considers fertility from within an adaptive framework. In some settings, groups are thought to engage in fertility competitions, in which only the most fertile groups survive. A sixth approach might enlist a coordination framework. Arguably, high fertility is a product of situations where the costs of a child are dispersed across a community while the benefits are centered on the child's biological parents. A communal setting of this sort establishes a collective action problem in which individual incentives are not aligned with community interests.

Other explanatory frameworks can easily be imagined. The point is, for any given outcome there are usually many possible explanations. Some may be truer than others; in this respect, explanatory frameworks are rivals. But all may be true, in varying degrees, or at different levels. If so, the various causal factors at work are likely to be interrelated in a complex fashion. Institutions may affect norms, and norms may also affect institutions, as seems likely in the previous example.

Formal Models

Sometimes, a theory is stated in formal terms, with an explicit set of assumptions (axioms) upon which a deductive structure is assembled. **Formal** theories are usually expressed in mathematical language, where a single equation or set of equations (a model) embodies the argument. Sometimes, the model can be solved, i.e., it offers a single solution or prediction. Sometimes, the assumptions must be narrowed in order to attain a solution. Insofar as it is possible to compute solutions for a formal model using various assumptions (e.g., imposing specific parameter values on the variables), we refer to the exercise as a *computational model* and to the various computations as **simulations**.

Whether an explanation can be represented in formal, mathematical terms depends upon its simplicity. This is not just a matter of the number of moving parts but also the extent to which each moving part can be understood as a "quantity." Some concepts, like *institutionalization*, are not very amenable to formal treatments.

Formal models often rest on **preferences** because they are relatively tractable (at least more so than norms and psychology). A preference refers to what an individual (or group) prefers across a range of options. Usually, it is assumed that preferences are *complete*, which is to say that for any two options the actor can decide whether option A is preferred to option B, option B is preferred to option A, or both are regarded as equal. In addition, it is usually assumed that preferences are *transitive*: if A is preferred to B, and B is preferred to C, then A is preferred to C. This allows preferences to be ordered, producing a **utility function**. When an individual's behavior follows this logic, she or he is said to maximize her or his utility. (Additional assumptions are sometimes added; but comparability and transitivity are almost always included in a preference-based explanation.) Although this framework may seem complex – and indeed some formulations are extremely technical and involve a great many assumptions – the core idea is quite simple: people's behavior is a product of their preferences.

Let us see how this framework might apply to vote choice. Consider an election conducted with single-member districts (a single candidate is selected from each electoral district) and winner-take-all (aka first-past-the-post) rules, where two parties (Democrats and Republicans) compete. We shall assume that voters' preferences may be understood according to their issue-preferences (about particular policies) and that these policies occupy a unidimensional issue-space from left (liberal) to right (conservative). For illustrative purposes, we also assume that voters are evenly distributed along this spectrum (although this assumption can be relaxed to get the same result). And we shall assume that ideological positioning by the parties is unconstrained by activist members, by their history, by the problem of credible commitment, by changes to voter turnout, or by other factors. Under these circumstances, where should the parties (and their candidates) position themselves?

Early work on voting employed a simple spatial model, illustrated in Figure 5.3, in order to understand why candidates in a general election might move toward the middle – understood as the median voter (that individual whose views lie in the center of the ideological spectrum, with an equal number of persons to his/her left and right). Consider panel (a), which offers a plausible description of the positions of the parties according to their aggregated personal preferences – with the Democratic Party on the left of the spectrum and the Republican Party on the right. This setting is not in equilibrium, however, because either party can enhance its position by moving to the center, as the Democratic Party does in panel (b). In this scenario, the Democrats win by a landslide simply by moving along the spectrum and thereby capturing more votes in the center. The assumption is that they lose no votes in doing so because voters to the left of the Democratic Party have no viable option that lies closer to their ideal-point. Of course, the Republican Party may also play this repositioning game. In panel (c), the Republicans move almost all the way to the middle, occupying a larger portion of the spectrum and assuring themselves a victory. Of course, this setting is also not in equilibrium because another move by the Democrats evens up the vote. Thus, under the terms of this simple model, the only stable equilibrium is one where both parties hug the center, as illustrated in panel (d).

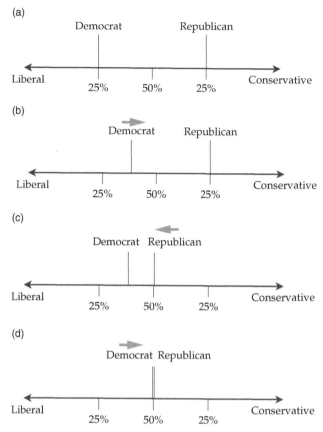

Figure 5.3 A spatial model of vote choice and party positioning

The intuition, then, is that if voters attempt to maximize their preferences (understood as policy preferences), they will vote for the candidate whose policy positions most closely mirror their own. In a two-party competition, parties (and candidates) maximize their vote-share by moving toward the center, generating a centripetal dynamic.

Here, issue-preferences structure candidate behavior, which in turn structures voting behavior. If most voters behave in this way we can use this simple folk wisdom to explain the results of an election.

Likewise, if we wish to explain why certain individuals or parties join together in a coalition, we might begin by examining their preferences, with the idea that those with similar utility functions are most likely to form enduring coalitions. The same logic may be employed to explain consumer choice, the structure of markets, the choice of marriage partners, social networks, and many other phenomena of interest to social science.

Of course, inferring what a person's true preferences are is not always an easy matter. One may ask directly (via a survey or interview). But people are not always forthcoming. Sometimes, they tell you what they think you want to hear or what they feel is most acceptable. They will rarely reveal preferences that go against the law or against social mores (see section on *Surveys* in Chapter 13).

One may also observe an individual's behavior. Typically, preferences predict behavior. If we observe how someone votes we are presumably observing their preferences at work. This approach to measurement is referred to as **revealed preferences**. Sometimes, however, people act strategically. Consider an election contest where three candidates, *A*, *B*, and *C*, compete for a single seat. Let us suppose that Bob's preference-ordering is $A>B>C$. However, he knows (from opinion polls) that *A*'s probability of winning is minuscule. Under these circumstances, Bob might opt for *B* even though *B* is not his first preference. On the basis of Bob's behavior, and knowing something about the situation, one can infer that Bob prefers *B* to *C*. But it is impossible to tell whether he prefers *A* to *B*.

Where asking and observation are impossible or for some reason flawed, one may try to infer preferences from other aspects of a person's situation. This approach may be reasonable if our focus is on the preferences of many people rather than on a single individual. In this case, it does not matter if our guesses about preferences are correct or incorrect for "Bob" so long as they are generally correct for members of Bob's group.

If one is trying to understand a series of decisions (taken by an individual or a group) in a particular sequence, a **decision-tree** model may be applied. This draws on a branch of math and economics known as decision theory. If actions by an individual or group depend upon the actions of others, the resulting model may be described as **game theory**. Here, each player is understood as playing a game insofar as their actions are strategic, with an eye to the probable behavior of others.

CONCLUSIONS

In this chapter, we have set forth a number of explanatory frameworks, summarized in Table 5.1. Although this typology is by no means comprehensive, it encompasses many of the arguments you are likely to run across in social science studies. The final section of the chapter discusses how frameworks interact with one another in the service of causal explanation. It also discusses – in a very general way – how and why explanations might be formalized in a mathematical model. This may prove helpful as you peruse the literature or construct your own arguments about a topic.

Naturally, every model of human behavior requires simplifying assumptions. And mathematical models are generally more reductionist than models elucidated in prose. On this ground, they may be criticized (for leaving out aspects that may be important for understanding an outcome) as well as praised (for their parsimony). This is the irreducible dilemma faced by any attempt to theorize about complex phenomena connected to human behavior.

The utility of any causal explanation – formal or non-formal, mathematical or non-mathematical – is contingent on the extent to which its assumptions are realistic and its predictions are testable. This brings us to the topic of the next chapter.

KEY TERMS

- Motivational frameworks
- Interests (that which benefits an actor)
- Norms (values, beliefs, ideology, culture, identity)
- Psychology (cognition, emotion, personality, genetics)
- Structural frameworks
- Material factors (financial resources, modernization, geography, technology)
- Human capital/demography (health, education, skills, migration, life-cycle events, demographic transition)
- Institutions (formal rules and organizations)
- Interactive frameworks
- Adaptation (feedback, competition, selection, evolution, efficiency, functionalism)
- Coordination (collective action, externalities, credible commitment, transaction costs)
- Diffusion (demonstration effect, exposure, ideas, information, knowledge, exposure)
- Networks (informal associational structures, social capital)
- Critical juncture
- Path dependence (contingent moments [critical junctures] leading to fixed trajectories)
- Formal models
- Simulation
- Preferences
- Utility function
- Revealed preferences
- Decision tree
- Game theory

Validity – closeness to real value

In the previous chapter we discussed general causal frameworks, the building blocks of a causal explanation. In this chapter, we focus on specific hypotheses, where one factor is thought to generate change in another factor.

We begin by clarifying the concept of causality. In the next section, we discuss the criteria of a *good* (well-constructed) causal hypothesis. The rest of the chapter is devoted to causal *analysis*. First, we outline the criteria that all causal research designs seek to achieve. Next, we discuss the problem of reaching causal *inference*.

This chapter is fairly complex. A number of new terms are introduced, some of which may be unfamiliar to the reader and some of which are used in slightly different ways in different disciplines. Although the vocabulary may seem bewildering at first, try to familiarize yourself with these concepts – which you are likely to encounter in your reading and in your future work. The topics covered here are critical for understanding how evidence is used to infer causality in social-science settings. Whether you are primarily a consumer or a producer of social science the following chapters bear a close read and a good think.

Causality

A causal hypothesis involves at least two elements: a *cause* and an *outcome*. A **cause** may be referred to variously as a *condition, covariate, exogenous variable, explanatory variable, explanans, independent variable, input, intervention, parent, predictor, right-side variable, treatment,* or simply "*X*." An **outcome** may be referred to as a *dependent variable, descendant, effect, endogenous variable, explanandum, left-side variable, output, response,* or "*Y*."

Whatever the terminology, to say that a factor, *X*, is a cause of an outcome, *Y*, is to say that a change in *X* generates a change in *Y* relative to what *Y* would otherwise be (the counterfactual condition), given certain background conditions (ceteris paribus assumptions) and scope-conditions (the population of the inference).

Now, let's unpack things a bit. As an example, we shall focus on the causal role of a worker-training program. A reasonable hypothesis is that participation in the program (*X*) will enhance an unemployed person's subsequent earnings (*Y*). If the relationship is causal, her earnings should be higher than they would be if she had never participated in the program. Let us represent the treatment, *X*, as a **binary** (dichotomous) variable, which takes one of two values. $X = 1$ (represented as X_T) means that the individual has attended the program (the treatment condition). $X = 0$ (represented as X_C) means that the individual did not attend the program (the control condition).

We shall refer to participants in the program as members of the **treatment group** since they receive the treatment (the worker-training program). Unemployed persons who did not participate in the training program – if they are similar to those who did – may be understood as a **control group**.

A **causal effect** (aka *treatment effect*) is the change in Y (ΔY or "delta Y") brought about by a change in X (ΔX). When X changes, Y must also change, at least probabilistically, if the relationship is causal.

When a treatment is binary, as above, ΔX refers to a change from 0 to 1, i.e., from the control condition (X_C) to the treatment condition (X_T), e.g., attending the worker-training program. It might also refer to a change from X_T to X_C, though in some cases this will not make a lot of sense (how does one un-learn what one has been exposed to in a worker-training program?). Some treatments are unidirectional; others are bi-directional.

When an outcome is continuous, ΔX affects the value of Y along an interval scale. Thus, we hypothesized that exposure to a worker-training program increases one's earnings. This hypothesis may be written as a statement of inequality ...

$$Y_T > Y_C$$

Read: "Earnings are higher for someone in the treatment group ($X = 1$) than for someone in the control group ($X = 0$)." Or, alternatively, "Earnings are higher for someone after they have been treated ($X = 1$) than before ($X = 0$)."

When an outcome is also binary, ΔX affects the probability (P) of Y achieving an outcome. Thus, one might hypothesize that exposure to a worker-training program increases the probability of employment ($Y = 1$), as opposed to unemployment ($Y = 0$). This may be written as

$$P(Y|X_T) > P(Y|X_C)$$

Read: "The probability of employment is greater conditional on having attended a worker-training program than conditional on not having attended such a program."

Estimating a causal effect involves comparing a *factual* (that which actually happened) with a **counterfactual** (that which might have happened). Continuing with our example, let us say that we wish to determine what effect (if any) a job-training program has on the earnings of unemployed people who have completed the program. We know what the program participants – the treatment group – earned before they entered the program and after they finished the program. But we do not know what they would have earned had they never attended the program. Unfortunately, this is precisely what we need to know if we are to estimate a causal effect. That is, we want to know whether members of the treatment group have higher earnings than they otherwise would have (had they never received the treatment).

Because causal effects depend upon counterfactuals that are not directly measurable they seem to require something on the order of a time-machine. Traveling back in time, one could replay events so as to observe the relevant counterfactuals. Thus, one could cancel the worker-training program and observe the earnings of those who would have participated in it, leaving everything else in the world as it is (ceteris paribus). In this fashion, one could obtain a measure of the true causal effect.

Lacking time-machines, we must resort to cruder expedients. Specifically, we must infer the unobservable counterfactuals – what-would-have-beens – from available evidence. For example, one might obtain an estimate of the causal effect by subtracting the earnings of members of the treatment group (Y_T) before completing the worker-training program (*Time at 0*) from their earnings after participating in the program (*Time+1*), expressed as . . .

$$Y_{T,Time+1} - Y_{T,Time0}$$

In this setting, one must be willing to believe that background conditions remained constant from *Time* to *Time+1* – a problematic assumption in many circumstances. One might also subtract the earnings of those in the treatment group from those in a suitable control group in order to get an estimate of the causal effect, expressed as . . .

$$Y_T - Y_C$$

Here, one must be willing to believe that members of the treatment and control groups are similar in all respects (relevant to their earnings) – also a difficult assumption, in most circumstances.

Causal inference is a tricky business, and you need to know the many tricks of the trade if you are to be successful at it. In subsequent chapters we will introduce a variety of research designs whose purpose is to arrive at a valid – and, if possible, reasonably precise – estimate of X's impact on Y.

It bears emphasis that whenever one asserts that X causes Y one is asserting that the actual probability of an event is increased by X, not simply a theory's predictive capacity. This is what distinguishes causality from description or prediction. To be causal, the factor in question must *generate*, *create*, or *produce* an effect. A correlation between X and Y does not necessarily indicate that a causal relationship exists; it may be spurious.

Of course, it is not always possible to specify precisely why X generates a change in Y. Yet, in identifying X as a cause of Y one is presuming the existence of some **causal mechanism** – understood here as the pathway or process or chain of intermediary variables by which X affects Y, illustrated as M in Figure 6.1. In our example, the mechanism might be the factual information about a particular occupation that is imparted in the worker-training program. Or it could be the job search skills that one learns as part of a program (such as how to construct a resume or how to present oneself in an interview). Or it could be general workplace comportment (how to relate to one's boss and co-workers). Lots of potential mechanisms might be identified, and any combination of them may be at work.

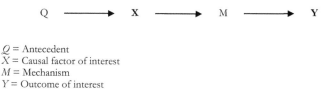

Q = Antecedent
X = Causal factor of interest
M = Mechanism
Y = Outcome of interest

Figure 6.1 A simple causal graph

Causal relationships occur against a background of other factors that also influence the outcome. In our example, many additional factors may affect earnings including experience, effort, and various demographic characteristics of the worker (race, sex, age, and so forth). These background conditions are generally assumed to hold constant. When one asserts that a particular causal factor, e.g., worker-training, increases earnings one is not asserting that other factors do not matter. One is asserting that participation in worker-training programs increase earnings, all other things being equal. This is known as the ceteris paribus assumption, and is implicit in all causal arguments.

Causal relationships are always bounded in some fashion; they do not exist everywhere and always. In this case, one would not expect worker-training programs to have much causal impact in a country where jobs (and promotions) are allocated by clientelistic networks. Likewise, one would not expect a worker-training program to affect earnings in a collapsing economy. So we might stipulate that the scope-conditions of the argument include an intact economy and meritocratic (or at least somewhat meritocratic) appointment and promotion practices. The scope-conditions of an argument may be understood as the area around the nodes in Figure 6.1.

One sort of background factor lies **antecedent** to the causal factor of interest. It affects Y indirectly, through X. In our example, the antecedent factor is that which causes a person to participate (or not) in a worker-training program, labeled Q in Figure 6.1.

In any causal argument, it is important to distinguish between factors that are *independent* or **exogenous** (causal in nature), and factors that are *dependent* or **endogenous** (outcomes). In Figure 6.1, the relationships are as follows:

- Q is exogenous to X, M, and Y
- X is exogenous to M and Y
- M is exogenous to Y

Likewise,

- Y is endogenous to Q, X, and M
- M is endogenous to Q and X
- X is endogenous to Q

As you can see, endogeneity/exogeneity is a relative matter.

Each factor in Figure 6.1 may be treated as an individual *variable* or as a *vector* (set) of variables. Although most of our examples will concern individual variables these examples can usually be generalized by treating the variable as a vector. Often, we are interested in combinations of causal factors, combinations of causal pathways, combinations of antecedent causes, and so forth (very rarely, we might be interested in combinations of outcomes).

By employing the language of "variables" our assumption is that each factor can vary (at least hypothetically) in the setting under study. We are not supposing that all variables are measurable. Nor are we supposing that all causal models are statistical in nature. Nothing in the foregoing passages necessitates a large sample or a probabilistic model. We find the language of variables to be a convenient means of simplifying and unifying our understanding of causation. It is not meant to impose a uniform approach to research design.

Causal Graphs

When attempting to tease apart correlational and causal patterns, and devise appropriate conditioning strategies, it is often helpful to diagram the expected relationship between two or more factors. The resulting diagram – an example of which is shown in Figure 6.1 – is known as a **causal graph**, a language of causal inference developed by Judea Pearl and others.

The notation used in this book does not exactly replicate Pearl's, but it is similar. Here, each node in a graph represents a variable (or factor). A one-sided arrow between nodes indicates a causal relationship from the origin to the terminus:

$X \rightarrow Y$ (X causes Y)

A two-sided arrow indicates a reciprocal causal relationship:

$X \leftrightarrow Y$ (X causes Y and Y causes X)

A line without an arrow indicates a covariational relationship that may or may not be causal:

$X–Y$ (X covaries with Y)

Note that when a node appears in a causal graph you may assume that it is measured (and "conditioned"), unless it appears in square brackets – in which case it is unmeasured (and perhaps unmeasurable). We make frequent use of these graphs in the coming chapters so it is important to have this language clear in your head.

Criteria of a Causal Hypothesis

Having defined causation minimally, and discussed various types of causal relationships, we turn to the ideal-type. What is a *good* causal hypothesis?

Recall from Chapter 2 that all arguments strive for *precision*, *generality*, *boundedness*, *parsimony*, *coherence*, *commensurability*, *innovation*, and *relevance*. Causal hypotheses also strive for *clarity*, *manipulability*, *precedence*, *impact*, and an identifiable *mechanism*. For convenience, all thirteen criteria applicable to causal theories are reproduced in Table 6.1. However, our focus in this chapter is on factors that are distinct to causal arguments.

Table 6.1   Causal hypotheses: criteria

ALL ARGUMENTS (Chapter 2)

Precision (specificity)
- Is it precise?

Generality (breadth, domain, population, range, scope)
- How broad is the scope?

Boundedness (population, scope-conditions)
- How well-bounded is it?

Parsimony (concision, economy, Occam's razor, reduction, simplicity)
- How parsimonious is it? How many assumptions are required?

Coherence (clarity, consistency; *antonym:* ambiguity)
- How coherent is it?

Commensurability (consilience, harmony, logical economy, theoretical utility; *antonym:* ad hocery)
- How well does it cumulate with other inferences? Does it advance logical economy in a field?

Innovation (novelty)
- How new is it?

Relevance (everyday importance, significance)
- How relevant is it to issues of concern to citizens and policymakers?

CAUSAL HYPOTHESES (this chapter)

Clarity (*antonym:* ambiguity)
- Is it clear what the envisioned variation on X and Y, background conditions, and scope-conditions are?

Manipulability
- Is the causal factor manipulable (at least potentially)?

Precedence (exogenous, foundational, independent, original, prime, prior, structural, unmoved mover)
- Is X separable from Y and prior to other causes of Y?

Impact (effect size, magnitude, power, significance, strength)
- How much of the variation in Y can X explain? Is the causal effect significant (in theoretical or policy terms)?

Mechanism (intermediary, mediator, pathway, process)
- How does X generate Y? What are the causal mechanisms (M)?

Clarity

We have defined causality as a situation in which a change in X (the causal factor of theoretical interest) generates a change in Y (the outcome of interest) relative to what Y otherwise would be, given certain background conditions and scope-conditions. It follows that a good causal hypothesis should provide **clarity** along each of these dimensions. Clarifying causal theories makes them more useful, as well as easier to test. Indeed, a theory that is ambiguous is impossible to verify or falsify; it is neither true nor false.

One issue is terminological. Writers may state that a causal factor, X, *leads to* an outcome, Y, *is related to* Y, *is associated with* Y, *influences* Y, *results in* Y, and so forth. Of these, only the last two are clearly causal in the sense in which we have defined the term. But all *may* be causal, depending upon the context. A simple suggestion for writers is to clarify whether an argument is intended to be causal or not. Intuition on the part of the reader should not be required.

A second issue is the specification of Y. To evaluate an argument we need to know the variation in Y that is the outcome of interest. Usually, this is apparent; but sometimes it remains ambiguous. There is a humorous tale of a priest who reportedly queried the notorious bank robber, Willie Sutton, about why he robbed banks. The miscreant patiently explained that this is where the money is. Evidently, the priest and the bank robber have different ideas about variation in Y. For the priest, it is robbing ($Y = 1$) versus not robbing ($Y = 0$). For Sutton, it is robbing banks ($Y = 1$) versus robbing other establishments ($Y = 0$).

A third issue is the specification of X, i.e., the change in X that is envisioned as a causal factor or *treatment*. If someone argues that worker-training programs cause wages to rise, the variation in X is presumably participation (X_T) versus non-participation (X_C) in a worker-training program. The latter may also be referred to as the causal counterfactual.

A fourth issue concerns the *background conditions* or *scope-conditions* of an argument. Under normal circumstances, it is not necessary to specify what these are. Sometimes, however, the background conditions of an argument are important enough, and ambiguous enough, that they really ought to be mentioned. For example, it may be important to specify that the causal role of worker-training programs in wages presumes a capitalist economy; no such causal effect can be expected in a socialist economy. It may be important to specify that the effect of worker-training programs is limited to workers who are currently unemployed, and does not extend (or may not extend) to those already employed. Further discussion of appropriate scope-conditions is found under the rubric of *boundedness* (Chapter 3).

Manipulability

In order to formulate a clear causal hypothesis it is helpful if the cause in question is **manipulable**, that is, if it can be changed by the researcher or by someone else.

Formulating the argument in this fashion – as an imagined manipulation – clarifies what the relevant change in X is, and what the background conditions might be.

As an example, let us return to the worker-training program. This treatment is fairly easy to manipulate because one can determine who is admitted into a program and who is rejected. Thus, when we say that a worker-training program has a particular causal effect we know what we are talking about.

By contrast, when someone argues that democracy has an impact on peace/war it is less clear what we have in mind. Naturally, it is helpful if we can specify how we are measuring "democracy." But this is not simply a problem of measurement. The problem is that it is difficult to envision circumstances in which a country democratizes while holding other relevant factors constant. Bear in mind that democratization entails a momentous shift in a country's political and social life and is apt to be accompanied by many additional factors that might impact the probability of peace and war. Consequently, it is not clear what the background (ceteris paribus) conditions of such an argument might be.

Similarly, to assert that "social capital causes economic growth" is ambiguous. We cannot directly manipulate the level of social capital in a community. Consequently, it is difficult to know what "increasing social capital" might mean in a specific setting.

Any causal argument that rests on attitudes, beliefs, or diffuse practices – including ideational arguments and cultural/ideological arguments – is also somewhat ambiguous, for we have no way of directly manipulating people's attitudes, beliefs, or diffuse practices. Of course, we can imagine manipulable treatments that would affect people's attitudes, beliefs, and practices. We might, for instance, ask subjects to read a passage, watch a video clip, listen to a tune, or participate in a staged intervention. These treatments might make the subject happy or sad, change their opinion on a subject, or prompt them to take some action. And they are readily interpretable as causes. However, in this scenario the causal factor is the manipulable treatment, while attitudes/beliefs/practices serve an intermediary role (as a presumed causal mechanism).

Some methodologists view manipulability as a necessary condition of any causal argument.[75] By this interpretation, arguments about the effect of democracy, inequality, race, and other abstract factors are not really causal in nature. This seems a little extreme. Instead, we will treat manipulability as a desirable trait, among others, and one that is best approached as a matter of degrees. Even non-manipulable causes – like attitudes, beliefs, and practices – have prior causes that are manipulable. Thinking carefully about these prior causes can sometimes help us to clarify an argument.

Precedence

A cause must be separable from the effect it purports to explain; otherwise it is tautological (circular). This seems obvious. Yet, on closer reflection, it will be seen that separation is a matter of degrees. To begin with, Xs and Ys are always somewhat differentiated from one another. A perfect tautology (e.g., "The Civil War was caused by the Civil War") is simply nonsense. One occasionally hears the following sort of argument: "The Civil War was caused by the attack of the South against Fort Sumter." This is more satisfactory. Even so, it is not likely to strike readers as a particularly acute explanation. Indeed, there is very little explanation occurring here, precisely because the X is barely differentiated from the Y (the attack against Fort Sumter was of course part of the Civil War). Equally problematic is an argument that links the Civil War to a warlike relationship between North and South, one that persisted from the 1850s to the outbreak of the conflict in 1861. Again, one is at pains to distinguish between cause and effect.

Generally, the greater the separation between cause and effect – the more distance lies between X and Y – the more useful the argument will be, and the more we are likely to regard X as a cause of Y. A good causal factor enjoys temporal precedence relative to other potential causes of an outcome.

Consider, if one proposed cause of an outcome is fully explained by something else, we shall regard the first as superstructural (epiphenomenal, endogenous) and the second as structural (exogenous, foundational). The second has better claim to the status of "cause." It embodies Aristotle's quest for an Unmoved Mover, a factor that affects other things but is affected by nothing.

Of course, every causal factor is affected by something. There are no unmoved movers. Yet, some factors are entirely (or almost entirely) explained by one or two other factors. Here, we are dubious about calling it a cause for it is mostly endogenous. By contrast, the causes of other causes are random or so numerous that they would be difficult to verify.

Consider Figure 6.1. If X is largely explained by Q (if most of the variation in X is due to variation in Q), then Q is probably more correctly regarded as "the" cause of Y. X is subsumed by Q. Once one knows the status of Q one can predict the status of X, M, and Y. X and M are not informative – except with respect to causal mechanisms, as discussed below.

If, on the other hand, Q explains only a small portion of X – which is a product of many factors, some of which may be purely stochastic – then X may properly be regarded as the cause of Y. It is not subsumed by Q.

The greater its precedence, the higher its standing among the various causes of some outcome. Indeed, debates about causal questions often rest on which causal factor is properly judged to come first. Which X explains all the other Xs?

Consider the various factors that have been proposed as explanations of long-term economic development, i.e., for explaining why some nations are rich and others poor. A short list of such causal factors would include geography, colonialism, domestic political institutions, technology, human capital, culture, population, and demographic transitions. Note that arguments among partisans of these different schools are not simply about whether a single factor – say, demography – has a large impact on long-term economic development. They are also, perhaps more importantly, about relationships among the various causal factors, namely which are independent and which are dependent. In this argument, geography has an important advantage: it is not easily explained. Indeed, geography approximates Aristotle's Unmoved Mover. Of course, there are geological explanations for why land masses were formed in certain ways, why rivers appear, why some are navigable and others are not, and so forth. However, these explanations would be quite complex and would involve a considerable amount of contingency. Geographic explanations would be difficult to explain away. By contrast, cultural explanations seem quite vulnerable, as they are often endogenous to other factors. Those who wish to restore the status of cultural explanation must show that a set of values and practices that impacted economic development is not superstructural, that it has causal independence in the long sweep of history.

Impact

Causal arguments strive to explain variation in an outcome. The more variation the causal factor explains – the greater the **impact** of X on Y – the more significant that argument is likely to be. This may also be articulated as a question of effect size, magnitude, power, or strength.

Necessary-and-sufficient causal arguments are compelling because they explain *all* the variation in Y, while remaining admirably concise. It is no wonder that they continue to be regarded as the ideal-type causal argument. By contrast, wherever there are exceptions to a causal argument, or where some factor other than X accounts for variation in Y, we can see that the argument is weakened: it no longer suffices to account for Y.

There are a number of ways in which the question of relative impact can be gauged. In a regression format, where the relationship between X and Y is assumed to be probabilistic, impact is measured by the coefficient (slope) for X or by a model-fit statistic such as R^2 for X, a vector of independent variables.

Of course, estimates of causal impact from an empirical model depend upon the specifics of that sample and model, and may or may not correspond to real-world impact. If the model is not realistic in this respect, then a separate evaluation of impact – perhaps in a more speculative mode – may be required. It is often helpful to consider the impact of X on Y in practical terms, e.g., as a matter of public policy. Could a significant change in Y be achieved by manipulating X? At what cost and with what opportunity costs?

The impact of X on Y may also be gauged by comparing its impact to other factors. If the impact of these other factors is well understood, this may provide a useful metric of significance (i.e., relative impact).

Whatever the metric of evaluation, the impact of X on Y is a key measure of success. One of the criteria of a good causal argument is that it explains a lot about the phenomenon of interest. It is not trivial.

Mechanism

We have said that causes generate – alter, change, condition, create, effect – outcomes. It follows that there must be a **causal mechanism**, or mechanisms, at work. The mechanism is "the agency or means by which an effect is produced or a purpose is accomplished."[76] It is the **causal pathway** (aka process, mediator, or intermediate variable) by which a causal factor of theoretical interest is thought to affect an outcome, illustrated by M in Figure 6.1. This might be a single factor, a large number of factors acting independently, a **causal chain** of discrete events, a continuous process (e.g., a billiard ball rolling across a table and hitting another ball) – in short, anything that is affected by X and that, in turn, affects Y.

Sometimes, the working of a causal mechanism is obvious and can be intuited from what we know about the world. For example, if product sales increase when the price is lowered we may infer that consumer decisions were influenced by price. Often, however, the mechanism operating within a causal relationship is obscure. For example, insofar as one might regard economic development as a causal factor (X) in democratization (Y) – rich countries being more likely to democratize or to consolidate their democracy – it is difficult to say which components of economic development might be causing this result. X might impact Y through income, infrastructure, urbanization, or education, and the mechanism might be interest-based or norm-based (or some combination of the two).

An $X \rightarrow Y$ hypothesis without a clear causal mechanism is an argument in search of an explanation. It may be true, but it will not be very meaningful, will be difficult to generalize upon, and may also be difficult to prove in a convincing fashion. We want to know *why* X causes Y, not simply that X causes Y.

Thus, it is incumbent upon the writer to clarify the causal mechanism(s) at work in a causal argument if it cannot be intuited from context. This may be accomplished in prose, in diagrams, and/or in mathematical models, and is implicit in the very act of theorizing, as discussed in the previous chapter.

Causal Analysis

Having established the nature of causal hypotheses, we turn to the problem of proof or demonstration. Given a specific hypothesis about the relationship of X to Y, how might one assess whether the relationship is actually causal (rather than merely correlative)? If it is causal, how might we estimate the causal effect?

In Chapter 4, we observed that all research designs strive for *validity*, *precision*, *sample representativeness*, and *sample size*. In this chapter, we focus on two additional criteria that are specific to causal analysis: *covariation* and *comparability*. For convenience, all six criteria are reproduced in Table 6.2.

Covariation

Empirical evidence of a causal relationship consists of patterns discovered in the data. Specifically, if a causal relationship between X and Y exists we expect to find **covariation** (association, correlation) between the two variables (probabilistically). If, for example, the causal factor of interest is a worker-training program (X), and the program has the hypothesized causal effect on wages (Y), we expect that the

Table 6.2   Causal research designs: criteria

ALL RESEARCH DESIGNS (Chapter 4)
Validity
- Is the estimate valid (true)?

Precision
- Is the estimate precise (reliable)?

Sample representativeness
- Is the sample representative of the intended population?

Sample size
- Is the sample large enough to overcome stochastic threats to inference?

CAUSAL RESEARCH DESIGNS (this chapter)
Covariation (association, correlation)
- Does X covary with Y?

Comparability (equivalence, unit homogeneity)
- Is each observation causally comparable to other observations in the sample?

earnings of participants (Y_T) will be higher than earnings of non-participants (Y_C) when measured a year after completion of the program.

Covariation between X and Y is thus a necessary condition of causality. That is to say, if we learn nothing about Y's probable value from looking at the value of X then X cannot be considered a cause of Y. Likewise, it is from this covariational pattern that we estimate a causal effect.

Imagine a hypothetical sample of 100 observations, each of which records a value for X, the causal factor of interest, and Y, the outcome of interest. In **conditioning** these variables we observe the value of Y for each value of X.

In the simplest case, both factors are binary. For all observations in which $X = 0$, we observe the values of Y, which we designate as Y_C. Next, for all observations in which $X = 1$, we observe the values of Y, designated as Y_T. Results of this test are contained in panel (a) of Figure 6.2. In this hypothetical sample, we observe a (positive) association between X and Y. That is, knowing the value of X, we can predict the value of Y (with some error).

Now, let us assume that Y is an interval variable, varying from 0–100. Again, we compare Y_T and Y_C. Results of this test are contained in panel (b) of Figure 6.2. Again, we see a covariational relationship. Knowing the value of X, we can predict the value of Y (with some error).

Finally, let us assume that both X and Y are measured along an interval scale stretching from 0–100. For each value of X, we record the values for Y. This produces a scatter plot, as shown in panel (c) of Figure 6.2. Once again, we observe a (positive) covariational relationship.

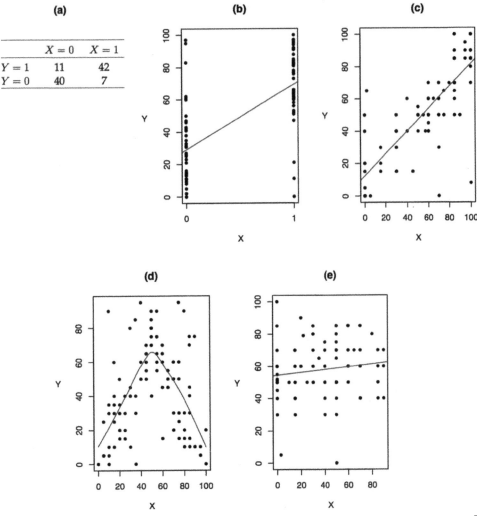

Figure 6.2 Covariational patterns

All of these hypothetical data distributions point to a positive (and statistically significant) relationship between X and Y. If the relationship were reversed – if the value of Y decreased with each increase in X – then a negative relationship would be in evidence. These are **monotonic** relationships insofar as an increase in X is always accompanied by an increase in Y or no change in Y, while a decrease in X is always accompanied by a decrease in Y or no change in Y.

All sorts of **non-monotonic** relationships are also possible. For example, the values of X and Y might be positive as X increases from 0 to 50, where they peak; from 50 to 100 the relationship might be negative, as shown in panel (d). This hump-backed (inverted-U) relationship may be quite common in the social world. The "Kuznets curve" is a well-known (but contested) relationship between economic development and inequality named after Simon Kuznets, who hypothesized that income inequality would increase during the early period of industrialization and then begin to decrease as a country became more developed.[77]

A final possibility is that there is no discernible pattern between X and Y, or at least none that can be distinguished from what **stochastic** (random) factors might produce. Such a situation is illustrated in panel (e) of Figure 6.2. In this situation, the null hypothesis (of no relationship) cannot be rejected.

Comparability

Finding a covariational pattern between X and Y does not assure that the relationship is causal. It might be merely associational. "Correlation does not equal causation," as the saying goes. If we find an association among unemployed persons between attending a worker-training program (X) and higher earnings (Y) it does not automatically follow that X causes Y.

In order to infer a causal relationship between X and Y from the covariation of X and Y across a set of observations we must be able to convince ourselves that other things are equal (the ceteris paribus assumption). That is, we need to be assured that the variation we observe in Y is a product of X and not of some other cause(s). If **causal comparability** is present across the sample, we can say that the estimate derived from the analysis is valid. So comparability is the specific feature of a research design that allows one to make claims about *validity*, an issue introduced (in a general fashion) in Chapter 4. If comparability does not exist then the pattern of X–Y covariation is spurious, i.e., characterized by systematic error or *bias*.

A more technical way of phrasing the assumption of comparability is that the **expected value** of Y for a given value of X should be the same across the studied observations throughout the period of analysis:

$$E(Y|X)$$

If this is the case, we can say that a group of observations is causally comparable (equivalent) with respect to a given hypothesis.[78]

If, for example, a set of unemployed persons is causally comparable with respect to a worker-training program then we shall expect them to experience roughly the same change in earnings when subjected to the same worker-training program. This must remain true throughout the period of analysis, i.e., from the first observation to the last (if several observations of the outcome are taken through time).

Our (minimal) understanding of causal comparability requires only that units be comparable to one another *on average*. Error (non-comparability) across units is satisfactory so long as its distribution is centered on the true mean (i.e., so long as the error is random).[79] That is, some persons may be positively affected by a worker-training program, while others weakly or even negatively affected. Yet, on average (across the sample), or in expectation, the effect of X on Y is assumed to be the same.

CONCLUSIONS

We began this chapter by defining the concept of causality at some length, with the assistance of causal graphs. In the next section, we introduced criteria intended to define a *good* (well-constructed) causal hypothesis – that which researchers strive to achieve (or ought to strive to achieve) in their work. This includes *precision, generality, boundedness, parsimony, coherence, commensurability, innovation, relevance, clarity, manipulability, precedence, impact,* and *mechanism* (see Table 6.2).

The chapter proceeded to discuss the challenge of causal *analysis*, i.e., the formulation of an effective research design in order to test a hypothesis. Here, we dwelt on the importance of *covariation* and *comparability*.

In subsequent chapters, we put these tools to work in the discussion of specific research designs. Experimental designs will be addressed in Chapter 7, non-experimental designs in Chapter 8, and case study designs in Chapter 9. Although these chapters address different topics, they are closely interrelated and build upon one another in a cumulative fashion. Indeed, all of the concepts introduced in this chapter will reappear in later chapters, so you will have a chance to review and to see how they apply in various research settings.

KEY TERMS

- Cause
- Outcome
- Treatment group
- Control group
- Causal effect
- Counterfactual
- Scope-conditions
- Antecedent
- Endogenous
- Exogenous
- Monotonic
- Non-monotonic
- Causal graph
- Clarity
- Manipulability
- Precedence
- Impact
- Causal mechanism
- Causal comparability
- Expected value
- Covariation

- Causal chain
- Causal pathway
- Conditioning
- Binary
- Stochastic

7

Experimental Designs

Recall (from Chapter 6) that estimating a causal effect involves comparing a *factual* (that which actually happened) to a *counterfactual* (that which might have happened). Returning to our perennial example, let us say that we wish to estimate the effect of a job-training program on the earnings of unemployed people after they have completed the program. Those who participate in the program are members of the **treatment group**. Non-participants are members of the **control group**.

Let us say that we know the earnings of participants and non-participants after completing the program. These are the factuals. What we do not know is what their earnings would have been if their roles had been reversed. These are the counterfactuals.

Although the only sure way to compare factuals with counterfactuals is to employ a time-machine, a well-designed experiment comes close to the mythical time-machine insofar as the control group exemplifies the (unobserved) counterfactual for the treatment group, and the treatment group exemplifies the (unobserved) counterfactual for the control group. Under certain conditions, this is a plausible scenario.

For present purposes, the defining criterion of an experiment is that the treatment is randomly assigned ("randomized") across subjects. We do not care who controls the experiment – the researcher conducting the study or someone else. (Sometimes, an experiment that unfolds naturally, without intervention by a researcher, is referred to as a natural experiment, as discussed below.)

We begin this chapter with a review of the problem of confounding as it applies to experimental research. We proceed to introduce various approaches to experimental research. The final section offers a series of examples of experiments conducted on a variety of diverse topics. Together, these sections should give the reader a sense of the opportunities for, and limitations of, experimental research in the social sciences.

Experiments With and Without Confounding

In its simplest version, a single treatment (e.g., a worker-training program) is randomly assigned to members drawn from a known population (e.g., unemployed people of a given age). That is, some are chosen to participate in the program (the treatment group) and others are chosen to become part of the control group. The causal effect of the program is measured by comparing annual earnings of program participants with annual earnings of non-participants one year after the completion of the program.

Since the **assignment** of the treatment is random, we can assume that all background factors that might affect earnings are equal (on average) across the treatment and control groups. The only difference between the two groups is that one has been subjected to the treatment and the other has not, as illustrated in Figure 7.1. Causal comparability is achieved, which is to say the **expected value** of the outcome is the same for each group, contingent upon its receiving the treatment or not (see Chapter 6).

C (control group)   T (treatment group)

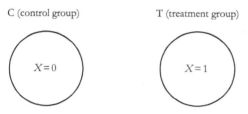

$X = 0$ $X = 1$

Figure 7.1 Experimental data without confounders: an illustration

$E(Y|X)$ is the same for treatment and control groups

In this situation, we can compare the factual with the counterfactual by comparing two factuals: the earnings of those in the treatment group with the earnings of those in the control group. If the program has the desired effect, those in the treatment group should have higher earnings, on average, than those in the control group. If there is no difference between the earnings of these two groups, or if the difference does not surpass that which might have been obtained through stochastic (random) factors, then we can conclude that there is unlikely to be a (positive) causal effect. And if the control group has higher earnings than the treatment group we may conclude that the program has adverse effects.

This simple data generating process may also be diagrammed in a causal graph. In Figure 7.2 (which builds on Figure 6.1), the following terminology applies. Q is the

[Z]   **Figure 7.2** Experimental data without confounders: a causal graph

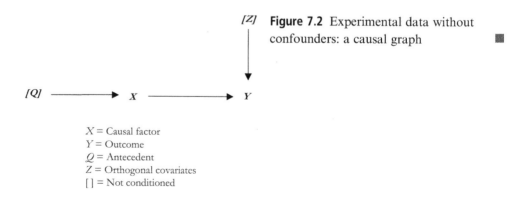

X = Causal factor
Y = Outcome
Q = Antecedent
Z = Orthogonal covariates
[] = Not conditioned

random assignment process. X is the assignment itself: $X = 0$ is understood as the control condition (C) and $X = 1$ as the treatment condition (T). Y is the outcome, i.e., earnings. And Z represents other factors that might impact the outcome, e.g., motivation, job skills, interpersonal skills, and luck. Note that in this graph Z is orthogonal to (uncorrelated with) X because the treatment has been randomly assigned: persons in the treatment group are assumed to have, on average, the same level of motivation, job skills, interpersonal skills, and luck as those in the control group.

Let us assume that the training program has a positive impact on earnings. If so, we should observe a pattern of data that looks something like the X/Y graph in Figure 7.3. The mean value of Y in the control condition $(\overline{Y}_C)$ is \$22,248. The mean value of Y in the treatment condition $(\overline{Y}_T)$ is \$32,915. We can therefore conclude that the causal effect of a hypothetical change from $X = 0$ to $X = 1$ is

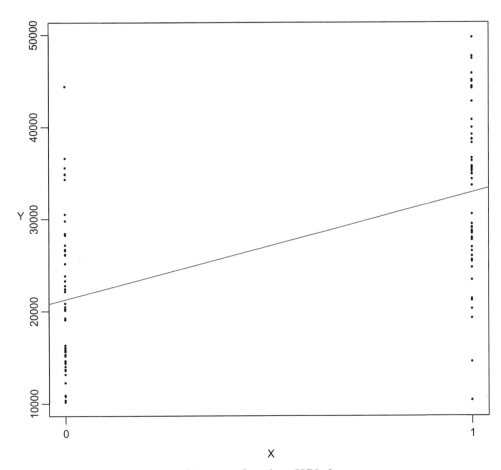

Figure 7.3 Experimental data without confounders: X/Y plot

$N = 100$. Mean value of Y_C: \$22,248. Mean value of Y_T: \$32,915. Difference of means: \$11,667.
t-test of statistical significance = –6.790.

given by the difference in means: $\overline{Y}_T - \overline{Y}_C$, or \$11,667. This may be regarded as an **average treatment effect** (ATE), since it averages results in the treatment and control groups. Implicit in this analysis is the idea that if one reassigned those in the treatment group to the control group, and those in the control group to the treatment group, and then ran the experiment again, the measured causal effect would be the same.

This is the simplest – and best – research design imaginable. We need only condition on two variables – X and Y – observing their covariation. (The problem of discerning when differences between treatment and control groups are greater than might be expected to occur as a result of chance – i.e., "statistical significance" – is postponed until Part IV.) Of course, we could decide to condition on orthogonal factors (Z) as well in order to increase the precision of our estimates. However, doing so would not affect our estimate of the causal effect, precisely because these additional factors are uncorrelated with X.

Non-Compliance

By assigning a treatment randomly, experiments avoid one sort of confounding. But they are still open to other sorts of confounders. Understanding these potential confounders is important not only for understanding of experimental research but also for our understanding of *non-experimental* research – since many of these confounders also appear in circumstances where a treatment cannot be randomly assigned.

One potential problem is **non-compliance**. Suppose that we have assigned unemployed persons to our treatment group but they refuse to attend the worker-training program, or they drop out before the program is complete (attrition). There is little that we can do to solve problems of non-compliance in many research settings. Yet, the effect is to render a treatment group in which some members have not been treated, i.e., they have not been exposed to the treatment or have been exposed to less of it than others, as illustrated in Figure 7.4.

Several approaches may be taken to this problem. One may regard the estimate of causal effects as an estimate reflecting **intention-to-treat** (ITT) rather than an ATE. This is a reasonable approach in settings where non-compliance is

C (control group)   T (treatment group)

$X = 0$ $X = 1$

Some units assigned to the treatment group are not exposed to the treatment. Non-compliers indicated by ⌀

Figure 7.4 Experimental data with non-compliance: an illustration

unavoidable and one wishes to take this into account in the final analysis. For example, a policymaker may wish to know what the causal effect of a worker-training program is likely to be on a population of unemployed people, given that some of those chosen to participate in the program are likely to drop out prior to completion. If attrition is inevitable, the ITT estimate may be more relevant than a (hypothetical) ATE estimate.

One may also choose to exclude non-compliers from the analysis. Thus, we might compare compliers in the treatment group with the (entire) control group. However, this raises a problem of comparison. Note that non-compliers are not likely to be similar to compliers; they may be less motivated to find work, for example. If we compare the compliers with the control group we shall be comparing apples and oranges, i.e., groups for which the expected value of Y, given X, is *not* the same.

One option is to try to identify those characteristics that differentiate compliers from non-compliers and then use these as controls in a regression or matching analysis. The purpose here is to identify subjects within the control group who are similar to compliers so that comparability is restored. However, it is often difficult to identify and measure those characteristics – especially if they are attitudinal (e.g., motivation). Another approach is to regard the random assignment to treatment and controls as an instrument in a two-stage analysis, as described in the next chapter (see *Instrumental Variables*).

A final option is to forget the control group entirely, focusing instead on a pre- and post-comparison of compliers in the treatment group. If one has a pre-treatment measure of earnings, this approach is feasible. However, it must be borne in mind that since the compliers are different from the non-compliers in key respects we cannot regard the estimate as representing an ATE. Rather, it should be understood as an **average treatment effect on the treated** (ATT). This means that the causal effect applies to units that are similar to those that actually received the treatment, but not to units drawn randomly from the population (in this case, the population of unemployed persons).

Contamination

A second potential problem with experimental designs occurs when the treatment and control conditions are not effectively isolated from each other, and thus are allowed to "contaminate" each other, as illustrated in Figure 7.5.

Contamination is rarely a problem in laboratory experiments precisely because experimenters can control all aspects of the situation. However, it is quite common in field experiments, where subjects in the treatment and control groups may intermingle or otherwise communicate with each other. (This distinction is introduced later in the chapter.)

Typically, contamination is caused when members of the control group manage to receive the treatment, or some aspects of the treatment. In our ongoing example, this might occur if participants who attend the worker-training program

C (control group)   T (treatment group)

$X = 0$ $X = 1$

$E(Y|X)$ is not the same for treatment and control groups

Figure 7.5 Experimental data with contamination: an illustration

communicate with those in the control group, thereby spreading their learning among those who are not supposed to be exposed to the treatment.

There is no easy fix for contamination unless one can successfully model the process by which contamination occurs – an uncertain prospect, in most settings. A better approach, if it is possible, is to redesign the experiment so that each group is effectively isolated from each other.

Compound Treatments

Sometimes, an experimental treatment combines two elements, only one of which is of theoretical interest. Because the treatment group is subject to both X (the factor of theoretical interest) and Z (the background factor), one cannot discern the independent effect of X on Y, which may be confounded by Z, as illustrated in Figure 7.6.

The most common scenario involves **researcher** (or **experimenter**) **effects**. This refers to a setting in which the subject is aware that she is part of a study and this knowledge alters her behavior. Since this is not the treatment of theoretical interest, it serves to confound the analysis.

For example, participants in a job-training program may be motivated to find a job simply because they know they are being studied. If so, this feature may

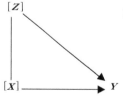

Figure 7.6 Causal graph of compound treatment confounding

X = Causal factor
Y = Outcome
Z = Confounder
[] = Not conditioned

generate differences in the outcome across treatment and control groups which have nothing to do with the content of the program and therefore offer a misleading picture of program impact.

A famous example occurred in a series of studies focused on workers at a General Electric plant in Hawthorne, Illinois. Here, it appears that workers in the treatment group applied themselves with greater diligence than those in the control group regardless of what the treatment consisted of. It was eventually determined that workers were responding not to the intended treatment but rather to the situation of being intensively monitored.[80] Experimenter effects due to the condition of being studied have been known ever since as **Hawthorne effects**.

Another form of researcher effect occurs whenever subjects are influenced by the ascriptive features or personality of a researcher. For example, respondents may react differently when interviewed by white and black surveyors, thus introducing an important confounding factor into any study of racial attitudes.

The best approach to compound-treatment confounders is to redesign the experiment to alleviate the confounder. If the problem is caused by researcher effects one may "blind" the subjects of an experiment so that they are unaware of their status as members of treatment or control groups. If one suspects that the researcher, rather than the subject, is instilling bias into the analysis then the researcher should be "blinded." And if both are suspected of introducing bias in the analysis, a double-blind protocol is desirable.

Of course, it is not always possible to achieve this research design feature due to practical or ethical constraints. Many social experiments are not truly *blind* (where subjects do not know whether they are in the treatment or control group), much less *double-blind* (where neither subjects nor researchers know who is in the treatment and control groups). And even when subjects are ignorant of their status they may respond to aspects of the treatment that are not of theoretical interest, thus introducing confounders into the analysis. Consequently, experimenter effects are difficult to avoid, and – worse – are not always apparent to the researcher.

An alternative is to subject the control group to the same "experimenter effects" as the treatment group, thus canceling out this feature of the design and rendering the two groups comparable. However, this may be difficult to implement.

Before concluding this section it is important to bear in mind that compound-treatment confounders are not limited to researcher effects. Other sorts of compound-treatment confounders will require different approaches.

Varieties of Experiments

We are accustomed to speak of experiments as if they all followed the same research design. This is true, but only to a point. While all experiments feature a randomized treatment (according to our adopted definition), other features vary, sometimes quite a lot. In this section, we review experimental designs, randomization mechanisms, and research settings.

Experimental Designs

Typology of Designs

There are many ways to establish an experimental protocol. However, most follow one of seven templates, summarized in Table 7.1. First, we need to introduce some notation that will be used in this table and in subsequent tables.

As previously, X_T refers to the treatment condition (e.g., program participation), while X_C refers to the control condition (e.g., program non-participation).

A *group* refers to a set of units (e.g., individuals) that are exposed to the same treatment/control conditions. This might be a simple control condition, a simple treatment condition, or a series of treatment/control conditions administered through time. Sometimes, there is no pure control group: all groups receive the treatment at different times or receive different treatments. Whatever the case, each group in a research design is represented by a Roman numeral ($I, II, \ldots$) in Table 7.1.

The size of a group – the number of subjects or units who are exposed to a particular treatment or set of treatments (or to the control condition) – is indeterminate. However, it is important to bear in mind that the randomization procedure is premised on the existence of a sufficient number of observations to overcome stochastic threats to inference. The greater the number of units, the greater our assurance that results obtained from a randomized design are not the product of chance. Indeed, the virtues credited to the technique of randomization become plausible only as the number of units increases. And this, in turn, means that the

Table 7.1 A typology of experimental designs

Design	Group						
1. Post-test only	I.		X_T	$Time_1$			
	II.		X_C				
2. Pre-test post-test	I.	$Time_1$	X_T	$Time_2$			
	II.		X_C				
3. Multiple post-tests	I.	$Time_1$	X_T	$Time_2$	$Time_3$	$Time_4$	$Time_5$
	II.		X_C				
4. Roll-out	I.	$Time_1$	X_T	$Time_2$	X_T	$Time_3$	
	II.		X_C		X_C		
5. Crossover	I.	$Time_1$	$X_T V_C$	$Time_2$	$X_C V_T$	$Time_3$	
	II.		$X_C V_T$		$X_T V_C$		
6. Factorial	I.		$X_C V_C$				
	II.	$Time_1$	$X_C V_T$	$Time_2$			
	III.		$X_T V_C$				
	IV.		$X_T V_T$				

I–IV	Groups
$Time_{1-N}$	Measurements of key variables through time
X_C	Control condition ($X = 0$)
X_T	Treatment condition ($X = 1$)
V_C	Control condition ($V = 0$) for second causal factor
V_T	Treatment condition ($V = 1$) for second causal factor

experimental method is implicitly a large-N method of analysis. (See discussion of *Sample Size* in Chapter 4.)

Data are generated when someone (e.g., the researcher) measures the value of X, Y, and relevant covariates (if any) for all units in the study. Thus, in a study of the impact of worker-training programs (X) on earnings (Y) the researcher might measure X and Y for each person in the sample before ($Time_1$) and after ($Time_2$) the intervention.

For each experimental protocol, an appropriate statistical test must be adopted for evaluating the impact of an intervention(s). This might be as simple as a *t-test* measuring the difference of means between two groups. It might involve a multivariate model incorporating additional factors to reduce background noise. Or it might be more complicated.[81] Typically, more complex models are required whenever confounders are suspected. Discussion of statistical models is postponed until Part IV; in this section we are concerned with issues of research design.

The simplest and most common experimental protocol is the **post-test only** design (#1 in Table 7.1). This involves a single treatment that is randomly assigned across the sample, creating two groups: the treatment group and the control group. Properly administered, only one feature – the presence or absence of treatment – differentiates the two groups. All relevant background features should be similar, on average, across the groups. A single post-test measures the outcome of concern at some point after the intervention.

Sometimes, observations are taken before and after the intervention, providing **pre- and post-tests** (#2 in Table 7.1). The potential effect of the treatment is calculated by comparing difference scores, i.e., differences on the measured outcome between the first set of observations (the pre-test) and the second set of observations (the post-test) for each group.

Sometimes, it is suspected that the effect of a treatment varies over time (after the initiation of the treatment), requiring **multiple post-tests** (#3 in Table 7.1) in order to track these variations. Indeed, wherever long-term causal effects are of interest multiple post-tests staged at regular intervals are advisable so that the endurance or attenuation of a treatment effect can be gauged.

Sometimes, it is desirable to stage an intervention across several sequences so that the same treatment is administered to all groups at different times. In varying the timing of an intervention, a **roll-out** design (#4 in Table 7.1) overcomes potential confounders that are coincident with the first intervention. Moreover, one is able to offer the treatment to all groups, which may be important for political or ethical reasons.

A **crossover** design (#5 in Table 7.1) may be employed if one is interested in testing sequencing effects. Does it matter whether X is introduced before V (a second treatment)? Sometimes, it does, and a crossover design allows one to test the possibility by constructing groups that are subjected to different sequences among the multiple treatments.

A **factorial** design tests the interactive effects of several categorical treatment variables (#6 in Table 7.1). In the simplest version, two binary causal factors are combined into four possible treatments. If, for example, treatments consist of $X =$ participation in a worker-training program and $V =$ small classes, these can be combined into four groups by randomizing across two dimensions, as shown in Table 7.1.

This concludes our itinerary of experimental protocols. Note that well-established names exist for only a few of these. For others, a variety of names (usually rather long and cumbersome) may be employed. Despite the lack of a standard terminology, the construction of these designs is remarkably consistent across diverse research settings. Most experimental designs may be understood as variants of the classics.

Randomization Mechanisms

Purposeful **randomization** of the treatment is the defining element of an experiment. By this, we mean that all members of the chosen sample have an equal opportunity of receiving the treatment (or the various treatment conditions, if there is more than one). This may be accomplished by choosing names from an urn, with a random number generator, or through some other method. In order to be fully realized, the goal of randomization must be intentional, which usually means that it is controlled by the researcher him/herself.

Sometimes, randomization is carried out within identified strata rather than across the entire sample. In this case, known as *blocking* (or sometimes as *matching*), units chosen for analysis are first stratified according to some background feature(s) relevant to the outcome of interest. Thus, an experiment on worker-training programs might stratify a sample of unemployed persons by race, sex, age, and parental educational attainment. Within each stratum, the treatment (e.g., participation in the program) is randomized. If the strata consist of only two units each (e.g., two students), then one is working with blocked-pairs (i.e., blocks of two). This is a common technique to limit background noise wherever background heterogeneity is great and sample size is limited.

Research Settings

Experiments may be carried out in a wide variety of settings. If the setting is constructed and controlled by the researcher it may be referred to as a **laboratory experiment**. If the setting is natural (i.e., more realistic) it may be referred to as a **field experiment**. However, there is no hard and fast distinction between these two types of settings, which are, after all, matters of degree. (What is a "laboratory"?)

To be sure, laboratory settings are likely to involve more researcher control, and this may in turn result in fewer threats to inference (e.g., by contamination). However, the simple fact of being conducted in a laboratory is no assurance that threats to inference have been removed. Likewise, the fact of being conducted "in the field" is no reason to believe that experimental protocols have been violated. Ultimately, it is up to the researcher – and the consumers of a study – to judge.

Some experiments involve nothing more than a survey instrument. The only difference between a **survey experiment** and a regular survey is that the former has a randomized treatment. That is, some respondents have been selected at random to receive a different version of the survey, generating a treatment version and a control version whose responses can be compared. The cheap and easy availability of online surveys (see Chapter 13) has contributed to the growing popularity of survey experiments in recent years.

Typically, the researcher controls the assignment of the treatment – the randomization procedure – as well as other design features of an experiment. Occasionally, a randomized treatment occurs naturally, i.e., outside the control of the researcher. This may be referred to as a **natural experiment**. For example, a government-run lottery assigns winners randomly from among those with lottery tickets (if the lottery is honest). Those who win may be considered part of a treatment group, while those who lose may be considered part of a control group. Researchers have nothing to do with it. So long as randomization has been achieved (with a fairly high degree of certainty) we shall regard it as an experiment. (If, on the other hand, random assignment is not achieved, or is highly questionable, we shall classify the resulting study as *observational*, as discussed in the next chapter.)

Examples

It remains to be seen how applicable the randomization approach might be to the research agenda of the social sciences. Indeed, the hard methodological question is not whether experiments work (there is little doubt that they do), but what they work for. As an entrée into this issue, we review four examples drawn from diverse fields: (1) employment discrimination, (2) corruption control, (3) historic election campaigns, and (4) gender and leadership. Each will be briefly discussed to give a flavor of the sorts of subjects that experimenters have tackled in recent years, as well as potential methodological difficulties.

Employment Discrimination

Employment discrimination is a policy question of obvious and enduring importance. Of course, few employers will admit to racially-based hiring practices.[82] This must be inferred.

One genre of experiment involves sending white and black (or male and female) applicants – matched in all respects and coached to answer questions in a similar fashion – into the same job interviews.[83] If white candidates experience higher success rates, this fact may be accorded to race-based discrimination. However, this procedure – known generically as an audit study – is subject to researcher bias. In particular, those conducting the experiments may act in ways that affect the employer's decision but has nothing to do with race per se. Note that since the pseudo-job candidates are aware of the objectives of the experiment they may (consciously or unconsciously) allow this to affect their behavior in the job interview. Black confederates may appear less eager to receive the job than white confederates because they believe this is how many black job candidates might behave or because they believe that this is how they will be perceived by the white employer. If so, then the reported results of the experiment are the product of experimenter effects rather than the treatment of interest (skin color), generating a compound-treatment confounder.[84]

In order to alleviate this potential bias, Bertrand and Mullainathan remove the experimenters entirely from the conduct of the experiment. Instead, they mail out hundreds of resumes in response to jobs advertised in the Boston and Chicago areas.[85] These applications differ in one key respect: some of the names on the resumes were distinctively African-American and the others identifiably white. The researchers find that applications with "white" names like Emily and Greg were more likely to be contacted by employers for a follow-up interview than applications with recognizably "black" names like Lakisha and Jamal.

This clever field experiment provides some of the strongest evidence to date of employment discrimination. However, it too may be subject to a compound-treatment confounder. Note that the names chosen by Bertrand and Mullainathan as typically black are also unusual. This is because African-American parents adopt a much wider array of names for their children than white parents. Nonetheless, it could be that the lack of employment success realized by "Lakisha" and "Jamal" – relative to "Emily" and "Greg" – is due to the fact that employers find these names strange. Persons with exotic names may be tagged by employers (probably unconsciously) as less trustworthy, less likely to take direction and work well with others, and so forth. And this, rather than their race per se, may account for differential hiring decisions.

Corruption Control

The causes of corruption are a central preoccupation among citizens and among scholars across the world. Yet, the question remains agonizingly diffuse. Studies generally build on cross-sectional analyses of countries (or states within a country), whose varying levels of corruption are measured through surveys of the public or country experts (e.g., the Transparency International and World Bank indices of corruption). If an institution is found to correlate with a higher level of corruption (taking all other relevant and measurable factors into account), then it may be interpreted as a causal relationship.[86] This genre of work is evidently open to the same, familiar objection: perhaps it is a merely correlational relationship, accountable to some unmeasured common cause.

In order to bring experimental evidence to bear on the question of corruption, Ben Olken observes levels of corruption in road projects spread across 600 Indonesian villages. Corruption is measured by a variety of direct methods – most interestingly, by sampling the cores of selected roads in order to determine whether materials used were standard or substandard (Chapter 5).[87] Two theories are tested. The first concerns the effect of an impending government audit, a top-down approach to corruption control. The second concerns grassroots participation in monitoring the road project, a down-up approach to corruption control. Each of these treatments is randomized across the 600 villages. Olken finds that the threat of an audit had a much greater effect in reducing corruption than institution of village-level monitoring (though both had some effect).

Historic Election Campaigns

Traditionally, the use of experimental methods has been understood as a prospective, rather than retrospective, exercise. Because the research is designed by the experimenter, it may help us shed light on general phenomena that pertain to the past, but it cannot shed light on particular events in the past. While generally true, there are exceptions to this rule.

The role of the infamous "Willie Horton" ad in the 1988 US presidential campaign has exercised scholars and pundits since the day it aired.[88] In the political advertisement, sponsored by a group loyal to George Bush's campaign, a black man, Willie Horton, is shown along with a voiceover explaining that Horton was released from prison on furlough by Massachusetts Governor Michael Dukakis, after which he proceeded to rape a woman and viciously beat her fiancé. Was this a "race-baiting" ad, or was it really more about crime? What sort of effect might it have had on the general public? And what, more generally, is the effect of attack ads that seek to capitalize on fear?

Tali Mendelberg's ingenious approach to these questions is to expose a sample of white college students to a laboratory experiment in which the treatment is exposure to the Horton ad, which is embedded within a news story.[89] (Students chosen for the experiment had little or no knowledge of the ad, and are thus unaware of its notoriety.) The control consisted of a similar news story, without the Horton excerpt. Mendelberg finds that the ad enhanced the salience of race, rather than crime, and interacted with existing prejudices so as to affect subjects' views on a range of issues in a more conservative direction.

Of course, this study is unable to determine (or even estimate) how long this effect lasted, how many voters it reached, and how many votes (if any) it changed. These very specific historical outcomes are beyond the scope of experimental methods to explore.[90] Even so, Mendelberg's influential study prompts us to consider ways in which experimental protocols might be enlisted to shed light on past events – a relatively new purview for the venerable experiment.

Gender and Leadership

Does the sex of a politician affect his/her policy decisions? The question has been much studied and much debated.[91] However, there is little strong evidence to show whether gender has effects on the quality of political decisions, primarily because observational data are replete with potential confounders. If we simply compare the behavior of male and female legislators we run the risk of confusing gender effects with other factors that happen to covary with the gender of a legislator, e.g., party identification, the character of the election, or the character of the district. And if the empirical comparisons are cross-country, the number of potential confounders is even greater. A recent study by Dollar, Fisman, and Gatti reports a negative correlation between representation of women in parliaments and corruption.[92] The causal question, raised pointedly by Chattapadhyay and Duflo, is whether this means that women are less corrupt (as Dollar et al. claim), or that "countries that are less corrupt are also more likely to elect women to parliament."[93] This gets to the heart of our topic.

To shed light on this issue, Chattapadhyay and Duflo take advantage of a federal law passed in India in 1993 requiring that one-third of all village council heads (an elective position) be reserved for women. Because the assignment of women to positions of authority is randomized (though not by the researchers), it is possible to interpret policy choices made by village councils under male and female leadership as an indication of the causal effect of gender. Prior to this, of course, it is necessary to determine what the varying preferences of men and women in West Bengal and Rajasthan, the two states under study, might consist of. This is accomplished by examining the types of formal requests brought to the village council by male and female citizens.

> In West Bengal, women complain more often than men about drinking water and roads, and there are more investments in drinking water and roads in [village councils] reserved for women. In Rajasthan, women complain more often than men about drinking water but less often about roads, and there are more investments in water and less investment in roads in [village councils] reserved for women.[94]

The authors find that these preferences are indeed reflected in the sort of public goods provided by governments in villages where a female council head is in charge – understood relative to villages in the control group, which are generally governed by men. In short, the sex of political leaders counts. Goods valued more highly by women are more likely to be distributed in villages where women hold important leadership positions.

The design features of this natural randomization are close to ideal. There are many units to study, the process of randomization seems to have been strictly adhered to, and there are viable outcome indicators by which one might judge the impact of the treatment. In short, the set-up in this experiment appears to be about as sound as one might have achieved even with an experiment that was controlled by the researcher.

Of course, the precise causal mechanisms at work in this setting are somewhat open to interpretation. Is the difference in policy outcomes between quota and non-quota villages a product of female leaders' desire to represent the interests of women in their constituencies or a product of the personal attributes and life-histories of the chosen female leaders? (Would well-off and politically empowered female leaders behave differently?) The authors try to address this question by running statistical analyses that control for various characteristics of female leaders, finding no effect. Even so, one may suspect that there is insufficient variation in these properties to provide a proper test. The general point is that once one moves from questions about the main causal effect (which is randomized) to questions of causal mechanism (which, in this case and most others, is not randomized) the precision and confidence of the analysis suffers accordingly. (This also provides a good example of a study in which experimental and non-experimental styles of analysis coincide.)

A final point of clarification is in order. Chattapadhyay and Duflo are careful to present their research as a test of gender quotas, not a test of gender per se. Note that it is the gender quota that is being randomized not the gender of specific political leaders or the gender of constituents within the studied communities (of course). What one may reasonably conclude from this experiment is that gender quotas influence public policy outcomes wherever gender preferences diverge (men and women in a community want different things) and one group is politically disadvantaged. We do not learn what features of gender are driving divergent preferences, either on the part of elites or of masses. What about "gender" affects public policy?

CONCLUSIONS

We have defined the experiment as a research design in which the treatment is randomly assigned across units. This avoids common-cause and circular confounders. But it does not solve threats to inference that arise after the treatment has been assigned – specifically, the problems posed by non-compliance, contamination, and compound treatments, as discussed.

Anticipating and identifying these confounders is, first and foremost, a matter of careful attention to the details of the research design and vigilant observation of the research as it progresses in real time. In this respect, constructing a sound experiment involves an ethnographic set of skills and resources. One must know one's subjects and one must be in a position to speculate what the reaction to a treatment might be in order to devise an adequate experimental test. Experiments cannot be constructed by rote adherence to an experimental handbook. Local knowledge, including qualitative evidence, is essential.[95]

In the event, some pre- or post-treatment threats to inference may be unavoidable. This does not mean that all is lost. Sometimes, adequate corrections can be applied ex post. However, these work-arounds usually involve the introduction of assumptions (e.g., about the nature of non-compliers) that are difficult to test empirically, and which therefore compromise the confidence with which we may regard an experimental finding. Insofar as an experiment depends upon "statistical" corrections, it begins to look more like observational research (the topic of the next chapter).

Before concluding, it is important to say a few words about *external* validity – the validity of experiments for a broader population of units (see Chapter 4). This is often regarded as the Achilles' heel of experimental research. Note that units chosen for experimental analysis are rarely sampled randomly from a known universe. Instead, subjects are taken opportunistically. As a result, it is often difficult to generalize the results of an experiment – whether conducted in a laboratory or in the field. This common feature of experiments is not coincidental. Because experimental work involves an intentional manipulation – subjects are "treated" – it is necessary to obtain consent. As such, many prospective participants are likely to demur, leaving the researcher with a less than random sample.

This does not doom the experimental method to triviality. Because of their generally high internal validity, experimental case studies have the potential to cumulate – *if* the protocols employed in these studies are standardized, and hence replicable across diverse settings. Multiple experiments on the same subject in different settings may help, ultimately, to bring a larger picture into focus if the key features of those individual experiments are commensurable with one another. In this fashion, we have learned from repeated field experiments what effects a variety of different treatments have on voter turnout (at least, in the United States).[96] The same replication may, over time, contribute to the cumulation of knowledge on other subjects of interest to social science. Of course, this will not happen quickly, or cheaply, and will require significant adjustment of scholarly incentives – which do not generally reward the faithful replication of extant studies.

Even so, some subjects are likely to escape experimental protocols. Try as one might, it will be difficult to test the impact of economic development on democratization in a randomized trial. It is not even clear how economic development should be operationalized, even if one could distribute it randomly throughout the universe of nation-states.

KEY TERMS

- Treatment group
- Control group
- Assignment
- Expected value
- Average treatment effect (ATE)
- Contamination
- Non-compliance
- Intention-to-treat (ITT)
- Average treatment effect on the treated (ATT)
- Researcher (or experimenter) effects
- Hawthorne effects
- Experimental designs (post-test only, pre-and post-test, multiple post-tests, roll-out, crossover, factorial)

Key Terms

- Randomization
- Laboratory experiment
- Field experiment
- Survey experiment
- Natural experiment

8 Large-*N* Observational Designs

There are many potential problems with experimental designs, as reviewed in the previous chapter. However, it is generally the case that experiments have a much stronger claim to internal validity than non-experimental research. Insofar as the latter can be justified it is either because experiments are impossible or because they lack external validity. As it happens, this is quite common. And this, in turn, accounts for the ongoing predominance of observational designs in the work of social science.

In this chapter, we review several approaches to the analysis of large samples without randomization. (The subsequent chapter addresses the analysis of *small* samples without randomization, i.e., case studies.) Five archetypal research designs will be distinguished: *cross-section* (CS), *time-series* (TS), *time-series cross-section* (TSCS), *regression discontinuity* (RD), and *instrumental variable* (IV), as summarized in Table 8.1.[97]

These terms are defined by the observed variation in X, the causal factor of interest, or the instrument by which the treatment is assigned. In a cross-section design, observed variation in X is across units; this is what provides leverage for causal inference. In a time-series design, observed variation in X is through time, typically with a single unit or case. In a time-series cross-section design,

---

Table 8.1 Large-*N* observational research designs

Cross-section (CS)
- Variation in X analyzed across units but not through time.

Time-series (TS)
- Variation in X analyzed through time but not across units (all units are exposed to the same treatment conditions, or there is only one unit).

Time-series cross-section (TSCS)
- Variation in X analyzed across units and through time (e.g., *panel*, *difference-in-difference*, and *pooled cross-section*).

Regression discontinuity (RD)
- Variation in X analyzed just above and below an arbitrary cutoff.

Instrumental variables (IV)
- Variation in Q affects assignment to treatment (X) but not the outcome (Y).

---

observed variation in X is both across units and through time. In a regression discontinuity design, observed variation is in X just above and below an arbitrary cutoff. In an instrumental-variables design, observed variation is in an instrument, Q, that affects assignment to treatment, X.

It is important to bear in mind that most of these terms also carry a narrower, more technical definition as a type of statistical model. For example, a cross-section in the statistical sense is an analysis in which a set of units is observed at a single point in time. A time-series in the statistical sense is an analysis in which a unit is observed over time. And a time-series cross-section is an analysis in which a set of units is observed laterally (across units) and longitudinally (through time). Here, our emphasis is on research design properties that might be conducive to causal inference. Note, for example, that a time-series (in the statistical sense) is not very useful unless there is observed variation in X contained within the time-series, so we define a time-series design in this fashion rather than as an iterated set of observations through time. As previously in this book, our emphasis is on the design properties of causal inference rather than on statistical methods of analysis (a topic postponed until Part IV).

That said, there is greater discussion of methods of statistical analysis in this chapter than in previous chapters. This is because correcting for the deficiencies of observational designs requires more complex methods of data analysis. While a well-constructed experiment can be analyzed simply by comparing the mean values of Y across treatment (Y_T) and control (Y_C) groups, reaching causal inference with observational data is not so simple. Bluntly stated: if you can't manipulate the treatment (ex ante) you need to do a bit of (ex post) data manipulation in order to arrive at results that can plausibly be regarded as evidence of a causal relationship. This means that we must introduce techniques of data analysis such as *regression* and *matching* – techniques that are not dealt with formally until Part IV. Readers who find this method of exposition confusing may wish to peruse the relevant chapters in Part IV prior to reading this chapter.

Cross-Sectional Designs

Consider the situation when a worker-training program is administered on a voluntary basis: all unemployed persons who wish to attend do so, and those who do not form the control group. A post-test taken one year after the completion of the program measures worker earnings for those who attended the program and those who did not. The design is illustrated in Table 8.2.

Superficially, this design is identical to the post-test only experimental design, illustrated in Table 7.1. However, under conditions of voluntary choice we are not likely to achieve comparability across the treatment and control groups, for those with greater motivation are likely to sign up, and their greater motivation – rather than the content of the program itself – may account for their superior earnings

Table 8.2   Cross-sectional design

Groups			
	I.	X_T	Time$_1$
	II.	X_C	

Time$_1$	Measurements of key variables after the intervention
X_T	Treatment condition ($X = 1$)
X_C	Control condition ($X = 0$)

relative to the control group. As such, the background factors are not the same across the two groups, a feature illustrated in Figure 8.1. Accordingly, the expected value of Y, given X, is not the same across the groups.

The problematic confounder in this case is a **common-cause confounder**, so called because it impacts both the causal factor (X) and the outcome (Y). In this instance, a highly motivated unemployed person is more likely to select into the treatment and is more likely to have higher earnings relative to those with lower motivation. The associated causal graph is illustrated in Figure 8.2.

There are several approaches to this sort of problem. The simplest and most common is to condition on Z, the potential confounder. What this means is that rather than simply looking at the relationship between X and Y we must now examine a multivariate relationship: $X \rightarrow Y$, holding Z constant.

This is easiest to explain if we assume that Z, like X, is binary. Let us say that motivation is a binary quality; one either has it or one does not; and let us imagine that this feature of a personality can be measured. This allows us to present the combination of possible values in a 2×2 matrix, as shown in Figure 8.3.

With this matrix, we pursue two sorts of comparisons. First, we compare values for the outcome, Y, when X_C ($X = 0$) and X_T ($X = 1$), holding Z constant at 0 (unmotivated people). By subtracting $Y_{X = 0, Z = 0}$ from $Y_{X = 1, Z = 0}$ we obtain the causal effect for all cases where $Z = 0$. Next, we do the same for the next row. Subtracting $Y_{X = 0, Z = 1}$ from $Y_{X = 1, Z = 1}$ we obtain the causal effect for all cases where $Z = 1$ (motivated people).

This may be achieved in the pencil-and-paper method we have just reviewed, or with **estimators** (e.g., regression or matching) that are capable of accommodating a

C (control group)   T (treatment group)

$X = 0$ $X = 1$

(Weakly motivated)   (Strongly motivated)

$E(Y|X)$ is not the same for treatment and control groups

Figure 8.1   Cross-sectional data: a typical scenario

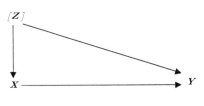

Figure 8.2 Causal graph with common-cause confounder

X = Causal factor
Y = Outcome
Z = Common-cause confounder
[ ] = Not conditioned

large number of confounders. Note that although the mechanics of punching buttons in a software program are easy, there are quite a number of assumptions wrapped up in this sort of analysis. Each must hold true, or the result will be **spurious**.

Returning to our exemplar, let us examine a few of the potential problems. First, we must assume that we have adequately accounted for the suspected common-cause confounder, motivation. Unfortunately, this is a difficult matter to measure. One cannot simply ask people whether they are highly motivated and expect to receive an honest answer. This is not simply because people may lie but also because people are not always aware of how motivated they are or how persistent they will be in pursuit of their goals. Of course, it would help if we measured motivation in a more sensitive fashion. Rather than a binary scale we could use an interval scale, stretching, let us say, from 0 to 100. One must then assume a particular function – say, linear or log-linear – to represent the relationship between motivation and earnings, and one must adopt a regression framework to conduct the analysis, involving additional assumptions (see Part IV).

Second, one must assume that one has accounted for all the additional confounders that may be present. Motivation is just one possible confounder. It could be that those who sign up for the worker-training program are more skilled – or less skilled – than those who do not. It could be that males, or whites, or Protestants, are overrepresented relative to the unemployed people who do not join the program. Each of these features may affect the outcome, measured as earnings, and thus may serve as a confounder. How is one to know whether one has included all of these factors as controls in the analysis? (What if some of them are impossible to measure?) This is referred to as **omitted variable bias**.

Third, one must assume that all those factors included as controls in the analysis actually are confounders. If they are not confounders they may introduce

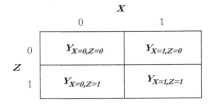

Figure 8.3 Conditioning on a common-cause confounder: an illustration

X = causal factor (0/1); Z = common-cause confounder (0/1); Y = outcomes (on average) for those subjected to the specified combination of values along X and Z.

$$X \longrightarrow Z \longrightarrow Y$$

Figure 8.4 Causal graph with mechanismic (post-treatment) confounder ■

X = Causal factor
Y = Outcome
Z = Mechanismic confounder

confounding to an otherwise valid analysis. This is apt to be the case if factors are measured in a post-treatment, i.e., after the treatment (the program) has been administered. Suppose, for example, that we measure motivation at the end of a worker-training program rather than at the beginning. In this instance, we might imagine that the motivation levels of unemployed persons participating in the program would be influenced by their participation in the program. If it is a well-run program they may feel more motivated to find work than they did at the outset. Indeed, this may serve as an important causal mechanism if the program has its desired impact. Conditioning on this factor in a multivariate analysis will block the impact of X on Y, resulting in an attenuated estimate and perhaps occluding the causal effect entirely, as illustrated in Figure 8.4.

Another potential problem posed by unwittingly conditioning on non-confounders is the **collider**. In its simplest version, a confounder is generated when one conditions on a factor that is affected by both the causal factor of interest (X) and the outcome (Y), as diagrammed in Figure 8.5. Consider the following scenario. In a bid to condition on all possible common-cause confounders in the analysis of a worker-training program one decides to include union membership as a covariate in the causal model. However, if union membership (Z) is affected by participation in the worker-training program (X) and by earnings (Y), a spurious relationship between X and Y is generated. That is, among union members ($Z = 1$) one will observe covariation between participation in the program and earnings that is not causal. Likewise, among non-union members ($Z = 0$) one will observe covariation between participation in the program and earnings that is not causal.

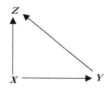

Figure 8.5 Causal graph with collider confounder ■

X = Causal factor
Y = Outcome
Z = Collider confounder

Finally, if entrance into the program is voluntary one can imagine that the outcome – earnings – might influence participation. For example, if the program is not free then those with higher earnings (prior to their current spell of unemployment) may be in a better position to participate. Even if it is free, they may be more likely to participate because they can better afford to forgo current earnings for

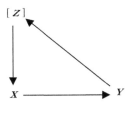

Figure 8.6 Causal graph with circular confounding

X = Causal factor
Y = Outcome
Z = Circular confounder
[ ] = Not conditioned

enhanced future earnings. Those with little or no savings may be obliged to accept the first job they find, presumably a low-paying job, rather than to attend a job-training program that promises higher rewards at some point in the future. This sort of circularity between cause and effect, illustrated in Figure 8.6, will also bias the analysis. In this case, it will result in a stronger correlation between X and Y than is warranted by the independent effect of X on Y. As with common-cause confounders, one may be able to restore comparability between treatment and control groups by blocking the circular path. In this case, that would require conditioning on pre-treatment income or wealth.

Example

Ethnic groups are everywhere, but only in some instances do they become fodder for politics, i.e., lines of cleavage between party groupings. Here lies a classic question regarding the construction of political identities. Daniel Posner surmises that the political salience of ethnic boundaries has a lot to do with the size of the ethnic groups relative to the size of the polity. Specifically, "If [a] cultural cleavage defines groups that are large enough to constitute viable coalitions in the competition for political power, then politicians will mobilize these groups and the cleavage that divides them will become politically salient."[98]

In order to pursue this hypothesis, Posner takes advantage of the arbitrary nature of political borders in Africa, where national boundaries are largely the product of intra-European colonial struggles rather than indigenous nation-building. This means that, unlike political boundaries in Europe, borders in Africa may be regarded as random elements of the political universe. The assignment problem is presumably (or at least plausibly) solved. In particular, Posner focuses on the border between Zambia and Malawi, which has separated members of two tribes, the Chewa and Tumbuka, since 1891, when these territories were held by the British (as Northeastern and Northwestern Rhodesia). As a product of this line-drawing exercise (conducted purely for administrative purposes, Posner says), Chewas and Tumbukas became very small minorities within the Zambian polity (7% and 4% respectively of the national population) and large minorities within the – much smaller – Malawian polity (28% and 12% of the national population).

Posner argues that this difference in relative size explains the construction of ethnic group relations in the two countries. In Zambia, Chewas and Tumbukas are allies, while in Malawi they are adversaries. This is borne out by surveys that Posner administers to villagers within each ethnic group on both sides of the border, and is also the received wisdom among scholars and experts.

Of course, a good deal of time elapses between the treatment (whose causal effect presumably begins with the initial partition of the territory in 1891, and accelerates after the independence of the two countries in 1964) and the post-test (in the early twenty-first century). Typically, institutional factors exert a small but steady causal influence over many years, so this is a reasonable way to test the theory of theoretical interest. And yet, whenever a great deal of time elapses between a treatment and an outcome of interest it is difficult to reach firm conclusions about causality. And when pre-tests are lacking, as they are (by definition) in all cross-sectional designs, inferential difficulties are compounded. In these respects, cross-sectional (post-test only) designs are a lot weaker than panel designs.

In Posner's study, even if the assignment problem is solved there are still a large number of potential confounders that threaten to creep into the research design after (or coincident with) the establishment of national borders. Specifically, any factor correlated with the treatment – "country" – is a potential confounder. It might well be, for example, that ethnicity is treated differently in Zambia and Malawi for reasons other than the sheer size of the ethnic groups. Posner looks closely at several of these alternative accounts including the actions of the colonial power, missionaries, ethnic entrepreneurs, and diverse national trajectories. This portion of the study draws on auxiliary evidence composed of causal-process observations (Chapter 10).

Posner does a good job of addressing the historical evidence. Even so, such confounders are difficult to dispense with, and stochastic threats to inference (factors that cannot be readily identified or theorized) are equally problematic. Under the circumstances, it might help to compare the politicization of ethnicity across small and large groups within each country, to study an ethnic group that is found in a large number of countries (e.g., Han Chinese), or to observe changes in the politicization of ethnicity as an immigrant community grows in size over time within a single country (a longitudinal design). There are many ways to skin this cat. Nonetheless, Posner offers an ingenious and plausible test of a difficult causal question.

Time-Series Designs

Having reviewed some of the complications faced by cross-sectional designs with non-experimental data, we can conclude the obvious: it is difficult to restore the virtues of randomization with a non-randomized treatment. Despite our best efforts, confounders may persist, or may be unwittingly generated by our attempt to overcome them. And, in the end, we have no way of knowing for sure whether we have achieved causal comparability between treatment and control groups, i.e., whether the expected value of Y, given X, is the same for both groups.

Another option dispenses with the control group entirely, focusing instead on the group receiving the treatment. This will be referred to as a **time-series design**. Instead of comparing the treatment and control groups one observes a group through time – before and after treatment – as a clue to causal relations. One may think of this as a treatment and control conditions observed through time rather than across groups. The pre-treatment condition exemplifies the "control" group and the post-treatment condition exemplifies the "treatment" group.

Typically, this involves a single unit (or case). However, occasionally a group of units are exposed to the same treatment condition(s) at the same time. Here, a number of units may be observed simultaneously. However, because X takes on the same values for all of the units there is no "control" group (in the usual sense).

Table 8.3 distinguishes three sorts of time-series research design. The simplest involves a single treatment with pre- and post-tests. For example, one might observe a group of unemployed persons who join a worker-training program, measuring their earnings before they join the program and again one year after they complete the program.

A second involves a single treatment accompanied by multiple pre- and post-tests. This is commonly referred to as an **interrupted time-series**. For example, one might observe the earnings of a group of unemployed people at monthly intervals for several years prior to, and after, they take part in a worker-training program.

A final variety involves the multiple iteration of a single treatment. This is known as a **repeated observations** (or *repeated measures*) design. For example, one might observe a group of unemployed persons who attend one or several worker-training programs over several decades, measuring their income every year.

Methodologically, these three designs are similar, though in some settings the interrupted time-series and repeated observations designs offer advantages over the simple pre- and post-test design.

In this context, the question of comparability concerns the status of the group prior to, and after, being exposed to the treatment (Figure 8.7). That is, the expected value of Y, given X, must be the same pre- and post-treatment, i.e., at $Time_1$ and at $Time_2$. Any violation of this criterion will introduce bias into the analysis.

Table 8.3 Time-series research designs

1. One group pre-/post-test	I.	$Time_1$	X_T	$Time_2$						
2. Interrupted time-series	I.	$Time_1$	$Time_2$	$Time_3$	$Time_4$	X_T	$Time_5$	$Time_6$	$Time_7$	
3. Repeated observations	I.	$Time_1$	X_T	$Time_2$	X_T	$Time_3$	X_T	$Time_4$	X_T	

I	A group
$Time_{1-N}$	Measurements of key variables through time
X_T	Treatment condition

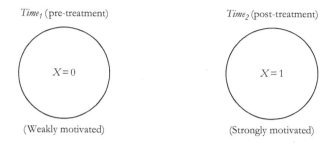

$Time_1$ (pre-treatment) $Time_2$ (post-treatment)

$X = 0$ $X = 1$

(Weakly motivated)   (Strongly motivated)

$E(Y|X)$ is not the same for the group, pre-and post-treatment

Figure 8.7 Time-series data: a typical scenario

Unfortunately, there are often confounders lurking in a time-series design. Consider the worker-training program. Some unemployed persons may undergo a marked increase in their level of motivation. This might arise from a conversation with a friend or family member, a religious experience, the birth of a child, or some other life-changing event. This increased motivation may incline them to (a) join a worker-training program and (b) apply themselves with renewed vigor to the arduous process of finding a job. As a result, we may find a spurious time-trend. Those who participate in worker-training programs may experience higher subsequent earnings not because they benefited from the program but rather because they are more motivated than they were in the pre-treatment period. The expected value of Y, given X, is thus not the same at $Time_1$ as it is at $Time_2$. The common-cause confounder is again motivation. However, in the time-series research design it is a *change* in motivation, rather than a static feature of individuals, that creates the problem.

As with any other design, any feature that correlates with the treatment and also affects the outcome is a potential confounder (if not conditioned). This is a common state of affairs in time-series designs simply because treatments are often temporally associated with other things that also impact an outcome. If one wishes to find a job one is likely to take multiple approaches to this problem. Consequently, it is difficult to parse out the impact of a worker-training program from all the other actions a highly motivated unemployed person might take. Likewise, if one is measuring a policy initiative at a state or national level it is likely that the policy initiative will be accompanied by lots of other policy initiatives, undertaken at more or less the same time. Consequently, it will be difficult to distinguish the causal effect of one from the causal effects of all the others.

Threats to inference in a time-series design include any temporal feature that affects the time-trend. For example, suppose that earnings are increasing across the board in a growing economy – a constant trend. At some point, a time-series design is implemented to test the impact of a worker-training program. If one simply compares earnings before and after the treatment within this group one is likely to find improvement. But this improvement may be due to the existing time-trend rather than the program itself.

One time-trend is so common, and so vexing, that it has a special name: **regression to the mean**. Commonly, we take action on a difficult matter only when the urgency is great. Individuals, like governments, wait for emergencies in order to institute reform. For an unemployed person, this might be the point when her bank account reaches zero. For a government, it might be the point at which societal unemployment reaches a particularly high point (in light of that country's historical experience). At such moments, heroic action is taken – the worker decides to sign up for a grueling job-training program, a government decides to institute an expensive worker-training program. Many things in life observe a cyclical pattern, and unemployment is probably one of these. So it will not be surprising if, subsequent to joining a worker-training program, the unemployed person finds work, or if, subsequent to instituting a worker-training program, the unemployment rate goes down. However, it would be a mistake to attribute these changes to the worker-training program. They are, instead, examples of regression to the mean, i.e., a return to a normal (average) state of affairs.

To be sure, there is some hope of handling the problem of pre-existing trends (but not omitted variables coterminous with the treatment). This can be accomplished with a careful examination of a trend-line, followed by corrective action. This requires a good deal of temporal data; a simple pre- and post-test will not suffice. Where the data are rich, an extensive set of operations has been developed for "de-trending" time-series data so that X's true effect on Y can be correctly estimated. It should be recognized that each of these operations involves significant, and difficult to test, assumptions about the data-generating process.[99] Time-series econometrics, even in the most sophisticated hands, is plagued with ambiguity. If the trend is complicated – involving, let us say, a long-term nonlinear trend, a short-term cyclical trend, and lots of stochastic variation – one will be at pains to estimate the true causal effect of X on Y.

At first glance, the repeated measures approach to time-series analysis appears to solve these problems. To be sure, if the unit returns to equilibrium after each intervention, then each intervention may be understood as an independent test of a given proposition. A single case observed longitudinally thus serves the function of a number of treatment and control cases, observed latitudinally. In effect, one tests and re-tests a single unit.

However, in many other situations common to social science there are enduring testing effects. Typically, the effect of an intervention is to change the unit experiencing the intervention. If so, the *tabula* is no longer *rasa*. Even if the unit remains the same, other contextual elements may vary from $Time_1$ to $Time_2$, rendering the second test non-equivalent to the first. This is why repeated measures designs often offer a poor substitute for a spatial control group.

Example

Time-series designs may be quite strong, especially if the factor of theoretical interest is subjected to multiple independent tests. An example of this procedure can be found in a study of employment discrimination conducted by Claudia Goldin and Cecilia Rouse.[100] We have already shown the potential of randomized experiments for analyzing the effects of employment discrimination in low-skill jobs. High-skill jobs offer a special obstacle to causal assessment because there are fewer positions, they are less standardized (and hence less comparable to one another), and the selection process is based on skills that are difficult to manipulate artificially, e.g., through audit or resume experiments. And yet, suspicion persists that a "glass ceiling" prevents the movement of women and minorities to the top of highly skilled occupations.[101]

An opportunity for testing this hypothesis arose recently when a number of orchestras instituted blind audition procedures. Before entering into the specifics of the study it is worth considering that a classical orchestra is perhaps the ideal prototype of a skill-based occupation. All that matters, or should matter, is how one plays an instrument. Moreover, there are shared standards about what constitutes good playing in the field of classical music. (It is conceivable that aesthetics are race- or gender-based, but this is not the general impression.) Thus, from a certain perspective, the producers of "classical" music fall into a sector of high-skill occupations that are *least* likely to exhibit discriminatory practices.

Goldin and Rouse exploit the change from non-blind to blind auditions in order to determine whether this shift in hiring practices has any effect on the propensity of women to attain positions in professional orchestras – where they were, and are, grossly underrepresented relative to their presence in the general populace. The study gains leverage on the problem by looking closely at variation before and after the initiation of treatment, a point in time that varies from orchestra to orchestra. Specifically, they compare the probability of a female orchestral candidate passing various stages in the interview process (from the first audition to the final audition and job offer) prior to the institution of blind auditing procedures and after the institution of blind auditing procedures. Data are collected for several decades prior to, and after, the change in hiring protocol. Thus, the analysis compares the success of female candidates in years prior to the change with their success in years after the change. Since the experiences of multiple orchestras are analyzed separately, this study may be understood as an interrupted time-series design, iterated for each orchestra under study.

The authors find that the existence of a screen separating the artist from the orchestral decisionmakers (and thus concealing the gender of the player) increased the probability that a woman would be hired severalfold. This seems to prove the thesis that women face obstacles to upward mobility that are due to their gender only, not to job-relevant characteristics. Indeed, it is difficult to identify any possible confounder in this research design. Of course, the analysis does not illuminate precisely why this form of gender discrimination persists. But it does show the power of time-series designs for estimating causal effects, at least in some circumstances.

Time-Series Cross-Section (TSCS) Designs

Having discussed the strengths and weaknesses of cross-sectional and time-series designs, we turn to a family of research designs that combines both sorts of comparisons – across units and through time. This will be referred to as a **time-series cross-section** (TSCS) design. Here, several observations are taken from each unit and there is variation in X through time (at least in some units) and across units. The TSCS design combines temporal and spatial comparisons.

Typically, a TSCS design involves repeated measurements from a set of units, observed through time. Thus, one might observe individuals, or nation-states, every year for 20 years, establishing a panel with 20 observations through time. Sometimes, there are missing data, i.e., some units are not observed for every time-period; this generates an *unbalanced* panel.

Sometimes, observations through time are not of the same units but rather of randomly chosen units from a larger population. For example, if one is constructing a TSCS analysis from survey data composed of a sample of 2,000 individuals drawn randomly from the US population every year over the course of 20 years, each annual sample (or panel) includes a different set of respondents. We shall refer to this sort of TSCS as a *pooled cross-section*.

TSCS includes a diverse family of research designs, as illustrated in the "miscellaneous" row of Table 8.4.

In order to focus our discussion we shall dwell on a simple variety of TSCS design known as the **difference-in-difference** (DD) design, illustrated in the second row of Table 8.4. Note that Group I receives the treatment while Group II exemplifies the control condition. Outcomes are measured prior to and after the intervention. Estimates of the causal effect derive from a comparison of the change in the outcome for the treated group with the change in outcome for the control group: ΔY (Group *I*) – ΔY (Group *II*). Hence, a difference-in-difference.[102]

Table 8.4 Time-series cross-section (TSCS) designs

1. Misc.	*I.*		X_T		X_C		X_T		
	II.	*Time$_1$*	X_T	*Time$_2$*	X_T	*Time$_3$*	X_C	*Time$_4$*	
	III.		X_T		X_T		X_T		
	IV.		X_C		X_C		X_C		
2. DD	*I.*	*Time$_1$*	X_T	*Time$_2$*					
	II.		X_C						

I–IV	Groups
Time$_{1-N}$	Measurements of key variables through time
X_T	Treatment condition ($X = 1$)
X_C	Control condition ($X = 0$)
Misc	Miscellaneous TSCS designs
DD	Difference-in-difference design

Suppose, for example, that we are comparing earnings for unemployed persons who (voluntarily) join a worker-training program with those who do not. We observe their earnings prior to starting the program (presumably, zero, unless we are measuring it several years prior) and again one year after the completion of the program. We then compare the change in earnings for the treatment and control group in order to estimate the causal effect (if any) of the program on earnings.

In some respects, this design looks very similar to a cross-sectional design. Yet, we are now looking at change over time between the pre- and post-tests rather than a simple post-test. To what extent does this make causal inference more secure?

In the cross-sectional design the assumption of causal comparability requires that all background factors that might impact the outcome be equal, on average, across the treatment and control groups. In the DD design, we require that all *changing* background factors be equal, on average, across the treatment and control groups. In most contexts, this is an easier assumption to satisfy. It is especially convincing if the time-period separating pre- and post-tests is relatively short and background factors change slowly. Under these circumstances, it seems plausible to suppose that causal comparability has been achieved.

Granted, any background factor that varies with X is still a potential confounder. So, if some subjects are propelled by a motivational change to (a) join the worker-training program and (b) get a job, this will generate a spurious result. But in other respects, the DD design is more robust than the corresponding cross-sectional or time-series designs. Threats from history (extant time-trends or regression to the mean) are not problematic so long as they affect both treatment and control groups equally. Circular confounding is less problematic because it is unlikely to affect the change in Y across treatment and control groups. Mechanismic confounders are still possible. However, because the number of potential confounders is much smaller in the DD design than in the corresponding cross-sectional or time-series designs, one is less likely to mistakenly condition on a post-treatment variable. In short, there is much to recommend the DD design (and its analogs in TSCS analysis) relative to cross-sectional and time-series designs.

One critical caveat must be inserted. Because the treatment is not randomized, one would not normally expect the treatment and control groups to be equal in all background characteristics that are relevant for the outcome. Specifically, we might not expect members of the control group to respond in the same fashion as members of the treatment group. Where self-selection is at work, those who choose to be exposed to a treatment are more likely to respond positively to that treatment. In this case, those who choose to attend a worker-training program may be in a better position to make use of that knowledge to find a job. Consequently, their gains from attendance may be greater than a typical member of the control group. It follows that a causal effect calculated with a TSCS design is often better understood as an average treatment effect for the treated (ATT) rather than an average treatment effect across the treatment and control groups (ATE).

Example

The effect on employment of minimum wage laws is a primary topic in labor economics. Despite multiple studies and a great deal of theorizing, the empirical issue remains elusive. As with other social science questions, a key methodological obstacle is the non-random aspect of the treatment. States (or countries) that set high minimum wages are also likely to be different in other respects from states (or countries) that set low (or no) minimum wages. These heterogeneous factors, relating to other labor market regulations, fiscal policy, or the character of societies and labor organizations, serve as potential confounders. The institution of labor market reforms may also be a response to features of macroeconomic performance, introducing threats from circularity.

In a widely cited paper, David Card and Alan Krueger approach this problem by focusing on an episode of policy change: the rise in minimum wages in New Jersey in 1992. Their data-collection strategy focuses on a single sector – fast-food restaurants – that is likely to be sensitive to changes in the minimum wage. Several hundred restaurants in New Jersey, and a neighboring state, Pennsylvania, are surveyed to determine whether levels of employment, wages, and prices underwent any change before and after this statutory change came into effect. Pennsylvania restaurants thus serve as the spatial control group. (Comparisons are also drawn between stores in New Jersey which paid more than, and less than, the newly instituted minimum wage. Since the former were unaffected by the rise in minimum wages, this group forms a second control group.)

Card and Krueger's empirical approach is a difference-in-difference model in which the change in fast-food employment in New Jersey (the treatment group) is compared with the change in fast-food employment in Pennsylvania. The analysis shows that changes in the two states through this period were quite similar, suggesting that a legislated rise in the minimum wage in New Jersey did not enhance unemployment in that state.

It is an impressive study, though – like all studies – not without potential difficulties. Questions might be raised, for example, about the representativeness of the chosen sector (is the total economy-wide effect of a minimum wage law reflected in the behavior of a single industry?). One also wonders about the tightness of the timeline (would the economic effects of an increase in minimum wages become manifest in the short space of eight months – the time elapsed between pre- and post-tests?). One wonders whether economic conditions in the two states were sufficiently similar to constitute a good paired comparison and whether the remaining differences were adequately modeled in the statistical analysis. It may also be questioned whether the research design incorporates enough power to constitute a fair test of the null hypothesis. (Has the positive hypothesis – that minimum wages affect labor market behavior – been given a fair chance to succeed?) At least one commentator has questioned whether the rise in minimum wages actually represents the factor of theoretical interest, or whether it should be regarded as an instrument for that underlying (unmeasured) factor – wages actually paid to workers.[103]

Some of these issues might have been overcome by slight alterations in the research design; others are inherent by virtue of the fact that the treatment cannot be directly manipulated.[104] The problem of non-random assignment haunts all DD designs (just as it does all other non-experimental designs). One can never be entirely sure, for example, that businesses in Pennsylvania (the control group) would have responded to a rise in minimum wages in the same manner as New Jersey. If not, then the generalizability of the finding is cast in doubt. One's doubts about causality are amplified wherever the treatment is non-randomly assigned because one worries that there might be something about the assignment of the treatment – some unmeasured factor – that differentiates the treatment group from the control group, and accounts for their responses. More specifically, one worries that the rate of change in the outcome might differ across the treatment and control groups. If this is the case, then the chosen comparison case (in this case, Pennsylvania) is not doing the job of an experimental control.

Regression-Discontinuity (RD) Designs

A regression-discontinuity (RD) design, in its simplest and most typical form, looks like an experimental post-test only or cross-sectional design. One group receives the treatment and the other the control condition, and a single post-test measures the outcome of interest, as diagrammed in Table 8.5. However, the details of RD design, i.e., how these groups come to be defined, are quite distinct.

Consider a worker-training program with a means-test. Only those who have been out of work for at least a year are eligible, and all such applicants are admitted. Let us imagine that this means-test is established after applications have been received (perhaps because of an unexpected budget cut). Thus, the program receives many applications from those who have been out of work for less than a year, and are thereby excluded from participation. This has the effect of establishing a clean cutoff between program participants and non-participants. While we can expect many background differences between the short-term unemployed and the long-term unemployed, we expect relatively minor differences between those out of work for 11–12 months and those out of work for 13–14 months. These groups should be similar in all respects that might impact the outcome of theoretical concern,

Table 8.5 Regression-discontinuity (RD) design

Groups				
	I.	X_T		$Time_1$
	II.	X_C		

$Time_1$	Measurement of key variable after the intervention
X_T	Treatment condition ($X = 1$)
X_C	Control condition ($X = 0$)

earnings. Since one group receives the treatment and the other does not, we have a situation that resembles a true experiment with randomized treatment.

Methods of analysis for RD designs vary. One may approach the observations lying just above and below the cutoff as equivalent on all background characteristics; in this case, a simple difference-of-means-test will suffice to measure the causal effect. Alternatively, one may include all members of the sample, downweighting observations lying further from the cutoff point. In our example, this would be accomplished by conditioning on *length of unemployment spell*. But the common characteristic of the RD design is its exploitation of an arbitrary cutoff point separating treated and untreated units.

Several potential weaknesses of the design should be noted. First, if the cutoff is not rigidly observed – if, for example, applicants who have been out of work for 11–12 months are admitted when members of the program staff judge that the applicant is especially needy – the comparability of observations lying on either side of the cutoff is likely to be compromised. Second, if the subjects in an RD design are aware of the cutoff rule they may be able to circumvent it, e.g., by lying on their applications. This will have the same effect, vitiating the comparison of treated/untreated units. Third, there must be sufficient units lying just below and just above the cutoff point – or, alternatively, one must have great confidence in the covariates (e.g., length of unemployment spell) utilized to control for dissimilarities. Finally, since the analysis centers on units lying near the cutoff point it may not be possible to generalize findings to units lying far from that point, limiting the generalizability of a study. These points notwithstanding, the RD design is still very attractive. Of all the observational designs reviewed here it probably lies closest in spirit and in fact to a randomized design (i.e., a true experiment).

Examples

As an example, let us consider Richard Berk and David Rauma's study of the California penal system.[105] In 1978, California extended unemployment insurance to recently released prisoners, in the hopes of easing their transition to civilian life and reducing rates of recidivism. Former inmates were eligible only if they had worked a requisite number of hours while in prison, thus setting up a cutoff point that provides the basis for an RD design. Subjects become part of the sample if they actually apply for benefits, which means that the analysis compares those who apply and are eligible for benefits with those who apply but are ineligible (presumably because they were unaware of their ineligibility). The data model assumes the following simple form:

Y : *Failure (re-incarceration)* =
X : *Benefits (the binary treatment variable)* +
Q : *Hours worked (the assignment criterion)* +
Z : *Control variables (background characteristics that might affect recidivism)*

On the basis of this procedure, Berk and Rauma conclude that members of the treatment group experienced 13% lower re-incarceration rates than those in the control group (i.e., those ineligible for the program), suggesting that providing post-prison assistance reduces recidivism by an appreciable degree.

A second example of the RD design is drawn from a recent study of labor unions. It is sometimes alleged that the formation of labor unions causes businesses to fail by imposing extra costs that cannot be recouped through enhanced sales, increased productivity, or changes in a firm's pricing structure. In order to test this proposition, John DiNardo and David Lee examine the fate of over 27,000 American firms over the course of a decade and a half. Noting that unionization occurs as a partial product of a secret ballot election (the results of which are publicly available), the authors use this cutoff to conduct an RD design in which firms where a union vote narrowly wins are compared with firms where a union vote narrowly loses. They find that a successful union election scarcely affects firms' subsequent survival rate; moreover, little evidence of a causal effect on employment levels, output, and productivity is discovered. (They also consider the possibility that the threat of a successful union drive may alter the wage structure, and hence a firm's chances of survival, prior to the vote for recognition.)

Some uncertainty necessarily remains about the randomness of the above-cutoff/below-cutoff comparison, as the treatment is not truly randomized. In particular, one must be wary of circumstances where participants in a sample are aware of the consequences of a threshold, and able to self-select. For example, in the RD design conducted by DiNardo and Lee, where the effect of unionization on firm survival, employment, output, productivity, and wages is tested, we must count the possibility that the failure/success of unionization drives are not random with respect to the outcomes of interest. Consider that workers in a union representation election may be conscious of the potential effect of their vote on the financial health of the firm. Management often argues that a union will put the firm at a competitive disadvantage and lead, ultimately, to a loss of jobs. Under the circumstances, workers may be more inclined to support unionization if they are convinced of a firm's strength, and less inclined if they feel that the firm is in a vulnerable position. If enough workers vote strategically on this basis, and if their hunches have some basis in fact (presumably they are familiar with their firm's market position), then the results of this RD design speak only to **local average treatment effects (LATE)**. That is, we may be willing to believe that firms that were/are unionized are no more likely to go bankrupt than firms that remain un-unionized, but we should not infer from this that unionization – if assigned randomly across the universe of firms – would have no causal effect on the probability of firm failure. (DiNardo and Lee are careful not to over-generalize from the limited data at-hand.)

Instrumental-Variable (IV) Designs

We have seen that the assignment of a causal treatment is often subject to confounding whenever the assignment principle is not random. A partial solution to this problem can sometimes be found if at least one factor influencing assignment to treatment is *not* subject to confounding. This "instrument" offers the opportunity of a two-stage analysis, setting up an **instrumental-variable** (IV) design.

Consider a worker-training program in which applicants self-select. A cross-sectional, time-series, or TSCS design is subject to potential confounding if the suspected confounders (e.g., motivation) cannot be measured and thereby conditioned. A regression-discontinuity design is not feasible because there is no cutoff for eligibility. However, among applicants, it is noticed that those living within easy travel distance to a worker-training center are more likely to matriculate and more likely to complete the program than those living at a further remove. Apparently, travel-time increases the opportunity costs of attending. Fortuitously, it is not a factor that applicants are likely to be aware of when applying, as they do not know the precise locations of multiple centers where worker-training programs are held within a metropolitan area, or the travel-time required to reach them. Travel-time for each applicant can be measured easily using Google's mapping algorithm, providing an instrument that predicts program participation.

Of key importance is that the chosen instrument does not affect the outcome directly and is not correlated with other factors (not controlled in the analysis) that affect the outcome. Travel-time must impact earnings only through the factor of theoretical interest, i.e., participation in the worker-training program. If, let us say, people living further away from worker-training centers are also further away from potential employers then the chosen instrument is subject to confounding and will render a biased estimate of the true causal effect. (In this case, it will bias the estimate downward, as those attending worker-training programs face a higher commute time to potential employers.) Let us stipulate that this requirement, sometimes referred to as an **exclusion restriction**, is satisfied.

In this situation, one can use the instrument (Q), to establish a predicted value for the causal factor of interest (X) that is free of confounding (Z). One then examines the covariation between $\hat{X}$ and Y, controlling for any additional confounders that can be identified and measured. A causal diagram of the relevant assumptions is embedded in Figure 8.8.

Example

A recent influential application of instrumental variables addresses the classic question of long-run economic development. Why are some countries so much richer today than others? Acemoglu, Johnson, and Robinson (hereafter AJR) suggest that a principal factor affecting secular-historical growth rates is the quality of institutions, i.e., the strength of property rights.[106] The methodological obstacle is that we have at our disposal no measure of institutional quality that is assigned in a fashion that is random with respect to economic development. Wealth and good institutions tend to go together. In order to surmount this difficulty, AJR construct the following causal story. Over the past several centuries, European colonial powers established strong property-rights protections in

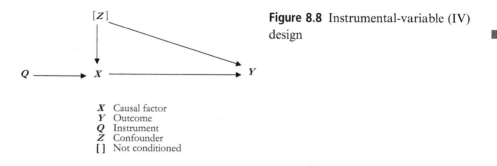

Figure 8.8 Instrumental-variable (IV) design

X　Causal factor
Y　Outcome
Q　Instrument
Z　Confounder
[ ]　Not conditioned

some parts of the world (e.g., North America) and not in others (e.g., most of Africa and Latin America). Schematically, they protected property rights in areas where large numbers of Europeans decided to settle and instituted "extractive" regimes in areas where Europeans were outnumbered by indigenous populations. This, in turn, was a factor of geographic circumstances such as the prevalence of tropical disease, which determined the likelihood of European survival in Africa, Asia, and the New World. Europeans settled, and thrived, where they had high survival rates. Estimates of varying mortality rates for European settlers in the course of the nineteenth century thus provide a suitable instrument for patterns of colonial settlement and, ultimately, for the quality of institutions that AJR presume the colonists are responsible for. This allows for a two-stage analysis, which may be simplified as follows:

$$X = Q + Z + e_1 \qquad [8.1]$$

$$Y = \hat{X} + Z + e_2 \qquad [8.2]$$

where X = property rights measured in the late twentieth century (expropriation risk), Q = the instrument (European settler mortality), Z = covariates (other causes of Y), Y = per capita GDP, $\hat{X}$ = the fitted values from Equation 8.1, and e = error terms for the two equations. (Intercepts are omitted.)

As with other corrections for non-randomized treatments, the IV technique is not without its difficulties. Indeed, the three assumptions outlined above seem rarely to be fully satisfied in empirical work. The chosen instrument, Q, may be weakly correlated with the theoretical variable of interest, X; Q may have an effect on the outcome, Y, *other than* through X; or there may be a common cause operating on both Q and Y (an unconditioned confounder). As with most modeling assumptions, these potential violations are difficult to test,[107] and perhaps best viewed as theoretical priors. For example, in the study explored above, critics have suggested that a common cause – geography – affects both settler mortality and current levels of economic development in ways not mediated by property rights.[108] If this story about the data generating process is true then the chosen instrument is not valid. Even so, the two-stage analysis is probably more convincing than any conceivable one-stage analysis for this particular problem; in this respect, and to this extent, the IV approach is useful.

A few limitations of this design should be noted. First, the requirements of the analysis – diagrammed in Figure 8.8 – are difficult to verify in most settings. Often, they are highly suspect on theoretical grounds. That is, one may wonder whether Q affects Y other than through X or whether other (unconditioned) confounders are associated with the relationship between Q and X or Q and Y.

Second, the IV analysis estimates a causal effect that relates to those units that are encouraged to receive the treatment due to the chosen instrument(s). This is referred to as a local average treatment effect (LATE), as distinguished from an average treatment effect. If the instrument (Q) is weakly correlated with the causal factor of theoretical interest (X), then the estimated LATE may have little practical or theoretical import. Moreover, it is rarely possible to identify the units encouraged into treatment by the instrument. Consequently, it may be difficult to say what sort of cases an IV result with a weakly correlated instrument would apply to.

It is easy to quarrel with many IV analyses found in the social sciences today. However, when the assumptions undergirding an IV analysis (as diagrammed in Figure 8.8) are plausible, the IV approach to causal inference is often more compelling than other observational research designs that might be adopted.

CONCLUSIONS

In this rather complex chapter we have introduced five research designs for use in situations where a treatment is not randomized (or is imperfectly randomized) and a large number of observations are available for statistical analysis. A cross-sectional analysis relies on comparisons across units at a single point in time. A time-series analysis relies on comparisons through time. A TSCS analysis enlists both latitudinal and longitudinal comparisons. A regression-discontinuity design compares units on either side of an arbitrary cutoff, which distinguishes treatment and control groups. An instrumental-variable analysis rests on a factor that influences assignment to treatment but has no direct effect on the outcome.

Each of these designs attempts to recapture the virtues of an experimental design. While this quest is noble, its achievement is a matter of doubt, as our discussion has shown. Even so, these designs often provide the best available method of analysis. Sometimes, an observational design is the only method that is practicable, or the only method whose results are likely to be generalizable to a larger population.

KEY TERMS

- Cross-section (CS)
- Time-series (TS)
- Time-series cross-section (TSCS)

- Regression discontinuity (RD)
- Instrumental variables (IV)
- Common-cause confounder
- Estimator
- Spurious
- Omitted variable bias
- Collider
- Interrupted time-series
- Repeated observations
- Regression to the mean
- Difference-in-difference (DD) design
- Local average treatment effect (LATE)
- Exclusion restriction

9

Case Study Designs

There are two ways to learn about a subject. One might study many examples at once, focusing on a few selected dimensions of the phenomena. We shall refer to this as an *extensive* approach, as laid out in Chapters 7–8.

Alternatively, one might study a particular example, or several examples, in greater depth. We shall refer to this as an *intensive*, or *case study*, approach – the topic of this chapter.

A **case** connotes a spatially delimited phenomenon (a unit) observed at a single point in time or over some period of time. It may be a political unit with a defined area of semi-sovereignty (e.g., empire, nation-state, region, municipality), organization (e.g., firm, non-governmental organization, political party, school), social group (as defined, e.g., by ethnicity, race, age, class, gender, or sexuality), event (e.g., foreign policy crisis, revolution, democratic transition, decision-point), or individual (e.g., a biography, case history).

However defined, a case must comprise the type of phenomenon that an argument attempts to describe or explain. In a study about nation-states cases are comprised of nation-states (observed over time). In a study that attempts to explain the behavior of individuals, cases are comprised of individuals. And so forth.

A **case study** research design is an intensive study of a single case or a small number of cases that promises to shed light on a larger population of cases. The individual case(s) is viewed as a *case of* something broader, just as large-sample analysis is also generally viewed as exemplary of a broader phenomenon. Thus, both intensive and extensive analyses generally make inferences from a sample to a population, even though the sample sizes are very different.

Case study research may incorporate one or several cases. The latter is a defining characteristic of **comparative historical analysis**, associated with the work of Barrington Moore, Theda Skocpol, David Collier, and James Mahoney. However, as the sample of cases expands it becomes less and less feasible to investigate each case intensively. The case study format is thus implicitly a small-sample format.

To be sure, large samples of observations may be drawn at a lower level of analysis, i.e., from within the case(s) of interest. Commonly, a case study focused on a nation-state will include **within-case** analysis focused on individuals, perhaps drawn from a survey. These observations may be analyzed in any fashion, using any of the research designs introduced in previous chapters.

Consider a case study of the democratic peace that rests on an intensive study of two (non-democratic) states that went to war. The cases of theoretical concern are nation-states. Yet, the researcher is likely to mobilize all sorts of within-case observations, some of which may be large in number (necessitating quantitative analysis) and others of which may be small in number (necessitating qualitative analysis).

It follows that case study research must enlist qualitative evidence at the level of the case because there are too few cases to allow for a statistical model. This is what makes it distinctive, methodologically speaking, and this is why one commonly equates case study research with qualitative analysis. However, *within-case* evidence may enlist small- or large-N samples. Consequently, case studies often combine qualitative and quantitative styles of research.

We begin this chapter by discussing case selection strategies, each of which is associated with a specific research design. Next, we briefly touch upon rules of thumb for *within-case* analysis. A concluding section discusses some of the trade-offs inherent in case study research.

In keeping with our focus in this section of the book we shall assume that the goal of the case study is to shed light on causal relationships. Readers should bear in mind that many case studies are descriptive in nature and thus omitted from this discussion.[109]

Case Selection

Case study research begins with a selection of cases that will be intensively studied. The reader will recall (from Chapter 4) that the ideal selection procedure for large-sample research is to sample randomly from the population of interest (or to include the entire population). This generates a sample that is very likely to be representative, and therefore good fodder for theories that encompass a broader population.

In case study research, however, cases chosen for intensive analysis are usually chosen in a non-random fashion. *Purposive* case selection enhances the likelihood that the chosen case(s) will provide leverage on the question of theoretical interest. Although purposive case selection may not achieve representativeness there is no assurance that random selection will do so either (by reason of stochastic error, which is extremely high in a sample limited to one or several cases). Given this, it is understandable why most case study researchers privilege causal leverage over representativeness.

In Table 9.1 we set out a variety of **case selection** strategies. This is not a comprehensive list, but focuses on those strategies that are most commonly employed.[110] These are understood according to their function, which might be *exploratory* (to identify a hypothesis, H_x) or *diagnostic* (to assess H_x). For each general aim or specific function there are several viable strategies of case selection, indicated by bullet points in Table 9.1.

Table 9.1 Case selection strategies

Goals/strategies	N	Factors	Criteria for cases
Exploratory (to identify H_X)			
• Extreme	1+	X or Y	Maximize variation in X or Y
• Deviant	1+	Z Y	Poorly explained by Z
• Most-similar	2+	Z Y	Similar on Z, different on Y
Diagnostic (to assess H_X)			
• Influential	1+	X Z Y	Greatest impact on $P(H_X)$
• Pathway	1+	X Z Y	$X \rightarrow Y$ strong, Z constant or biased against H_X
• Most-similar	2+	X Z Y	Similar on Z, different on X & Y

N = number of cases. H_X = causal hypothesis of interest. $P(H_X)$ = the probability of H_X. X = causal factor(s) of theoretical interest. $X \rightarrow Y$ = apparent or estimated causal effect, which may be strong (high in magnitude) or weak. Y = outcome of interest. Z = vector of background factors that may affect X and/or Y.

Column 2 specifies the number of cases in the case study. It will be seen that case studies enlist a minimum of one or two cases, with no clearly defined ceiling. Column 3 clarifies which dimensions of the case are relevant for case selection. This may include the causal factor (X), background factors that may serve as confounders (Z), and/or the outcome (Y). Column 4 specifies the criteria used to select a case(s) from a universe of possible cases.

In the following sections, we outline each case selection technique, offer one or two examples, and suggest ways in which cases might be chosen from a large population of potential cases. Before beginning, three general points should be underlined.

First, case selection criteria can usually be understood *cross-sectionally* or *longitudinally* (through time). For example, the test of "deviance" might be a case's status at a particular point in time, or its change in status over an observed period of time. Usually, the latter is more informative for purposes of in-depth case analysis. A case that happens to be deviant may have undergone a change at some point in the past, or perhaps its deviance is a product of changes in other cases. By contrast, if we can ascertain the point of inflection – the time at which a case becomes deviant – we can focus subsequent study of the case on this time-period. This is usually more informative. Wherever possible, researchers should choose cases based on their values through time rather than their value at a particular point in time.

Second, virtually all case selection strategies may be implemented in an informal, "qualitative" fashion or in a formal, "quantitative" fashion. The qualitative approach involves reviewing potential cases known to the researcher according to the criteria listed in Table 9.1. The quantitative approach involves translating the criteria in Table 9.1 into an *algorithm* that can be applied to a large sample of potential cases. Case selection algorithms are an excellent, and probably under-utilized, tool for selecting a pool of potential cases. However, the algorithmic choice should probably not be followed slavishly in the final selection of cases, which usually depend upon details of the research context that are hard to represent in an algorithm.

Third, it is important to emphasize that case study analysis is never entirely restricted to the cases chosen for intensive analysis. Other cases always form a basis of comparison. These comparisons might be explored informally through *shadow cases*. Or they might be explored explicitly by integrating data from a large number of additional cases in a large-N cross-case model – a multi-method (aka *mixed-method*) approach to research. Thus, while case selection is important we want to emphasize that generalizations based on case study research usually rest on an empirical base that extends beyond the cases that are intensively analyzed.

Exploratory

Many case studies aim to identify a hypothesis and are therefore **exploratory**. Sometimes, the researcher begins with a factor that is presumed to have fundamental influence on a range of outcomes. The research question is, what outcomes (Y) does X affect? More commonly, the researcher works backward from a known outcome to its possible causes. The research question is, what accounts for variation in Y? Or, if Y is a discrete event, Why does Y occur? The researcher may also have an idea about background conditions, Z, that influence Y but are not of theoretical interest. The purpose of the study, in any case, is to identify X, regarded as a possible or probable cause of Y. The most common exploratory techniques may be classified as *extreme*, *deviant*, or *most-similar*, and will be explored in detail below.

Extreme

An *extreme* case design maximizes variation on a variable of interest, either X or Y. This may be achieved by a single case or by a set of cases that, together, exhibit contrasting outcomes.

Looking more closely, one may discern three versions of the extreme case. The first exhibits extreme values on X or Y (or ΔX or ΔY), which is then compared – formally or informally (through "shadow" cases) – with the norm. Thus, in a study of democratization one might examine a country that transitions quickly and completely. Likewise, studies of welfare state development often focus on the world's largest welfare states, located in Northern Europe. Studies of war often focus on one of the two world wars. Studies of genocide often focus on the Holocaust. It is almost second-nature to identify phenomena by their most extreme manifestation.

A second version applies when an input or output is conceptualized in a binary fashion and one value (generally understood as the "positive" value) is especially rare. Case studies of democratization generally focus on regime transitions – continuity being the more common condition. Case studies of war generally focus on wars – peace being the more common condition. Case studies of revolution generally focus on revolution – non-revolution being the more common condition.

Note, again, that the rare value is – explicitly or implicitly – compared with the normal value, either by comparing a case to itself through time or by comparing a case to other (less intensively studied) cases.

A third approach to achieving variation in the outcome is to choose cases lying at *both* tails of the distribution, i.e., *polar* cases. Here, comparisons can be made directly across the chosen cases. For example, a study of war may focus on cases exhibiting peace *and* war.

Deviant

In many settings, what one knows about the background causes of an outcome can help identify useful cases. A deviant (anomalous) case deviates from an expected causal pattern. The purpose of a deviant case study is to explain the deviant case – and, in so doing, to explain other cases, providing a generalizable hypothesis about the phenomenon under study.

For example, Cuba is the only country in the Americas that shows no signs of democratization at the present time, constituting an anomaly in the region. A study of this case might reveal something new about the causes of democratization.

Another example is provided by Werner Sombart's (1906/1976) classic study, *Why is There No Socialism in the United States?*, often regarded as the first study of American exceptionalism. The United States seemed deviant to Sombart at the turn of the twentieth century because, despite the advance of capitalism, it failed to exhibit the expected rise of a sizable socialist party. In explaining this non-event, Sombart called attention to the consciousness of American workers, which seemed favorably disposed to capitalism and to the American system of government.

Most-similar (exploratory)

Sometimes, one can identify cases that exhibit strong similarities on background conditions (Z) but divergent outcomes (Y). The generic label for this research design is most-similar, aka Method of Difference.

To apply this approach to the study of democratization one might compare neighboring countries that exhibit different regime outcomes. For example, in the 1990s Mali, one of the world's poorest countries, introduced multi-party elections. Although threatened by an insurgency in the north of the country and a recent military coup, Mali's democratization has so far survived though it shows signs of disrepair. Other countries in the region such as Burkina Faso, Guinea, Mauritania, and Niger have taken no steps to open up political competition, despite sharing many geographic, cultural, and historical features with Mali. This sets up a most-similar comparison in which the question of interest is posed by this striking juxtaposition of different outcomes among similar circumstances.

Diagnostic

Case studies may also perform a **diagnostic** function – helping to confirm, disconfirm, or refine a hypothesis (garnered from the literature on a subject or from the researcher's own ruminations) and identifying the generative agent at work in that relationship. Specific strategies may be classified as *influential*, *pathway*, or *most-similar*, as discussed below.

Since all elements of a causal model – X, Z, and Y – are generally involved in the selection of a diagnostic case, the reader may wonder what is left for case study research to accomplish. Actually, a good deal remains on the table. Diagnostic case studies may assess:

- *Measurement error:* Are X, Z, and Y properly measured?
- *Scope-conditions:* Is the chosen case rightly classified as part of the population? What are the appropriate scope-conditions for the hypothesis?
- *Causal heterogeneity:* Are there background factors that mediate the $X \rightarrow Y$ relationship?
- *Confounders:* Is the actual data generating process consistent with the chosen causal model? What is the assignment mechanism? Are there pre- or post-treatment confounders?
- *Causal mechanisms:* What is the pathway (M) through which X affects Y?

Of particular interest is the latter feature – the mechanisms (M) connecting X to Y (if indeed the relationship is causal). Mechanisms not only help to confirm or disconfirm a hypothesis, they also explain it, since in specifying a mechanism we also specify the generative process by which X causes Y. Note that when there is no strong prior theoretical expectation about the nature of the mechanism the case analysis assumes an open-ended, inductive quest – to identify M. When there is a theoretical expectation, the analysis assumes a deductive format – to test the existence of a pre-specified pattern thought to be indicative of M. This is sometimes referred to as *congruence testing*, *pattern-matching*, or *implication analysis*.

In sum, there is quite a lot to occupy a case study researcher engaged in a diagnostic case study, even though preliminary values for X, Z, and Y are known. Information gleaned from a case study may be used to confirm, reject, or refine a theory or to revise a cross-case model, e.g., by helping to re-specify that model.

Influential

An *influential* case is one whose status has a profound effect on the (subjective) probability of a hypothesis being true, $P(H_x)$. We may understand influence in a counterfactual fashion. That is, if values for key variables – X, Z, M, or Y – for that case were to be reassigned, our assessment of $P(H_x)$ would change. Because the values for this case matter more than the values for other cases, intensive analysis is warranted. Case study analysis is likely to affect our assessment of the hypothesis – either strengthening or weakening $P(H_x)$.

The most influential case is one that, by itself, falsifies a hypothesis. This is possible if the proposition is strictly deterministic. Suppose that $X = 1$ is regarded as a necessary condition of an outcome, $Y = 1$. A falsifying case would have the attributes $X = 0$, $Y = 1$. If, on the other hand, $X = 1$ is regarded as a sufficient condition of an outcome, $Y = 1$, a falsifying case would exhibit the attributes

$X = 1$, $Y = 0$. (Necessary and sufficient conditions are mirror images of each other; which terminology one uses is a matter of clarity and convenience.)

The most prominent deterministic hypothesis in political science today is probably the democratic peace – the idea that democratic dyads do not wage war on each other. There are a number of possible exceptions to this "universal" law including the Spanish–American war, the Kargil War, the Paquisha War, Lebanese participation in the Six Day War, the French–Thai war, and the Turkish invasion of Cyprus. Each has drawn considerable attention from supporters and skeptics of the democratic peace hypothesis. Thus far, this research has not yielded a knockout blow to democratic peace theory. There is a problem of measurement insofar as apparent exceptions are often hard to classify cleanly as democratic/ autocratic or peaceful/belletristic. More fundamentally, many researchers take a probabilistic view of the theory – in which case a few exceptions are not so worrisome for the theory. For present purposes, what is important is that these cases are influential. Whether the theory is interpreted as deterministic or probabilistic, these cases have greater bearing on the validity of the theory than other cases that might be chosen for intensive analysis, which explains their centrality in the ongoing debate over the democratic peace.

Note that while influential cases are usually outliers – and in this sense appear to mirror deviant cases (discussed above) – they may also be conforming. Indeed, they may *define* the relationship of interest (e.g., least-likely cases, discussed below). What makes a case influential is not its fit with the causal model but its influence on the model. Likewise, even when an influential case is deviant the purpose of these two genres is quite different. A deviant case is designed for discovery (to identify a new hypothesis) while an influential case is designed for diagnostic purposes (to assess an existing hypothesis).

Influential cases may take the form of *crucial* cases if certain background conditions hold. If the goal is to prove a hypothesis the crucial case is known as a *least-likely* case. Here, the hypothesized relationship between X and Y holds even though background factors (Z) predict otherwise. With respect to the democratic peace hypothesis, a least-likely case would be a dyad composed of two democratic countries with background characteristics that seem to predispose them to war but nonetheless are at peace. If the goal is to disprove a hypothesis the crucial case is known as a *most-likely* case. Here, the hypothesized relationship between X and Y does not hold even though background factors (Z) predict that it should. With respect to the democratic peace hypothesis, a most-likely case would be a dyad composed of two democratic countries with background characteristics that seem to predispose them to peace (e.g., they are rich, culturally similar, and economically co-dependent), who nonetheless engage in violent conflict. Distinguishing most- from least-likely cases depends upon the hypothesis, which may be formulated in different ways. For example, if one chooses to frame the outcome as "war" rather than "peace" (an arbitrary decision, in most respects) then the terminology is flipped. The logic that informs the crucial case remains the same.

Pathway

A *pathway* case is one where the apparent impact of X on Y conforms to theoretical expectations and is strong (in magnitude), while background conditions (Z) are held constant or exert a "conservative" bias. This might also be called a *conforming, typical, online,* or *illustrative* case since it conforms to, typifies, or illustrates a causal relationship of interest. Generally, the chosen case is *positive,* i.e., where $X = 1$ and $Y = 1$, with the assumption that these sorts of cases embody change through time that might be fruitfully studied.

In a setting where the relationship between X and Y is highly uncertain – perhaps because it has not yet been (or cannot be) tested in a large-N cross-case format – the pathway case serves an illustrative function. By showing that the theory fits the chosen case, the case study illustrates the contents of the theory and demonstrates its plausibility. If it works here, the logic goes, it may apply elsewhere. For example, in presenting the theory of path dependence Paul David (1985) draws on the curious case of the "QWERTY" keyboard. This peculiar arrangement of keys was adopted by the developers of the typewriter as a way to slow down the action of the keys so they wouldn't jam up – a constant problem on early typewriters, even with the QWERTY arrangement. Later on, as technology advanced, typewriters could accommodate faster keyboard action and developers suggested new arrangements of the keyboard that promised to speed up the typing process. However, David shows that these innovations never caught on. The QWERTY system had "locked in" with both consumers and producers, illustrating the theory of path dependence.

In a setting where the relationship between X and Y is well established, the pathway case is usually focused specifically on causal mechanisms (M). An example is provided by Edward Mansfield and Jack Snyder's (2005) research on regime transitions and war. The authors find a strong relationship between (incomplete) democratization and bellicose behavior in their cross-national analysis. To ascertain whether their hypothesized causal mechanisms are actually at work in generating this relationship they look closely at ten countries where the posited covariational pattern between X and Y clearly holds, i.e., where democratization is followed by war.

Most-similar (diagnostic)

When employed for diagnostic purposes, the most-similar design consists of a pathway case (as above) plus a control case, which exhibits minimal variation in X and Z. That is, chosen cases exhibit different values on X, similar values on Z, and different values on Y.

As an example, let us consider a recent study by Karen Lutfey and Jeremy Freese (2005). The authors are interested in uncovering the mechanisms at work in a persistent, and oft-noted, relationship between socioeconomic status and health. Poor people experience poor health, which is presumably – at least in some respects – a product of their poverty. (Illness may also contribute to poverty, but we shall not consider this feedback loop here.) Lutfey and Freese compare high and low status individuals who suffer from diabetes, with the knowledge that the latter are more likely to succumb to the effects of the disease. This is accomplished by focusing on two endocrinology clinics, one located in an affluent neighborhood and the other in a poor neighborhood. Cases are thus selected on X (patient socioeconomic status) and Y (mortality rates from diabetes), with the assumption that other background factors that might contribute to mortality (Z) are equivalent across the clinics. The focus of the study is on factors inside the clinic (continuity of care, in-clinic educational resources, bureaucratic organization), outside the clinic (financial limitations, occupational constraints, social support networks), and among the patients (motivation, cognitive ability) that might affect compliance with an exacting medical regime. These are regarded as prima facie causal mechanisms in the relationship between SES and health.

Omnibus Criteria

In addition to criteria that allow us to distinguish among case selection procedures, several additional criteria apply broadly to the selection of cases. Omnibus criteria include (1) *intrinsic importance*, (2) *data availability*, (3) *logistics*, (4) *case independence*, and (5) *sample representativeness*. We introduce these criteria last, though not out of lack of respect. Indeed, these features often outweigh the others. While the diversity of case selection procedures is emphasized in Table 9.1, case selection also has some generic features.

Intrinsic Importance

The selection of cases is often influenced by the (perceived) *intrinsic importance* of a case. Some cases – such as world wars, genocides, key inventions, revolutions – matter more than others because they have an obvious world-historical significance. Others matter because they are important for a specific group of readers. We presume that every social group or organization is interested in its own history, and this may justify the choice of cases. These sorts of case studies are sometimes described as *idiographic*. However, *most* case studies have an idiographic feature or element, which is to say that the researcher is interested in saying something about the chosen case(s) as well as about some larger subject. It is only the latter that qualifies a study as a case study (following our definition), so we are not concerned with studies that are not generalizable in any fashion. Or, to put the point more finely, we are concerned only with the elements of a study that are generalizable.

Data Availability

Any case chosen for in-depth analysis must afford enough *data* to address the question of interest. If sources are unreliable, scarce, or for one reason or another inaccessible, the case is of little value. Recall that the purpose of a case study is to extend our knowledge beyond what it is possible to explore in a large sample. One important way that a case extends our knowledge is by providing information on things that we cannot measure, or cannot easily assemble, across a large number of units. This includes *within-case* evidence.

Logistics

The availability of data is, in turn, often a product of the researcher's personal attributes – his or her language facilities, connections, and previous acquaintance with a region, time-period, or topic. We assume that these *logistical* features are taken into account – implicitly if not explicitly – in any case selection process. Sometimes, it is referred to as *convenience sampling*, though researchers may be loath to admit that they have chosen one case over another simply because it is easier to study the former than the latter. Nonetheless, if a researcher has special access to Site *A*, but not Site *B*, we should be grateful if she chooses *A* over *B* (so long as other criteria are not sacrificed). And we must acknowledge the fact that many cases find their authors, through some serendipitous process that could scarcely be predicted or replicated, rather than the reverse. Darwin did not select the Galapagos Islands from a universe of potential cases.[111]

Case Independence

Chosen cases should, ideally, be *independent* of each other and of other cases in the population. If cases affect each other they are not providing independent evidence of the proposition. This may be referred to as Galton's problem, interference, or a violation of the stable unit treatment value assumption (SUTVA) (see Chapter 23). (The exception would be a situation where inter-action across cases happens to be the subject of investigation, as it would in a study of diffusion.)

Sample Representativeness

Although case studies are focused on one or several cases they also aim (by definition) to represent features of a larger population. Some cases are chosen primarily because of their presumed representativeness (aka *typical* cases) – though one should not imagine that typicality assures representativeness. For most case studies, representativeness is just one of several attributes of concern. Note that deviant cases perform their function – identifying new causes of *Y* – only if they are representative of a larger population. (If the result of a deviant case study is to develop an idiosyncratic explanation – pertaining only to the chosen case – it is not very useful.) Likewise, influential cases are likely to be dismissed – as lying outside the population of the hypothesis – if they are too idiosyncratic.

Within-Case Analysis

Once cases are chosen, they must be analyzed for clues into causal inference. Within-case evidence might be gathered longitudinally (the case observed over time) or from a lower level of analysis ("inside" the case). Evidence enlisted for this analysis might draw on any sort of source, e.g., primary sources, secondary sources, interviews, ethnography, or standardized surveys, as discussed in Chapter 13. And techniques for analyzing that evidence might be primarily qualitative or it might combine qualitative and quantitative techniques. In short, reaching causal inference with case study evidence is not so different from reaching causal inference with large-N samples of observational data, as discussed in Chapter 8. Do not imagine that you are entering a different universe.

However, one element is somewhat distinctive. Case study research must rely, at least in part, on qualitative evidence drawn from a single case or a very small number of cases. (Studies based on large samples may also incorporate qualitative evidence, but they need not do so; and when they do so the use of qualitative evidence is apt to be different from its use in case study research – where the data are focused, by definition, on one or several cases.)

Since this is the most distinctive feature of case study research it is important to spend some time discussing how one might draw inferences based on this sort of data. Our suggested "rules of thumb" cover several interrelated topics: the identification of a hypothesis or theory, testing theories, analyzing temporal relations, and examining background assumptions.

Identifying a Hypothesis/Theory

Insofar as a case study is generalizable it must center on causes that might conceivably apply elsewhere. Idiosyncratic causal factors should not be major protagonists in the narrative.

The problem is that it is not always easy to discern which factors might be generalizable, and the same cause may be differently framed. For example, a key event in the Spanish transition from autocracy to democracy in the 1970s was the "Moncloa Pact" (so named because it was signed at the prime minister's residence by that name), which brought key actors – politicians, political parties, and trade unions from differing ideological perspectives – into formal agreement on how the economy might be handled during the transition. As such, it is a particular event with a particular context. But it might also be framed as an example of a more general phenomenon – a political pact, which some political scientists view as instrumental to the process of democratization. O'Donnell and Schmitter (1986: 37) define a pact as "an explicit, but not always publicly explicated or justified, agreement among a select set of actors which seeks to define … rules governing the exercise of power on the basis of mutual guarantees for the 'vital interests' of those entering into it."

In order to be considered as general causes a factor must be stated in a manner that has plausible application to other cases in a larger population. At the same time, in order to make sense of what actually happened in the case – including confounders, mechanisms, and alternate outcomes – the researcher must also keep track of the specifics. Common nouns generalize, while proper nouns particularize. Both play important roles in a case study. But their respective roles should not be confused. Make clear – to yourself, and to readers – which factors are potentially generalizable and which are not.

Testing Theories

Once a hypothesis has been identified (an original hypothesis or one drawn from someone else's work), it is important to canvas widely for rival explanations. This canvas should include extant work on the particular case under examination, general theoretical frameworks that might be brought to bear on the subject, as well as your own intuition. Try to anticipate rival explanations that critical readers of your work might construct.

For example, if the theory of interest focuses on the role of political pacts in democratization then you must consider alternative narratives that might account for the trajectory of the case(s) you have chosen. Alternate theories of democratization include modernization (more developed societies are more likely to democratize), diffusion (countries in democratic neighborhoods are more likely to democratize), polarization (ideologically polarized societies are less likely to democratize), and so forth.

Where rival causes can be (convincingly) eliminated as factors in a particular case, this elimination serves two important functions: (1) it eases concerns about potential confounders, and (2) by the logic of elimination, it enhances the likelihood that X is the cause of Y. For example, if Linz and Stepan can prove that democratization in Spain was not caused by diffusion this cannot serve as a confounder and their favored explanation – resting on social pacts – becomes more plausible.

To test a theory – your favored theory and rival theories – it is vital to examine all relevant hypotheses suggested by the theory. For example, O'Donnell and Schmitter (1986: 38) write that pacts

> are typically negotiated among a small number of participants representing established (and often highly oligarchical) groups or institutions; they tend to reduce competitiveness as well as conflict; they seek to limit accountability to wider publics; they attempt to control the agenda of policy concerns, and they deliberately distort the principle of citizen equality ... At the core of a pact lies a negotiated compromise under which actors agree to forgo or underutilize their capacity to harm each other by extending guarantees not to threaten each others' corporate autonomies or vital interests. This typically involves clauses stipulating abstention from violence, a prohibition on appeals to outsiders ...

Each one of these assertions constitutes a hypothesis that may be affirmed or disconfirmed by looking closely at a case (assuming the evidence is available to do so).

Of course, it is not always easy to uncover specific, falsifiable hypotheses embedded in a theory, particularly if that theory is stated in very general terms. This may be facilitated if the theory is articulated in a formal model, but even formal models can be differently interpreted. In any case, for a theory to be falsifiable it must issue predictions about the world. And these predictions, or hypotheses, must be applicable to the case under investigation if the case is to adjudicate among rival explanations.

When testing those rival explanations, treat them fairly – not as "straw men." In order to dismiss a rival explanation it must be given a good chance to succeed. For example, do not dismiss a probabilistic theory with a single counter-example (a case or instance where the theory appears to be wrong). Think about the rival explanation as a proponent of that theory might think about it. This requires approaching your topic fresh, without all the baggage (preconceptions) you may have acquired as you developed your argument. What must be true about the case under investigation if the theory is true?

Often these hypotheses center on the causal mechanisms of the theory (M) – what lies "inside the box" between X and Y. For example, Michael Ross (2001: 327–28) suggests three mechanisms that might generate a relationship between resource wealth and autocracy:

> A "rentier effect" ... suggests that resources rich governments use low tax rates and patronage to relieve pressures for greater accountability; a "repression effect" ... argues that resources wealth retards democratization by enabling governments to boost their funding for internal security; and a "modernization effect" ... holds that growth based on the export of oil and minerals fails to bring about the social and cultural changes that tend to produce democratic government.

Case study analyses of the resource curse have focused on each of these putative mechanisms in an attempt to determine their veracity.

Another sort of test involves units at a lower level of analysis. For example, studies of the resource curse sometimes examine patterns across regions *within* a country. In this fashion, Goldberg, Wibbels, and Mvukiyehe (2008) focus on Texas and Louisiana, two American states that experienced revenue windfalls from oil resources, in order to take a closer look at the interrelationship between resource wealth and democracy. They confirm that revenue riches lead to a decline in political competitiveness, and also discuss the possible causal pathways. In their words, "mineral rents provide cheap revenues that incumbent politicians use to purchase clientelistic support while keeping direct taxes on citizens low. It is this combination of low taxes and extensive public outlays that seems to contribute to politicians' persistence in office" (Goldberg, Wibbels, and Mvukiyehe 2008: 506).

Temporality

To tease apart causal relations within a single case, clues derived from the temporal ordering of events are essential. And to judge temporal relationships a chronological timeline of relevant events is indispensable. Sometimes, authors construct chronologies in a list format. Sometimes, key events will be portrayed in a causal diagram. But always, there is an accompanying narrative explaining who did what to whom, and when. Juan Linz's (1978) analysis of the breakdown of democracy in Spain during the 1930s involves a meticulous assemblage of historical facts including the changing composition of the legislature (disaggregated by ideological faction), the duration of cabinets, and the role of key actors in each event.

A chronology should begin *before* the causal factor of interest and extend all the way up to the outcome of interest, and perhaps beyond. Note that a qualitative analysis of X's relationship to Y is in some respects like a quantitative time-series analysis. The longer the temporal relationship can be observed, the greater our opportunities for gauging X's impact on Y, and identifying potential confounders. It is, however, unlike a time-series analysis insofar as one is unlikely to be able to observe X and Y throughout the whole period; or, it is irrelevant to observe them over a long period because they are not changing. In this setting, which often characterizes qualitative analysis, the relevant "covariational" features are the initial change of X and the eventual change in the outcome. What is left to observe are the factors that may have contributed to ΔX and ΔY. So, look for things that preceded X and things that lie in between X and Y.

The latter are the essential features of what has come to be known as *process tracing*, represented by M in this book. A good chronology includes all relevant features of M. It is complete. Unfortunately, it is not always apparent how to interpret completeness or continuity, i.e., which features are suitable for inclusion in a chronology and which features may be considered redundant. But one may assume that completeness exists when the connection between the events included in a chronology is tight – such that it is easy to see how a phenomenon evolved from step 1 to step 2, and step 2 to step 3, and difficult to see how any confounder could have disrupted that path.

The model of dominoes has served as a metaphor for the ideal. If one wishes to fully explain how the first domino is causally connected to the last domino one would want to construct a chronology of dominoes that includes each domino's fall – the events leading up to, and causing, the outcome of interest. In this simple example, each domino serves a gateway function and there is only one pathway (flowing through all of these gates). Factors that seem to carry a "necessary" or "sufficient" quality should always be included in a chronology. When in doubt, the inclusion of ancillary details is not damaging, and certainly less damaging than the accidental exclusion of crucial details.

Examining Background Assumptions

A final goal of case study research – whether undertaken on its own (a stand-alone case study) or in tandem with a cross-case study (a multi-method study) – is to shed light on background assumptions. All causal models assume causal comparability. The expected value of Y must be the same for all observations in the sample, conditional on observables. For large-N samples, this is understood in a probabilistic sense: $P(Y|X)$ is the same, on average, for all cases and for observations within a case (if the case is observed over time). For small-N samples, this is understood in a deterministic sense. Thus, any possible threat to this assumption for the studied cases is potentially damaging for the inference that the researcher wishes to draw.

Special attention to the assignment mechanism is warranted, as this is a source of bias in many social science analyses. Where X is not intentionally randomized by the researcher – as it is not, by definition, in observational studies – one must worry about assignment bias (or selection bias, as it is sometimes called). The blessing is that case studies are often especially insightful in providing insight into the assignment principle at work in a particular instance.

For example, Jeremy Ferwerda and Nicholas Miller (2014) argue that devolution of power reduces resistance to foreign rule. To do so, they focus on France during World War II, when the northern part of the country was ruled directly by German forces and the southern part was ruled indirectly by the "Vichy" regime headed by Marshall Petain. The key methodological assumption of their regression discontinuity design is that the line of demarcation was assigned in an as-if random fashion. For the authors, and for their critics (Kocher and Monteiro 2015), this assumption requires in-depth case study research – research that promises to uphold, or call into question, the author's entire analysis.

Strengths and Weaknesses

Like all research designs, the case study method has characteristic strengths and weaknesses. These may be assessed relative to large-N cross-case analysis, the topic of Chapter 8. As such, researchers face a series of tradeoffs, summarized in Table 9.2.

It should be stressed that each of these tradeoffs carries a ceteris paribus caveat. Case studies are more useful for generating new hypotheses, *all other things being*

Table 9.2 Case study and large-N research designs

	Case study	Cross-case study
Validity	Internal	External
Research goal	Deep	Broad
Causal insight	Mechanisms	Effects
Population	Heterogeneous	Homogeneous
Variation in X & Y	Rare	Common
Data	Concentrated	Diffuse
Hypothesis	Generating	Testing

equal. The reader must bear in mind that additional factors also rightly influence a writer's choice of research design, and they may lean in the other direction. Ceteris is not always paribus. One should not jump to conclusions about the research design appropriate to a given setting without considering the entire set of criteria, some of which may be more important than others.

Case studies generally have stronger claims to internal validity than to external validity. It is difficult to claim representativeness across a larger population when a sample consists of only a single case or a handful of cases (see Chapter 4).

Relatedly, case studies are generally more useful when the population of interest is moderate in size (e.g., countries in South America [$N = 13$]) and less useful when the scope of the research encompasses an enormous number of units (e.g., people in South America [$N > 400$ million]).

Case studies are generally more effective in shedding light on causal mechanisms than in measuring causal effects. This is because the X/Y relationship is generally defined in a way that can be accessed with a large sample, while the mechanism (M) connecting X to Y is often harder to observe and hence to test in a large sample.

Case studies are generally more useful when there is a great deal of heterogeneity in the population of interest. Consider that cross-case analysis is premised on cross-unit comparability (unit homogeneity). Cases must be similar to each other in whatever respects might affect the causal relationship that the writer is investigating, or such differences must be controlled for. Uncontrolled heterogeneity means that cases are "apples and oranges"; one cannot learn anything about underlying causal processes by comparing their histories. Case study researchers are often suspicious of large-sample research, which, they suspect, contain heterogeneous cases whose differences cannot easily be modeled. "Variable-oriented" research is said to involve unrealistic "homogenizing assumptions."[112] Under circumstances of extreme case heterogeneity, the researcher may decide that she is better off focusing on a single case or a small number of relatively homogeneous cases. Within-case evidence, or cross-case evidence drawn from a handful of most-similar cases, may be more useful than cross-case evidence, even though the ultimate interest of the investigator remains on that broader population of cases.

Case studies are generally more useful when variation on key parameters is limited (e.g., revolution or school shootings) and less useful when variation on key parameters is ubiquitous (e.g., economic growth, election results). Rare events call for case studies, while common events militate toward cross-case analysis.

Case studies are especially useful when data are available only for one or several cases (even though the phenomenon itself may be ubiquitous). We might have good reason to focus on the history of Sweden or the United Kingdom if we wish to study long-term demographic developments, for the history of available demographic records in these countries is much longer than the corresponding statistics for most other countries. By contrast, if for all units the same quantity and quality of information is available, a cross-case analysis may be more informative.

Finally, and perhaps most importantly, case study research is generally more useful at an early stage of analysis, where a study serves an exploratory role – perhaps identifying a new outcome or a new causal factor of interest. Once a specific hypothesis has been identified the task is to test that hypothesis in a falsifiable fashion. For this purpose, large-N cross-case research is usually more useful.

In short, lots of things might incline one toward a case study analysis, and lots of things might incline one toward a large-N style of analysis, as summarized in Table 9.1. It all depends.

In this context, it is worth noting the current trend toward combining these styles of research in a single study, i.e., *multi-method* research (see Chapter 10). This may allow the researcher to take advantage of the virtues of intensive and extensive styles of research without suffering the corresponding vices. It follows that when considering the utility of the following case selection strategies the reader should consider them as stand-alone research designs *or* as possible additions to a large-N research design, such as those introduced in Chapters 7–8.

KEY TERMS

- Case
- Case study
- Comparative-historical analysis
- Within-case
- Case selection
- Multi-method
- Exploratory
- Diagnostic

10

Diverse Tools of Causal Inference

This section of the book has covered a lot of ground. We have presented a variety of causal frameworks (Chapter 5), defined the problem of causal inference (Chapter 6), and introduced an itinerary of research designs, which we classified as experimental (Chapter 7), large-N observational (Chapter 8), or case study (Chapter 9).

This short chapter summarizes some of the themes discussed in this long, and complex, part of the book. We begin by reviewing the problem of confounding, and the various types of confounding that impede causal inference. Next, we review the panoply of research designs discussed in previous chapters, illustrating their interrelationship in a tree diagram, and discussing whether there is a "best" research design. We conclude by discussing the multi-method approach to research.

Identifying and Avoiding Confounders

Causal inference is possible only if confounders can be avoided or controlled in the analysis. Recall that we adopted a very broad definition of confounding, including any factor that produces a spurious (or biased) association between X and Y.

This idea may be rendered in a more concrete fashion using the language of causal graphs. A causal model will generally render a valid estimate if the "**frontdoor**" path from X to Y is unblocked and any existing "**backdoor**" paths from X to Y are blocked. Simply stated, a causal model should allow no covariation between X and Y except that which is a product of X's causal impact on Y. This is another way of describing *causal comparability*, i.e., the expected value of Y for a given value of X is the same for all units throughout the period of analysis. (You will see that there are many languages by which to express the same general idea.)

Five types of confounders, introduced in previous chapters, are recapitulated in Figure 10.1. In each case, Z stands for the confounder, generating a backdoor path from X to Y. Recall that in interpreting these graphs one must distinguish settings in which Z is conditioned from settings in which it is not (indicated by square brackets). In some settings, a confounder is created because a factor is *not* conditioned, in other settings because it *is* conditioned.

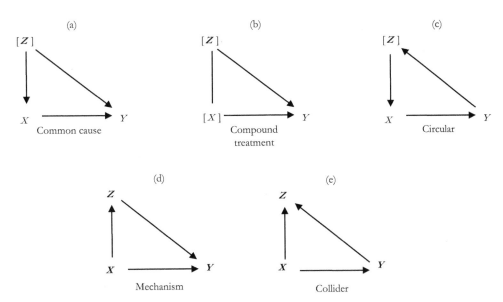

Figure 10.1 Typology of confounders using causal graphs

X = Causal factor
Y = Outcome
Z = Confounder
[ ] = Not conditioned

Panel (a) illustrates a **common cause confounder**, which has a causal effect on both X and Y. Panel (b) illustrates a **compound-treatment confounder**, where Y is affected by X and Z, whose effects cannot be distinguished from each other because they cannot be separately conditioned. Panel (c) illustrates a **circular confounder**, where Y affects X through Z. Panel (d) illustrates a **mechanismic confounder**, where an intervening factor (Z) between X and Y is conditioned. Panel (e) illustrates a **collider confounder**, produced by conditioning on a factor (Z) that is affected by both X and Y.

These confounders apply to any estimation strategy that relies on measuring the direct causal effect between X and Y.[113] The estimation of an unbiased causal effect generally depends upon unblocking the frontdoor path from X to Y (by refraining from conditioning on factors endogenous to X) and blocking the backdoor path(s) from X to Y (by conditioning on factors that block those paths, if they exist).

Research Designs

There are many ways to investigate a causal relationship between X and Y. As a way of pulling together our knowledge on this crucial aspect of social science methodology, we shall look at a particular research question and various

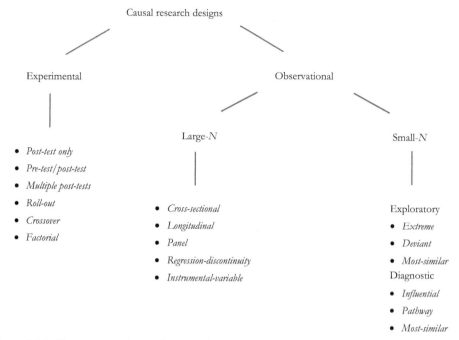

Figure 10.2 Taxonomy of causal research designs

approaches that might be taken to it. Research design options are summarized in a taxonomic fashion in a tree diagram, shown in Figure 10.2.

The general research question focuses on factors that enhance, or mitigate, the probability that unemployed persons will land well-paying jobs. The more specific hypothesis is that worker-training programs play a role in this process.

Experimental designs (large-N). *Assumption:* the researcher can assign the treatment across a large number of units. *Units of analysis:* individuals.

- **Post-test only**. Randomize the intervention across groups, forming a treatment group (unemployed persons who attend the worker-training program or programs) and a control group (unemployed persons who do not), whose earnings are compared at some point after the intervention.
- **Pre-test/post-test**. Randomize the intervention across groups, forming a treatment group (unemployed persons who attend the worker-training program or programs) and a control group (unemployed persons who do not). Measure earnings before the intervention and after the intervention, comparing the change in earnings for the treatment group with the change in earnings for the control group.
- (We forgo a description of other experimental research designs, as they are less common.)

Observational designs (large-N). *Assumption:* the researcher cannot assign the treatment, but X and Y can be measured across a large number of units. *Units of analysis:* individuals.

- **Cross-sectional**. Compare the earnings of unemployed persons who attended a worker-training program with those who did not, controlling for other factors.
- **Longitudinal**. Compare the earnings of unemployed persons prior to their participation in a worker-training program with their earnings after their participation.
- **TSCS**. Compare the change in earnings of (initially) unemployed persons who participated in a worker-training program with the change in earnings of (initially) unemployed persons who did not participate in a worker-training program, measuring earnings prior to the program start and at some point after the completion of the program.
- **Regression-discontinuity (RD)**. Identify a worker-training program that operates with an income threshold – a maximum income beyond which applicants are not accepted. Let us say that the maximum capacity for the program is 1,000 and that 2,000 or so apply. Applicants are prioritized according to income so that the poorest 1,000 applicants are accepted and the rest put on a waiting list. (This means that the threshold cannot be known by participants in advance.) Now, compare the earnings (among those who applied to the program) of those whose income falls just below (and therefore attended the program) and above (and therefore did not attend the program) at some point after the program is completed. Alternatively, compare the change in earnings of these two groups.
- **Instrumental-variable (IV)**. First, identify a feature that (a) enhances the likelihood of an unemployed person attending a worker-training program and (b) has no impact on earnings and is not correlated with other things that might impact earnings. Second, analyze the probability of attending a worker-training program (X) using this instrument along with any additional exogenous factors that may affect earnings. Third, test the hypothesis of interest by regressing earnings on the predicted (fitted) value for X along with any other exogenous covariates.

Case study designs (small-N – where N refers to cases rather than observations). *Assumptions:* the researcher cannot assign the treatment and data are not available for a large number of units, or it is inconclusive.

- **Exploratory** (there is no a priori hypothesis). *Units of analysis:* individuals.
  - **Extreme**. Select a small sample of long-term unemployed persons in order to identify some hypotheses about why they have been unable to land a job.
  - **Deviant**. Select a small sample of long-term unemployed persons who seem like they would be good candidates for employment, e.g., they

are well-educated, mature, and members of the majority social group. Identify some hypotheses about why they have been unable to land a job.

- **Most-similar.** Select several persons who were unemployed for long periods of time and are similar on background characteristics (e.g., education, social class, ethnicity) – some of whom found work and others of whom did not. Try to discover the reason(s) for their divergent success/failure.

- **Diagnostic**. *Units of analysis:* worker-training programs.
  - **Influential**. Select a worker-training program that exemplifies the state-of-the-art, and has clients who seem poised for success, but has very low rates of success in finding jobs for its clients. Try to identify why the anticipated result is not achieved, e.g., whether there is an important mediator.
  - **Pathway.** Select a worker-training program that initiates a change from a traditional method of training to the new method without any other changes to the program. Compare outcomes, as well as attitudes and performance of administrators and participants, before and after the adoption of the new method.
  - **Most-similar.** Select several worker-training programs that are similar in background features, some of which initiate a change from a traditional method of training to a new method. Compare outcomes, as well as attitudes and performance of administrators and participants, before and after the adoption of the new method.

And the Winner Is ...

With these options before us, the question naturally arises: what is the *best* research design? This issue was raised initially in a very general fashion in Chapter 1. Here, we take up the issue in the context of research designs for causal inference.

Restricting ourselves to issues of internal validity the question has a simple answer. The best research design is one where the treatment has been randomized (i.e., an experiment) so long as various post-treatment confounders can be avoided or satisfactorily dealt with (ex post).

Recall that in experimental research the treatment is randomly assigned to treatment and control groups. So long as subjects are compliant, treatment and control groups are kept apart, and compound treatments are avoided, the study can generally claim to have attained causal comparability. That is, the expected value of Y conditional on X will be the same across treatment and control groups. In this fashion, an unbiased estimate of the causal effect can be obtained.

Naturally, it is not always possible to randomize a treatment of theoretical interest. And naturally, one is also concerned with the validity of a study with respect to a larger population (external validity). For these reasons, social scientists often resort to observational data. Indeed, observational studies continue to constitute the vast majority of social science work.

Among observational research designs, one rightly gives priority to those that successfully mimic the virtues of an experiment. That is, the treatment is assigned in a manner that may be regarded as random with respect to potential confounders. It is "as-if" random. This sort of setting may be referred to as a **natural experiment** or (more loosely) a *quasi-experiment*.

As an example, let us consider a study by Susan Hyde that attempts to determine whether election observers deter vote-buying and other elements of voter fraud. The 2003 presidential election in Armenia offers an ideal subject of analysis, for in this election international election observers were allocated in a fashion that, she argues, is equivalent to a true randomized experiment. Hyde explains:

> In this particular election, delegation leaders [from various international monitoring groups] gave each team of short-term observers a preassigned list of polling stations to visit during election day. These lists were made with two objectives in mind: (1) to distribute the observers throughout the entire country ... and (2) to give each observer team a list of polling stations that did not overlap with that of other teams.[114]

These objectives were pragmatic in nature and unlikely to be correlated with any confounders. That is to say, the polling stations visited by international monitors were similar, in all important respects, to polling stations that were left unmonitored.

In order to measure the impact of these observers on the incidence of fraud, Hyde compares the incumbent vote in districts with observers to those districts without observers. The assumption is that the incumbent party is the principal instigator of vote-buying and intimidation. On the basis of this analysis, which follows a cross-sectional design, Hyde concludes that the deterrent effect of international observers is significant in both rounds of that election.

Let us return for a moment to the method of assignment. Although random-number generators were not used and Hyde herself had no control over the process, she argues that the choice of sites was orthogonal to (uncorrelated with) any possible confounders. Under the circumstances, it seems fair to regard this as a natural randomization with the desirable characteristics of a classic experiment. One element of doubt remains: because the experimenter does not control the assignment process she may never know for sure whether it is truly random, or just *apparently* random. This is why the distinction between a true experiment and a natural experiment is important to maintain.

Even under the best of circumstances, a natural experiment is not as convincing as a true experiment. More crucially, incidents of natural randomization such as the Armenian presidential election of 2003 are extremely rare. Alternatively, one might say that many situations appear to bear the marks of natural randomization but we simply do not know for sure and lack any means of decisively proving or disproving the point. Although one can often compare background characteristics, even if one finds that these characteristics are comparable across treatment and control groups it could be that other – unmeasurable – characteristics are not comparable. Likewise, if one finds that treatment and control groups are dissimilar on some background characteristics it could be that these characteristics are irrelevant to the X/Y relationship of theoretical concern, and thus may be disregarded.

Because of this, the designation natural or quasi-experiment is likely to remain a vague moniker. All observational research – whether large-N or small-N – aims to capture the virtues of the true experiment, either by happenstance (as in Hyde's case) or by the implementation of a procedure intended to restore random assignment to a non-randomly assigned treatment, e.g., by blocking covariates that might serve as confounders, by limiting analysis to some portion of a sample that is not subject to confounders, by focusing on longitudinal rather than cross-sectional variation, by focusing on observations that fall just above and below an arbitrary cutoff point (regression-discontinuity designs), or by isolating a feature that affects assignment to treatment but is not affected by confounding (instrumental-variable designs). If we accept that the chosen technique restores randomness to the assignment of treatment we are inclined to designate the research design as a natural experiment. If not, then not.

Consequently, the terms "natural experiment" and "quasi-experiment" must be treated with caution. They are only as convincing as the assumptions that surround a particular research setting and accompanying research design. Nonetheless, they focus our attention on a feature of causal inference that is absolutely critical. If the assignment process is non-random the association between X and Y is quite likely to be spurious and will need to be corrected.

But the goodness of a research design is not simply a matter of non-random assignment to treatment. There are many additional elements at work in the construction of a strong research design. This returns us to the main theme of the book. The best research design is the one that maximizes *all* the various criteria of causal inference (see Chapter 6). Best means best-possible, i.e., the best that could be achieved under the circumstances. The goodness of a research design is therefore assessable not by reference to some abstract standard but rather by reference to all possible research designs that might be devised to address the same research question. In some settings, this might be an experiment, in other settings it might be a large-N observational design, and in other settings it might be a case study. It all depends.

Thus, rather than trying to arrange research designs in a neat hierarchy it is probably more helpful to consider which design offers the best fit for a particular causal hypothesis. A good instrumental-variable (IV) analysis is better than a flawed pathway-case study, just as a good pathway-case analysis is better than a flawed IV analysis. And what makes these analyses strong or weak is the extent to which the assumptions required for each research design are met in a given instance.

Multiple Methods

In selecting among research designs one can anticipate methodological tradeoffs. One method might be good at achieving internal validity but with questionable external validity. Another method might speak clearly to a larger population of concern but with questionable internal validity. This is just one example of the tradeoffs one may encounter in the work of social science.

In light of such tradeoffs a natural solution is to employ multiple research designs within the same study. Ideally, each design compensates for weaknesses in the others. This is known generically as **multi-method** (aka *mixed-method* research or *triangulation*).

For example, in pursuing the impact of worker-training programs one might construct an experiment to test the causal effect, coupled with close observation of the participants in order to understand the causal mechanisms at work. One might also construct a study that enlists non-experimental data from extant worker-training programs to figure out whether the estimated causal effect from the experiment conforms to estimated causal effects from actually existing programs. Here, the experiment sits front-and-center but is complemented by other designs.

Now consider a question that is probably more suited for observational research: the impact of economic development on democratization. Here, the point of departure is perhaps a TSCS study of countries in which one searches to discern a relationship between economic development, proxied by per capita GDP, and regime-type. This might be complemented by case studies of countries that have undergone rapid economic development in order to try to understand the mechanisms that may be at work in this relationship. One might also construct experiments – or take advantage of natural experiments – in which some facet of economic development is manipulated in order to perceive its effect on political life or political attitudes. For example, one might compare regions of a country targeted for economic development with other regions not targeted for growth, observing the way in which regional politics evolves. This is a strong research design if ceteris paribus conditions are upheld, i.e., if everything else is more or less equal across the chosen regions.

Often, the most convincing approach to solving a causal problem enlists multiple methods, each of which fulfills specific goals. The sum of these different approaches may add up to a more convincing explanation than is possible when a single method is employed in isolation. Of course, conducting multi-method research is time-consuming and demands a lot of the researcher, who must cultivate diverse methodologies. Sometimes, multi-method approaches are best undertaken by multiple people, each of whom brings specialized skills to the project. Alternatively, one can think of the accumulated literature on a subject as presenting a multi-pronged approach insofar as each study brings different tools to the question.

Medical research provides a good example. Typically, research on a disease begins with the identification of a set of symptoms, which clinicians are able to classify as a particular disease-type (new or old). This spurs the collection of observational data, drawn initially from sources that are readily available. Clinicians work intensively with patients suffering from the disease, administering treatments and noting responses as best as they can (the case study method). They may also study subjects who are exposed to the disease but do not contract it (a deviant-case approach to case study research). Epidemiologists collect data from populations, attempting to identify larger patterns from a statistical analysis encompassing many data points. Biologists work at the micro-level, seeking to identify disease patterns within the cell (a form of within-case analysis, focused on causal mechanisms). Eventually, from one of these research streams, a potential treatment is devised and researchers construct an experiment to test it – first with animal subjects and then, if the results are promising, with human subjects.

In this fashion, medical research benefits from diverse methodological approaches. Each is based on distinct technical and substantive expertise, often housed in different disciplines, e.g., medicine, biology, chemistry, public health, and medical anthropology. Despite the diversity of methods, they take part in a single conversation about a topic – say, HIV/AIDS – which, over time, often leads to progress on that problem. Methodological diversity does not pose an obstacle (or at least, not an insuperable obstacle) to problem-solving.[115]

Unfortunately, this sort of multi-method community of scholars does not exist in many corners of social science. Because research programs are generally uncoordinated (leading to different choices across the various dimensions of research design), and because scholars are entrenched in different research communities (publishing work in different journals and often not citing members of a rival methodological camp), work conducted in different modes does not always cumulate. Instead, it simply accumulates. However, we should still regard the multi-method research community as a goal to aspire to, and the field of medical research offers a good exemplar of what might be achieved in other areas.

CONCLUSIONS

Causality has been a popular topic for applied and theoretical work in social science, statistics, and philosophy in recent years. Many insights have arisen from this work, as reflected in the text and in the set of references listed as part of the online materials for this book. Anyone hoping to make sense of contemporary work in the social sciences will need to grapple with the wiles of causal inference.

At the same time, one must bear in mind that causal knowledge is not the only sort of knowledge that one might acquire about the social world. Other forms of knowledge – i.e., descriptive, predictive, normative, and prescriptive, as outlined in

Chapter 2 – are also valuable. These styles of analysis often accompany causal analysis; indeed, description is a prerequisite for any causal argument. However, description is not only a precursor for causation. Sometimes, we want to know what X is – rather than (or in addition to) what causes X or what effects X has on something else. We close this section of the book with a reminder that good social science is not reducible to causal knowledge. And good methodology is not reducible to methods of causal inference.

KEY TERMS

- Frontdoor
- Backdoor
- Common cause confounder
- Compound-treatment confounder
- Circular confounder
- Mechanistic confounder
- Collider confounder
- Natural experiment
- Multi-method

III | Process and Presentation

In this section of the book we consider the process of research, as it is conducted, and the presentation of research, once it has been conducted. Chapter 11 discusses how to read works of social science (i.e., books and articles produced for an academic audience). Chapter 12 offers advice on how to find a topic for a research paper. Chapter 13 lays out various strategies for gathering data. (Since this is a large topic this is an especially long chapter.) Chapter 14 discusses the task of writing. Chapter 15 addresses the task of public speaking. Chapter 16 offers a short discussion of ethical issues associated with the research process.

As you can probably appreciate, these tasks are closely interwoven. Reading social science will help you develop a topic for your research and will help you develop a sense for how to construct your own project. Likewise, writing social science will help you appreciate the strengths, and realize the weaknesses, of other studies. Public speaking is another form of communication, closely linked to writing. Sometimes, a good way to write is to express an idea out loud (or sotto voce); sometimes, it is best to write it out first. There are lots of synergies. So these chapters – and their associated activities – are best approached together.

11 Reading and Reviewing

This chapter is devoted to reading and reviewing the social science literature on a topic. Here, we discuss how to distinguish social science sources from other sorts of work, how to locate and survey the literature on a chosen topic, how to read strategically, how to read critically, how to figure out complex arguments, how to construct a systematic review of the literature on a topic, and how to take notes as you go along. These are closely linked topics so you will find a good deal of overlap across these sections.

As you read social science you may be struck by the dry tone of the literature, especially in journal articles. (Books usually attempt to include some divertissement to relieve the tedium of pages and pages of prose.) Remind yourself that what is exciting about science – any science – is getting closer to the truth. The mode of exposition is secondary, and generally remains in the background. Indeed, it is important to adopt a dispassionate tone to discourage other factors from interfering with the logic of the argument. This is why authors generally avoid personal anecdotes, jokes, heavily symbolic or allegorical language, and other narrative devices.

Of course, there is a person behind the prose, and perhaps it would aid the cause of science if some personal elements – such as his/her motivations for studying a subject – were made explicit. But, for better or for worse, this is not the accepted scientific mode of communication in most social science fields. Bear with it.

In any case, new media are opening up new modes of communication, many of which are more personal in nature and less tightly structured. On virtually any given topic you can now find blogs (discussed below) or lectures and debates preserved on YouTube, as well as other multi-media presentations. The medium is changing, though the austere format of journal articles is likely to remain the workhorse of social science for the foreseeable future.

Identifying Social Science Sources

Reading social science presumes that one can identify works of social science from the mass of other sources out there in print and on the World Wide Web. This brings us back to an earlier discussion. What is it that distinguishes social science from other genres such as casual conversation, journalism, or partisan rhetoric?

In Chapter 1, we stipulated the following. First, social science involves the systematic application of reason and evidence to problems with explicit attention to method and to possible sources of error. Second, it is accompanied by realistic estimates of uncertainty with respect to whatever conclusions are drawn from the evidence. Third, it attempts to provide a comprehensive treatment of a subject within whatever scope-conditions are defined by the study. All relevant information should be included; none should be arbitrarily excluded. Finally, social science adopts a disinterested posture with respect to all goals except the truth. Its purpose is to get as close to the truth as possible, in all its complexity, rather than to provoke, entertain, elucidate moral truths, or advance polemical claims.

Studies with these characteristics generally appear in academic venues, i.e., in scholarly journals and working papers, in academic reports, and in books published by university presses. The audience for this sort of work is comprised of academics, policymakers, and members of the public with a special interest in the subject matter. Occasionally, a work of scholarship crosses over to a broader audience. Jared Diamond's classic *Guns, Germs, and Steel* broke through the usual boundaries separating scholarly and popular work.[116] However, this is fairly rare, and likely to remain so. The features that define social science also limit its appeal to a broader audience.

It may seem as if we are defining the genre of social science in a circular fashion: social science writing is what social scientists write and read. This is generally the case, but not always. Social scientists have many opportunities to write for the general public outside the genre of social science. They may write editorials, blog posts, speeches, manifestos, or articles for the popular press. They may tweet. They may even compose short stories, novels, and films. Each of these genres offers a somewhat different set of opportunities and constraints. Each has distinctive rules. However, while these forms of writing may deploy aspects of social science and may lean heavily on social science research they do not fall into the genre of social science as we usually understand it. Just because a work includes the phrase "social science studies say..." does not make it social-scientific. In order for it to be an example of social science the study must possess the characteristics listed above.

Consider the case of Paul Krugman, a Nobel laureate who has become a prominent liberal pundit, weighing in on all manner of political debates in the United States. His scholarly work, published in economic journals and academic presses, falls clearly into the genre of social science. His polemical work appears in newspapers and online, and occasionally in books. While the latter draws on academic research it is of a very different character.

Usually, readers will have no trouble discerning popular and academic genres – though occasionally they are somewhat blurred. In any case, it will be helpful to briefly review the variety of venues that are available as you research a topic. These include (a) journals, (b) books, and (c) working papers and blogs.

Journals

Every academic discipline boasts a handful of top journals that help to define that field or subfield. You should become familiar with these journals, as they will help you to identify important work in your area of research. Sometimes, this literature is rather technical and may not be easily accessible to those without advanced training. One of the purposes of this chapter is to assist in making sense of scholarly language – though it is important to bear in mind that some of the background knowledge required to process an academic journal article is, by its nature, highly specialized and therefore impossible to survey in a general textbook.

Books
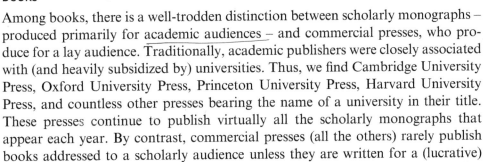

Among books, there is a well-trodden distinction between scholarly monographs – produced primarily for academic audiences – and commercial presses, who produce for a lay audience. Traditionally, academic publishers were closely associated with (and heavily subsidized by) universities. Thus, we find Cambridge University Press, Oxford University Press, Princeton University Press, Harvard University Press, and countless other presses bearing the name of a university in their title. These presses continue to publish virtually all the scholarly monographs that appear each year. By contrast, commercial presses (all the others) rarely publish books addressed to a scholarly audience unless they are written for a (lucrative) textbook market.

The imprimatur of a book – by a scholarly or commercial press – is thus an important clue to its contents. However, it is less useful than it used to be. The reason for this is that academic presses are under pressure to publish books with crossover potential (i.e., books that might reach a general readership). Likewise, academics are less motivated to publish traditional academic monographs, as the task of scholarly communication is increasingly performed by journals. In most fields, books are now regarded as an occasion to reach a broader audience (and not coincidentally, to make some money). Thus, for a variety of reasons fewer academic monographs appear every year, and the books that do get published by academic presses are more likely to paint on a large canvas with an orientation to the general reader.

Working Papers and Blogs

Because of the slow pace of academic publishing most studies appear initially as working papers. They may be posted on a conference website, on the author's homepage, on the website of a sponsoring organization or an aggregator like the Social Science Research Network (SSRN). Unpublished papers are of varying quality. Of course, published papers are also of varying quality, but the variance is greater in papers that have not passed the threshold of peer review. Bear in mind that some authors post papers at a very early stage, while others wait until a paper is ready to publish before making it available to the world. You must be the judge.

With respect to blogs the situation is even more confused. Some b written for other academics and consequently employ all the acrony phrases, and technical verbiage that distinguish a field or subfield. They presume a lot of "inside" knowledge and thus may be less accessible to outsiders than journal articles, where a formal style of presentation is adopted and where acronyms are explained and points are fully referenced. Nonetheless, academic blogs play an increasingly important role in scholarly debate, and sometimes they go down a lot easier than a turgid journal article. A short list of widely used academic blogs is included in the online materials for this book, for illustrative purposes. They may or may not offer a good entrée into the scholarly literature on a subject you are researching. But they are certainly worth a try.

More generally, the benefit of drawing upon unpublished papers and blogs is that you are able to get closer to the frontiers of knowledge on a topic. The drawback is that those frontiers are wild and untamed. Here, you will find undigested ideas, weakly supported claims, and brainstorms that may never gain acceptance in the academy. Because there is no official process of vetting (with the exception of a few working papers or conference-series papers that operate like journals), you will need to decide upon the quality of the work and whether it merits inclusion in your survey of a subject. One clue is the academic standing of the author, which you may be able to judge by his/her academic position, prior publications, or overall reputation.

General Observations

By way of conclusion to this discussion, let us return to the central distinction between "academic" and "popular" genres of writing. It should be clear that we are not casting aspersions on the latter. We have greater admiration for Martin Luther King's *Letter from Birmingham Jail* (one of the world's most inspired polemics against racism) than Gunnar Myrdal's *An American Dilemma* (a learned monograph on the same subject).[117] However, this chapter is not about how to write jeremiads against injustice. It is a chapter about how to read and write social science. As such, Myrdal's book is relevant and King's letter is not (except as a primary source). Our purpose is not to subsume or belittle other realms of discourse but rather to improve the practice and understanding of social science discourse. As a first step, it is important to understand the content and the boundaries of the genre known as social science.

Surveying the Literature

Having defined social science – at least in a rough-and-ready way – we arrive at the problem of identifying the literature on a particular topic. This used to be an extraordinarily time-consuming task undertaken at the library, where one would laboriously page through hard-copy indexes such as the *Reader's Guide to Periodical Literature* and the card catalog, followed by a hunt through the stacks for relevant books and articles (which would then need to be photocopied). Things are more efficient nowadays. Sometimes, a trip to the library is still required in order to get advice from a librarian or to obtain a book or article that is unobtainable in electronic form. But a good deal of the work can be conducted with a computer, providing one has access to e-journals, e-books, and specialized databases. (Usually, access to these proprietorial sources must be obtained through a library or university.)

Four computer-assisted approaches are generally helpful for this task: (a) *recent publications*, (b) *search terms*, (c) *citation searches*, or (d) *other venues*. As you pursue them, you may find it useful to maintain an updated list of references and/or a folder on your hard-drive where you keep PDF copies of relevant articles and reports.

Recent Publications

The best way to start your literature review is to identify a book or article that includes a survey of the relevant literature. Of course, all studies will include citations to the literature. But some are more useful for this purpose than others. Especially useful are books – if they contain a chapter that reviews the literature and an extensive bibliography – and review articles. A good place to look for the latter are journals that specialize in literature surveys.

A thorough literature review on your topic vastly simplifies your task. Indeed, it may be sufficient, unto itself. However, one must bear in mind that a literature review is only as current as its publication date. If it is several years old, you will be obliged to comb through the literature in subsequent years. Likewise, be aware that the person conducting the review has a point of view, like everyone else. Their review of the literature may be undertaken in order to show that some aspect of the literature on a topic is weak or biased. This may be true, or it may not. In any case, the author may neglect other aspects of the subject since they are less relevant to his/her argument. You should not assume that a literature review covers all aspects of a question. This will require further work. However, a search through the references of a literature review should provide a good jumping-off place.

Search Terms

A second approach to surveying the literature focuses on keywords. Think about different terms that articulate various aspects of your topic. These are useful search terms which may be plugged into Google Scholar, Web of Science (which includes the Social Sciences Citation Index), or some other database that is perhaps more focused on your area of concern. Some topics are nicely summarized in a set of key terms; these terms return items associated with that topic and only that topic. Unfortunately, many topics do not have this characteristic. When key terms are entered into a search engine they return all sorts of irrelevant material, or no relevant material. You may have to experiment a bit with different search terms before you find the right word, or the right combination of words.

Citation Searches

A third approach is contingent upon identifying at least one scholarly work that bears directly on your topic. If it is a classic work, one that defines the topic in question, you are in luck. This may be entered into Google Scholar, Web of Science, or some other database and should return all relevant material published after that classic work. The reason for this is that classic works on a topic are likely to be cited by other work on that topic.

Other Venues

A final approach involves a grab-bag of other web-based venues. You may find a Wikipedia article on your topic. While Wikipedia articles are of varying length and quality, many are carefully written and (even if they are not) they often contain a smattering of references to the relevant literature. Likewise, you may find websites maintained by scholars or hobbyists to be useful. If a subject is frequently taught, you may locate syllabi from those courses. This is a good way to identify entry-level readings, though rarely is a course syllabus detailed enough to satisfy a literature review.

General Observations

How widely should one survey? Sometimes, a topic generates work in multiple fields. It would be difficult to restrict one's survey of the literature on social capital or democracy to a single discipline. Other topics are restricted to a single discipline or sub-discipline. Worker-training programs are solidly within the purview of labor economics, though the topic has repercussions in sociology, education, and public policy.

How far back in history should one survey? In principle, the cumulative nature of science obviates the reading of older works, since their arguments and findings should be subsumed by more recent studies. As it happens, the cumulative character of science is more apparent in the natural sciences than in the social sciences. In the social sciences ideas tend to be recycled with each generation, perhaps with a slight change of terminology or theoretical focus. Gaining a sense of this intellectual history is important if one is to distinguish cycling from progress. Likewise, reading the history of a subject may open new windows into that topic, allowing one to see the "obvious" in a new and perhaps illuminating way. A deep reading of the literature on a topic is not simply a means of extracting classic quotations for an epigraph (though it performs that function as well).

Once you have identified a body of work, try to identify the most relevant studies, i.e., those that are most influential (as judged by number of citations or by what other authors say about them) and those that bear most directly on your particular topic. This smaller set of articles and/or books bears close reading.

Reading Strategically

— skim liiceriviik!

By virtue of your own background research (above) or by virtue of a specific class assignment, you now have an article or book to read. How shall you go about this?

Bear in mind that social science is not a sphere of activity in which close reading of texts is always advised. Occasionally, a topic is so dominated by a classic work that anyone working in that field is obliged to master the details of that classic work. But social science is not like literature or philosophy, where texts are intended to be dissected and where each turn of phrase merits attention. Sometimes, a close reading bears fruit. However, the time invested in a close reading must be weighed against the time that might be spent on other activities – such as skimming another hundred articles on the same general topic.

You must learn to read *strategically*. Typically, readers pick and choose which aspects of a study they are interested in or how deeply they wish to engage a particular work. In order to determine how you should approach this book or article you need to have a clear idea of what you hope to get from it.

Let us briefly survey some possibilities. If you are constructing your own review of the literature it may be sufficient to read the abstract of an article or the back-jacket blurb of a book. Perhaps all you need to know is what the study is about and what its main findings are. If the study in question contradicts your own argument or your own prior beliefs about a subject, you may wish to look closely at the evidence and the author's interpretation of that evidence. If you are reading the study for a class then you need to think about how much detail it is necessary to remember, and what sort of issues your instructor might wish you to focus on. Some classes are focused on substantive issues, others on methodological issues, and so forth. If you are asked to write a review of, or make a presentation based on, a study, then obviously you will need to understand that study in fine-grained detail. In short, there are many purposes for reading social science and each will entail a different level of engagement.

Regardless of your strategic purpose, it will be helpful to know a bit about how social science studies are put together. This is easiest with articles, which tend to follow a uniform template. (Books are more variable, though much of what we have to say is also applicable to scholarly monographs.)

Most scholarly articles are accompanied by an *abstract*. The abstract lays out the general subject, the argument, and the evidence – all in the space of a single paragraph or several short paragraphs. This is immensely useful and probably bears reading, even if you also read the innards.

The *introduction* of an article generally repeats the abstract, with additional verbiage and citations to the extant literature. It lays out the importance of the subject matter, says a bit about work that has already been conducted on it, and the author's contribution to that literature. Finally, there will be signposting – an outline of what is to follow.

The *theory* section lays out the argument, usually combined with a more in-depth engagement with the literature. Sometimes, the theory will be presented in narrative format as well as in a formal (mathematical) model.

This is usually followed by an *empirical section(s)*, which presents the evidence. Typically, this is the lengthiest part of a social science study, and may be supplemented by an *appendix* where descriptive statistics, specialized issues, or robustness tests are dealt with in greater detail. (Nowadays, this appendix is likely to appear online somewhere else rather than as part of the published article.)

The *conclusion* of an article typically repeats the main findings, comments on the limitations and broader ramifications of the study, and points out directions for further research.

This is the formula for a social science journal article. The utility of a common format is that you can easily skim a social science journal article, knowing where to look for what you wish to find. Naturally, there are exceptions. Some articles do not have a well-defined "theory" section; they proceed quickly to the evidence. Some articles do not have a well-defined empirical section; their emphasis is on building theory. But most articles assume the foregoing format, which is explored at greater length in Chapter 14.

Reading Critically

Social scientists are generally pretty smart, and the work that gets published in top journals and top university presses is generally of high quality. However, it is not flawless. And sometimes, it is very flawed. In any case, you need to read critically. This does not mean that you should try to knock down every study you encounter. It means that you should learn to identify the limitations of each piece of research. Sometimes, authors are forthright and will point out these limitations in their discussion. Sometimes, these limitations or contradictions will be hidden or mentioned only obliquely. (The author may not even be aware of them.) Suffice to say, in order to be an intelligent consumer of social science you need to cultivate a critical eye.

While there is no recipe for deconstructing social science, a few standard questions should be asked of any study. With respect to the *theory*, one might ask:

- Is it clearly stated?
- Does it address an important problem?
- Is it original, or in what ways is it original? (Or does it tell us something that we already know, or that has already been established by prior research?) Does the author properly credit other work that contributes to the theory? What body of work is the author arguing *against*?
- Is it properly bounded? (Are the scope-conditions clear, and defensible?)
- Is it specific enough to be falsified?
- How should we classify the theory? Is it, for example, primarily descriptive or causal?

- If the argument is causal, what general causal framework does it invoke?
- If the argument is causal (and if the research is non-experimental), what is the envisioned counterfactual? (What is the expected variation in X and what impact does this variation have on Y?) Has the author correctly identified the causal mechanism(s) at work?
- Are there underlying assumptions that must be satisfied for the argument to hold?

These questions elaborate on points laid out in Chapter 2 (for all theories) and Chapter 6 (for causal theories).

With respect to the *research design*, one might ask:

- How would one characterize it, in general terms? (Is it experimental or observational? Large-N or small-N? If the former, is it properly classified as a TSCS, cross-section, . . .?)
- Does it fit well with the theory? Does it constitute an easy test or a hard test?
- Are there potential problems with the research design? Is the author's proposed account of the data correct? Is there another way to account for the observed pattern of data? Is the research design prone to stochastic error or to systematic bias? Are there potential confounders that are not effectively controlled for in the analysis?
- Is the sample representative of a defined population? To what larger population are the results generalizable?
- Are there better research designs for addressing the author's research question?
- Is the finding original? How does it fit with other work on the subject? If it is at variance with other work, which finding is most credible? Can these research streams be reconciled?

These questions bring us back to fundamental issues of research design, as introduced in Chapter 4 (for all research designs) and Chapters 6–10 (for causal analysis).

Figuring It Out

As you read the social science literature you will occasionally get stuck. That is, you will be unable to figure out what an author is trying to communicate, or you have a general idea but are not sure that you are correctly interpreting the text.

Sometimes, this is because the text itself is not clear and thus open to various interpretations. (This touches on a leitmotif of this section of the book – the importance of communication skills in social science.) Sometimes, it is because the text is written for readers who possess a good deal of background knowledge about the subject or the method.

A common stumbling block is unfamiliarity with technical terms. Once upon a time it was important to have a lexicon – a specialized dictionary – at your side, with key terms in your field or subfield defined. Nowadays, you can usually solve this problem by Googling the term and finding the appropriate Wikipedia article or other online source. Of course, these online sources are of varying quality, so you must exercise judgment. Note also that key terms can mean quite different things in different contexts. Reading several definitions can usually help to sort this out.

Another common stumbling block is a mathematical formula or model that is beyond your present capabilities. Unfortunately, learning enough algebra to understand a formal theoretical model or a proof, or learning enough probability theory to understand a statistical model, is a time-consuming venture. These are matters best learned in the structured context of a course in math or statistics (something you might want to consider as you plan your future coursework).

You may take comfort in the fact that this aspect of an article or book is (generally) carefully vetted by expert reviewers. It is rare to find mathematical errors in a published work, especially if it is a top-notch journal or press. Problems are much more common in interpretation. What does the theoretical or statistical model mean? How does it bear on the theory and the evidence? What is the data generation process (the process by which the data the author is analyzing has come to be)? Does the chosen statistical model correctly describe that data? Is the research design appropriate for the task?

Of course, knowing the math will help you resolve these sorts of questions. However, you can still address those questions by reading the author's (verbal) explication of the model. If the point at issue is a statistical model that is not well-explained by the author you may wish to consult Part IV of this book, or take a look at a stats textbook or an online reference source (suggestions are included in the online materials for this book).

Reviewing the Literature

We have now discussed how to identify a work of social science, how to identify studies of a particular topic, and how to read those studies strategically and critically. A remaining task is to review that literature in a systematic fashion.

There are essentially three versions of the literature review. The first involves combining results from multiple quantitative analyses of the same subject – published separately – in order to determine the overall causal effect of a variable, taking sampling error and other sorts of error into account. This is known as a meta-analysis, and is beyond the purview of the book.

A second sort of review is prefatory to an original piece of research (usually conducted with primary sources). Its purpose is to situate that research within a broader literature, showing how the author's work provides an original contribution to (some aspect of) that literature. This will be discussed in Chapter 14.

The third sort of review is a *general* review of the literature on a topic, where the author's sole purpose in the paper is to survey that literature. This is equivalent to the sort of article one might find in any of the "Annual Review" journals (listed in the online materials). You might wish to peruse one of these as an example of how to conduct such a survey of the literature.

Literature reviews of this sort are commonly assigned in seminar courses, as they can be conducted without access to primary sources and provide an opportunity for students to integrate a large amount of material, perhaps spanning the entirety of the course. They may serve a number of purposes. For example, they may serve to illustrate how scholars have conceptualized a topic, what research designs they have employed, and what data sources they have used. They may serve to identify recent trends in research or the trajectory of a subject over a longer period of time (its intellectual history). They may serve to identify inconsistencies and controversies within the literature, perhaps offering a reconciliation of divergent positions. They may serve to identify omissions in scholarly work on a topic, areas that are relatively untouched by serious research, or areas that are fraught with methodological problems. They may identify hidden biases in a subject. They may identify hypotheses that bear further research, thus pointing the way to future work on a subject.[118]

Note that a literature review is also an original contribution to that literature, for it synthesizes that literature in a new way, pointing out strengths and weaknesses or new approaches that may not have been apparent. Occasionally, a cogent literature review becomes a canonical reference, reorienting a field in a new direction.

Think carefully about your overall argument before you begin, and modify it as you go along, as necessary. A plausible place to begin is by defining the scope of the review. Like research with primary data, the literature review must have clearly established scope-conditions. It must be bounded in a logical fashion. This is equivalent to establishing the population of studies that the review is intended to encompass. For example, you must decide the temporal scope of the review. Many reviews limit their purview to recent work, e.g., work published over the past two decades. Others are more ambitious, intending to uncover the intellectual history of a topic. You must also decide what sort of literature you wish to include: Published and/or unpublished material? Articles and/or books? Scholarly and/or popular sources? All social science fields, or just one or two? Other scope-conditions relate to the topic itself, which may be defined broadly (e.g., "democracy") or more narrowly (e.g., "democratization in Latin America").

Having defined the purview of the review, you must now integrate the literature that falls within that purview. This means painting a broad picture, citing as many studies as possible while discussing the details of only a few. These few should be chosen carefully. Usually, they exemplify a general feature that one finds in the literature; they are examples of a broader trend. Alternatively, they may offer an unusual – and especially fecund – line of inquiry, opening up a new approach to the subject. In any case, a good literature review summarizes a vast literature with little expenditure of prose. It is synoptic. That is, it reduces the subject to a few fundamental parameters.

These parameters might be theoretical. For example, one might argue that the literature on democratization employs two very different types of explanations in the effort to explain why some countries democratize and others do not (or why they democratize at different times). The first sort of explanation is structural, focusing on distal causes of democracy such as geography, colonial heritage, social inequality, and modernization. The second sort of explanation is proximal, focusing on short-term causes or mechanisms such as elite bargains, social movements, civil conflicts, military interventions, and the sequences by which different political institutions develop over time. This distinction is fundamental, and allows one to categorize all studies as part of one or the other camp.

Another way of dividing up the subject is methodological. One might point out that studies of democratization can be classified into four approaches: country case studies, sub-national studies, large-N cross-national studies, and experimental studies.[119]

One might also divide up a subject by looking at various ways of operationalizing its key concept(s). Thus, one might distinguish among studies of democracy that utilize binary measures of democracy (e.g., the Democracy/Dictatorship index), ordinal measures of democracy (e.g., the Freedom House indices), or interval measures derived from latent-variable analyses (e.g., the Unified Democracy Scores[120]). If one is exploring country and regional studies of democracy, one might divide up the subject by *geographic area* – Latin America, Africa, Middle East, Asia, and so forth.

There are many ways to analyze any given subject. This is what distinguishes one literature review from the next, though both may be focused on the same general subject. Different authors often identify different lines of cleavage, calling attention to different aspects of a topic.

Taking Notes

As you read, it is a good idea to take notes. Some readers take notes on whatever they are reading, regardless of whether they have a clearly designed purpose for the notes, ex post. For these readers, taking notes is a form of diary-keeping.

However, most readers are strategic in their note-taking. If one's purpose is to prepare for a class discussion or an exam one's notes will consist of points that are relevant to those tasks. If one's purpose is to construct a paper – an original piece of writing – one's notes should assist in that process. In either case, taking notes enhances your engagement with the text. It makes reading an interactive process. Thus, regardless of your immediate purpose in reading a text (whether it is to prepare for a discussion, an exam, or a paper), use note-taking to allow your mind to roam freely.

Nowadays, there are many ways to take a note. You may mark up a hard copy. You may mark up a PDF or Kindle text. You may insert notes in a text file. Or you may employ various citation managers (BiblioExpress/Biblioscape, Endnote, Mendelay, ProCite, RefWorks, Reference Manager, Zotero), most of which also allow you to maintain notes on each source in the database.

Importantly, if you are using a text file to take notes make sure you have a good system for keeping track of which idea or quotation comes from which source (and what page in that source). Any sloppiness in your record-keeping is likely to lead to plagiarism if the notes are later incorporated into a paper. (See section on plagiarism in Chapter 14.) Also, make sure to mark clearly which ideas are copied verbatim from a source (within quotation marks), so they can be distinguished from ideas that you have paraphrased based on your reading of a source (suitably transformed so that they do not reflect the author's original rendition). In order to distinguish ideas that are clearly your own from those that need to be footnoted, you might want to preface the former with your initials. This will help when you return to your notes, whether this is a week later or several years later.

CONCLUSIONS

Social science offers an important set of resources on a wide range of topics. It is not the last word on these topics, and rarely is it the first word. However, social science sources are almost always worth consulting.

Consider the alternative. If you rely entirely on journalistic work on a topic – e.g., articles appearing in newspapers, popular journals, books produced for a general audience, or a non-academic website – you will be reading someone else's digest of the social science literature on that topic. An article on crime will tell you what the author knows, based on his or her perusal of the literature and perhaps some interviews with academics who have conducted research on the topic. But the author of such an article is unlikely to have a deep knowledge of the scholarly literature, and – given space limitations – must produce a brief and schematic report.

This is probably not a good way to make up your mind on a complex subject. Without delving into the scholarly literature you will not be in full possession of the facts, even if – especially if – those facts are disputed.

Unfortunately, the literature of social science is not always readily accessible to the non-specialist – hence, the widening gap between social science and popular writings on most topics. This chapter is intended to help bridge that gap. We have discussed how to distinguish social science sources from other sorts of work (of a less scientific nature), how to locate and survey the literature on a chosen topic, how to read strategically, how to read critically, how to figure out complex arguments, how to construct a systematic review of the literature on a topic, and how to take notes as you go along. We hope that these tips will prove useful to you as you survey the literature on topics of your choosing.

KEY TERM

• Meta-analysis

Brainstorming

How does one go about identifying a fruitful research question and, ultimately, a specific research hypothesis? This is the very early exploratory phase, when one quite literally does not know what one is looking for, or at. Arguably, it is the most crucial stage of all. Nothing of interest is likely to emanate from research on topics that are trivial, redundant, or theoretically bland – no matter how strong its research design components are.

Methodologists generally leave this task to the realm of metaphor – bells, brainstorms, dreams, flashes, impregnations, light bulbs, showers, sparks, and whatnot. The reason for this lack of attention is perhaps because beginnings are inherently unformulaic. There are few rules or criteria for uncovering new questions or new hypotheses. Methodologists may feel that there is nothing – nothing scientific, at any rate – that they can say about this process. Karl Popper states the matter forthrightly. "There is no such thing as a logical method of having new ideas," he writes. "Discovery contains 'an irrational element,' or a 'creative intuition.'"[121]

Accordingly, what we have to offer in this chapter is more in the character of a homily than a framework. It reads like an advice column. We urge you to Study the Tradition, Begin Where You Are, Get Off Your Home Turf, Play With Ideas, Practice Disbelief, Observe Empathically, Theorize Wildly, and Think Ahead.

This advice is largely commonsensical and by no means comprehensive. It cannot help but reflect our own views and experiences, though we have drawn extensively on the writings of other scholars. Nonetheless, it may help to orient those who are setting out on their first journey, or who wish to begin again.

Study the Tradition

Consider the state of the field on a topic. What are the frontiers of knowledge? What do we – collectively, as a discipline – know, and what don't we know? We doubt if anyone has happened upon a really interesting research topic simply by reading a review of the extant literature. However, this is an efficient method of determining where the state of a field lies and where it might be headed.

In exposing oneself to the literature on a topic one must guard against two common responses. The first is to worship those that have gone before; the second is to summarily dismiss them. We advise a middle path. Respect the tradition, but don't be awed by the tradition either. Try stepping outside the categories that are conventionally used to describe and explain a subject. By this we mean not simply arguing against the common wisdom, but also thinking up new questions and new issues that have not been well explored.

As you peruse the literature, be conscious of what excites you and what bothers you. Which issues are under-explored, or badly understood? Where do you suspect the authorities in a field are wrong? What questions have they left unanswered? What questions do you find yourself asking when you finish reading? Where does this line of research lead? Sometimes, typically in a conclusion or a review article, scholars will reflect upon the future direction of research; this, too, can be useful.

Sometimes, it is necessary, due to time-constraints, to limit oneself to the recent literature on a subject. However, time permitting, there is something to be gained by going deeper, delving into the "classics," i.e., the founding texts of a field or subfield.[122] This is useful because it sometimes prompts one to think about familiar subjects in new ways, because classic works tend to be evocative (raising questions), and because it is a reminder that some things have, in fact, been done before. Every subject has an intellectual history and it is worthwhile to familiarize yourself with this history.

As C. Wright Mills began his study of elites, he consulted the seminal contributions of Lasswell, Marx, Michels, Mosca, Pareto, Schumpeter, Veblen, and Weber.[123] In commenting upon this experience, Mills reports:

> I find that they offer three types of statement: (a) from some, you learn directly by restating systematically what the man says on given points or as a whole; (b) some you accept or refute, giving reasons and arguments; (c) others you use as a source of suggestions for your own elaborations and projects. This involves grasping a point and then asking: How can I put this into testable shape, and how can I test it? How can I use this as a center from which to elaborate – as a perspective from which descriptive details emerge as relevant?

Not every topic is blessed with such a rich heritage; but some are, and there it is worth pausing to read, and to think.

Begin Where You Are

Charles Sanders Peirce points out, "There is only one place from which we ever can start ... and that is from where we are."[124] The easiest and most intuitive way to undertake a new topic is to build upon what one knows and who one is. This includes one's skills (languages, technical proficiencies), connections, life-experiences, and interests.[125]

Hopefully, your chosen topic resonates with your life in some fashion. This is often a source of inspiration and insight, as well as the source from which sustained commitment may be nourished and replenished over the life of a project. C. Wright Mills writes:

You must learn to use your life experience in your intellectual work: continually to examine and interpret it. In this sense craftsmanship is the center of yourself and you are personally involved in every intellectual product upon which you may work. To say that you can 'have experience,' means, for one thing, that your past plays into and affects your present, and that it defines your capacity for future experience. As a social scientist, you have to control this rather elaborate interplay, to capture what you experience and sort it out; only in this way can you hope to use it to guide and test your reflection, and in the process shape yourself as an intellectual craftsman.[126]

Because the business of social science is to investigate the activities of people, any personal connections we might have to such people – your subjects – may serve as useful points of leverage. It will be helpful if you can establish a personal connection – however distant – with the phenomena you are studying.[127]

Sometimes, our connection with a topic is motivated more by ideas than by personal connections. We are naturally drawn to subjects that are horrifying or uplifting. Many research projects begin with some notion – perhaps only dimly formulated – about what is wrong with the world. What real-life problem bothers you?[128]

The desire to redress wrongs also helps to keep social science relevant to the concerns of lay citizens. We all begin, one might say, as citizens, with everyday concerns. Over time, we come to attain a degree of distance from our subject. Thus, our roles as citizens and scholars inform one another.

Of course, at the end of a project one must have something to say about a topic that goes beyond assertions of right and excoriations of wrong. The topic must be made tractable for scientific inquiry. If one feels that the topic is too close to the heart to reflect upon dispassionately then it is probably not a good candidate for study. As a probe, ask yourself whether you would be prepared to accept the results of a study in which your main hypothesis is proven wrong. If you hesitate to answer this question because of normative pre-commitments you should probably choose another subject.

As a general rule, it is important to undertake questions that one feels are important, but not projects in which one has especially strong moral or psychological predilections for accepting or rejecting the null hypothesis.[129] For example, one might be motivated to study the role of worker-training programs because one is concerned about the problem of unemployment. But one probably should not undertake a study of worker-training programs to demonstrate that they are a good or bad thing. To do this would be to prejudge the answer to your research question.

Get Off Your Home Turf

While the previous section emphasized the importance of building upon one's personal profile (skills, connections), it is also vital for scholars to stray from what is safe, comfortable, and familiar – their home turf.

Consider that academia is not now, and likely never will be, a representative cross-section of humankind. At present, the practitioners of social science are disproportionately white, Anglo-European, and male. They will probably always be disproportionately privileged in class background. Evidently, if members of these disciplines restrict themselves to topics drawn from their personal experience little attention will be paid to topics relevant to underprivileged groups.

Equally important, advances in knowledge usually come from transgressing familiar contexts. After all, local knowledge is already familiar to those who live it. Whatever value might be added comes from moving beyond established categories, theories, and ways of thinking. A good ethnography, it is sometimes said, renders the exotic familiar *or* the familiar exotic. The same might be said of social science at large. Try to think like a stranger when approaching a topic that seems obvious (from your "home turf"). Likewise, do not be afraid to export categories from your home turf into foreign territory – not willfully, and disregarding all evidence to the contrary, but rather as an operating hypothesis. Sometimes, the application of a foreign category is illuminating.

Novel descriptive and causal inferences often arise when an extant concept or theory is transplanted from one area to another. For example, the concept of *corporatism* arose initially in the context of Catholic social theory as an alternative to state socialism. It was later adopted by fascist regimes as a way of legitimating their control over important economic and social actors. More recently, it has been seen as a key to explaining the divergent trajectories of welfare states across the OECD, and for explaining the persistence and resilience of authoritarian rule in the developing world.[130] There are endless ways of adapting old theories to new contexts. Sometimes these transplantations are fruitful; other times, not.

Most important, try to maintain a conversation with different perspectives on your subject. What would so-and-so say about *X*? If this does not drive you mad, it may serve to triangulate your topic.

Another sort of boundary crossing is that which occurs across disciplines, theories, and methods. The trend of the contemporary era seems to be toward ever greater specialization, and to be sure, specialization has its uses. It is difficult to master more than one area of work, given the increasingly technical and specialized techniques and vocabulary developed over the past several decades.

Yet, it is worth reflecting upon the fact that many of the works that we regard today as pathbreaking have been the product of exotic encounters across fields and subfields. Indeed, all present-day fields and subfields are the product of long-ago transgressions. Someone moved outside their comfort zone, and others followed. Note also that the social sciences are not divided up into discrete and well-defined fields. So, try reading inside, *and outside*, your area of training.

All academic work is theft of one sort or another. So long as the sources are well-documented one need not fear the charge of plagiarism. And thefts sometimes produce novel insights. Another word for this sort of theft is creativity.

Play With Ideas

The literature on invention and discovery – penned by science writers, philosophers of science, and by inventors themselves – is in consensus on one point. Original discoveries are usually not the product of superior brainpower (i.e., the ability to calculate or reason). Robert Root-Bernstein is emphatic:

> Famous scientists aren't any more intelligent than those who aren't famous. [Moreover,] I'm convinced that successful ones aren't right any more often than their colleagues, either. I believe that the architects of science are simply more curious, more iconoclastic, more persistent, readier to make detours, and more willing to tackle bigger and more fundamental problems. Most important, they possess intellectual courage, daring. They work at the edge of their competence; their reach exceeds their grasp . . . Thus, they not only succeed more often and out of all proportion; they also fail more often and on the same scale. Even their failures, however, better define the limits of science than the successes of more conventional and safe scientists, and thus the pioneers better serve science.[131]

The key question, as Root-Bernstein frames it, is "How can one best survive on the edge of ignorance?"[132]

Although the art of discovery cannot be taught (at least not in the way that the technique of multiple regression can be taught), it may be helpful to think for a moment about thinking. The act of creation is mysterious; yet, there seem to be a few persistent features. Arthur Koestler, synthesizing the work of many writers, emphasizes that discoveries are usually "already there," in the sense of being present in some body of work – though perhaps not the body of work that it had heretofore been associated with. To discover is, therefore, to connect things that had previously been considered separate. To discover is to think *analogically*.

> This leads to the paradox that the more original a discovery the more obvious it seems afterwards. The creative act is not an act of creation in the sense of the Old Testament. It does not create something out of nothing; it uncovers, selects, re-shuffles, combines, synthesizes already existing facts, ideas, faculties, skills. The more familiar the parts, the more striking the new whole. Man's knowledge of the changes of the tides and the phases of the moon is as old as his observation that apples fall to earth in the ripeness of time. Yet the combination of these and other equally familiar data in Newton's theory of gravity changed mankind's outlook on the world.[133]

What frame of mind does this require? How does one think analogically? This trick seems to have something to do with the capacity to "relinquish conscious controls," to block out the academic superego that inhibits new thoughts by punishing transgressions against the tradition.[134] Above all, one must feel free to make mistakes.

> Just as in the dream the codes of logical reasoning are suspended, so 'thinking aside' is a temporary liberation from the tyranny of over-precise verbal concepts, of the

axioms and prejudices engrained in the very texture of specialized ways of thought. It allows the mind to discard the strait-jacket of habit, to shrug off apparent contradictions, to un-learn and forget – and to acquire, in exchange, a greater fluidity, versatility, and gullibility. This rebellion against constraints which are necessary to maintain the order and discipline of conventional thought, but an impediment to the creative leap, is symptomatic both of the genius and the crank; what distinguishes them is the intuitive guidance which only the former enjoys.[135]

It might be added that what also distinguishes the genius and the crank is that the former has mastered the tradition of work on a subject. Her liminal moments are creative because they take place on a foundation of knowledge. In order to forget, and thence recombine features of a problem, one must first have a first-hand familiarity with the facts.

Practice Disbelief

One can't think without words, but sometimes one can't think well with them either. Sometimes, ordinary language serves to constrain thought-patterns, reifying phenomena that are scarcely there. When we define, Edmund Burke commented, "we seem in danger of circumscribing nature within the bounds of our own notions."[136] Language suggests, for example, that where a referential term exists a coherent class of entities also exists, and where two referential terms exist there are two empirically differentiable classes of entities. Sometimes this is true, and sometimes it is not. Just because we have a word for "social movement" does not mean that there are actually phenomena out there that are similar to each other and easily differentiated from other phenomena. Ditto for "social capital," "interest group," and virtually every other key concept in the social science lexicon. Words do not always carve nature at its joints. Sometimes, they are highly arbitrary ("constructed"). Likewise, just because we have a word for some phenomenon does not mean that cases of this phenomenon all stem from the same cause. It is not even clear that the same causal factors will be *relevant* for all members of the so-named set of phenomena.

The reader might respond that, surely, concepts are defined the way they are because they are useful for some purposes. Precisely. But it follows that these same concepts may not be useful for *other* purposes. And since one's objective at early stages of the research game is to think unconventionally, it is important to call into question conventional language. For heuristic purposes, try assuming a nominalist perspective: words are merely arbitrary lexical containers. As an exercise, put brackets around all your key terms ("social movement"). Now try to redescribe the phenomenon of interest using different language.

A parallel skepticism must be extended to numbers, which also naturalize phenomena that may, or may not, go together in the expected fashion. Here, the claim is more complicated. First, the use of a number is explicitly linked to a dimension – e.g., temperature, GDP, number of auto accidents – that is thought to be relevant in some way. Moreover, the imposition of a numerical scale presupposes a particular type of relationship between phenomena with different scores on that variable – nominal, ordinal, interval, or ratio (Chapter 3). But is it *really*? More broadly, is this the dimension that matters for understanding the topic in question? Are there other dimensions, perhaps less readily quantified, that provide more accurate or insightful information? While GDP is the conventional measure of economic development it could be that other aspects of modernization are more relevant for explaining an outcome of interest. An obsessive focus on GDP may serve to obscure that relationship.

Another sort of conventional wisdom is contained in **paradigm-cases**. These are cases that, by virtue of their theoretical or everyday prominence, help to define a phenomenon – the way Italy defines fascism, the Holocaust defines genocide, the United States defines individualism, Sweden defines the welfare state, and the Soviet Union (for many years) defined socialism. Paradigm-cases exist in virtually every realm of social science inquiry. They often provide good points of entry into a topic because they are overloaded with attributes; they operate in this respect like ideal-types (Chapter 3). Yet, because they anchor thinking on these topics, they are also thought-constraining. And because they are also apt to be somewhat unusual – even extreme – examples of the phenomenon in question, they may present misleading depictions of that phenomenon.

With respect to words, numbers, and paradigm-cases – not to mention full-blown theories – it is important to maintain a skeptical attitude. Perhaps they are true and useful, perhaps only partially so, or only for certain purposes. To test their utility, try adopting the Socratic guise of complete ignorance (better labeled as thoroughgoing skepticism). Once having assumed this pose, you are then free to pose naïve questions of sources, of experts, and of informants. It is a canny strategy and can be extraordinarily revealing – particularly when "obvious" questions cannot be readily answered, or are answered in unexpected ways.

Observe Empathically

One technique of discovery is empathic, or (to invoke the philosophical jargon) hermeneutic.[137] Here, one employs observational techniques to enter into the world of the actors who are engaged in some activity of interest – playing ball, drafting a bill, murdering opponents, casting a vote, and so forth – in order to understand their perspective on the phenomenon. Of course, this is easier when the actors are our contemporaries and can be studied directly (i.e., ethnographically). It is harder, and yet sometimes more revealing, if the actions took place long ago or are removed from direct observation, and must be reconstructed. In any case, non-obvious perceptions require interpretation, and this interpretation should be grounded in an assessment of how actors may have viewed their own actions.

Consider that the process of understanding begins with an ability to recreate or reimagine the experiences of those actors whose ideas and behavior we wish to make sense of. Somehow, a link must be formed between our experiential horizons and the horizons of the group we wish to study. This may involve a form of role-playing (what would we do in Situation X if we were Person Y?). Some level of sympathy with one's subjects is probably essential for gaining insight into a phenomenon. This may be difficult to muster if the subject is grotesque. No one wants to empathize with Nazis. But the hermeneutic challenge remains; some way must be found to enter into the lives and perceptions of these important historical actors in order to explain their actions, however repellant they might be.

Theorize Wildly

Rather than working single-mindedly toward One Big Idea, you might consider the benefits of working simultaneously along several tracks. This way, you avoid becoming overly committed to a single topic, which may turn out to be unavailing. You can also compare different topics against one another, evaluating their strengths and weaknesses. "Have lots of ideas and throw away the bad ones," advises Linus Pauling.[138]

At the same time, you should do your best to maintain a record of your ideas as you go along.[139] Take a look at this idea-diary every so often and see which projects you find yourself coming back to, obsessing about, inquiring about. The objective should be to keep your mind as open as possible for as long as possible (given the practicalities of life and scholastic deadlines). "Let your mind become a moving prism catching light from as many angles as possible."[140]

Historians of natural science identify productive moments of science with the solving of anomalies – features of the world that don't comport comfortably with existing theories.[141] If these anomalies can be solved in a more than ad hoc manner, the frontiers of knowledge are pushed forward. Perhaps a new paradigm of knowledge will be created.

Another technique for theorizing wildly is to juxtapose things that don't seem to fit naturally together. Theorizing often consists of disassociating and reassociating. One version of this is to examine a familiar terrain and think about what it resembles. What is "X" an example of? Charles Ragin calls it "casing" a subject.[142]

Another tactic is to examine several diverse terrains in order to perceive similarities. Can colonialism, federalism, and corporatism all be conceptualized as systems of "indirect rule"?[143]

A fourth tactic is to examine a familiar terrain with the aim of recognizing a new principle of organization. Linnaeus famously suggested that animals should be classified on the basis of their bone structures, a new principle of classification that turned out to be extraordinarily illuminating.[144] In the realm of social science, scholars have provided organizational schemes for political parties, bureaucracies, welfare states, and other social phenomena.

A fifth technique for loosening the theoretical wheels is to push a conventional idea to its logical extreme. That is, consider an explanation that seems to work for a particular event or in a particular context. (It may be your idea, or someone else's.) Now push that idea outward to other settings. Does it still work? What sort of adjustments are necessary to make it work? Or consider the logical ramifications of a theory – if it were fully implemented. What would the theory seem to require?

Theories are tested when they are pushed to their limits, when they are tried out in very different contexts. Root-Bernstein observes that this strategy leads, at the very least, to an investigation of the boundaries of an idea, a useful thing to know. Alternatively, it may help us to reformulate a theory in ways that allow it to travel more successful, i.e., to increase its breadth. It may even lead to a new theory that explains the whole empirical realm.[145]

In theorizing wildly, it is important to keep a list of all possible explanations that one has run across in the literature, or intuited. As part of this canvas, one might consider some of the more general models of human behavior as discussed in Chapter 5. Sometimes, these abstract models have applications to very specific problems that might not be immediately apparent. (How might the topic of romance be understood as an exchange? As an adaptation? As a product of diffusion?)

Once achieved, this list of possible explanations for phenomenon Y can then be rearranged and decomposed (perhaps some propositions are subsets of others). Recall that theoretical work often involves recombining extant explanations in new ways. Your list of potential explanations also comprises the set of rival hypotheses that you will be obliged to refute, mitigate, and/or control for (empirically) in your work. So it is important that it be as comprehensive as possible.

In order to figure out how to correctly model complex interrelationships it is often helpful to draw pictures. If one is sufficiently fluent in graphic design, this may be handled on a computer screen. For the rest of us, pencil and paper are probably the best expedients. Laying out ideas with boxes and arrows, or perhaps with Venn diagrams or decision trees, allows one to illustrate potential relationships in a more free-flowing way than is possible with prose or math. One can "think" abstractly on paper without falling prey to the constraints of words and numbers. It is also a highly synoptic format, allowing one to fit an entire argument onto a single sheet or white board.

Think Ahead

All elements of the research process are intimately connected. This means that there is no such thing as a good topic if that topic is not joined to a good theory and a workable research design. So, the choice of a topic turns out to be more involved than it first appears. Of course, all of the elements that make for a successful piece of research are unlikely to fall into place at once. And yet, one is obliged to wrestle with them at the very outset.

Recalling the elements of your topic – containing, let us say, a theory, a set of phenomena, and a possible research design – it is vital to maintain a degree of fluidity among all these parts until such time as you can convince yourself that you have achieved the best possible fit. Beware of premature closure. At the same time, to avoid endless cycling it may be helpful to identify that element of your topic that you feel most committed to, i.e., that which is likely to make the greatest contribution to scholarship. If this can be identified, it will provide an anchor in this process of continual readjustment.

Consider the initial decision of a topic as an investment in the future. As with any investment, the payoff depends upon lots of things falling into place. One can never anticipate all of the potential difficulties. But the more one can "game" this process, the better the chance of a payoff when the research is completed. And the better the chance that the research will be completed at all. (Really bad ideas are often difficult to bring to fruition; the more they advance, the more obstacles they encounter.)

Although the prospect may seem daunting, one is obliged to think forward even at the "just getting started" stage of research. Try to map out how your idea might work – what sort of theory will eventuate, what sort of research design, and so forth. If everything works out as anticipated, what will the completed project be like?

An obvious question to consider is what *results* a study is likely to generate. Regardless of the type of study undertaken there will presumably be some encounter with the empirical world, and hence some set of findings. Will the evidence necessary to test a theory, or generate a theory, be available? Will the main hypothesis be borne out?

Sometimes, a failure to reject the null hypothesis means that the researcher has very little to show for her research. Conventional wisdom has prevailed. Other times, the failure to prove a hypothesis can be enlightening. Sometimes, a topic is so new, or a research design so much more compelling than others that came before, that *any* finding is informative. This is ideal from the perspective of the scholar's investment of time and energy, as it cannot fail to pay off.

In any case, you should consider how your anticipated findings might be situated within the literature on a topic. How will it be perceived? What will be its value-added?

In test-driving your idea you should also keep a close eye on yourself. See if your oral presentation of the project changes as you explain it to others (e.g., your friends and classmates). At what point do you feel most confident, or most uncertain? When do you feel as if you are bull-shitting? These are important signals with respect to the strengths and weaknesses of your project. Indeed, the process of discussing your ideas – aside from any concrete feedback you receive – may force you to reconsider issues that were not initially apparent.

Most important, try to evaluate the feasibility of your project. Your work is probably subject to a hard deadline, so construct a realistic time-schedule with that deadline in mind. As you construct that schedule, be aware that research and writing generally demand more time than one imagines they will. Alternatively, you may identify a back-up plan – a shorter version of the project that can be implemented if the full-scale version turns out to be unrealistic.

CONCLUSIONS

Published work in the social sciences presents a misleading appearance of order and predictability. The author begins by outlining a general topic or research question, then states a general theory, and from then proceeds to the specific hypothesis that will be tested and her chosen research design. Finally, the evidence is presented and discussed, and concluding thoughts are offered.

This is nothing at all like the progress of most research, which is circuitous and unpredictable – hardly ever following a step-by-step walk down the ladder of abstraction. One reason for this is that knowledge in the social sciences is not neatly parceled into distinct research areas, each with specific and stable questions, theories, and methods. Instead, it is characterized by a high degree of open-endedness – in questions, theories, and methods.

There is no Archimedean point of entry to this maze. One might begin with a general topic, a research question, a key concept, a general theory, a specific hypothesis, a compelling anomaly, an event, a research venue (e.g., a site, archive, or dataset), a method of analysis, and so forth. Accordingly, some research is problem- or question-driven, some research is theory-driven, some research is method-driven, and other research is phenomenon-driven (motivated by the desire to understand a particular event or set of events). These are obviously quite different styles of research – even though, at the end of the day, each study must be held accountable to the same methodological criteria, as laid out in Parts I and II of the book.

There is no right or wrong place to start; all that matters is where you end up. And yet, where one ends up has a lot to do with where one starts out. Students are rightly wary of the consequences of choosing a bad topic – one that, let us say, promises few interesting surprises, has little theoretical or practical significance, or offers insufficient evidence to demonstrate a proposition about the world. No matter how well executed that research might be, little can be expected from it.

Because the selection of a good topic is difficult, careful deliberation is in order. In this arduous process, advice is welcome – from friends, family, teachers, advisors, experts in the field. Solicit all the feedback you can. But make sure that, at the end of the day, you are comfortable with the choice(s) you make.

KEY TERM

- Paradigm-cases

13 Data Gathering

Insofar as social science research rests on an empirical base it involves an encounter with **data**. Data may be qualitative or quantitative. It may be numerical, textual, visual, olfactory, auditory, or artifactual. It may be drawn from primary or secondary sources. It may be collected by the researcher or by someone else. "Data" is understood here in the broadest sense, including any sort of evidence that serves as the empirical basis for understanding and explanation.

In this chapter we lay out various methods of gathering data, a topic that is important for both producers and consumers of social science. Note that in order to judge the quality of a study you need to be familiar with the data-collection method that underlies the analysis.

Data-gathering methods may be classified broadly as *obtrusive* or *unobtrusive*. **Obtrusive methods** comprise standardized *surveys* as well as less structured interpersonal settings such as *interviews, focus groups,* and *ethnography*. **Unobtrusive** measures include those that are *surreptitious* and *ex post*. After outlining these techniques of data collection we discuss the problem of *data assessment*: how do we know that our data (or someone else's) is true?

Before launching into the chapter, a few caveats and clarifications are in order.

First, each section of the chapter is cumulative. For example, many of the ingredients of a good survey are also ingredients of a good interview, focus group, or ethnography. This explains why the section on surveys is somewhat longer than the later sections of the chapter. It also means that this chapter should probably be read from front to back rather than browsed in a selective fashion.

Second, each method will be treated as a stand-alone technique of data collection. However, readers should be aware that in the course of conducting a study it is common to combine several data-collection strategies. Where a multi-method approach is adopted, the strengths and weaknesses of each strategy should be understood within that context.

Third, *experiments* and *case studies* are regarded in this book as research designs rather than data-gathering techniques and are therefore discussed in Part II rather than in this chapter. (The distinction becomes clear when one considers that experiments and case studies may be implemented with a variety of data-gathering tools, as outlined here.[146]) Note also that strategies of gathering data might be understood as strategies of *measurement*, so the topics discussed here overlap those introduced in Chapter 3.

Fourth, any data-gathering effort must wrestle with fundamental tasks of all empirical analysis. Researchers must reflect upon (a) the basic *unit of analysis* (e.g., persons or countries), (b) the units that will be included in the *sample* and the size of the sample, (c) the *population* that the sample is drawn from, and (d) the extent to which the sample is likely to be *representative* of that population. These issues were presented in Chapter 4.

Finally, a note on terminology. People who gather data may be referred to as *ethnographers, facilitators, interviewers, investigators, researchers,* or *surveyors* – depending upon the context. People who provide data may be referred to as *coders, informants, interviewees, participants, raters, respondents,* or *subjects* – again, depending upon the context. Each of these terms has a somewhat different connotation. However, the distinction of importance for present purposes is between data *gatherers* and data *providers*. Terms that fall within each of these categories will be used interchangeably.

Standardized Surveys

A great number of methodological issues are sometimes grouped together under the rubric of **survey research**. However, many of these issues are not limited to standardized surveys, as they also apply to other styles of data gathering. Thus we deal with issues of sampling in Chapter 4, issues pertaining to scaling and indexing in Chapter 2, and issues pertaining to causal analysis in Part II. The following section is limited to the construction of a survey instrument – understood as a standardized questionnaire with limited response-options – and its implementation. (Open-ended questions are discussed below under the rubric of *Interviews*.)

There are many variations on the survey instrument. *Surveys* ...

- May be conducted in person, by phone, by mail, by email, or by website
- May be conducted by an interviewer, an automated voice, or self-administered (via hard copy or computer)
- May be administered in a public space (e.g., laboratory, street) or in a private space (e.g., the respondent's home)
- May involve members of the general public, a subset of the public, elites, or experts
- May focus on the attitudes and behavior of the respondent or on some objective feature of the world (*coding*)
- May or may not offer compensation
- May incorporate large or small samples
- May be of any length and duration
- May be implemented once (producing a *cross-section*), multiple times with the same respondents (a *panel*), or multiple times with different respondents drawn from the same population (a *pooled time-series*)

Each variation in survey design involves distinct challenges and opportunities, and may require special strategies of implementation or analysis. You should consider carefully the impact of different choices on (a) response rates (the likelihood of those contacted agreeing to participate in the survey), (b) completion rates (the percentage of respondents who successfully complete the survey), (c) sample representativeness (vis-à-vis the population of interest), (d) possible biases in responses, and (e) the time and cost involved in the implementation of a survey.

Medium, Location

A survey may be administered in person, by phone, by mail or email, or by website. The administrator may be a "live" surveyor, an automated voice, or a computer. The location may be a public place (e.g., a laboratory or street) or a private place (e.g., a respondent's home).

With the spread of computers and access to the Web it is now possible to administer many surveys online. Here, the surveyor may take advantage of online sites like Survey Monkey that allow the researcher to set up a survey instrument using existing templates and to collect responses in a convenient data format.

However, choices among these various options have important consequences. For example, implementing a survey by email or website effectively excludes those who don't have access to the Internet or who feel uncomfortable with the medium. It may, however, give the respondent a greater sense of anonymity and thus may prompt more honest responses than one would get in a person-to-person exchange (where an interviewer is administering the survey by phone or in person). Of course, the situation is probably reversed in societies where the Internet is routinely monitored; there, respondents may feel more comfortable talking directly to a researcher (whose bona fides they can judge) rather than to a machine.

Wherever a survey is administered "live" by an interviewer there is a possibility of **interviewer bias**. That is, responses may be influenced by the interviewer. A good deal of research has been conducted on this point. It has been shown, for example, that responses are often affected by the sex and race of the interviewer, or by the power relationship between interviewer and respondent.[147] Even subtle inflections of an interviewer's voice may serve as a cue to the respondent.[148] Issues such as these are often difficult to overcome, even if interviewers are well trained and attentive. (Neither the interviewer nor the respondent may be entirely aware of such biases.)

Another problem is **social desirability bias**. The presence of an interviewer may prompt the respondent to answer a question in a way that she or he feels is most appropriate and acceptable, even when it does not accord with her or his true preferences. This is a common problem with surveys that touch on issues of race, sexual behavior, corruption, and other sensitive topics. Of course, this sort of bias may also be present in a self-administered survey. However, it is apt to be more problematic when an interviewer is present – in person or at the other end of a phone line.

A self-administered survey (via hard copy or computer) eliminates interviewer bias and may reduce social desirability bias. However, this format requires more of the respondent. If respondents are illiterate they will be unable to participate. And if they are bored or annoyed by the questions they are likely to quit before completing, or pay little attention to their answers. Accordingly, response rates and completion rates tend to be lower for self-administered surveys than for comparable surveys administered person-to-person.

Respondents

Respondents for a survey may be drawn from the general public or from some subset of the public, e.g., a minority group, teenagers, or those who have tested HIV-positive. These sorts of respondents may be regarded as members of the *mass public*, i.e., lay respondents.

A rather different sort of respondent is a member of an *elite* group, e.g., a business leader, political leader, or leader in a profession. Elites tend to be much less accessible, which is to say that response rates and completion rates will be lower. Moreover, elites are unlikely to respond to monetary compensation (or will require a great deal of compensation). Obtaining an elite interview may therefore require a lot of work, and perhaps some special connections or some quid pro quo arrangement (something you can do for them). Typically, elites are more willing to engage in an open-ended conversation than in a standardized survey, as they may not consider the latter a good use of their scarce time. If they are willing to submit to a survey it may be necessary for the researcher to administer it in person or over the phone.

A third sort of respondent is an *expert* in some area. This sort of respondent qualifies for inclusion in a survey because of their knowledge or experience, not their position or demographic characteristics. A wide range of surveys are focused on experts. Here, the goal is usually to obtain specialized knowledge of some topic rather than the personal predilections of the respondent. For example, researchers wishing to judge the ideology of a political party or the quality of democracy in a country often call upon experts to code these features of a polity. Typically, these experts are trained in social science or have some professional position that qualifies them as experts in this area. This sort of coding is useful whenever (a) it is difficult to reduce a subject to objective indicators and (b) when members of the general public are not very knowledgeable about that subject. While surveys geared for experts can assume a higher level of knowledge about the subject, one should not lose sight of the fact that experts are people too. That is, they may be subject to the same problems of non-response, non-completion, and bias as members of the general public.

Compensation

In order to recruit respondents, and to minimize non-response and non-completion, it may be necessary to offer some compensation to those who agree to undertake a survey. Respondents may be paid directly for their work or may be offered the opportunity to win a prize. One option that is increasingly popular among survey researchers is to recruit respondents through *Mechanical Turk*, a website owned and maintained by Amazon. Here, one may find respondents willing to fill out surveys on a wide range of topics for a nominal sum.

Arguably, those who are paid for their work are more likely to take it seriously. However, one must also consider how it might affect the sort of people who agree to take the survey and the sort of answers they provide. Consider a survey that focuses on the respondent's willingness to donate blood. Suppose that one of the questions is about monetary compensation for blood donations. The answer to this question may be affected by the structure of the survey, in which the respondent has already agreed to sell his or her services for a price.

Introductory Statement

When contacting potential respondents, and/or at the start of a survey, several important issues must be covered. The potential respondent should be informed of . . .

- The topic of the survey. (This is a complicated issue, as you are under an obligation to inform the participant; at the same time, you don't want to reveal anything about the survey that might compromise the possibility of obtaining unbiased responses.)
- The method by which the respondent was selected.
- Requirements for participation, e.g., the time required, the format, and any special instructions.
- Compensation (if any).
- Sponsorship of the survey, i.e., the identity of the principal investigator (PI), the identity of the interviewer (if different from the PI), and the funding agency (if any).
- Use to which the data will be put.
- Whether survey results will be made public or otherwise made available to the respondent.
- Whether the respondent will be granted anonymity (no one associated with the survey knows his or her identity) or confidentiality (no one except members of the project team know his or her identity), and what measures will be taken to assure this.
- The voluntary nature of their participation. The respondent may refuse to answer any question and may exit the survey at any time.
- Specific Institutional Review Board (IRB) procedures that may apply, e.g., an explicit statement by the respondent that she or he is willing to undertake the survey.
- Researcher contact information (email, telephone, address), in case the respondent has further questions. The potential respondent should also be encouraged to ask questions about any of the foregoing, if something is unclear.

Some of these points are commonsensical. Others are informed by ethical imperatives, as discussed in Chapter 16.

Questionnaire

The content of a survey – including all text, pictures, or other media as presented to the respondent – will be referred to collectively as the **questionnaire**. The questionnaire may consist of several questions or several hundred questions. Accordingly, it may require just a few minutes or several days to complete. A longer survey will probably result in lower response and completion rates, and may mean that respondents pay less attention to the questions and their responses. However, some respondents are willing to bear with a lengthy survey, especially if administered in-person and/or accompanied by some sort of compensation. Surveys conducted in the developing world sometimes last several hours. Members of the mass public in rich countries, as well as elite respondents (everywhere), are usually less generous with their time.

The first few questions on a survey are usually designed to ease the respondent into the situation, to make them feel comfortable with the format, and to establish a rapport with the interviewer (if any). Sometimes, it is important to collect personal information about the respondent, e.g., age, sex, residence, occupation, and so forth. These are usually easy questions for the respondent to answer. However, these apparently bland factual questions are sometimes sensitive and may also serve to "prime" the respondent for what is to follow.

Priming (or framing) refers to a statement or question that affects later responses. Suppose, for example, that a respondent is asked about his/her age in an early question and then, later on, is asked about his/her feelings about the government's social security program. It is quite possible that the first question affects responses to the second question. This may be desirable; sometimes, a researcher wishes to prime certain topics. Or it may be undesirable. Either way, it is important to be aware of the way in which question-ordering affects the responses one receives. This may be tested systematically by reversing the ordering of questions (or removing questions) and administering each version of the survey to randomized treatment and control groups – a *survey experiment* (as discussed in Chapter 7).

If one wishes to neutralize the priming effects of question-ordering one can also randomize this feature of a survey, assuring that equal numbers of respondents receive a survey in which Question *A* precedes Question *B* and Question *B* precedes Question *A*. This solution, however, may interfere with a natural ordering of topics. If questions on a survey skip from topic to topic without any apparent logic, respondents may become confused.

Equally important is the way in which a question is posed. Consider the following statement intended to elicit a respondent's position on abortion: *Abortion is wrong*. It seems obvious that one will obtain different sorts of answers to this question depending on how individual respondents interpret it. One might ask: Does abortion mean in all cases or just for particular situations? Some might respond to "wrong" in terms of it being a moral question while others may see it as a legal question. We have given a stark example of this, but even slight differences in question wording (e.g., substituting "reproductive choice" for "abortion") may be sufficient to alter the number of people who support a women's right to abortion and thus may be claimed as political fodder for those who are fighting political battles on this issue. The answer may then be construed to indicate differing levels of support for abortion in the population.

Are some questions more correct than others? It is usually wise to steer clear of a question that seems to prejudge the correct response, i.e., a question that is framed in a "biased" manner. One probably would not pose a question about abortion by asking whether the respondent is for or against "killing babies." On the other hand, it may be revelatory to ask the question in this inflammatory way – so long as the results are not systematically misinterpreted. Consider that someone who is willing to defend abortion when the question is posed in such an extreme manner is probably a very strong supporter. If the goal of the survey is to gauge varying levels of support, a "biased" question such as this may be quite fruitful.

Note also that some topics like abortion are difficult to address in an unbiased fashion. Supporters and opponents of abortion are unlikely to agree on the proper wording of a survey question. When polls on a subject appear to conflict it is often because they are asking a question in different ways or have not provided enough clarity in the question or response options to attain a valid response from all respondents. A useful approach in this situation is to pose a series of statements or questions that offer a variety of opinions on a subject or a variety of ways of framing a subject. One may also preface these statements with "Some people say …" or "There is debate over the question of …" to indicate that the surveyor is not taking sides in the dispute. On the other hand, asking a range of questions on an issue will require a lot of space on the survey. Regardless, to avoid interpretation problems, it is important that the question is phrased so as not to lead respondents and that the question provides the full range of possible outcomes. The American National Elections Study wording of the abortion question attempts to do exactly that. Here they ask: "Which one of the opinions on this page best agrees with your view?" And they provide the following response choices:

1   By law, abortion should never be permitted.
2   The law should permit abortion only in case of rape, incest, or when the woman's life is in danger.
3   The law should permit abortion for reasons other than rape, incest, or danger to the woman's life, but only after the need for the abortion has been clearly established.
4   By law, a woman should always be able to obtain an abortion as a matter of personal choice.

If the goal of the researcher is to measure variation across a population – rather than a point estimate for the population at large – it may not be necessary to introduce multiple questions about the same topic. Consider the four questions on abortion listed above. Now imagine that there is a latent concept – degree of support for the right to abortion – that one is attempting to measure. If this latent concept underlies responses to all the questions then it ought to be manifested in answers to all of these questions. That is, those with strong support for the right to abortion will give the "pro-abortion" response regardless of how the question is posed; those strongly opposed to the right to abortion will give the "anti-abortion" response regardless of how the question is posed; and those who are ambivalent will give responses that lie in between the "pro" and "anti" positions. In this scenario, altering the question affects the level of support but not the *distribution* of support. (In regression analysis, the intercept changes but not the slope of the regression line. See Chapter 19.) In this manner, one may be able to ascertain variation in opinion across a population with a single question – so long as responses to that question allow for the expression of degrees of support, e.g., a Likert scale (introduced below). One may also combine questions about the same general topic into an index, as discussed in Chapter 3.

Constructing a good question requires keen intuition about how respondents are likely to interpret and respond to that question. It is vital that respondents interpret the meaning of the question in the same way. So the survey researcher must consider how a question might be interpreted by respondents, bearing in mind possible differences in education, age, culture, or other background factors. If respondents understand a key term (e.g., "abortion") differently, then one has a problem of non-equivalence. The same responses actually mean different things. Suppose some people understand abortion as any interruption of pregnancy prior to birth, while others understand it as an interruption prior to the first trimester. Here, people who say they oppose abortion may be opposing different sets of practices. Some may support the right of a woman to interrupt a pregnancy prior to the first trimester; others may not.

Insofar as survey questions attempt to delve into difficult and contested issues they are inevitably subject to problems of interpretation. It is the responsibility of the surveyor to minimize such ambiguities, without sacrificing the topic of interest. To this end, here are some helpful tips.

- State questions and answers in the simplest and most natural way possible.
- Questions (and accompanying explanations) should be no longer than they need to be.
- Avoid technical jargon (unless your respondents are experts). If you must include a technical term, provide a definition.
- Be wary of terms that can mean different things (e.g., "inflammable").
- Avoid double-negatives (e.g., "Do you oppose the abolition of taxes on cigarettes?").
- Do not combine several disparate elements in a single question (e.g., "Do you support democracy and the rule of law?").
- If you wish to employ an abstract concept (e.g., "liberalism"), also include some questions that probe into that concept in a specific context (e.g., "Do you favor increasing government support for education?").
- Use vignettes (short stories that illustrate a concept) whenever a concept may be unclear. However, be aware that vignettes necessarily introduce a lot of

background noise, which may affect responses in ways that diverge from the concept of interest.

- Adopt questions from other (reputable) surveys wherever possible – assuming they serve your goals and satisfy other requirements, as above. These questions have been vetted. Also, results obtained from your sample can be directly compared with those obtained from other surveys if the questions (and accompanying responses) are identical. (Make sure to acknowledge this borrowing, lest you be accused of plagiarism.)

Response-Categories

A standardized survey specifies a set of responses that are available to the respondent. These may reproduce any type of scale (see Chapter 3). The scale may be *nominal* – Yes/No. It may be *ordinal* (Strongly agree, Agree, Neither agree nor disagree, Disagree, Strongly disagree), a particular kind of ordinal scale known as a **Likert scale**. It may be *interval*, as in the "feeling thermometer" response which asks a respondent to register their agreement/disagreement on a scale of 0 to 100.

The interval scale is the most sensitive, and thus is generally most helpful in discerning small differences among respondents. However, an interval response is not always appropriate. One cannot ask someone to indicate whether they are male or female on a 100-point scale. Likewise, there are many circumstances in which ordinal-level categorical responses are more natural than interval-level responses. Arguably, it is easier for a respondent to understand a Likert scale than a feeling thermometer.[149] If the respondent does not understand what a "10" on a 100-point scale means, or if different respondents interpret it differently, a good deal of noise will be introduced into the survey instrument. So, sensitivity to fine differences is not always the most important consideration. Consider also that a set of questions may later be combined into a single *index*, using techniques discussed in Chapter 3.

Knowledge, Certainty, and Salience

A survey is free to inquire about anything the surveyor wishes (so long as it doesn't violate ethical norms). And many respondents will be happy to oblige the surveyor with an answer (perhaps because they believe that is what is required of them). But this does not mean that the respondent knows or cares much about that issue, or is very certain about his or her response. Thus, when we read that $X\%$ of Americans support NAFTA (North American Free Trade Agreement) we must process this fact with a grain of sodium chloride (salt).

There are ways of ascertaining the knowledge, certainty, and salience of an issue to the respondent. One can add questions of a factual nature intended to gauge a respondent's knowledge of an issue. (What does NAFTA stand for?) One can ask the respondent directly about his or her knowledge of a subject or its salience to him or her. One can offer a "Don't know" (DK) or "No opinion" option. One can ask a follow-up question about the respondent's confidence in their response.

Prior questions may also serve a *screening* function, i.e., only those who demonstrate knowledge of a subject are asked the next question. Alternatively, one may be interested in how knowledge or salience affects responses to a question, in which case the respondent would be required to answer both questions.

Note that including a DK option may dramatically change the results if the distribution of uncertain respondents across the response-categories is not uniform. Thus, if those who oppose NAFTA are strong in their opposition while those who claim to support NAFTA are not sure, many of the latter may opt for the DK option, thus altering the distribution of positive/negative responses.

Sensitive Subjects

In the context of survey research – where there is ordinarily no opportunity to gain the trust of respondents or to judge their responses in a contextual fashion – there are nonetheless ways of accessing sensitive subjects.

Perhaps the most important step is to guarantee the anonymity of the respondent by omitting their name from the survey. Unfortunately, in an electronic age it is hard to convince a skeptical respondent that his or her anonymity will be respected. Consider that whatever mode of contacting is employed – in person, mail, email, or Web – involves a potential sacrifice of anonymity. In some countries, spies may pose as surveyors, and respondents are not generally aware that academic "IRB" protocol (discussed in Chapter 16) imposes strict requirements on any research on human subjects.

One can also adopt an anonymous setting for the survey, which may be administered by mail or online. This may do more to reassure the respondent of his or her anonymity, even though in reality the respondent probably has greater assurance of anonymity in a public setting like a mall or park (so long as the respondent does not reveal his or her identity).

Another approach involves the construction of the questionnaire. One may frame sensitive subjects as questions about other people, e.g., "Do you think that other employers use race as a criterion for making hiring decisions?" The assumption here is that those engaged in activities that are denigrated by society (e.g., discrimination or corruption) will be inclined to see these activities as widespread, as this may assuage feelings of guilt or shame.

One may also enlist an experimental survey design in order to mask individual identities.[150] The **list experiment** begins by sorting respondents randomly into two groups, each of which is given a small set of questions to ponder. The questionnaires are identical except that the treatment group is given one additional question of a sensitive nature (e.g., pertaining to racism or corruption). Respondents are then asked to report the total number of questions that they agree (or disagree) with, but not their answers to any specific question. Since the treatment and control groups are assumed to be comparable in all respects except the one additional question asked of the treatment group, any differences in responses across the two groups (i.e., in percentage of "agree" answers) may be attributed to this question. The innovation of the method is to allow for accurate aggregate-level results while avoiding any possibility of linking an individual with a specific answer.[151]

Another experimental survey research technique varies the questions on a questionnaire in small ways so as to gauge the effect of a carefully chosen treatment. For example, in order to probe hidden racism Paul Sniderman and colleagues construct surveys that inquire about respondent views of government's responsibility to assist those in need. In one version of the **split-sample survey** the scenario involves an unemployed black worker, while in another version it involves an unemployed white worker. The scenarios (i.e., the questions) are identical, with the exception of the race of the worker, and so are the two groups (which have been randomly chosen). Thus, any differences in response across the two groups may be interpreted as a product of the treatment.[152]

Longitudinal Data

Most surveys are conducted once, producing a cross-section of those surveyed. However, longitudinal data may be generated from a one-shot survey by asking people about past events. For example, demographers may ask female respondents how many times they have given birth, whether any of these children died, and the approximate dates of these events. In this fashion, they may reconstruct a time-series of births and child mortality for each respondent (which can then be combined to construct fertility and mortality rates for a sampled population).

Of course, researchers must be wary of asking questions about the past that the respondent only dimly recalls. Indeed, studies have shown that many memories are false, or only vaguely rooted in reality. Selective memory may privilege events that are highly salient or that resonate with the image we currently have about ourselves and about the world.

Another approach is to survey the same people multiple times, e.g., twice (perhaps before and after a planned intervention), every day for several months, every month for a year, or every five years for several decades. This is known as a **panel design**.[153]

Surveys may also sample repeatedly from the same population (but not the same people) over a period of time. For example, the well-known National Election Study (NES) and General Social Survey (GSS) draw national samples of the American public every few years. This is generally referred to as a **pooled cross-section**.

Note that a panel design provides information on individual-level changes. One can tell who changed their attitudes or behavior and when, which may offer insight into why they did so. However, over time, the panel may become less representative of the population of interest. Consider a panel of citizens observed over several decades. Let us suppose that the panel was chosen randomly in 1980 (using one of the techniques of probability sampling reviewed in Chapter 4) so as to represent the American electorate, and that respondents are asked every several years about their views on various issues pertaining to racial equality. We can easily ascertain who is changing their views in this issue-area and when (approximately), and we can also track other features of these individuals (e.g., their education, income, and place of residence), which may provide clues about their changes (when contrasted to respondents whose views remained constant). However, over time the panel becomes less and less representative of the general population. (Young people are missing, for one thing.)

A pooled time-series, with observations taken at the same intervals (e.g., every several years), provides an accurate indicator of population-level changes. Each sample is representative, which means that the composition of the sample changes as the population changes. If we wish to know how the views of the American public at large are changing on issues pertaining to racial equality, this is a preferred source of information. But it is often difficult to piece together the reasons for changes over time; for that purpose, a panel design is more useful.

Summary

If you are developing your own survey you should be aware that a good survey takes a long time to develop. Think carefully about each of the issues raised in this section. If possible, conduct a **pilot test** prior to scaling up to the full sample. If you don't have time or money for a pilot test, ask your friends – or someone from your target population – to complete the survey and then get their feedback on it. Try to straighten out points of confusion. Gauge how long it takes to complete and decide whether this is a reasonable duration. See if other improvements can be introduced. And remember that once the full survey is initiated there is no opportunity for further revision.

When *interpreting* survey results (yours, or someone else's) all of the issues raised in this section bear consideration. By way of a summary, it may be helpful to consider the strengths and weaknesses of surveys as instruments for the measurement of attitudes and behaviors (whether of elites or mass publics).

Surveys are powerful instruments for measuring changes in opinion or behavior over time so long as the survey instrument remains constant over time (i.e., the questions themselves, the available responses, question-ordering, and any other feature that might affect responses to the question or the representativeness of the sample). We can tell when a population is changing its views on matters of racial equality, for example (though it is possible that some of those changes reflect changing perceptions of what is appropriate behavior rather than changes in gut-level attitudes and behavior).

Surveys are also powerful instruments for comparing the attitudes or behavior of different groups with respect to the same issue-area, for we can directly compare their responses to the same questions. The caveat is that they must understand the questions in the same way.

Surveys are less impressive as tools for summarizing opinion when a topic is not salient to the population that is being surveyed. Although respondents can render an opinion on virtually anything, if that is what they think they are expected to do, it is unclear what this opinion might mean and how it should be interpreted. Any survey of the mass public in the United States that focuses on NAFTA faces this problem. By contrast, a survey of the Mexican mass public on the same subject may be more meaningful, as it is a high-salience issue in Mexico.

Surveys are also problematic for summarizing a population's view of very complex issues like racial equality. Even if a survey (or, better yet, a series of surveys) asks a battery of questions, exploring different facets of the subject and using both abstract concepts as well as specific scenarios, it will be difficult to summarize these findings in a concise manner. We are accustomed to reading survey reports that $X\%$ of the public supports racial equality, or abortion rights, or democracy. But it is exceedingly unclear what this means, given that slight changes in the wording of the question or the number of response-categories may fundamentally alter the point estimate. The reason we face this problem is fundamentally conceptual rather than empirical. Since we have no agreement on what racial equality, abortion rights, or democracy means we are certainly not going to be able to measure these concepts with great precision.

One final weakness deserves emphasis. Because they are standardized in question and response-type, surveys can inform only on issues that are incorporated into the questionnaire. The survey researcher must first identify a problem, craft a questionnaire to explore that problem, a sample to test it, and so forth. But the surveyor will hardly ever learn of a new problem that she or he hadn't anticipated in the first place. As Donald Rumsfeld might say, surveys can tell you what you know and what you don't know, but they cannot tell you what you don't know you don't know. This is because there is (generally) no place on a standardized survey for respondents to speak freely. And this, in turn, provides a nice segue to techniques of data gathering that are more exploratory in nature.

Less Structured Interpersonal Settings

We began this chapter with surveys because they are the most structured method of data collection (from persons) – and, hence, the easiest to discuss from a methodological perspective. Other methods of gathering data are less structured – a feature that may be regarded as a strength as well as a weakness.

The lack of structure also means that these methods are more difficult to generalize about. An interview, focus group, or ethnography may be successfully conducted in many ways, and different techniques may make sense in different settings. It is difficult to establish a set of instructions for such varied contexts beyond the obvious admonition to "be sensitive to local context."

Another important difference between surveys and less structured interpersonal data-gathering techniques is that the former generally employ large samples – often a probability sample drawn from a known population – and the latter generally employ small samples, which are rarely drawn in a purely random fashion from a known population. The issue of sampling is discussed in Chapter 4 and will not be returned to, except to note that the sorts of generalizations one can make when a sample is small and perhaps unrepresentative are limited – or must be hedged with caveats. Of course, one must also bear in mind that large samples and random sampling are not always possible when data gathering depends upon less structured interpersonal settings.

A final difference between the survey and less structured modes of data collection is that the former generates quantitative ("dataset") observations while the latter is apt to generate qualitative observations that do not fit neatly into a matrix format (these are sometimes referred to as "causal-process observations").

Of course, qualitative data can sometimes be standardized so as to conform to a rectangular dataset. Indeed, a lot of data that we think of as quantitative is a product of qualitative judgments. For example, an index of democracy such as those produced by Freedom House and Polity rests on judgments about how each country fits into a coding template. An index of ideology may rest on instances of natural speech, as recorded by newspapers or parliamentary records. Qualitative can become quantitative, as discussed in Chapter 16. In this section, however, we are concerned with the initial qualitative format of the data, which usually takes the form of natural language or visual images and is recorded by the researcher.

Despite their different formats, the reader should be aware that many of the points raised about surveys also pertain to these less structured settings. For example, any time data is obtained from human subjects the battery of topics addressed in the *Introductory statement* should be covered. Likewise, other considerations for surveys may also apply to interviews, focus groups, and ethnography. This section of the chapter thus builds on the previous sections.

Interviews

A survey **interview** involves a standardized questionnaire and a limited set of possible responses. Other sorts of interviews are less structured. That is, there may be a standard set of questions that one wishes to pose to all respondents; however, there are no pre-set response-categories, and respondents are urged to respond in a way that makes sense to them (so long as it addresses the question). There may be a "yes" or "no" answer, but there is also room to explain – if necessary, at some length – one's choice. It is this explanation, as much as the simple response, that is of greatest interest. This sort of exchange may be referred to as a *qualitative, unstructured, conversational, in-depth,* or *open-ended* interview, as distinguished from a survey interview.

The best interviewers are probably journalists; this is, after all, what they do for a living. So, as you study the art of interviewing think of yourself in the role of an investigative journalist. The only difference – and it is an important one – is that the social scientist is not interested in a possible headline in tomorrow's paper or in the misdeeds of individual but rather in piecing together a larger story and an explanatory theory. (This should help to put your informant at ease.)

In seeking out respondents, you may want to begin with those who are closest at hand. That will allow you to gather background information that could prove useful in later interviews. It will also allow you to hone your skills as an interviewer and revise your *interview schedule* or *protocol* (the set of questions or topics that you wish to raise). Interviews are often difficult to set up and may be even more difficult to repeat. You may get only one shot to interview a big shot, so make sure you've done some preliminary interviews prior to entering that situation.

In constructing a sample of respondents, the researcher may be less concerned with representativeness (since the sample is unlikely to be sufficiently large to generate a precise estimate of population characteristics) than with other characteristics. For example, if the focus of the research is a particular event the researcher may want to locate those who are (or were) most directly involved in that event. For those focused on inter-state conflicts, the most useful respondents are usually those who are (or were) present when crucial decisions were made. As first-hand observers, they possess critical knowledge. Another sort of knowledge is possessed by those who experience violence directly, e.g., survivors of genocide. They, too, are first-hand witnesses to history, though it is history "from below" rather than history "from above."

Typically, the researcher will be looking for the respondent's sense of an entire situation or an entire community, not simply his or her own story or perspective. A key informant may prove especially useful insofar as that person has intimate knowledge of a community or a topic, is willing to share that knowledge, and has credibility as a source (a matter addressed below).

> Many research projects have been 'made' by ... that rare, reflective inside informant who seems to know just about everything ... and has thought about it and reflected on it ... They are often marginal to the setting or scene being studied and are often seen by others ... as 'lay intellectuals,' thinkers, eggheads, or know-it-alls.[154]

One must be wary of relying too heavily on any single informant, or a group of informants who share a single perspective or set of interests. But the point remains: not all informants are equal. Some will reveal things, or a breadth of detail, that others are not privy to or are not reflective enough to recognize.

Triangulation is the key to successful investigative journalism, as it is to historical investigations and detective work. When facts are uncertain, try asking around. Robert Wade reports the following experience when investigating corruption in irrigation systems among several dozen south Indian villages.

> Only gradually, from conversations with dozens of engineers, government officials from other departments and farmers did it become apparent that a 'system' was at work, which probably had an important impact on how canals are operated and maintained. In particular, once some degree of trust was established, farmers often volunteered information about how much they had to pay the Irrigation Department; and while one would discount their figures in one, two or three instances, the regularity in farmers' statements across many villages did suggest that something

more than wild exaggeration or generalisation was involved ... This led to cautious, always informal enquiries of officers in other departments and of irrigation staff themselves, as part of wider conversations about the sorts of difficulties they saw themselves facing in doing their jobs well. These conversations, it should be noted, were with irrigation staff from outside the area of detailed fieldwork as well as with many serving within it, and covered the way 'the department' and 'the government' worked in the state as a whole, as well as in the specific district. Some of the engineers were thoroughly disgruntled at the situation they were caught in, and since disgruntled people tend to exaggerate the reasons for their discontent, one had to be cautious about accepting details from any one person at face value. Again, as with farmers, it is the regularities in the individual comments and incidents, and the consistency in the orders of magnitude (as between, for example, what a district Collector told me a Superintending Engineer had told him he had had to pay to get a one-year extension, and what an Assistant Engineer in one Division – in another district from the first case – said in strictest confidence his Executive Engineer had had to pay to get the transfer) that gives confidence in the correctness of the broad picture.[155]

A sample of interviews should include those who are likely to have different factual knowledge and different viewpoints on a topic. If the topic is political, the sample should include those of varying political persuasions. If the topic includes a set of identifiable stakeholders, make sure to interview those with varying stakes in the outcome. If the topic is more general, make sure to include those who occupy varying positions within that community, organization, or network – the high and the low, the nodes and the spokes. In this fashion, and taking account of the proportion of these informants in the general population, one may construct a rough sense of how "representative" one's sample might be.

Interviews may be formal affairs, where an appointment is secured, a designated time is allocated, and a formal setting is employed (e.g., an office). Alternatively, interviews may occur on the fly and in a serendipitous fashion, e.g., when a researcher encounters a valued informant in an elevator or at a night club.

The interviewer may present him- or herself in a professional manner. This effect is enhanced by a business suit, a dignified comportment, and a formal style of address. (In some languages, formal and informal styles of address are marked by different verbs.) It typically commences with a formal handshake and the distribution of business cards. Alternatively, the interviewer may adopt a more personal approach, dropping formalities, talking "person to person," and emphasizing similarities between his or her life experience and the informant's.

Each approach has costs and benefits. The benefit of professionalism is that one may be more likely to receive a "serious" response, one that is thoughtful and considered. One is also better able to retain a dispassionate view of the subject at hand, thus retaining objectivity and not overly influencing the informant's responses.

The cost is that the informant may be more guarded, less forthcoming. Likewise, the benefit of an informal approach to interviewing is the possibility of getting beneath the surface, i.e., to a piece of information or an emotion that the informant normally would not show (at least not to an outsider). Of course, one should be careful about lending too much importance to chance utterances, especially if the informant is inebriated.

One solution to this dilemma is to pursue both approaches, seeing what works in a given context and whether the stories that one obtains converge or diverge. You may conduct the formal interview in a professional manner and then repair to a local bar or café, where you can continue the conversation in a more informal fashion.

The relative power and status of interviewer and respondent are important matters to consider. If the respondent has higher status it may be important for the interviewer to adopt formal dress and demeanor in order to gain respect. The interviewer needs to emphasize that, despite our different positions, "We are both professionals." If the respondent occupies a lower status, it may be important for the interviewer to adopt a demeanor that is informal and sympathetic, not forbidding. The implicit message is, "We are both regular people." Choices in dress and comportment thus serve as tools to level the playing field, establishing the possibility of trust and reciprocity between interviewer and respondent.

Bear in mind that the interviewer/interviewee relationship depends on many factors that the interviewer can scarcely control. In addition to social status, it depends on gender roles. It depends on the extent to which the interviewer occupies an "outsider" or "insider" position. And so forth. Background factors such as these are likely to establish parameters of expected and acceptable behavior on the part of the interviewer. Trespassing across these boundaries may involve risk and is likely to attract attention away from the interview itself, so it is not something to be trifled with. Equally important, it is likely to affect the sort of answers that you get and the degree of frankness and cooperation you receive. "Interviewer effects" are likely to be more intense than in a standardized survey since so much depends upon interpersonal dynamics between interviewer and interviewee.

If social boundaries prove too confining it may be wise to enlist a confederate with the desired social characteristics who can conduct the interview. In some cases, this will be required even to gain access to an informant. For example, in some Muslim societies it would be considered extremely inappropriate for a male to ask questions of a female.

A critical decision is whether to record the proceedings – generally with audio but conceivably with video as well. Technologically, this is as easy as placing your smartphone on the table in front of you (and making sure to meet in a quiet place without a lot of background noise). It offers the advantage of preserving a verbatim recording, relieving you of the necessity of taking notes, and allowing (for you) a more natural, conversational style. A verbatim recording may come in handy at some later date if the informant disputes what she or he has said or there is a question of how to interpret a passage.

On the other hand, your informant must approve of a live recording. Equally important, she or he must feel comfortable talking in front of a microphone. Most people, even if they are accustomed to speaking before a crowd, will choose their words more carefully if a live recording is being made. They may be less likely to share intimate thoughts, criticize others, or give out potentially damaging information. In short, the interview is likely to elicit less information, especially if the subject is a sensitive one.

Before beginning an interview, make sure you have reviewed any relevant background information. Go into the interview knowing as much as you can learn about the person you are interviewing and the topic at hand so that you don't waste the informant's time (and yours) with background facts that could have been gathered from the Web. You may wish to bring some notes if you don't have these background facts at the top of your head.

You should also have (in your mind or in an accessible format) a list of questions or topics that you want the informant to address. Think about the natural order of presentation and the direction the conversation might take. Generally, it makes sense to begin with easier questions of a factual nature and then to proceed to those issues that are either more sensitive or more complicated.

In order to establish rapport, one is well advised to start an interview with some friendly banter – whatever you think will make the informant feel at ease. Wait until you think the informant is ready to begin. Then proceed to discuss the issues listed in the *Introductory Statement* (above).

It is especially important to clarify for the informant why you are interested in interviewing him or her (taking up a considerable amount of their precious time) and why the topic of your research matters. This satisfies curiosity and allays suspicion. It also serves to establish reciprocity – the basis of trust. If the informant is convinced of the importance of your research and your seriousness as a researcher, she or he may feel an obligation to assist and be more likely to trust your professional integrity (e.g., to protect the informant's identity and not to quote out of context). Likewise, the informant will feel that she or he is participating in a venture that may have some impact on the world – in addition to contributing to someone's CV or helping them complete a class assignment. Instead of the informant helping the researcher (a one-way avenue), both of you can be engaged in a project, e.g., helping to better understand a subject of mutual concern such as democracy or environmental degradation. This is the relationship of reciprocity that you wish to establish.

Of course, you don't want to reveal too much about the nature of your research, as this may prejudice your informant's responses. If you tell the informant that you are investigating pollution caused by a power plant, you cannot follow this up with a question about whether the power plant has produced a lot of contaminants.

The issue of confidentiality must be treated with care. It is always preferable to cite a source by name rather than as Informant #32. However, people are often less inclined to speak for the record than off the record, for obvious and understandable reasons. If an informant is unwilling to be associated with specific statements you may ask permission to include his or her name among a set of informants, listed at some point in your study. If the list is long, and includes those who occupy similar positions (and thus can be expected to have a similar knowledge base), it will be difficult for anyone to link up a name with a specific statement. Of course, you will need to be careful about how you write the narrative; specific details may give away the identity of the informant. Another approach is to agree to go "on record" with some portion of the interview and "off record" with other portions.

Once these preliminaries have been completed, you will need to set an appropriate pace for the interview. This depends upon your (and your informant's) time-constraints and on the topic you wish to address. Given the opportunity, some people will talk for hours on any given subject. This can be a blessing or a curse. If there is a specific topic that you wish to see addressed, and time is limited, you should make this clear at the outset. Don't let the informant waste your interview hour regaling you with stories of his or her college days. Some people will not respond to subtle hints and will need to be interrupted.

On the other hand, if time is plentiful and you want the informant to free-associate, then let the conversation wander. The benefit of an open-ended interview format is in allowing the conversation to flow, so don't try to impose too much order on the proceedings. Doing so may discourage the informant from speaking frankly, and will restrict your opportunity to discover things that lie outside the range of your interview schedule.

An open-ended interview is ostensibly a conversation, so protocol normal to a conversation applies. Make sure you are responsive to the speaker, nodding your head, uttering brief replies ("oh really?"), and showing your appreciation in other ways. Restate key points from time to time so as to confirm that you've correctly understood; this also serves to maintain focus and to show interest. Express ignorance or confusion if you wish to elicit an explicit articulation of a key point. Encourage elaboration where more detail is required.

Signpost clearly when you wish to transition to another topic so that the respondent doesn't feel jerked around like a dog on a short leash. Where appropriate, reveal information about yourself. This should serve to build rapport but should not exert pressure on your respondent to suppress his or her views.[156]

Make clear to the respondent that there is no "correct" or expected answer, perhaps by pointing out that the issue has aroused controversy, with many respectable people supporting each position. The respondent should feel comfortable to express his or her own perspective. Likewise, the respondent should not feel that she or he is expected to know the answers to all questions posed by the interviewer.

As the conversation proceeds, probe for signs that the respondent is uncomfortable, or may be holding out or equivocating on a subject. This does not mean that you should necessarily press forward on these subjects; ethical constraints may require that you respect an informant's privacy. However, if the informant occupies an elite position, and the subject of your query is directly related to official duties in that position, it may be appropriate to adopt a prosecutorial approach. In any case, pay close attention to the informant's facial expressions, gestures, and tone of voice. See if you can "hear between the lines." Likewise, if parts of a person's narrative don't hold together, or don't square with what you have heard or read from other sources, you should be able to call attention to this in a friendly manner.

In some respects, the qualitative interview is poorly suited to deal with sensitive subjects, as there is no pretense of anonymity. On the other hand, there is an opportunity to build trust between interviewer and respondent and this may serve to reassure the latter that confidentiality will be maintained. It may also make the respondent more comfortable in revealing sensitive information. Likewise, the interviewer has an opportunity to judge the veracity of the respondent, to fill in information that is hinted at but not explicitly formulated. Needless to say, these options are not available to survey researchers.

As the interview proceeds, try to assess how credible your informant is – or, more specifically, on which topics she or he might be authoritative and on which she or he might be biased or uninformed. This judgment should rest on everything you know about the informant (position, age, training, . . .), on everything you have learned from other sources about the topic, and on your own intuition. You might want to take notes on these matters so that you don't forget, as the credibility of sources is one factor that may incline you to weight one version of reality over another as you construct your own narrative of events.

When completing an interview, make sure to thank the informant for their time and ask whether it might be permissible to contact them for a follow-up interview or simply to straighten out some aspect of the interview that you, in retrospect, find confusing. You may also wish to ask about other potential subjects whom you might contact for further information.

Gratitude is obligatory, as the respondent has just spent a good deal of time with you and may have related some difficult material. Make sure that your last word or gesture is a positive one and that you don't give the respondent the impression that they have been exploited for the purpose of advancing your research.

Focus Groups

A **focus group** comprises a set of respondents who are brought together to discuss an issue. Rather than a dyad – interviewer and respondent – there are a handful of people who interact with one another, with cues from the focus group leader, the facilitator.

As in a one-on-one interview, there is a schedule of questions the facilitator asks the group to reflect upon. However, there is more latitude for free-flowing conversation than there would be with just two people in the room. Each participant reacts to what others have to say, and the discussion is more likely to move off in unpredictable directions.

In a focus group the role of the facilitator is minimized, at least on the surface. He or she is just one of several in the group, occupying a less obtrusive position than he or she would in a one-on-one encounter. The hope is that participants are more conscious of each other than of the facilitator. In this way, interviewer effects – e.g., affirmation bias – may be mitigated.

Another goal of the focus group is to access thoughts and emotions that might not come to light in the dry, professional atmosphere of a survey or interview. A focus group should make a subject come alive, eliciting responses that reach beneath the surface. Granted, with some subjects people are more likely to talk openly in the confidential environment of a one-on-one interview. However, with other subjects the group may provide a degree of anonymity that is essential for free-flowing conversation. Participants can blend in with the crowd.

The size of a focus group varies, though six to ten participants is a typical number. Beyond that number, the discussion format is apt to become unwieldy and the facilitator will have to play a more active role in keeping order and directing the flow of discussion. Likewise, participants may feel self-conscious since they are speaking in front of a large group. In a smaller group (say three to four), the format is also more likely to be dominated by the facilitator. The ideal size of a focus group is probably the size at which participants feel most comfortable and in which discussion can sustain itself without frequent cues from the leader. Naturally, the leader will need to intervene if the discussion takes a dilatory turn (away from the chosen topic).

More important than the size of a group is its composition. Typically, the objective is to bring together persons with shared experiences or perspectives, people who are similar to each other in relevant respects. (Ideally, they do not know each other, though sometimes this cannot be avoided.) If one were studying ideology, one would look for people who share a similar ideology. If one were studying academics, one would bring together people in the same discipline. For many subjects, it makes sense to select a group with similar demographic characteristics – age, social class, ethnicity, gender, and so forth. The more homogeneous the group, the more likely it is that participants will trust each other and feel comfortable speaking freely with each other. Likewise, they may feel comfortable articulating thoughts that would be unacceptable, or incomprehensible, in a more heterogeneous setting.

A core assumption of the focus group methodology is that opinions are formed in interaction with others – particularly, those within one's immediate social group (people like oneself). This is why a survey or interview may not get at the truth of the matter – because the respondent does not know the truth (i.e., his or her truth) until he or she has discussed the matter with those in his or her reference group.

However resonant a particular focus group experience might be, it is best not to rely too heavily on a single session. Bear in mind that the direction of discussion may be influenced by a particularly voluble or persuasive participant in the group. Likewise, the views of one group may be idiosyncratic, even if members are drawn from a seemingly homogeneous population. Thus, it is best to iterate the process several times, observing similarities and differences across the sessions.

Even if one assembles multiple focus groups, one should be cautious about drawing inferences about a larger population. First, it is important to appreciate that the number of participants in a set of focus groups is not the same as the number of participants in a survey. Because the former are not isolated from each other, the expression of their views cannot be considered independent. And because they are not independent, the true "N" (sample size) is considerably less than the number of people who participated. Second, since the setting is not controlled by the facilitator, each focus group is a little different. Specifically, the stimulus – that which participants are responding to – is inconsistent, and responses are correspondingly difficult to summarize. This lack of standardization inhibits one's ability to generalize. Finally, because participation in a focus group is a time-consuming and demanding exercise (by comparison with a short survey, let us say), and because it tends to draw on smaller and highly homogeneous (but perhaps hard to define) populations, it may be difficult to draw participants randomly from a known population (or the random selection procedure may be marred by very high non-response). Without a random sample, generalization to a population is problematic, as discussed in Chapter 4.

However, the goal of a focus group is usually more exploratory (hypothesis-generating) than confirmatory (hypothesis-testing). For example, several decades ago a group of researchers conducted focus groups in the United States and the United Kingdom in order to explore citizens' perceptions of citizenship. They discovered, among other things, that discussion within the American focus groups often centered on civil rights (freedom of speech, religion, movement). By contrast, discussion in British groups often emphasized social (economic) rights. This corroborates standard narratives about American and British political cultures. Noting the shortcomings of focus groups as a tool for generalizing across large populations, the authors regard the exercise as a useful first step in a larger empirical study.[157]

Once a key hypothesis has been identified it may be possible to test it in a more systematic fashion with a survey, an experiment, or with unobtrusive data. Sometimes, the main purpose of the focus group is to develop a survey instrument, i.e., to understand how best to frame a set of questions on a standardized survey. Sometimes, the purpose is to develop a marketing strategy for a product or a candidate. Sometimes, the purpose is to delve into deep-seated norms and values that might not be apparent from surveys or interviews. There are lots of uses for focus groups, both in the world of commerce and in the academic and policy worlds.

Ethnography

Ethnographic research – aka **participant observation** – may be understood as an extension of interviewing and focus grouping, including aspects of both. As such, much of what we have said in previous sections applies here as well.

However, interviews are limited to one or two respondents and focus groups are limited to a small group. Both techniques are circumscribed, having a pre-set period of time and a schedule of questions to address. The roles of researcher and informant are clearly delineated.

By contrast, ethnography is immersive. The researcher goes to a site – perhaps living there for a period of time and in any case observing and engaging in activities similar to those of the subjects under investigation. The time-period is indistinct; the location is "local" (wherever that happens to be). The delineation between researcher and subject is blurred, for the researcher functions as both participant and observer in the context she or he wishes to understand.

As such, ethnographic research is less structured. Naturally, a particular ethnographic context may be very structured, and most are. But the structure stems from whatever rules and norms apply in that setting. If the researcher is studying a construction site and serves as a construction worker in order to gather information, his or her time will be rigidly monitored according to the responsibilities of the job. But there is nothing in the method itself that mandates a particular structure. The mandate is to work, to hang out, to blend in, to "go native" – whatever that may mean in the chosen context.

It follows that there is no technical manual laying out rules for how to succeed as an ethnographer. Nonetheless, certain challenges are ubiquitous and some vague rules of thumb for dealing with these challenges may be adduced. That said, one can probably learn more by absorbing stories "from the field" than from reading a list of do's and don'ts. So, if ethnography is on your agenda, spend some time browsing through the list of suggested readings posted online with other materials for this book. And talk to people with experience in the setting you wish to explore. They can probably tell you more that is useful than a general textbook can hope to relate.

We have already quoted the folk wisdom that the task of a good ethnography is to render the strange familiar and the familiar strange. Classically, the topic of an ethnography is a setting that is exotic (to the anticipated readers of the ethnography). Anthropologists study naked tribes-people of the sort one is accustomed to see featured on the cover of *National Geographic*. Sociologists study poor and immigrant communities and distinct subcultures within our society. This is most people's image of ethnography, and it illustrates something important about the enterprise. After all, those of us who inhabit the educated middle classes of the West need to understand other cultures around the world, if for no other reason than the fact that our actions vitally affect those who are different from us. Presumably, the field visits of anthropologists and sociologists also serve to inform other cultures of *our* way of life, and thus open a two-way avenue of cross-cultural communication.

A second sort of ethnography makes the familiar strange. That is, it focuses on a subject that is common enough (in our life-world), and which we think we understand. But it illuminates some aspect of that subject that surprises us. Into this category one might place Richard Fenno's work on members of the US Congress, Robin Leidner's study of fast food restaurants, and Amy Best's study of American teens (cited in the References).

Once one has chosen a research question and a site of investigation, the researcher must gain access to that site. Successful ethnographic work depends upon entry into the community under study – i.e., being treated as an insider (if not entirely as an equal). If people don't accept you, they won't trust you with their secrets. (This is also somewhat true of interviewing. But it is especially true for work of an ethnographic character.)

Gaining insider status does not necessarily mean that the researcher is "one of them." After all, your role as a researcher and your (presumably temporary) status in the community probably sets you apart from the community you are studying. In addition, there may be differences of sex, class, education, language, religion, and so forth. But you must be considered enough of an insider so that informants can speak freely, without censoring their language.

Gaining this status is the first task of an ethnographer. It may be attained by an introduction from an insider. For example, Daniel Posner began his fieldwork with the Chewa and Tumbuka peoples, who inhabit the border area between Zambia and Malawi, by requesting permission from local chiefs. Without such permission, many villagers might have been reluctant to participate in the study.[158] If you have connections, even distant ones, you may wish to exploit them to gain entry to your community of interest.

Insider status may sometimes be attained by signing up through some formal process as a member of a firm, a group, or an organization. It may be attained by hanging out in places where your subjects pass time, and doing what they do.

Sometimes, gaining entrée to a group happens by serendipity. In one of the most celebrated (and entertaining) accounts of ethnographic work, Clifford Geertz relates how he came upon a Balinese cockfight as it was raided by police (cockfighting being illegal in Indonesia). Fleeing from the authorities, he and his wife were sheltered by some villagers, thereby gaining their trust (and occasioning some degree of good-humored ribbing).[159]

Whatever the method of entrée it will probably take some time before you are trusted. Becoming part of a corporate group is a complex process. On the one hand, you probably should avoid becoming too closely allied with a particular faction, as it will impede your access to (or bias your encounters with) other factions. Likewise, try to avoid taking strong positions on matters that members of the group care about.

On the other hand, if the group is factionalized, and perhaps in a hierarchical fashion, participating in that group may require identifying with one of the factions. And your official duties (if any) may also require it. You cannot be a bricklayer and a plumber on a construction site. You cannot be a lawyer and a secretary in a law firm. You cannot be a Crip and a Blood.

Collecting data at an ethnographic site should be accomplished in as unobtrusive a fashion as possible, lest it mark you as an outsider and impede the natural flow of conversation. You may be limited to taking notes at the end of the day. But each setting is different. And in some settings – e.g., a law office – there may be nothing at all unusual about recording an interview or typing on a laptop.

In any case, keeping accurate and detailed field notes is an essential part of the ethnographic exercise. These should include both the specifics of what you observe and learn from conversation, and also more general observations that seem to explain or tie together the threads of people's lives and understandings. This includes causal understandings of a situation.

Determining how long your fieldwork at a given site should last is a delicate question. Evidently, you want to have obtained as much insight into your research question as possible before leaving. Specifically, you want to fully exploit your informants' knowledge and experience. And you want to have fully plumbed the diversity of this knowledge and experience, contacting all members of the community who might provide new information or a new perspective on your subject.

A clue to this point of completion is redundancy. At a certain point in your fieldwork you will probably feel that you are no longer surprised by what you see and hear. Things that were once strange have become familiar. You can predict what informants are going to say on various subjects. And you have fully gained the trust of your informants, so that you are pretty sure they are revealing all that they know. This is the point at which further ethnographic research on this site is probably redundant. Of course, it may be necessary to return at some later date, or to re-initiate contact with key informants. Memories may fade, facts on the ground may change, and new ideas may germinate. Keep your links to the community strong.

If you have informants with a taste for social science – or for your particular topic – it is a good idea to get their feedback on what you have written while it is still in draft form. (The exception would be situations in which your study may be deemed offensive to some members in the community, or when you might face strong pressure to change elements of the narrative to suit particular individuals.)

Unobtrusive Measures

A final category of data is gathered in an **unobtrusive** manner, i.e., those whose attitudes or behavior are being observed are not aware of the fact or are not aware of the scholarly purpose to which it is being put. This may also be referred to as *non-reactive data* collection since the subject has no opportunity to react to (or be influenced by) the data-collection process.

A chief advantage of this mode of data collection is the avoidance of one sort of researcher effect, i.e., bias introduced by contact with the researcher. We have discussed the problem of social desirability bias, in which subjects answer questions in a way that they think the researcher will approve or in a way that they feel is appropriate, thus disguising their true beliefs or behavior. We have also discussed the problem that researchers may consciously or unconsciously influence the subjects of their research. Finally, we should mention the "Hawthorne effect" (see Chapter 6), that the mere fact of being studied may affect the way in which a subject behaves. These biases may result from any interpersonal method of data collection, i.e., from surveys, interviews, focus groups, or ethnography.

Unobtrusive data is free of these sorts of biases and on this account may be described as more objective than data collected by obtrusive techniques. However, it is not immune from other forms of researcher bias. Arguably, the most important form of bias arises from the selective use of data, i.e., when a researcher focuses on data that conforms to his or her hypothesis and ignores data that does not. Likewise, the researcher must interpret the *meaning* of chosen measures, which is rarely apparent. It is one thing to count up instances of a phenomenon and quite another to interpret it.

Finally, bias may be introduced by the original method of data collection or storage, whatever that may be. Recall that in order to reach the researcher the activity of interest must be generated and preserved in some fashion. Whatever persons and institutions are in charge of the collection and preservation of this data necessarily impose their own goals and purposes, which presumably affects the kind of data that is collected. Original data collectors are not immune to bias or sloppiness. All of these factors must be carefully considered as one attempts to judge the veracity and representativeness of data gathered by others. So it is not the case that unobtrusive measures can be considered more objective than obtrusive measures, though they are subject to somewhat different biases.

What, then, does "unobtrusive" data consist of? The category is residual, including all data-gathering techniques in which subjects are unaware of their status as subjects. This is a large category, and no one can pretend to offer a comprehensive accounting of it. Nonetheless, all data gathered without the knowledge of participants can be classified as **surreptitious** or **ex post**.

Surreptitious Measures

An ethnographic style of research normally involves a direct – obtrusive – encounter between researcher and the subjects she or he is studying. However, it is sometimes possible to study behavior without direct engagement.

One might observe activity taking place in a public space – a park, bus station, café, or nightclub – without participating in that activity. Alternatively, one might talk to people but without revealing one's purpose and while maintaining a low profile. Accordingly, the researcher's identity remains obscured and subjects are presumably unaffected (or less affected) by the researcher's presence. (Ethical considerations occasioned by surreptitious observation are discussed in Chapter 16.) For example, Tim Pachirat penetrated the "distant and concealed" world of the industrialized slaughterhouse, working undercover for nearly six months in order to provide a first-hand account of the kill floor from the perspective of those who work there.[160]

The same opportunity is sometimes afforded in experimental studies. For example, in a "dropped-letter" research design the experimenter leaves addressed letters in a public place to see how frequently they are taken by an anonymous bystander to a post office box. (Variations on this design include leaving cash in the letter, forgetting to add a stamp, and so forth.) Response rates may be interpreted as a sign of public-spiritedness. For example, in one set of experiments researchers place letters in classrooms where economics is taught, comparing their response rates to those from other disciplines in an attempt to determine whether studying economics minimizes public-spiritedness.[161]

In Chapter 7, we discussed an experiment of employer bias conducted by Bertrand and Mullainathan in which hundreds of resumes were sent out in response to jobs advertised in the Boston and Chicago areas.[162] The resumes differed in one key respect: some of the names on the resumes were distinctively African-American and the others identifiably white. The researchers discovered that applications with "white" names like Emily and Greg were more likely to be contacted by employers for a follow-up interview than applications with recognizably black names like Lakisha and Jamal, suggesting employment bias by race. In such settings, subjects' behavior under treatment and control conditions may be observed unobtrusively. (Note, however, that most experiments involve the explicit participation of subjects in a research protocol. Likewise, ethical considerations usually require informed consent, as discussed in Chapter 16.)

Ex Post Measures

A second genre of unobtrusive data involves observations that occur *ex post* (after the fact). The event of interest may be broadcast, published, or distributed in some other fashion (e.g., on the Web). It may be produced for a variety of reasons, e.g., commercial, artistic, entertainment, political, personal expression, or academic. It may be concurrent or may have been produced eons ago. It may consist of text, sound, film, or some other artifact. All historical research is, by definition, ex post.

All such data is properly classified as unobtrusive so long as the researcher has nothing to do with its creation and so long as the creators are not aware of the researcher's presence. Let us consider some examples, focusing our attention on hard-to-measure phenomena such as corruption, ideology, and alcoholism.

How corrupt are elites in politics around the world? Although one can gain a general sense of the subject by interviewing citizens, it is difficult to arrive at a more precise measure of elite corruption for the simple reason that this behavior is hidden from view. Cross-national indices such as the Corruption Perceptions Index produced by Transparency International measure the perceptions of citizens and businesspeople, which may or may not reflect actual practices. An alternative approach to this question focuses on the behavior of diplomats. Top diplomats from virtually every country in the world are permanently stationed in New York City, the headquarters of the United Nations. Here, they face a constant temptation. Because diplomats and their families enjoyed immunity from parking offenses (prior to 2000) they could park their cars anywhere they liked in this crowded city – where legal parking spots are exceedingly scarce – without worrying about parking tickets. Some took advantage of this perquisite, and others did not (or did so irregularly). Noting that New York City keeps records of unpaid parking fines, Ray Fisman and Ted Miguel compared the number of unpaid fines accrued by diplomats from countries around the world. Since payment is effectively voluntary, an unpaid fine may be interpreted as a sign that the diplomat (or a member of his or her family) did not feel a moral obligation to observe parking regulations or to compensate the city for infractions. This, in turn, may be interpreted as a measure of the degree to which elite corruption is practiced, and condoned, in countries around the world.[163]

What is the ideology of a legislator? It is a classic conundrum, for subjects – especially those holding elite positions – often have strong reasons to camouflage their true policy preferences. Moreover, the question itself may be difficult to articulate and hence open to multiple interpretations. One person's definition of "conservative" may be quite different from another's. One approach relies on behavioral measures, i.e., on what legislators do rather than on what they say. One of the most important things that legislators do is to vote on bills. Thus, when attempting to analyze the ideal-points of members of the US Congress researchers may examine patterns of correspondence among voting records, under the assumption that those who vote together share the same ideology. This is the basis for the widely used "NOMINATE" score developed by Keith Poole and Howard Rosenthal.[164]

How widespread is alcoholism and how has the rate of alcoholism changed over time? Alcoholics do not always declare themselves as such; they may not even admit that they have a problem. And surveys on such topics do not extend back very far, in any case. So, if we want to chart the rate of alcoholism in a country we shall have to rely on more subtle measures. One option focuses on reported rates of liver disease. Since alcoholism is a principal cause of liver disease, when disease rates fluctuate it may be interpreted as a change in the rate of alcoholism.[165]

Potential sources for ex post data are many and various, as our discussion suggests. Amidst this variety, one important distinction – between *primary* and *secondary* sources – deserves discussion.

Primary sources refer broadly to material produced by the actors under study (without prompting by a researcher). These might consist of official papers, minutes from meetings, memoranda, letters, emails, blog posts, field notes, diaries, autobiographies, newspaper reports, government documents, testimony in public hearings, works of fiction, photographs, films, handbills, flyers, pottery shards, and so forth. There is no limit, in principle, to what might be considered a primary source. Parking tickets, as employed in the Fisman/Miguel study, would be classified as primary, as would Congressional voting records or hospital records of liver disease.

Secondary sources, by contrast, are produced by those who are studying the actors of theoretical interest. Typically, this takes the form of published articles and books, though it may also take any of the forms traditionally associated with primary sources (as listed above).

Note that the distinction between primary and secondary sources depends upon the use to which a source will be put. Imagine a blog devoted to legislative activity in the US Congress. In the context of a study of the US Congress the blog is appropriately understood as a secondary source. In the context of a study of popular impressions of the US Congress the blog is rightly classified as primary material. The primary/secondary distinction is thus always relative to some specific research goal.

Unless you are studying some very new or very neglected topic it will be fairly easy to gain access to secondary sources. (For help in identifying relevant secondary sources see Chapter 11.) Primary sources, unfortunately, are often more obscure. Historical sources may exist only in a particular archive, and are thus accessible only to those who can travel to that archive. Even then, gaining access to archives may require personal connections, and finding what you want in a large archive can be a very long process – especially if it is not well organized or the librarians working there are unresponsive. Of course, the challenges of archival work are also what make this sort of research rewarding. One never knows precisely what one is going to discover. Some documents may have been untouched for hundreds of years. Even the librarians working there may be unaware of their existence, or their import. So, for those with vast patience who enjoy combing through diverse documents (often hard to decipher) and artifacts looking for new insights to the past, an archive offers the pleasure of a scholarly treasure hunt.

In any case, historical material is increasingly accessible to non-archivalists. Internet archives such as Google Books are in the process of digitizing the world's printed knowledge, putting them online for all to view. Works published before the 1920s are generally freely available, as they are no longer under copyright protection. Those under copyright may be partially accessible, or may be available for purchase. Sometimes, the most obscure sources are only a few clicks away. In addition, libraries contain vast holdings in microform or microfiche formats (which require special viewers). So, do not assume that lack of access to an actual archive means that you cannot do research with primary documents. Books, newspapers, and other printed materials (including artwork) from another historical era or another part of the world are often readily obtainable.

Data Assessment

Having introduced various techniques of data collection, we turn to the problem of assessment. Is the data, as collected and assembled by the researcher, valid? Does it accurately represent the phenomenon of interest? Or is it biased in some fashion?

Social science is focused on the attitudes and behavior of human beings. But attitudes are not directly observable, and behavior is not meaningful until it is given a context and an interpretation. Consider various events of interest to social scientists such as murder, mortality, voting, coups d'états, and consumer purchases. These are countable – and hence readily measurable – phenomena. But our interest in these phenomena is not merely in their incidence but also in their meaning, and more specifically in their causes and effects. This requires us to interpret the meaning hidden in observable behavior, raising an oft-noted problem of social science that may be referred to as the **interpretive** (or *hermeneutic*) **challenge**.

Sometimes, the meanings of actions are relatively easy to intuit. But often – more often than not – they are hard. For example, in investigating the topic of corruption we face the problem that those who engage in corrupt activities try hard to conceal these actions and, perhaps equally important, are often informed by different understandings of corruption. It is quite different if an act of patronage is seen as a moral obligation (e.g., to help kith or kin) as opposed to an act of self-aggrandizement. Because questions of meaning and intentionality are often central to our understanding of a phenomenon they are also central to the task of data gathering.

The same difficulties are encountered with many other social science subjects, e.g., clientelism, crime, democracy, discrimination, economic output, happiness, human rights, identity, ideology, intelligence, nationalism, prejudice, public opinion, utility, and wellbeing. We have trouble measuring these things because actors have strong incentives to misrepresent themselves and because actors often have differing understandings of their own actions or experiences. They lie *and* they disagree. Sometimes, they don't have a good understanding of their own conduct, or they misremember things they did or said or thought. (Beware of selective memories!) So the interpretive challenge is recalcitrant.

Regardless of the technique by which data for a study is gathered, it is important to keep sight of the active role played by the researcher. Data does not speak for itself. Structured data collection procedures such as surveys allow the researcher to set the agenda. Even when subjects are encouraged to articulate their sense of what is going on it is the researcher who must synthesize this information across sources and articulate it in a narrative. Although qualitative data-gathering processes generally allow more space for the subject to express him- or herself it is not clear that, in the final product (i.e., in the study itself), the researcher plays any less of a role than she or he does in a study based on quantitative data. Arguably, the only difference is that the researcher intercedes in the process at different stages. When constructing a survey, the researcher's role is apparent in the choice of questions to include in the survey. When utilizing in-depth interviews, focus groups, or ethnography, the researcher's role is more prominent at a later stage – when sifting through the gathered information and deciding which is relevant to the study and which should be ignored. When utilizing unobtrusive measures, the intervention of researchers generally occurs at two stages. At the primary data-collection stage someone is probably responsible for collecting the data, thus imposing his or her imprimatur. If the data accrues as part of a natural process – e.g., archeological remains – then researchers impose their stamp on the process only after the fact.

Having acknowledged the active role of the researcher in collecting data, we must also acknowledge that researchers do not occupy a position of objectivity, separate and apart from the processes that they investigate or the world that we all inhabit. Researchers, like everyone else, have material interests, emotional bonds, prior commitments, and cultural baggage that allow them to see certain things in certain ways but not other things or in other ways. Naturally, researchers try to visualize as many aspects of a problem as they can. But human flexibility, and creativity, is limited. The point is that social science is a human product, created by humans. As such, it is appropriate to regard scientists, and scientific products, with a degree of skepticism. In particular, in light of the intimate – and often hidden – role that investigators play in the collection of evidence, we must look closely at the process of data collection to see what things may have been missed, misstated, or wrongly stated. There is as much mischief in the process of data collection as in the process of data analysis.

In the following section, the task of data assessment is broken down into three problems: *divergent sources* (can divergent sources be integrated?), *replicability* (can the data be reproduced by others?), and *validity tests* (does the data conform to patterns that we believe to be true?).

Divergent Sources

Any reconstruction of reality rests on the veracity of one's data, and the veracity of data rests in part on the believability of one's sources. This is true whether the source is qualitative or quantitative, contemporary or historical, primary or secondary.

Typically, different sources will tell somewhat different stories about a topic. One source claims that Actor A pulled the trigger; another says that it was Actor B. One source says that British colonialism was brutal and rapacious; another says that it was relatively enlightened. The problem of evaluating divergent social science evidence is no different from the problem of evaluating journalistic, historical, or criminal evidence. Sources matter, and because they matter social scientists must judge the quality of their sources.

In making these judgments the following considerations come into play:

- *Relevance:* The source speaks to the question of theoretical interest.
- *Proximity:* The source is in a position to know what you want to know. They are close to the action.
- *Authenticity:* The source is not fake or doctored, or under the influence of someone else.
- *Validity:* The source is not biased. Or they are biased in ways that (a) are readily apparent and can therefore be taken into account or (b) do not affect the theoretical question of interest.
- *Diversity:* Collectively, the chosen sources exemplify a diversity of viewpoints, interests, and/or data-collection methods, allowing one to triangulate across sources that may conflict with one another.

We shall now explore these issues in greater detail, with particular attention to problems of bias.

Data gathered in an obtrusive fashion is subject to researcher bias. Subjects may tell the researcher what they think she or he wants to hear, or what they think is appropriate in a given context. Data gathered in an unobtrusive fashion is usually mediated by someone other than the researcher. This fact also warrants caution. In particular, if one is viewing an event through the eyes of later analysts one must be aware of whatever lenses (or blinders) they may be wearing. Their interpretation of the activity might not be the only possible interpretation, or they may have made errors of a factual nature.

Even where primary sources are available, one must be wary of the data-collection process. Consider that the main source of information about crime, rebellion, and political protest in previous historical eras comes from the official records of police investigations. Police and military authorities have a natural interest in suppressing unrest, so it is not surprising that they keep close records of this sort of activity. Thus an extensive set of records accumulated by French authorities during and after the uprising of the Paris Commune, including interrogation of key actors in the rebellion, provide the most important primary source for our understanding of that key event.[166] Likewise for other episodes of rebellion, protest, and crime throughout recorded history. Needless to say, one would not want to uncritically accept the authorities' interpretation of these events (though one would not want to reject them out of hand either).

A combination of primary and secondary sources should give one a more complete view of what is actually going on than could be garnered from either genre on its own. Just as one should be wary of relying solely on secondary sources one should be equally wary of relying solely on primary sources. There may be secrets that later observers have uncovered that would help one interpret events occurring long ago or far away.

But the problem of interpretation stemming from source material is only partially captured by the hallowed distinction between primary and secondary sources. It is not simply a matter of getting closer to or further from the action. It is also a matter of the perspectives that each source brings to the subject under investigation. A contemporary example is offered by Christian Davenport and Patrick Ball (2002: 428) in their research on state repression in Guatemala. As part of this research, conducted over the past few decades, they reviewed "17 newspapers within Guatemala, documents from four human rights organizations within as well as outside of the country, and 5,000 interviews conducted by the International Center for Human Rights Research within Guatemala." Sorting through this material, they find recurring patterns. Specifically, "newspapers tend to focus on urban environments and disappearances; human rights organizations highlight events in which large numbers of individuals were killed and when large numbers were being killed throughout the country in general; and ... interviews tend to highlight rural activity, perpetrators, and disappearances as well as those events that occurred most recently."[167] In short, each source has a distinct window on the topic, which sheds light on some particular facet of the topic. None are wrong, but all are partial. And this, in turn, stems from the position each of these sources occupies. The authors summarize:

> [N]ewspapers, tied to both urban locales/markets and authorities, tend to highlight events that occur within time periods of excessive state repression (i.e., within years in

which the overall number of killings is highest). This identification/distribution occurs predominantly in an environment where the regime is not overly restrictive. These sources become useful in documenting obvious behavior or that which is deemed politically salient within a specified political-geographic context. At the same time, journalistic sources may be relatively weaker at identifying events in more remote areas that occur during periods of relatively less state repressiveness and that are relatively smaller in scale ... In contrast, human rights organizations in Guatemala tend to highlight violations where they are most frequent, most destructive (i.e., where they injure the most individuals at one time), and where the context is most dire (i.e., during historical periods when individuals are generally being killed in the greatest numbers and when political openness is limited). As a result, these sources are useful in comprehensively trying to document human rights abuses – especially those of a particularly destructive nature ... Finally, interviewees tied inexorably to their homes, loss, revenge, and/or healing tend to highlight events that took place in the area with which they are most familiar. ... Interviewees also favor highlighting the perpetrator who abused the victim(s) and specifically what was done during the violation. As a result, such sources are useful for identifying what happened and who did it within particular locales.[168]

Typically, diverse sources will reveal different aspects of a problem. These differences are "tied to where the observers are situated, how they collect information, and the objectives of the organization."[169] If these sources can be combined, as Davenport and Ball endeavor to do, the researcher will usually be able to put together a more complete picture of the phenomenon under study – in this case, the location, extent, and type of human rights violations occurring within Guatemala.

Sometimes, however, observers have frankly discordant views of a phenomenon, which cannot therefore be pieced together to form a coherent whole. Occasionally, this is the product of a false document, i.e., a document written by someone other than who the author claims to be, or at some other time or set of circumstances. The authenticity of sources must be carefully monitored. This old piece of advice becomes truer still in the electronic age, as the provenance of an e-document is probably easier to forge or misrepresent, and harder to authenticate, than hard-copy documents.

More commonly, discordant views of the historical record are rooted in divergent interests or ideologies. Consider that the interests of state authorities must have come to bear in their collection of data on crime and disorder, as discussed in our previous example. The potential biases of sources must therefore be carefully judged whenever a researcher uses those sources to reach conclusions on a subject.

This is not to suppose that some sources are thoroughly biased, while others are thoroughly reliable. More typically, each source is reliable on *some* features of an event but not on others. It is the researcher's task to figure out who can be relied on, and for what sort of information. Figuring this out is a matter of understanding who they are, what they are likely to know (and not know), and what their stakes and preconceptions might be.

Sometimes, knowing the potential bias of a source is sufficient to establish an upper or lower bound for the information in question. For example, one might surmise that any human rights violations admitted by organs of the state, or organs closely affiliated with the state, would provide a lower bound. Likewise, estimates provided by zealous human rights advocacy organizations may be regarded as an upper bound. Somewhere in between these extremes (but not necessarily in the middle!), one might suppose, lies the true value.

Note that in searching for a "consensus view" on a particular question of fact or interpretation it is not sufficient to enumerate sources according to their views. Suppose that five sources take one view of a matter and three take another. This does not necessarily offer vindication of the first view. For one thing, it is never entirely clear when one has fully exhausted the sources on a subject. More important, some sources are probably in a better position to know the truth. Others may have no first-hand knowledge of the matter, and thus simply repeat what they have heard elsewhere. So, although it is good to keep tabs on who says what, do not imagine that all testimony can be weighted equally.

The issues raised in this section are often difficult to evaluate. How is one to know whether a source is biased, and in what ways? If you are having trouble reaching conclusions on these issues, consult someone who has worked intensively with the sources you are dealing with. This sort of source-expertise – even if they know little about your chosen topic – is immensely helpful, precisely because so much of the business of sourcing is context-specific. Someone with knowledge of one historical era may be unhelpful in elucidating another historical era, for example. Someone with experience working in a particular part of the world, or working with a particular sort of research subject (e.g., trial attorneys or wholesale merchandisers), may help you distinguish between reliable and unreliable sources.

Also, bear in mind that judgments about sources are rarely final or definitive. That is why every work of social science includes a long clarificatory section focused on the nature of those sources. It is long because it is complicated. And it is complicated because sources – through which we understand the world – do not speak for themselves. More precisely, they may speak for themselves but their speech requires interpretation.

Replicability

All knowledge should be **replicable**. This is a core goal of science. Narrowly construed, replication means that someone (other than the original researcher) should be able to access the data used in a study and repeat the procedures of the original analysis – whether qualitative and/or quantitative – working their way from the evidence to the author's conclusions. If this is not possible, i.e., if there is insufficient information to allow for this replication, then the value of a work is limited for it cannot be verified or falsified. One must simply take it on faith that the evidence gathered for a study supports the author's conclusions.

In order to facilitate the goal of replication it is important for researchers to preserve their data and to make it available to others once the study is complete – either on their own website, on a journal website, or on the website of a data repository. It is also important to include careful notes about the sources of that data as well as various decisions the researcher makes in collecting, coding, and analyzing data. This may be contained in the study itself, in an appendix, or in a companion document. If the analysis is quantitative, a "do" file should be included showing the set of operations performed on the data to obtain the results shown in tables and texts of the study.

Achieving replicability is often harder in qualitative research than in quantitative research. If a study is based on qualitative interviews or ethnography it may be difficult to preserve the original data collected by the researcher. Likewise, it may be difficult to re-collect the data since informants may be no longer available or the setting has changed so much that it is not possible to repeat the study in its original context. Even so, the researcher's field notes should be preserved and made available to others (insofar as this is possible without compromising the identity of subjects). Clear and specific citations of primary and secondary sources should help to achieve replicability in work based on sources that are already in the public domain, e.g., books, articles, material posted on the Web, and archival sources. Future historians should be able to follow the trail of footnotes left by their predecessors. (This process is likely to become much easier if the use of hypertext links located in online texts replaces hardbound texts.)

The obligations of a researcher extend to what can reasonably be achieved, and standards may differ for different styles of research. Likewise, the researcher must bear in mind ethical constraints such as informant confidentiality, as discussed below. This may require masking the identity of informants prior to releasing data to the general public.

Validity Tests

In order to assess the quality of data we may also apply **validity tests**. Broadly speaking, a validity test is one that compares the pattern of data under review to some other pattern that we believe to be true. Common approaches include face validity, case-based strategies, convergent validity, and causal validity.

Face validity refers to an obvious or intuitive appeal. If one is attempting to validate an index of democracy one might begin by considering countries that everyone (or almost everyone) agrees are democratic or non-democratic to see if they are correctly classified. If the index classifies Sweden as a democracy and North Korea as a non-democracy, this conforms to most people's sense of the world and may be regarded as a simple validity test. If, on the other hand, the index classifies Sweden as a non-democracy or North Korea as a democracy, one might have serious questions about the index.

Case-based strategies examine key cases to see if the coding for these cases is factually correct. For example, scholars of Central America have shown that the scores allocated to these countries by Freedom House and Polity are often patently erroneous. This sort of investigation rests on a scouring of primary and secondary sources for the countries in question, including local newspapers, government documents, and US diplomatic correspondence, as well as interviews with local informants.[170]

Convergent strategies attempt to validate an indicator by comparing it with other measures that are deemed to be valid measures of the same concept. A high correlation demonstrates convergent validity; a low correlation suggests poor convergent validity. Convergent validity studies have shown that the leading indicators such as Freedom House and Polity are highly intercorrelated, rendering a Pearson's r correlation of 0.88 across all countries in recent decades, and this has been interpreted as evidence that all such indicators are valid. Of course, the operating assumption is that additional indicators of a concept are themselves valid. If the measures that compose a convergent validity test are subject to bias the technique holds little promise.

Causal strategies attempt to validate a measure by looking at its relationship to an input or output to which it is presumed to be causally related. Suppose one is attempting to validate an index measuring the freeness and fairness of elections based on reports by election observers. One also has data on the percentage of the vote obtained by the winning party. If the index classifies an election as free and fair when the winning party obtains 100% of the vote one might have reason to doubt the veracity of the index. We expect that if an election is truly free and fair, some people will dissent. This is a causal assumption about the world. But it carries important ramifications for our assessment of the index.

CONCLUSIONS

Getting good data is critical to doing good social science research. *Garbage in, garbage out* – as the phrase goes. And judging the quality of data is critical to judging the quality of a piece of research. The more you know about various data-collection processes the better you will be able to produce social science and judge the findings produced by others.

To this end, this chapter introduced a variety of techniques for data collection, distinguishing between those that are obtrusive (surveys, interviews, focus groups, and ethnography) and those that are unobtrusive (surreptitious measures and ex post measures). We then discussed the task of data assessment, including divergent sources, replicability, and validity tests.

KEY TERMS

- Data
- Obtrusive methods

Key Terms

- Survey research
- Interviewer bias
- Social desirability bias
- Questionnaire
- Priming
- Likert scale
- List experiment
- Split-sample survey
- Panel design
- Pooled cross-section
- Pilot test
- Interview
- Focus group
- Participant observation
- Unobtrusive methods
- Surreptitious (ex post) data
- Primary sources
- Secondary sources
- Interpretive challenge
- Replicability
- Validity test
- Face validity
- Convergent strategies
- Causal strategies

14 | Writing

Sometimes, the task of writing is regarded as separate and independent from the study of social science. In this view, writing is a skill taught in English, rhetoric, or composition courses while theorizing and analyzing are reserved for courses in social science.

People who hold this view may also regard writing as an art (and hence the province of the humanities) in contrast to the task of analysis, which they may regard as more scientific (and hence the province of the social sciences). They may even be a bit suspicious of eloquent prose, regarding it as a sign of sophistry (a subtle, superficially plausible, but generally fallacious method of reasoning). From this perspective, the cultivation of style is a substitute for sound analysis – "mere rhetoric," as the phrase goes.

We can all agree that substance should trump style in the realm of social science. Yet, in order to communicate ideas must be put into words. If an author is unable to do so the reader must put the pieces of an argument together him- or herself, with much effort and possible misunderstanding. A poorly written study is one that is poorly executed. It will have less impact on the world, and – if it has any impact at all – may have an impact that is different from what the author intended. Communication skills thus matter a great deal to the progress of social science.

Moreover, the act of communicating is impossible to separate from the act of reasoning. We think through prose. This recalls E. M. Forster's question: "How can I tell what I think till I see what I say?"[171] In our own experience, writing out an argument usually leads to a reconceptualization of that argument. One cannot express an idea cogently without first understanding that idea, and one cannot understand an idea until one has effectively expressed it. Bad writing is usually a symptom of a deeper malaise.

Of course, everything depends upon how one chooses to define "good writing." Some purely stylistic components of writing such as spelling, grammar (norms of usage), and word-choice are indeed rather superficial in nature and do not necessarily reflect on the logic of an argument or the thoughtfulness of the writer. Nonnative writers will always face difficulties in these areas, especially if their chosen language is English – arguably, the world's most idiomatic language.

We urge you to think about writing in a more holistic way, incorporating spelling, grammar, and word-choice along with argumentation and organization. In *this* sense, writing is inseparable from thinking. And in this sense, writing is not an isolated skill, like penmanship, that can be separated from one's overall expertise as a social scientist. Writing is a vital part of the skill-set that one expects all social scientists to possess.

The first section of the chapter identifies various writing genres that you may encounter, each of which follows somewhat different rules. The second section is about organization. The third section encompasses considerations of style, including grammar. The fourth section is about integrating sources clearly, honestly, and creatively. The fifth and final section is about editing.

Prior to reading this chapter, we shall assume that you have identified a topic for research – which may be assigned or may be of your own choosing (see Chapter 12). It is worth reiterating that the topic of a paper is the most consequential part of the resulting work; do not skip lightly over this crucial decision. Likewise, we shall assume you are familiar with the criteria pertaining to social science arguments and research designs, as discussed in Parts I and II of the book.

Genres

There are many kinds of written documents and hence many diverse – and occasionally conflicting – criteria for good writing. As an entrée to this chapter it may be helpful to identify some of these genres, and their distinctive aims.

Perhaps the most important distinction lies between fiction and non-fiction. Evidently, we are concerned with writing that aims to represent reality in a factual manner. Of course, fiction may contain valuable truths. A compelling novel, poem, or play may be more real than a non-fiction treatment of the same material, at least in certain respects. However, because the former is not intended to reproduce a factual reality its construction follows very different rules.

Within the vast category of non-fiction we can recognize a number of sub-genres based on the venue for which a work is produced. These include (a) short papers or theses written in pursuit of a degree, (b) academic journal articles, (c) longer monographs (including dissertations and books) written for an academic audience, (d) books written for a general audience, and (e) memos, reports, press releases, and website content produced for a business, government agency, or non-profit organization. What we have to say in this chapter is relevant to all of these genres. But it bears most directly upon (a) short papers or theses written in pursuit of a degree.

Another way to categorize non-fiction genres hinges on the *substance* of the writing rather than its venue. Here, one may distinguish the following genres: (a) general accounts, (b) book reviews, (c) literature reviews, (d) policy reports, and (e) monographs. Here, we briefly review their goals and usual formats.

A *general account* seeks to encompass all aspects of a topic, or at least all those that might be of interest to a lay audience (non-experts, who are presumed to know little about the topic). For example, a general account of democracy might encompass the following topics: (a) the definition and measurement of democracy,

(b) the origins and spread of democracy since ancient times, (c) the process by which countries democratize, (d) the exogenous causes of democratization, and (e) the effects of democracy. This is a lot to deal with, evidently, and even a book-length treatise is likely to skim lightly over these topics. Encyclopedia articles must be even more concise. For this reason, general accounts are often employed for textbooks or for books and articles addressed to a popular (non-specialist) audience. A general account offers a point of departure for more focused work.

A **book review** offers a synoptic overview and discussion of a chosen book. Book reviews appear on all subjects and in many academic and non-academic venues. Typically, a review begins by summarizing the main theme or argument of the book under review, along with the evidence. The review will also seek to place the book within a larger context, i.e., as part of an intellectual current, identifying elements that are novel or held in common with that tradition. Finally, there is an attempt to identify the book's strengths and weaknesses. Laudatory reviews emphasize the former; critical reviews emphasize the latter. Generally one finds a mixture of both.

A **literature review** discusses work that has accumulated on a particular subject. For example, one might review studies of democratization or of social capital. Where a large literature has developed – as on these topics – the author may seek to further limit the scope of the review, e.g., to recent work, work published in a particular subfield, or work with a narrower focus. For further discussion the reader is referred to Chapter 11.

A **policy report** is written to provide direction and guidance for citizens, policy-makers, or members of an organization who require guidance on a topic. Prior to reaching this goal the report may contain a good deal of descriptive, causal, and/or predictive analysis. However, its primary goal is prescriptive, i.e., to suggest a concrete course of action. Thus, a report commissioned for a government office might begin by relating the history of a policy problem, including past attempts to deal with it and evaluations of their relative success, before concluding with a policy recommendation. Policy reports, unlike work in other genres, are meant to be acted upon.

A **monograph** encompasses studies with a highly focused topic and a concise argument or theory, which might be descriptive, causal, and/or predictive. This is the mainstay of academic work, as discussed in previous chapters. It also segues neatly into our discussion of essay organization.

Organization

Grammar (rules of usage), spelling, and other niceties of the English language should be observed, as discussed in a later section of this chapter. But this is the most obvious, and in some ways least essential part of an essay's style. More important is a clear argument (as discussed in Chapter 2) and a logical organization.

In order to facilitate this we suggest keeping an outline of how you think the paper will proceed. This outline might be extremely detailed – including, let us say, virtually every point that you wish to make – or it might be brief and schematic. You might experiment with both approaches to see what works best for you.

Of course, this outline will probably be revised as you work your thoughts out on paper (or on the computer). This is the thinking-through-writing process that we have discussed. Nonetheless, at any given point in time you need to have a general idea of how all the pieces of your paper fit together. You may keep this outline in a separate document or on a separate screen (if you are working with two screens), and revise it continually as you go along. All your notes (including your ideas and your citations and quotations from the literature) should fit somewhere within this outline.

One way to move from a mass of notes toward a draft is to write headings and sub-headings for each idea. This will then translate into sections, or paragraphs, of the paper. In any case, it will help you keep track of the flow of your narrative.

Sometimes, one has difficulty putting together an entire outline. It isn't clear where the pieces fit, or even whether they all fit. Rather than spending hours and hours fiddling with the outline you might try another approach, based on the sections that you envision for the paper. Sometimes, you know that there will be a section on "apples" and a section on "oranges" but you don't know which will come first, and the appropriate ordering does not become apparent until the sections are written. In this instance, you should probably write the sections first (or at least some of them) and then return to the outline, in the hope that these sections can be fit together into a coherent narrative. This is equivalent to working on various sections of a puzzle separately and then putting them together at a later stage.

One of the hardest tasks is discarding good ideas and juicy quotes. However, this process of tossing things out is essential. It is often what distinguishes a focused, well-constructed essay from one that is disjointed and hard to follow. You should appreciate that any creative work will generate ideas that don't fit within the rubric of a single topic. This is inevitable. It is akin to the sketches that an artist produces prior to the final work, or the false leads that a detective pursues prior to finding the culprit. There is always some "waste product." Do not think of it as waste, however, for it is essential to the creative process. The point is that in order to create a well-crafted product you need to be able to recognize the parts that don't fit and have the discipline to toss them out, or file them away for a future project.

When constructing an outline, bear in mind that most social science papers follow a similar organizational format. The prototype looks like this:

   I. *Introduction*
  II. *Literature Review*
 III. *Thesis*
 IV. *Methods*
  V. *Evidence and Supporting Arguments*
 VI. *Conclusion*
VII. *End Matter*

In a longer paper – say, over five pages – it is helpful to separate different sections of an argument by headings, as below. (Additional sub-headings may be added, as needed.)

Introduction

Introductions contain the body of an essay in a highly abbreviated form. Typically, introductions (a) explain the meaning and importance of the chosen topic, (b) review the literature on that topic, (c) state the main argument along with the method of analysis and the evidence that will be brought to bear, and (d) outline how the topic will be addressed.

Let us discuss each of these objectives, in turn.

Introducing a subject means, first of all, explaining that topic to your reader. Some topics are self-explanatory. Others require a long preamble and perhaps the definition of key terms. Naturally, much depends upon the audience one is writing for. In any case, one must build on common ground, i.e., features of the world – and terminology – that your readers are likely to understand.

Typically, one says something about the significance of the chosen topic. Why should we care about your topic (and by extension, your paper)? Why does it matter? Some topics are intrinsically interesting, touching on themes that lots of people care about. Others need to be connected to things that your reader is likely to care about. For example, the topic of "party identification" seems at first glance to be a relatively obscure preoccupation of political scientists. However, you may be able to claim that the strength or weakness of party identification in a country has important consequences for politics and policy.

Even with topics that are intrinsically interesting it may be important to establish the present-day relevance of that topic. For example, if you are writing about genocide some readers may assume that this refers to events that lie firmly in the past. It may be important to remind readers that genocides have occurred as recently as 1994 (Rwanda) and – according to some observers – are occurring right now (e.g., in Syria).

The significance of a topic may derive from a particular problem that it addresses. If so, it is natural to begin with a statement of this problem. For example, one might launch an essay by making reference to the problem of polarization in contemporary American politics, perhaps citing some authorities on the subject and making clear why you think it is a problem. Having set the context, and drawn your reader in, you can then state how your chosen topic addresses that problem, explains it, or perhaps suggests a solution to it.

At some point in an introduction you should outline briefly what others have written about your topic. This review of the literature might occupy several sentences or, at most, several paragraphs. If a longer review is required it must be postponed until a later section of the paper (see below).

Against this backdrop, tell the reader in a few sentences or a paragraph what your thesis is, and what sort of evidence and method of analysis will be employed to prove it. Recall that a good thesis usually contains some element of novelty. This might be the argument itself if it is at variance with what most authorities on a subject have been saying or with what most people believe. If the thesis is not entirely new – and of course no thesis is completely unique – the novelty of a study may lie in the evidence. Perhaps a new terrain is being explored, or an especially strong test of an established theory is on display. Or perhaps material is being synthesized in a new way. In any case, a thesis is more interesting and useful insofar as it points out things that are not readily apparent. A paper should add something to the sum total of human knowledge. You should make this clear in the introduction.

Finally, provide an outline of the paper. Don't shy away from straightforward sign-posting techniques: "First, I will address the question of *X*. Next, I will . . ."

Introductions generally occupy at least several paragraphs, perhaps as much as two pages. They should in any case consume no more than one-tenth the length of your paper. They are, after all, introductions. If your introduction stretches beyond that consider either cutting the excess or moving it to another section.

Literature Review

Every paper has a section in which the literature on a subject is reviewed. Sometimes, this is incorporated into the Introduction or the Thesis section (above and below). Sometimes, it stands alone.

In any case, it is vital to establish what sort of work has already been conducted on a subject before the author can introduce his/her own perspective on that subject. Literature reviews establish what *they* say and what *they* have done, thus situating the author's own work and the originality of that contribution.

The author must acknowledge his or her forebears graciously; there is nothing as discrediting as a crass and stingy review of the literature that pours ridicule on everyone who has worked on a subject. By the same token, the author must be careful to distinguish his or her work from those who came before. If one is meekly following in a well-established tradition one cannot claim to be making much of a contribution. One should honor, but not worship, one's forebears. This is the delicate balance – between hubris and timidity – that every writer must strike.

There are at least two dimensions to every social science literature review. The first focuses on the argument, i.e., the theory. The second focuses on the analysis, i.e., the empirics. A contribution can be theoretical and/or empirical. Most reviews of the literature offer a little bit of both.

Thus, an author might begin by tracing the lineage of the chosen theory – to what extent is it original or derivative? To what extent is he or she agreeing or disagreeing with the standard view of a subject?

Next, an author might tackle the empirical elements of previous research. What sorts of material have been examined by scholars, and with what methods? What are the strengths and weaknesses of these empirical efforts? In what ways are they limited or open to question?

The literature review may seem daunting, and it commonly occupies a good deal of time. However, it is usually the *least* important part of a paper. As such, you should take pains not to get too wrapped up in it. Try to summarize the extant literature as succinctly as you can. If the literature is substantial, this will require a good deal of bundling. Since you cannot afford to discuss each study individually you will need to group them according to some schema. "Group A focuses on Topic 1, Group B focuses on Topic 2, . . ." and so forth.

Another approach is to capture important characteristics of many studies in a table, with studies listed across each row and their characteristics listed across each column. An example is provided in Table 14.1. Here, salient features of recent studies focused on the relationship between development and democracy are summarized, including the outcomes employed to measure democracy, the research design, the period of analysis, and the main finding.

Table 14.1   Cross-national studies of development and democracy

Study	Democracy Indicator	Analysis	Period	Finding: Development affects...	
				Democratization	Consolidation
Acemoglu et al. 2008	Polity 2; PR	TSCS with country FE, IV	1500–2000	0	0
Boix and Stokes 2003	BMR	TSCS	1850–1990	+	+
Epstein et al. 2006	Based on Polity 2	TSCS with Markov estimation; survival analysis	1960–2000	+	+
Przeworski and Limongi 1997	DD	TSCS	1950–1990	0	+

Democracy indicators

BMR   Boix, Miller, and Rosato (2013)
DD   Democracy–Dictatorship (Cheibub, Gandhi, and Vreeland 2010)
PR   Political Rights (Freedom House 2007)
Polity 2   Marshall and Jaggers (2007)

Analysis

TSCS   Time-series cross-section design
FE   Fixed effects model
IV   Instrumental-variable analysis

Finding

0   No consistent relationship between development and democracy
+   Positive relationship between development and democracy

Thesis

If the thesis (aka theory, main argument) of a paper is very simple it may be incorporated into the introduction. If it is more complex, it deserves a section of its own, or may be combined with the literature review. Here, you have space to lay out the theory in its entirety. Make sure to be clear about what you are arguing. Any ambiguity on this score will injure your cause. Recall that the purpose of a social science paper is not to leave the reader dangling, as one might in a work of rhetoric or fiction. Readers of social science have very little patience. If you wait until the middle or end of the paper to reveal the punchline you will lose some readers and annoy the rest.

Sometimes, one does not become fully aware of the thesis until one has already written a rough draft of a paper and put it aside for a few days. It is common to see thesis statements in concluding paragraphs. Once you realize this, a simple reorganization of the paper should be possible (swapping text from back to front).

If the thesis is complex, with many interacting parts, it may be helpful to construct a diagram, summarizing the key features, as suggested in Chapter 2. Regardless of how many moving parts it has, the argument should be summarizable in a few sentences. If it is longer than that, we suspect it is too long – which is to say it needs to be pared down, simplified, or presented in a more unified manner.

Although parsimony is important, you should not feel pressured to over-simplify the argument. Where caveats, clarifications, and scope-conditions are needed, make sure that they are fully articulated. It is important not to claim too much as this will make your case less persuasive. Sometimes it is helpful to distinguish between a "home turf" where you are pretty sure your argument is correct and a larger turf where its application is more speculative. (This distinction may conform to the distinction between sample and population, as discussed in Chapter 4.)

Method

If the method employed in a study is fairly straightforward it can be folded into the following section (*Evidence and Supporting Arguments*). If it is more complicated it should be accorded a section of its own. This is where you explain how you collected your data, how you analyze it, what methodological problems you face, and how you intend to overcome them.

Note that these methodological questions are equally important in quantitative and qualitative research. In a case study (see Chapter 9), you need to explain how you chose your case(s) and what method(s) you are employing for analyzing data drawn from that case(s).

Evidence and Supporting Arguments

The body of the paper is composed of your defense of the thesis. Here is where you present evidence and supporting arguments that are intended to convince the reader that you are right. Evidence is broadly interpreted, including any species of "data" discussed in the previous chapter.

Each portion of the paper should address a different facet of the author's thesis. Generally, one saves the most important and/or the most complicated parts for last. But this is a matter of taste. Sometimes, a cumulative logic is at work, demanding that some issues be presented first and others later.

In arguing for your thesis imagine possible responses from those who might be inclined to skepticism. How might you convert this sort of reader to your argument? Remember that in order to convince the skeptics you will need to deal not only with the evidence and arguments that support your case but also those that do not. Omission of contrary evidence is generally damning to an argument for it suggests that the writer is not aware, or has not fully considered, the facts of the case. Thus, you need to show why these points are wrong, overstated, or counterbalanced by opposing arguments or evidence. Since the thesis is your purpose for writing, if you do not argue your thesis effectively you have not achieved your stated objective.

Note, however, that a social science paper is not a legal brief, a debate, or an exercise in rhetoric. One wishes to convince, naturally, but not by misrepresenting the truth. One's purpose is to shed light on a subject, honestly and with as much completeness as you can muster (given time and space constraints). This is how science advances. There is no honor in convincing readers of a false thesis. The writer, therefore, has a strong professional obligation not to overstate the evidence in support of a thesis and to acknowledge arguments and evidence that contradict it.

Conclusion

One is obliged to sum things up in some manner. In a short paper, this summation should be brief. Remind the reader what you have argued and what you have proven. Clarify, as well, the limits of your thesis, its scope-conditions, if you have not already done so. If there are weaknesses in the argument that you have not already addressed, now is the time to acknowledge them.

Traditionally, the concluding section of a paper approaches the subject from a broader perspective, exploring possible implications of the thesis. What does your argument imply? If true, what predictions flow from it? What debates does it relate to? What additional topics might it be applied to?

Conclusions are often speculative, as you can see. They set forth ground for future research by pointing out various extensions of the subject. Here, it may be appropriate to discuss some of the thoughts and questions you had as you conducted your research – things that couldn't be proven or that didn't fit neatly into your paper but which are nonetheless connected to your subject and might be of interest to readers.

End Matter

At the end of a paper one generally finds a References section, providing full citations for all in-text references. (Naturally, if you choose to employ full references in the body of your paper – as footnotes or endnotes – you do not need a separate References section.) There may also be an Appendix, or even several appendices. An appendix is typically used to provide further detail on sources, descriptive statistics, robustness tests, or other information pertaining to the analysis. Sometimes, Tables and Figures are listed at the end of the document, rather than in the body of the paper. This is a matter of choice, though our personal preference is to integrate tables and figures into the body of the paper, where they are more accessible.

Variations

Having presented the prototypical organization of a social science paper it is important to note that these features can be aggregated or disaggregated in various ways. For example, one might merge the Literature Review and/or Thesis sections into the Introduction. Alternatively, one might split the Evidence and Supporting Arguments section into several sections, each devoted to a separate analysis. Much depends upon how much you have to say about each of these topics. Sections should be roughly similar in length, though this is not a strict standard. It is much more important to carve up the paper into logically distinct parts than it is to create parts of equal length.

Style

Social science is similar to rhetoric insofar as its goal is to persuade. However, unlike other genres, the work of persuasion in social science is carried by the logic of the argument and the strength of the evidence. Fancy turns of phrase, evocative metaphors, a compelling narrative, provocative observations – these sorts of adornments are not essential, and may detract from the presentation of a theory and evidence to support that theory.

It follows that expository styles appropriate for popular journals, or even highbrow journals like the *New Yorker*, are not always appropriate for social science. The job of a social-scientific study is to contribute to the development of a body of knowledge, not to entertain. Our stylistic motto might be summarized as follows: To hell with beauty, let's try to communicate some truth.

Of course, there is no reason why the art of evocative writing must be sacrificed on the altar of clarity. One can be clear, organized, and also entertaining. However, wherever the two might conflict, intelligibility should take precedence.

The use of technical language – including mathematical symbols – also imposes a sacrifice of intelligibility, at least for those without the requisite technical knowledge to follow the argument. To remedy this problem, we suggest that everyday language be employed in works of social science wherever possible.

We recognize that a technical vocabulary is often essential insofar as it is clearer (less ambigous) or more concise than the analogous term or phrase in everyday language. That said, it is important that writers summarize technical issues in everyday language at some point in a study – perhaps in the introduction or conclusion – so that the latter is accessible to lay readers.

Note that if social science is to have any effect at all on society we must be able to translate our wisdom into the vernacular. It is no use discovering the benefits and drawbacks of an electoral system if one cannot influence public debate on electoral reform. Knowledge about the effects of public and private investment does not bring any benefits at all if economists are the only holders of that knowledge.[172] Whatever sociologists may learn about the sources of racism will not help anyone overcome this condition if sociologists are the sole repositories of this truth.

More generally, whatever arguments are developed in specialized venues of social science must eventually filter down to a broader audience. In order to make sure that this occurs, or at least has some chance of occurring, social science must be intelligible to the lay reader. We must do our best to bring social science to the people.

Rules

Language, in common with math, chemistry, music, and any sporting event that you can imagine, has rules. Without rules, language is meaningless; indeed, it is no longer language at all but simply a random set of words without meaning (or with a wide range of possible meanings). When writing emails, tweets, texts, and in other contexts we may apply these rules loosely. However, in a formal setting it is important to abide by the formal rules of the English language, perhaps with an occasional change of pace to provide dramatic or comic relief.

Spelling, usage, word-choice, and all the delicate mechanics of language are essential to effective communication. You will not convince your reader that you know what you are talking about and have thought seriously about the subject if there are careless mistakes of punctuation or spelling. This is a serious "image" problem, and you need to protect your credibility. Matters of form are also likely to affect the substance of the argument. But even if they are peripheral, stylistic mistakes will affect the rhetorical power of your paper – your ability to persuade.

As you think about grammatical rules bear in mind that writing is not a paint-by-numbers exercise. Regrettably, it is not possible to issue a set of rules that would tell you everything you need to know about proper sentence structure. Good writing is a matter of developing sensitivity to the English language, a process that develops over a lifetime. English is also a highly idiomatic language, so rules of grammar don't take one very far. In any case, good writing in any language involves much more than following correct rules of grammar. It involves choosing the best word from among several near-synonyms. It involves finding the right way to phrase an idea, the right organization for a set of related ideas, and the proper mix of general statements and supporting examples. This is what differentiates a persuasive and powerful essay from one that is merely grammatically correct.

While it is impossible to learn good writing by memorizing a set of rules, here are some bits of advice – drawn from a variety of sources – that are worth paying close attention to.

- Good writing is possible only if one has a good idea of the audience one is writing for. For most purposes, you may assume an audience of your peers. As you sit before the computer screen, imagine yourself writing to other members of your class.
- Don't assume knowledge of specialized topics. Do your best to explain things in a way that non-specialists can understand. Then, you may proceed to technical details that only specialists will be able to appreciate. (We have already discussed the rationale for this prescription.)
- Avoid jargon wherever possible. "Jargon" refers to technical or abstruse vocabulary for ideas that can be communicated just as accurately and parsimoniously with everyday words. If you wish to vary the vocabulary in an essay by introducing an unusual word, use this word only once or twice. *Chew* can be repeated; *masticate* should be used sparingly. Granted, some technical words have no ordinary-language counterpart. These are permitted, and indeed are often indispensable. Make sure that these technical terms are carefully defined at the outset of the paper, lest you lose your audience.
- Don't talk down to your reader. Fancy words and phrases often come out sounding pretentious. Likewise, explaining the obvious suggests that you have a low opinion of the reader. Find an appropriate voice, one that conveys respect.
- Don't let your prose get in the way of the logic of the argument. Overly long sentences with multiple clauses are hard for the reader to follow. Try to write as simply as possible – without sacrificing the complexities of your topic.
- Colloquial phrases are sometimes funny (dammit). But they should be kept to a minimum.
- Use adverbs like "very," "extremely," or "unbelievably" sparingly. They sound shrill and don't add much to a sentence.
- Avoid a polemical or conversational style. The tone should be even, measured, and scholarly.
- Use examples wherever a statement might not be entirely clear, or simply to avoid the arid effect of an unrelieved series of generalizations.
- Avoid deterministic language, unless it is clearly justified. Most things in the social-science universe are probabilistic, rather than invariant.
- Don't overstate your argument. In debates and in courtroom arguments one is enjoined to give no quarter, to contest every point. Academic writing is different. Here, you are enjoined to acknowledge the limitations of your own position and the possible utility of arguments offered by others. Your purpose is to reach the truth, not vanquish opponents. And reaching the truth is usually a communal endeavor. This does not mean that compromise is always warranted, or that the truth always lies in the middle. It means, very simply, that you should worry about getting things right, not about settling scores. It means that you should indicate uncertainty wherever uncertainty is indicated, using appropriate qualifiers and caveats.
- Turn on, and pay attention to, the grammar promptings that your word processor provides. Also, take a look at this page, which clarifies a basket of

words that are often confused with each other (such as *there*, *their*, and *they're*): www.englishchick.com/grammar/grconf.htm

- Thesauruses are now available online or as part of word-processing programs. Don't hesitate to use them. But don't use them too often as it will slow down your writing and, worse, may encourage you to write in an ungainly manner. Words drawn from a thesaurus tend to be poorly chosen and stick out inappropriately in a paper. In order to use a word correctly you need to be familiar with it, which is to say you need to have seen that word in a natural context several times. In this way, you maintain control over the medium.
- Avoid brackets (" ") wherever possible. Irony is not well-conveyed by the use of a scare-quote. A new term, if questionable in some way or if under definition, may be placed in brackets when it is first introduced. (Note the use of "jargon" above.) Afterwards, it should be used without the brackets.
- Each paragraph should contain a single idea. Typically, this idea is expressed in the first sentence of the paragraph. This allows your reader to skim your paper by reading the first sentences of each paragraph, which function as headings in an outline. Of course, no one follows this format slavishly, and to do so would probably end up sounding rather stilted. However, as a rule topic sentences should not be hidden in the middle of paragraphs. They should be placed at the beginning, or (occasionally) at the end.
- The length of a paragraph is less important than its logical coherence. Some will be long and others will be short, depending upon how much verbiage needs to be packaged within that container.
- You may think of paragraphs as separate slides within a PowerPoint presentation; each should address a different facet of the argument. Establish breaks between paragraphs when you move to a new idea.
- Work hard on your transitions from one paragraph to the next and from one section of the paper to the next. If there are no transitions, your reader will have difficulty following the narrative.
- State your points as concisely as possible and avoid redundancy. Delete words that are not needed, perhaps because they are implied by other words. Replace phrases with words, where possible. Alter sentences so that they are stated positively rather than negatively (eliminate *not*).[173]
- The main point of an essay should appear in the introduction, in the conclusion, and – in varying ways – within the body of a paper. This is justifiable redundancy – although each appearance should be phrased somewhat differently. Other points should appear only once in the course of your essay. If you find that a given issue is treated on several occasions, you should think about reorganizing the essay to eliminate this redundancy. Another way to deal with this problem is to refer back to earlier points ("as stated above"). This relieves you of the necessity of repeating a point ad nauseam while allowing you to point out continuities and connections.
- Differentiate clearly between (a) what others say, or what is generally understood to be true about a subject (background knowledge), and (b) what you – the

author – say about that subject (the argument). The first is established in the introduction or the literature review section of a paper; it provides the point of departure. The second is the author's contribution to that subject – where she or he extends or contests established wisdom. If you confuse (a) and (b) your readers will be confused and perhaps also annoyed. Consider the difference between "Alcoholism is a principal cause of unemployment," and "I argue that alcoholism is a principal cause of unemployment." The first statement suggests that this is a truth that most people – or at least most knowledgeable experts on the subject – accept. The second statement suggests that this is the author's perspective, which knowledgeable observers may contest, and which the author will try to prove in the course of the essay.

- Length is probably the least important element of any paper. Granted, one is often constrained to work within arbitrary page or word limits set by a journal or by an instructor. However, bear in mind that this is an entirely arbitrary matter, established for convenience. Above all, do not confuse length with quality. Longer is not necessarily better; indeed, it may be worse. Pascal once apologized to a correspondent, saying "The present letter is long, as I had no time to make it shorter." Writing concisely usually requires more care and attention than writing at length about a subject. One must pick and choose.

To summarize, the object of your paper is to persuade the reader, to communicate. So try to be as clear and straightforward as you can, without trivializing your ideas or patronizing your reader. The secret to what is generally regarded as good non-fiction writing probably has less to do with prose style than with clear thinking.

Sources

Ideas come from somewhere; they are not invented out of whole cloth. (If they were, they would probably be pretty absurd, and wouldn't constitute good social science.) So don't be ashamed of taking ideas from other places. Everyone does it. Social science is theft.

The point is to give full attribution wherever borrowing occurs if the piece of information is not already common knowledge. (You don't need to footnote that the sun rises in the East and sets in the West.) This is a matter of honesty, as well as a matter of scholarly cumulation. Recall that your paper builds on a skein of existing knowledge. Only through accurate documentation can the reader distinguish the writer's original contribution from those of others. Likewise, your arguments build on evidence, and in order to establish the veracity of the evidence you present, readers must be able to trace it back to a source. Correct use and acknowledgment of source materials is therefore vital to any research project.

Thus, if you use material drawn from something aside from your own first-hand experience, and the material is not common knowledge, give credit to your source. If you quote directly, even a word or phrase, use quotation marks and a citation. If you paraphrase (i.e., take the ideas and put them into your own words), cite the source.

If you take ideas or words from sources without attribution you may face disciplinary action – including expulsion – from a college or university, or you may lose your job. You should also bear in mind that the current state of information technology assures that a paper that you write today may remain in the public domain for the rest of your life. This means that decades from now someone may discover an episode of plagiarism, committed in your youth, which jeopardizes your position, not to mention your standing in the community. There is a lot at stake. So, if you are in doubt about whether a citation is necessary, play it safe by citing the source or consult your instructor for further guidance. Once your paper is turned in, the reader has the right to assume that whatever appears in the paper, unless otherwise indicated, is your own work or is common knowledge.[174]

Naturally, even with appropriate citation you do not want to take your entire argument from someone else. What you should be taking from your sources are bits and pieces: a fact here, a point there – whatever bears upon *your* argument. You will need to refer to multiple sources; otherwise, you can hardly avoid relying excessively on one person's work. Creativity, in this context, means putting together the material presented in the text in a new way in order to answer a question that is at least slightly different from the authors' point of view.

In citing evidence, don't simply cite an author's view that such-and-such is true. Research is not a polling of authors. If four out of five authors say something is true it still may be false. Of course, it may be helpful to establish what the prevailing wisdom on a topic is. However, in bringing evidence to bear you must be sensitive to whether a particular source is authoritative. An authoritative source is a source that is, for one reason or another, well suited to weigh in on a given topic – an eye-witness, an expert, and so forth. For these sources, direct quotations may be appropriate.

Even so, such authorities must often be viewed with suspicion. In general, you should avoid quotations, especially long ones. Try to paraphrase instead (put things in your own words). This, of course, still requires a citation.

Note that the purpose for which a source is being cited determines what sort of source is most useful or most authoritative. If you are attempting to demonstrate that a certain mood pervades a society, or that a certain event received a great deal of attention, then citing popular media (newspaper, wide-circulation magazine, best-selling novel, television report) may be the best source. You might also cite an academic study that studied these popular media in a systematic fashion. If, on the other hand, you are trying to demonstrate a non-obvious point about the world – a descriptive, predictive, or causal inference – then an academic source is probably more authoritative than a popular source.

Although most sources are in written form they may also be in the form of personal communication with the author (interviews, discussions, and so forth).

This raises a final, but extremely important, point: if you talk with friends and classmates about your paper and this discussion leads to an exchange of ideas (substantive ideas, not just stylistic/organizational ones) you need to cite these sources just as you would a book or article. If you got the idea for an argument from Cindy Walker, Cindy Walker should appear in a citation where this argument is presented. Otherwise, you are plagiarizing.

How many sources/citations are necessary? This is an oft-repeated question, to which our oft-repeated response is: it depends. It depends on what it is you are trying to prove, on what sources are out there, and on whether it is possible to cite one or two sources as examples of what is out there. Citations, like pages of text, are not to be judged by their quantity. More is not necessarily better. There are over-referenced papers and under-referenced papers. However, you are more likely to be sanctioned for the latter than for the former. So, if you must err, err on the side of over-referencing.

Note that if you find a well-referenced article or book that reviews the academic literature on a subject it may be sufficient to cite this one source, rather than all the additional sources that are cited therein. You may indicate in your citation that this particular source offers a good review of the literature ("for a comprehensive review of the literature see Smith 1989").

Quotation Formats

If a direct quotation exceeds a sentence or two you should set it off in the text in a block quotation, such as the following:

> This is a block quotation, with larger margins than the rest of the text. Sometimes, a smaller font is also employed, as it is here. In any case, no quotation marks are necessary. Simply type the quotation into the block, and include the citation as you normally would (Smith 1989: 45).

In adapting a quotation for use in a paper you may need to alter it in small ways. If you drop words from the quoted passage, indicate the missing text with ellipses. For example, Smith (1989: 45) writes, "Ellipses are important ... but sometimes ignored." The deleted words are situated in between "important" and "but."

If you insert words into a quotation, this is signaled by square brackets. For example, Smith (1989: 45) writes, "Ellipses [in a published paper] are important ... but sometimes ignored." The added words are in brackets.

If a quotation includes a misspelled word or grammatical error you should indicate this by inserting (*sic*) after the error. For example, Smith (1989: 45) writes, "Ellipses are important ... but sometimes ignord (*sic*)." This indicates to the reader that the error is in the original.

Occasionally, you may need to employ quotations marks within a quotation. This is handled with single quotes. For example, Smith (1989: 45) writes, "You should remain financially independent. Following the words of Shakespeare, 'Neither a borrower nor a lender be.'"

Citation Formats

There are many citation formats. You should learn the format that is most common in your field, or that which your instructor advises. As a default, you may follow the formatting style used in this book – described below – which is similar to most formats used in the social sciences today.

In the text, or in a footnote, list the author's name in parentheses, followed by the year your edition of the work was published, followed by the page number of the quotation or idea you are citing (Smith 1989: 45). If you are citing a whole book, which is to say an idea or argument that consumes an entire book, then you may omit the pagination (Smith 1989). Information from several sources may be combined in a single parenthetical note (Smith 1898; Washington 1945). Within a parenthetical citation, author last names are alphabetized (Smith comes before Washington). A work with multiple authors should cite each author (Smith, Wilson, and Crane 1989) unless the number of authors is greater than three, in which case cite only the first author followed by *et al.* (Smith et al. 1989). A citation drawn from a source without an author may be cited by the name of the organization or journal that published the work (*The Economist* 1989: 45). Information obtained from a personal communication should be cited in a footnote and needn't appear in your bibliography. For example, *Footnote:* Roger Smith, personal communication (5/31/1989). When a person has authored several pieces in the same year these may be distinguished by letters (Smith 1989a, 1989b, 1989c). Very long lists of citations, or extensive substantive comments of a parenthetical nature, should go into footnotes. Do not use endnotes, unless instructed to do so (they are hard to follow).

At the end of your paper include a References section including all works cited, with complete citations, as follows.

Books:
Smith, Arthur. 1989. *My Great Idea*. New York: Random House.

The same author with several works published in the same year:
Smith, Arthur. 1989a. *My First Great Idea*. New York: Farrar, Straus.
Smith, Arthur. 1989b. *My Second Great Idea*. New York: Random House.
Smith, Arthur. 1989c. *My Third Great Idea*. New York: Farrar, Straus.

Edited books:
Smith, Arthur (ed.). 1989. *A Series of Chapters about My Great Idea*. Washington: Crane Russak.

Book chapter in edited volume:
Smith, Arthur. 1989. "His Great Idea Stinks," in Arthur Smith (ed.), *A Series of Chapters about My Great Idea* (Washington: Crane Russak), 55–66.

Works with multiple authors:
Smith, Arthur, Philip Smith, and Rose Smith. 1989. *Our Great Ideas*. New York: Farrar, Straus.

Collective authorship
The Economist. 2004. "Great Ideas that Aren't Really so Great." 2004. *The Economist* (August 15), 44–46.

Translated works:
Smith, Arthur. 1989. *My Great Idea*, trans. Hugh Smith. New York: Farrar, Straus.

Newspaper articles:
Smith, Arthur. 1989. "My Great Idea, in Brief." *New York Times* (May 31), 44–55.

Journal articles:
Smith, Arthur. 1989. "My Great Idea Dressed Up as Social Science." *American Political Science Review* **11**.1: 44–55. [11 refers to the volume #; 1 refers to the issue #; 44–55 is the pagination.]

For the web:
Work that has appeared, or will appear, in printed form (e.g., the *New York Times* on the Web), can be cited as if it were printed material (as above). If there is no printed version, or the printed version has different pagination or is otherwise altered from the Web version, construct a bibliographic entry that approximates your entry for books and articles. At the end of the entry, give the exact Web address from which you downloaded the material and the date that you downloaded it.

In handling citations you may wish to employ software that is either incorporated in your word processing program or can be imported to it. Popular citation software (aka bibliographic software, citation managers, or reference managers) includes *BiblioExpress/Biblioscape*, *Endnote*, *Mendelay*, *ProCite*, *RefWorks*, *Reference Manager*, and *Zotero*. These programs import citations from databases and websites, build and organize bibliographies, and format citations (according to your choice of format). They may also allow you to take notes on articles and to save other files (e.g., PDFs). Note that most of these programs are proprietary, so you will need to purchase the software or employ a site license.

Editing

The skill of writing is learned primarily by writing, not by reading about writing. That is why this is a short chapter rather than a long one (though there is no harm in reading longer treatises such as those listed at the end of this chapter).

However, the act of writing, by itself, is unlikely to advance your skills. You also need feedback. You should look closely at the comments you receive from your teachers. Request that they comment on the *form* of your essay, not simply its content.

Be aware that very few writers – even professional writers – get it right the first time. Good writing depends upon *rewriting*. Usually it is better to write quickly, in a stream of consciousness, rather than to slave over sentence structure the first time a sentence is formed. Editing, in any case, is essential. Careful proofreading can tell you where things work and where they're not so clear or convincing. Reading the paper aloud to yourself may also alert you to stylistic problems that look innocent enough on the written page but sound awkward or confusing when spoken.

If you can enlist a friend to read the paper – one who will give honest feedback without sparing your feelings – this is often extremely helpful. By the time you have written a paper you are perhaps *too* familiar with the subject matter to be an objective judge of your communication skills. Someone with no knowledge of the topic is in a better position to tell whether you have done a good job of getting your point across. If he or she doesn't get it, or has to struggle to understand it, then you have done a poor job.

As you proofread, make sure that you are actually addressing your thesis in some way in every paragraph. You may wish to keep a sentence-long copy of your thesis taped to a wall next to you as you write so that you can remind yourself of your argument. This is a good way to identify and eliminate dilatory points.

CONCLUSIONS

By way of conclusion, let us review the most important criteria of all social science papers, whether written for a classroom assignment, for the completion of an advanced degree, or for publication. These may be summarized in the following questions.

1 Is there a thesis and is it clearly stated?
2 Is the thesis significant? Does it matter?
3 Is the thesis adequately argued or proven (within the constraints imposed by time, resources, and available sources)?
4 Is the study innovative with respect to theory, method, or findings? Does it expand our knowledge of the chosen subject?
5 Is the essay well written, i.e., cogently organized, grammatically correct, stylistically elegant, and citing all appropriate sources?

Flaws in one of these categories may be compensated by virtues in others, but generally speaking an essay must satisfy all five in order to qualify as excellent. This chapter has focused primarily on the fifth, though we have stressed repeatedly that matters of form can never be neatly separated from matters of substance.

Writing is the perhaps most important basic skill that the social sciences and humanities impart, and the skill upon which the liberal professions (law, medicine, academics) and business still depend. Getting good grades, getting into the graduate or professional school of your choice, getting a job, and succeeding in that line of work will rest, in part, on your ability to put your thoughts on paper clearly and persuasively.

Freshman English classes give you a start on the road to good writing. However, writing must be practiced continually or the skill atrophies. It is in your interest to pay attention to writing as a craft, and to practice that craft as frequently as possible.

Whatever its role in enhancing your career, good writing is also inherently rewarding. If you wish to influence the world – to change the way people think about something, to offer a new idea or solution – you will need to find a way to communicate that idea to the public, or to some portion of the public with a special interest in what you have to say. Doing so will probably require you to put your words into a coherent, organized format, e.g., a memo, article, essay, or book. If you think that your argument matters then the communication of that argument matters. One without the other will not go very far.

KEY TERMS

- Book review
- Literature review
- Policy report
- Monograph

15 | Speaking

Having surveyed the craft of writing, we turn to the craft of speaking, the oral form of language. Good speaking is somewhat different from good writing. Of course, one can simply read a prepared text, in which case the difference virtually disappears. But this does not generally qualify as good speaking in an academic or professional context – unless, that is, it is carefully honed to appear as if it is extemporaneous.

People expect a "live" performance. Your presence should be real, unmediated. Naturally, it may be mediated by various technologies and it may be pre-recorded; but it should feel as if it is happening right here and right now. This is the dynamic quality of public speaking. It is a special quality that is probably hard-wired in our brains and therefore carries a resonance that cannot be simulated with prose.

Public speaking is inextricably linked to comportment, i.e., how you carry yourself. Every time you make a public intervention you convey a vision of yourself. It is this persona that people tend to remember. Thus, when we say "speech" in this chapter we intend to include all the visual cues that accompany speech – dress, gaze, posture, gestures, and so forth.

In ancient times, speech was the preeminent art of persuasion. Rhetoric meant speech, and only secondarily prose or poetry. That prioritization is easy to understand in the context of a predominantly oral culture.

Nowadays, the craft of public speaking has fallen into desuetude (though some writing courses also include a component devoted to public speaking). People still talk, but speech is no longer cultivated as a professional activity, with a few exceptions such as moot courts in law school. This is unfortunate because speech is no less important today than it was a century ago. Perhaps it is destined to become more important over time as online lectures and YouTube videos replace written texts, and video calls and video conferences replace email. The spoken word may turn out to be mightier than the written word.

In any case, whether you are a good speaker or a poor speaker is likely to affect how successfully you can get your ideas across – not to mention getting good grades, landing a job, and succeeding in your chosen profession. To be sure, college courses generally don't allocate much credit for participation. Nor is an employer likely to admit that she or he hired someone because they present themselves well. However, we suspect that oral presentation matters a lot more than instructors, or employers, are willing to admit – or are even aware of.

Following is some advice culled from various sources and from our own experience. This advice is framed primarily around the task of delivering a formal presentation – a talk or lecture. At the end of the chapter we discuss the complementary role: how to participate in discussion as an audience member.

Be aware that everyone comes to the task of public speaking with different strengths and weaknesses. For some people, fear of speaking before an audience is the main obstacle; for others, unfamiliarity with English. Some have lots of experience; others do not. Tailor the following advice to your own circumstance.

Your Public Image

Your public image must fit the setting, i.e., the audience and the topic. If your topic is genocide, don't wear something garish. If the setting is professional, dress professionally. If you're not sure it probably won't hurt to over-dress. Likewise, adopt a form of address that is consistent with the setting. Don't speak colloquially unless the occasion is sufficiently relaxed to allow for it.

People are sometimes offended if the speaker is more informally attired than the audience, or if the speaker adopts an informal tone. These visual and verbal cues may be taken as a sign of disrespect, especially if you are younger than most members of the audience or from a different social class or cultural background. The greater the distance (chronological, cultural, economic, whatever) between you and them, the more important it is to convey respect in your choice of clothes, your bearing, and your words.

At the same time, the most important part of establishing a public image is finding a stage presence that feels comfortable *to you*. After all, you're the one that has to wear the suit (or whatever it is that you choose to wear) and you're the one who must inhabit the persona that you establish. If you are comfortable you will be relaxed, and the audience will likely be too. What makes audiences squirm is when they can see that the speaker is uncomfortable. So, be comfortable with yourself and try to convey that comfort to the audience – without being arrogant. A fine line separates confidence from conceit.

Format

Most talks in academic and professional settings last 30–40 minutes and are followed by a question-and-answer period, which may last a half hour or as long as people remain in the room. Even if your host tells you that there is no time-limit you should still impose a limit on your talk. Our own experience suggests that 30–40 minutes is about the upper limit of what most people are willing to sit through in an academic or professional setting. After that, they get fidgety. If you go on longer you are likely to lose the audience – literally and or figuratively.

You will also lose the opportunity to hear their input because you have used up all the time available.

So time your talk carefully. And remember that it usually takes longer to do things "live" than in a practice session. Cut material mercilessly, honing things down until you can get through your talk in an unhurried fashion in the allotted time.

Naturally, the protocol obtaining at a talk will vary according to the setting. Among economists, it is common to pepper the speaker with all sorts of questions – often critical – which may be launched at any point during the talk. In other settings, audience members generally limit themselves to points of information, waiting for the speaker to finish before offering comments and criticism.

The smaller the group the greater the opportunity for informal back-and-forth between speaker and audience. Sometimes, the assembled group is so small that there is little separation between speaker and listeners; it is like speaking to friends in a living room.

Make sure that you know what the established format is and that your presentation conforms to it (more or less). If the ground rules are unclear and you wish to establish some parameters, make sure you do so at the beginning of the talk.

Visual Aids

Nowadays, presentations are usually accompanied by PowerPoint slides or some equivalent technology. For most settings, including most academic settings, this is strongly advised. PowerPoint allows you to present the main ideas along with other visual materials such as graphs, data tables, pictures, perhaps even video clips. This is all to the good. But don't let the slides get in the way of the talk, and don't let it replace you as the center of attention. It's OK to glance at the screen from time to time, to draw the audience's attention to it. But we suggest focusing mostly on the audience, encouraging them to watch you along with the projected images.

It is worth spending a bit of time putting your slides together. Think carefully about each slide and try to minimize the number of words and images on each one. Concision is even more important for slides than it is for prose. Try to group related ideas on the same slide, so as to limit the number of slides you show.

You may prepare additional slides as back-up, in preparation for specific questions that your presentation does not cover. These can be kept in a separate file or at the end of your slide-show. They are the presentational equivalent of an appendix.

Graphs, figures, and pictures are often helpful – if they contribute to your argument. But don't feel obliged to insert colorful filler if it does not relate to the argument. This will detract from your task and you are less likely to be taken seriously.

Likewise, if the statistical tables you are presenting are too large to fit on a slide (and be read by those in the back of a room), consider printing out copies for members of the audience, or at least for those who may be interested. In some settings, this is important. You don't want to find yourself in a situation where you have to answer queries by saying "Trust me, it's in the fine print."

Practice

There is an old saying, variously attributed, about the game of golf. "Golf," says the pro, "is a game of luck. And the more I practice, the luckier I get."[175] This is true of most things, and it is certainly true of public speaking.

If you are faced with an important occasion such as a class presentation, you probably should practice your talk multiple times. You may even wish to write it out as a script. However, you certainly don't want to memorize the script, as it will probably come out in a "canned" fashion (unless you are an extremely skilled performer). Instead, make sure you become familiar with the key points, the key terms and phrases, and have your notes on-hand as back-up if you freeze on the spot. The best way to practice is to give the talk to friends, a mock-up of the real thing. Try to make this as realistic as possible so that you can simulate the experience. If you expect questions from the audience, instruct your friends to ask questions (without sniggering).

Know Your Audience

With speaking, as with writing, it pays to know your audience. In a classroom setting, you have the advantage of intimate familiarity. Of course, you don't want to pander, even if it pleases the room. While your classmates may be looking for diversion, your professor is probably looking for you to grapple with a social science topic in a serious fashion. So, bear this in mind.

Likewise, in a public setting where you don't know everyone – perhaps you don't know anyone – think carefully about the sort of person that is likely to be present at this event. What is their background? How much do they know about your subject? What will they find interesting, and perhaps unexpected? What will they find humorous? What, more importantly, might they find offensive?

It helps to know in a general way what your audience is expecting to get from your presentation. Of course, you may not be able to give them precisely what they wish. But knowing what they want will help you craft your talk. At the very least, you can address their expectations and try to reframe them to suit your own interests and capacities, and your own sense of what is important.

In any case, you should be clear at the outset about what you aim to deliver in the talk, and make sure you achieve those goals. Set your own expectations. This is usually sufficient. Unmet expectations are much more problematic when a talk fails to deliver on its own terms; that is, questions or problems raised at the outset or suggested by the topic are not adequately addressed.

Speak Naturally (and, if Possible, Grammatically)

Spoken English is different from written English (as, we assume, the spoken version of any language is different from its written version). When speaking extemporaneously one can scarcely avoid grammatical mistakes. One may not find exactly the right word at the tip of one's tongue. This is perfectly understandable. However, your goal should be to emulate correct speech.

Minimize your use of "ugggh" and other space-fillers. Don't be afraid of dead air in your talk. No one should talk continually for a half-hour, and the introduction of a few open spaces will give your audience a chance to breathe (figuratively) and will heighten the drama of what follows.

Try to suppress colloquial expressions. For example, employ the locution "like" only when comparing things – not, like, when pausing in the middle of a sentence.

Emulating correct written English does *not* mean that you must speak in long sentences with lots of polysyllabic words. Extemporaneous speech should be natural, not stilted. If you use words that are usually encountered only in a written form your audience is likely to be confused.

Relate to the Whole Room

Do your best to relate to the audience (and to the camera if it is being filmed). This means scanning the room to make eye contact with as many people as you can as you speak. Of course, you may not actually be making eye contact. Generally, when one is speaking to a large room one tries *not* to focus on anyone in particular, as it tends to be rather distracting. Instead, let your gaze wander about the room so that everyone is made to feel involved. If you look only at one part of the room, those sitting elsewhere are bound to feel neglected. They may even feel that the speaker does not care for them, or that the speaker is playing favorites. Of course, there are generally some persons in the room who are more active in asking questions and making comments than others, and these windbags may be sitting in the same place. This is all the more reason to scan the rest of the room, so others feel that they are part of the enterprise and that the speaker is not responding only to the blowhards.

Another way to engage members located far away is to wander up and down the aisle, or pace back and forth at the front of the room. A moving target enlivens the show. (But there is no need for stage antics.) Make sure that those in the back of the room can hear you. One may even start a talk by asking this question: "Can you hear me?" This also gets the back of the room engaged, sending a message that the speaker recognizes them and cares about their participation.

Entertain (a Little)

In a public speech (as opposed to an academic paper), people generally expect some divertissement – a joke, a story, a bit of narrative to relieve an otherwise tendentious argument. This will help you win your audience over, and keep them awake. Typically, the speaker opens with a joke.

Years ago, one of the authors attended a talk by Peter Skerry, a noted political scientist. After being introduced, Skerry remarked: "Some of you are probably expecting me to open with a joke. Well, I don't have one. So, if anyone feels obliged to laugh, now is your opportunity to do so." This brought guffaws. He had won us over by calling attention to the absurdity of the begin-with-a-joke protocol.

Of course, there is a well-grounded reason for beginning with a joke. Like most rituals, it plays a sociological function. Humor is well suited to establishing rapport and relieving situations of stress. The beginning of a talk is a situation in which these two functions must be performed. Otherwise, everyone feels awkward.

Jokes are funny when they play off context. Canned jokes generally fail, especially when the teller is not a professional comedian and the setting is not a comedy club. So, in introducing humor to your talk, think about what is funny in the setting in which you find yourself.

Further back in time, one of us attended a talk by Mervin Field, the founder of the Field Poll, a leading polling firm in California. Field was being introduced by Merrill Shanks, and Shanks was reading from a page with a long list of accolades, which seemed to include everything Field had accomplished since he was toilet-trained (which was quite a lot). This went on for some time. Finally, Shanks finished and gave the floor to Fields. Fields shuffled up to the front of the room, leaned over to Shanks with his hand cupped in a mock attempt to shield his words from the audience, and stage-whispered: "I hope you didn't have any trouble reading my handwriting."

Jokes are fun when they're funny. However, you should not allow humorous comments to upstage your argument. An academic or professional setting is quite unlike other settings insofar as the main focus must remain the subject matter. Some speakers are able to integrate humor and story-telling seamlessly into a talk without drawing attention away from the subject matter. But this is a finely-honed skill and it is easy for the novice to get carried away. When in doubt, opt for a sober presentation rather than a hilarious one. Otherwise, people will come away from your talk guffawing, but they will not take you – or your ideas – seriously. You want them to remember the punchline of your talk, not the punchline of your joke.

Calm Your Nerves

For those who are inclined to get a bit queasy when we look out over a hundred heads, here is some advice.

If you mis-speak – forgetting a noun or mispronouncing a word – correct yourself and move on. There is no need to call attention to it. If appropriate, you may wish to joke about it. No one will care about these verbal slip-ups, so do not allow them to distract you.

As you look out over the room people will be in various stages of attention and inattention. Some will be eyeing you closely; others will be fiddling with their phones or reading. There is not much you can do about this, and you shouldn't imagine it reflects upon you or your performance. Likewise, some members of the audience may leave while you are speaking. Again, this may have nothing to do with you; they may have a previous engagement, or they may have discovered they are in the wrong room. Any number of factors might be at work. But you should be aware that this reflects badly on the audience, not on you, and other folks in the room are likely to be sympathetic to you if they observe it.

Another feature of public speaking that you may find disconcerting is that most members of the audience will not react to what you are saying. They will stare, passively, as if watching TV. Those in the back of the room may feel invisible, exactly as they do when watching television. This is likely to strike the speaker as odd. When we speak to people we generally expect them to respond, verbally or facially. Non-response is generally interpreted as a sign of extreme rudeness, if not autism. But public speaking is different. Although it is live, and although there should be some interaction between speaker and audience, the speaker often drones on for some period of time without cues from the other side. Indeed, the speaker may have no idea how the audience is receiving the talk until it is over. Part of becoming a practiced speaker is getting used to speaking into a vacuum. Alternatively, locate a few people in the audience who appear to be following you closely, nodding sympathetically, laughing at your jokes. Pretend that you are speaking to them and forget about everyone else in the room. (Of course, you still need to cast your eyes across the whole room so no one feels excluded.)

Foster Exchange

The most important piece of advice for effective public speaking in academic or professional contexts is not to think too much about yourself. As you stand in front of the room, think instead about the reason you are there. That is, focus on the subject matter. Your function is not to display yourself for public acclaim (or disapprobation). This is not a beauty contest, nor is it a contest of brains. Your purpose is to communicate important information about a subject that you know something about (more, at any rate, than most members of the audience). This is your reason for being there.

Likewise, members of the audience are not antagonists – even if some of them behave in an antagonistic way. They are your allies in the search for the truth, which is – always, and necessarily – a communal venture. So, when you start your talk enlist these allies. Tell them that you hope your presentation leads to a lively discussion and that you welcome their input.

Granted, you might prefer a quiescent audience that passively accepts whatever you serve up – better yet, an audience that erupts into applause the moment you have finished speaking. However, this sort of response is not going to contribute to your thinking on the topic. Your quest for knowledge will not be enhanced.

Forward movement in a field usually begins with debate. And one debate leads to another. This is what academic and professional discourse is all about, or should be about. Thus, debate is what you should expect and what you should look forward to when you make a presentation in an academic or professional setting. It is a sign that your audience is taking you seriously. By contrast, if the room falls silent when you are done speaking, or if you receive polite responses but no searching questions, this is a sign that people are not engaged with your work. They don't get it, or they don't care.

If debate erupts after a talk you can assume that you have successfully engaged your audience. They are convinced that the subject is important and that what you have to say about it is important, even if they don't agree with you or if they agree with the general argument but are critical of some aspect of your presentation. This is the sign of a successful talk. It is hoped that the discussion leads to insights, for you and for the members of the audience. In this fashion, our collective knowledge of a subject is advanced.

Be Gracious

When handling debate, be gracious. Even if they hold views that you find repugnant, remember that they are human beings, and as such worthy of respect and understanding. They may have good reasons to hold the views they hold. In any case, to respect a person does not mean that you respect everything that she or he says or does. It is possible – and, arguably, essential – to accord respect to persons who have violated fundamental human rights. It follows that you should also respect those with whom you have ideological, substantive, or methodological disagreements.

It is tricky, to be sure, to convey a sense of respect for someone while arguing vehemently with them. You may need to monitor your words and gestures carefully, for it does not come naturally. Generally, when we argue about something that argument is accompanied by a degree of hostility toward the person we are arguing with. We strike an antagonistic pose. We roll our eyes, look away, or find ways to express contempt for the person we are confronting. These ingrained responses must be controlled, for they tend to personalize the conflict and lead away from any possibility of rational debate or reconciliation. Each side digs in and refuses to cede ground.

Remind yourself that the purpose of academic and professional debate is to find the right (or best) answer, not to win an argument or to prove one's intellectual superiority. The true intellectual is one who seeks truth, not one who seeks victory. Learn how to argue with someone (or with a whole room) without conveying contempt or dismay.

You may find it helpful to preface your response to a critical comment with a disarming comment like, "That's an interesting point, . . ." This turn of phrase should not be over-used or applied in situations where it is patently inapplicable. However, it is always good to begin by acknowledging the interlocutor's perspective. Everyone wants to be acknowledged. And as the speaker you have special powers in this domain.

Another point to bear in mind is that disagreements are less invidious when they are openly acknowledged. So whenever you think that you might be saying something that others would take issue with, call attention to this fact. In doing so, you confer respect upon those who hold this opposing view. It is a rhetorical bowing of the head or doffing of the cap.

The most noxious statements are unacknowledged assumptions. Indeed, people generally take offense not when they disagree with your argument but when they disagree with your premises. This recalls the witticism: *When did you stop beating your wife?* What is annoying about the question is the assumption contained in the predicate. Anyone addressed in this manner is apt to be driven into frenzy.

Likewise, do not assume that members of the audience share your ideology or your worldview. It is common in social science settings to find a predominance of liberals and leftists, so much so that speakers may easily assume that everyone in the room shares this political perspective. Imagine how uncomfortable someone with more conservative views might feel if the basis of a comment – perhaps intended to be humorous – is the wrongness of their politics.

Audience Participation

Thus far, our comments have been addressed to situations in which you are called upon to make a formal presentation (a talk or lecture). Most of this advice is also applicable to situations in which you participate as a member of an audience, e.g., in a classroom setting where someone else (a teacher or fellow-student) is holding the floor. Be respectful of your audience; be mindful of how you present yourself; consider the audience and the context carefully; use various techniques for combating nervousness; and so forth. However, there are some distinctive features to audience participation that deserve special consideration.

Participation is a formal component of some courses. Even where it is not accorded a portion of your grade, your participation is likely to affect the teacher's opinion of you as a person and a scholar. As such, it may influence your grade in subtle ways and it will certainly influence any letter of recommendation that you are able to extract from the instructor. (Nota bene: this letter may be much more important for your future prospects than the grade you receive in the course.) Instructors, like the rest of us, tend to remember personal interventions more vividly than written work. Or, perhaps, they all blend together.

In any case, participation is a vital part of your education. If you participate regularly in class discussion you are more likely to enjoy the course, to remember its content, and to think creatively about the subject.

Talking extemporaneously on a subject works the brain, just as making a structured presentation does, but in somewhat different ways. Talking "from the floor" allows you to think in a relatively unstructured fashion about a topic, without having devoted countless hours of preparation. In formulating your words you may find yourself thinking about things differently. You may come to new insights. This is what the classroom experience is all about, or should be all about. (Regrettably, some classes consist of canned lectures delivered to passive audiences, who stare at their notes or computer screens, struggling to stay awake.)

You may think of questions and comments as an unwanted intrusion on a well-crafted presentation. You may wonder about your capacity to engage a complex subject, which the speaker has been studying for many years and about which others in the room may have superior knowledge. You may fear embarrassment.

This is entirely the wrong attitude. Bear in mind that an academic talk is not a finished work of art meant to be observed from a distance like a dance performance, a symphony, or a play. It is a *participatory* art form where little distinguishes the speaker from the audience, except that the former happens to be in front of the podium and the latter are seated around a table or in some arrangement in the hall. Where eminent people sit in the audience, their response to the presentation is often more eagerly anticipated than the speaker's own presentation. Regardless of who is in attendance, the hall generally comes alive in the Q&A (question-and-answer) period. This is what academics look forward to for it is the dynamic part of the talk, where an argument is put to test and where new ideas are vetted. By contrast, the talk itself may be a formality, especially if the speaker's argument is well known. So, rather than thinking of participation as auxiliary to the talk you might think of the talk as auxiliary to the discussion. A formal presentation facilitates productive debate, focusing the discussion – usually on matters that are in dispute, leaving other issues (those that everyone more or less agrees upon) in the background, where they belong. A talk without Q&A is like a symphony without a crescendo.

In an educational environment, where the speaker is an expert and the audience are novices, the situation is slightly different. There is more separation between speaker and audience, for one thing. However, it is still the case that the format of live presentation is served only if there is some interaction. Indeed, without such interaction between speaker and audience (or among audience members) there is nothing to distinguish a live lecture from one that is viewed on video or streamed online. There must be a purpose for bringing speaker and audience together in one place. That purpose is for the two parties to interact.

Likewise, intervening regularly in class discussion will serve your educational goals. You are likely to feel more involved, more motivated, and more engaged in the class. (At the very least, your instructor will have that impression, and this will serve you well at the end of the semester.)

Note also that instructors generally appreciate questions and comments, even critical ones. There is nothing so discouraging as talking to a silent – and apparently indifferent – room. If you show the lecturer that you are following what is going on, and thinking independently about the material, she or he is likely to be grateful. And you are likely to be rewarded – and certainly not punished – for having spoken your mind.

Naturally, it is more difficult to participate in a cavernous hall, where the number of audience members precludes a lot of talk from the floor. Some courses are structured so as to facilitate a good deal of student participation; others are not. With that caveat, we would encourage you to participate whenever it is possible and appropriate to do so.

In planning your interventions, here are some guidelines to follow:

- If there is an assigned reading for that day, make sure that you have read it.
- Listen carefully to the lecture and discussion prior to intervening.
- Avoid repeating points that have been raised previously (unless you have something new to say about them).
- Make sure that your question or comment is germane. It should follow the previous point. If it refers back to something covered earlier, point this out. And if others are wishing to engage the current topic, let them have their say before changing the subject. (Sometimes it is helpful to employ the *one finger/two finger rule*. Raising one finger indicates that you have a new point to make. Raising two fingers indicates that your comment follows the previous comment. Two fingers trump one finger, facilitating the logical flow of discussion.)[176]
- Do not think of participation simply as a matter of "saying something." There are insightful comments and questions, and there is also drivel. Consider what you want to say before raising your hand, especially in a large hall. You may even jot down a few notes, which you can refer to as needed.
- Be judicious in the use of anecdotes drawn from your personal life. We all have stories, but these stories are not always relevant to the subject matter. In an informal setting (e.g., a coffee-house) it is appropriate to indicate your personal connection to what a speaker has to say. But it is not good form in an academic setting – unless, that is, the anecdote moves the discussion forward. There must be a point to any story – whether drawn on your experience or someone else's.
- Don't dominate the discussion. If you have spoken already and others have not yet had a chance, wait for a few moments before raising your hand or cede the floor if you see that others wish to be involved.
- Don't be afraid to make a mistake. Making mistakes is part of the learning experience. If you do not allow yourself to make mistakes you are preventing yourself from learning. We make mistakes all the time. There is nothing wrong with a wrong answer. Oftentimes, the most productive sort of answer or question is one that reveals what is *not* clear in a presentation, and is thus on everyone's mind.

CONCLUSIONS

Some people enjoy speaking to a crowd. Others detest it. We suspect that the difference between the two is that some are more comfortable in the spotlight than others, and this in turn is largely a product of familiarity. After all, most of us like attention. And this is an opportunity to get a lot of attention, and perhaps some accolades as well.

There is a common view that good speakers are born rather than raised. We don't think this is any truer than the idea that good writers or good mathematicians are genetically endowed. In any case, whatever your native capabilities, there is probably a lot that you can do to improve your speaking ability. Indeed, the fact that public speaking is neither taught nor systematically practiced in most academic settings suggests that, for most of us, there may be great room for improvement. We can become much better speakers if we put our minds (and voices) to the task.

To that end, this chapter has introduced a number of tips that may prove useful to you as you work to improve your presentation of self, and your presentation of ideas. Here, as elsewhere, practice is important. Unlike some other skills, this one cannot be mastered on your own.

Ethics refers to formal and informal codes of behavior, i.e., the rightness or wrongness of an action as judged by a community. In the present context, we are of course concerned with ethical norms that apply to the activity of social science.

Ethical concerns are often raised in conjunction with experiments, where some subjects are assigned to a treatment condition and others to a control condition. If the treatment condition is potentially dangerous – or potentially beneficial – there are obvious ethical concerns. Why should one group of subjects be singled out in a wholly arbitrary fashion? What could justify such an intervention?

While they may be less apparent, ethical concerns also impinge upon other aspects of social science, e.g., to the collection of data from human subjects by observational methods, data analysis, and the dissemination of data and results. Arguably, everything that one might do, or refrain from doing, has ethical implications. Consequently, we take a broad view of the subject.

The chapter begins by discussing the *juridical* conception of ethics – centered on statutes, legal precedents, and institutional rules. Next, we discuss the central importance of protecting human subjects. Finally, we explore the activity of social science as an ethical sphere of action. What is right (moral) conduct for a social scientist?

Juridical Ethics

The juridical conception of ethics refers to rules one is obliged to follow as a member of a university, a profession, or a country. Universities in the United States are obliged, as a condition of receiving federal funding, to establish a set of procedures to govern research with human subjects. This involves the formation of an **Institutional Review Board** (IRB) to apply the protocol and to approve specific research proposals submitted by students or university employees. (IRBs may also be referred to as ethics review boards.) All research on human subjects is subject to approval by the IRB. Even research that does not involve human subjects – such as historical research – may require IRB exemption. Thus, IRBs have become an integral part of scientific research at all American universities – at least, all universities that receive federal funding.

Those interested in the general goals of the IRB process are advised to take a look at the Belmont Report issued by the National Commission for the Protection of Human Subjects of Biomedical and Behavioral Research in 1979. This document informs all IRB processes.

Similar protocols have been developed in universities outside the United States and within businesses and research organizations, though there is considerable variety in procedures and methods of enforcement. Likewise, since every university in the United States sets its own procedures, and empanels its own IRB, there is considerable variety even across American universities.

Researchers are well advised to familiarize themselves with IRB requirements wherever they are situated. The penalty for not abiding by these regulations may be severe, as it constitutes a very explicit form of professional misconduct and may be grounds for dismissal. In addition, professional associations generally publish a code of ethics. Membership in an association implies an acceptance of this code, and violation of the code may, in principle, result in expulsion from the association.

Protection of Human Subjects

The vital importance of protecting human subjects became apparent to the world in the wake of the Tuskegee syphilis experiment in which black victims of the disease in rural Alabama were studied by the US Public Health Service for several decades without treatment and without even being informed that they had contracted the disease.

At the present time, protection of human subjects is vested primarily in IRBs, as discussed above. The principles underlying the IRB process are laid out in the **Belmont Report**, which reviews two main topics: informed consent and assessment of risks and benefits. (A third topic, the selection of subjects, is somewhat less important and is largely subsumed under the former. Quotations in the following paragraphs are from the Belmont Report.)

Informed consent refers to the principle that "subjects, to the degree that they are capable, be given the opportunity to choose what shall or shall not happen to them." Consent procedures may involve signing a form or otherwise giving explicit consent to the researcher.

Evidently, subjects cannot make informed choices unless they are informed of the nature of the activity they are participating in. This involves, at the very least, information about who is sponsoring the study, what its goals are, how long the process will take, what will be required of them, and any costs or benefits that they might realize as a result of participation. In addition, they should be given an opportunity to ask questions and to withdraw their participation at any point.

The quandary of informed consent is that, quite often, a study may be compromised if the participants in that study are fully informed of its research goals. For example, in any experiment subjects' choices are likely to be affected if they are told what the experiment is about. Imagine conducting a study of cheating in which subjects are given the opportunity to cheat on an exam. If subjects are informed of the purpose of the experiment no one is likely to cheat (and if they do, one may wonder about how to interpret this behavior).

The issue of informed consent is thus a delicate one. Sometimes, it is deemed sufficient if the participant is informed of the general topic undertaken by the researcher, described in a diffuse manner that is unlikely to affect how the informant responds to stimuli. Regardless of prior knowledge, participants should be fully informed (de-briefed) about the specific purposes of the experiment when their participation is completed.

Special consideration must be taken for subjects who are minors, mentally impaired, unfamiliar with the language, or for some other reason unable to exercise informed consent. Likewise, if subjects feel special obligations or pressures to serve as participants in a study, perhaps because they are being enlisted by someone in a position of authority (e.g., their professor) or perhaps because their peers are participating, the goal of informed consent may be thwarted. Informed consent "requires conditions free of coercion and undue influence," whatever those may be.

A somewhat lower bar for informed consent may be granted for research subjects who occupy positions of prominence and power (e.g., political leaders). The assumption is that by virtue of the public nature of their profession and the generally recognized need to subject such individuals to special scrutiny, prominent individuals have less claim to privacy than others (at least as regards features of their life that are relevant to their public duties).

The assessment of *risks* and *benefits* is perhaps the most complex aspect of human subjects research. Risk may involve possible "psychological harm, physical harm, legal harm, social harm [or] economic harm." In a large study, with thousands of participants and (let us imagine) a long questionnaire, it is quite possible that some untoward consequence will result to a few of the participants. The most likely sort of harm is psychological. Insofar as research involves topics that are sensitive – at least to some subjects – those subjects may experience distress as a result of their participation. If they are already in a condition of anxiety, fear, or depression, that distress may be especially severe and may have consequences for them or those they are intimate with.

It is fatuous to suppose that social science research – or, for that matter, medical research – could be conducted without doing any harm to anyone. The avoidance of harm must be considered a relative matter, and must be judged against the possible benefits to be gained from the research.

The Belmont Report specifies:

- Brutal or inhumane treatment of human subjects is never morally justified.
- Risks should be reduced to those necessary to achieve the research objective. It should be determined whether it is in fact necessary to use human subjects at all. Risk can perhaps never be entirely eliminated, but it can often be reduced by careful attention to alternative procedures.
- When research involves significant risk of serious impairment, review committees should be extraordinarily insistent on the justification of the risk (looking

usually to the likelihood of benefit to the subject – or, in some rare cases, to the manifest voluntariness of the participation).

- When vulnerable populations are involved in research, the appropriateness of involving them should itself be demonstrated. A number of variables go into such judgments, including the nature and degree of risk, the condition of the particular population involved, and the nature and level of the anticipated benefits.
- Relevant risks and benefits must be thoroughly arrayed in documents and procedures used in the informed consent process.

One important mechanism for limiting harm to subjects is to guarantee anonymity or confidentiality. **Anonymity** means that the researcher has no knowledge of the identity of subjects under study, who remain anonymous. Most surveys do not require the name of the respondent, so a limited form of anonymity is usually possible. However, there may be identifying information contained in the survey, so researchers will need to be careful about releasing this information if they have guaranteed anonymity to their subjects.

Confidentiality means that the researcher is aware of the identity of subjects but promises not to reveal it to others. This may be accomplished by keeping names in a separate database (perhaps even on a separate computer) and referring to subjects only by an assigned number or pseudonym. Again, the problem of identifying information must be handled carefully.

The Belmont Report has been quoted extensively because of its broad impact on the conduct of IRBs and on the consideration of ethical norms pertaining to the protection of human subjects. However, the diffuse nature of the mandate to protect human subjects, and the largely autonomous work of IRBs within institutions throughout the world, leads to considerable unevenness of application. Inevitably, some valuable studies with (arguably) few negative implications for human subjects never gain approval, and some not-so-valuable studies with negative implications for human subjects gain approval. The process is not perfect.

Moreover, everyone covered by an IRB protocol is obliged to spend a lot of time satisfying these procedures, a (relatively) unproductive use of academic resources. At the same time, those living *outside* IRB regimes – such as researchers working for international NGOs such as the World Bank, private sector businesses, or journalists – have very little oversight.

It is troubling that studies with an academic objective receive much closer ethical scrutiny than activities undertaken for commercial or journalistic purposes. For example, if a company wishes to conduct a survey, focus group, experiment, or participant-observation study in order to market-test a new product the researchers engaged by that company are unlikely to undergo a rigorous IRB process. If the same study were taken by a student or professor within a university they would be required to be IRB compliant. This divergence of standards is difficult to justify.

Broader Ethical Issues

Ethics pertaining to social science begins with the protection of human subjects. That is why it is commonly associated with the process of data collection, and especially with obtrusive approaches to data collection such as experiments with a manipulated treatment. However, ethical considerations do not end there.

In conducting social science research one is (hopefully!) affecting others in society. Some research is directed explicitly at policymakers or at the general public. Even if it is directed at other academics the general expectation is that it will, eventually, have an echo in the broader society of which academics are a part. If this weren't the case – if we engaged in social research purely for our own edification or entertainment – the enterprise wouldn't be very satisfying. For most of us, there is an expectation that our ideas will change the world, even if only modestly.

It follows that a complete consideration of social science ethics involves a consideration of social science's role in society and how that role might be fashioned in the best possible way.

Arguably, the contribution of social science to society lies in its capacity to elucidate useful truths, i.e., insights into topics that citizens and policymakers care about. To the extent that members of the various social science tribes are successfully performing this task we might say that they are acting ethically. To the extent that they are not, we might say that they are violating an implicit ethical obligation to be of service to society.

The question then becomes, which features of social science – which norms and rules – are conducive to elucidating useful truths? The answer, we would suggest, are all those features generally regarded as part of social science methodology, as laid out in this book.

Of course, some norms are not universally agreed upon. The point remains that insofar as a norm promotes useful truths it is rightly accompanied by an ethical imperative. Consider a norm that most practitioners would probably agree upon such as *replicability*. Replicability is generally regarded as promoting the advancement of science. Likewise, violating this ideal by failing to cite sources, to make available one's data, or to leave a trail that other scholars can follow, is regarded as destructive of scientific advance. If we cannot replicate studies we cannot cumulate knowledge on the subject those studies address. Consequently, a violation of this methodological principle is generally regarded as a gross violation of academic norms. This is just one example of how methodological rules carry normative freight. They are not just bees in a methodologist's bonnet.

It may seem odd to associate methodology with ethics. After all, methodologists occupy an academic niche far removed from the field of moral philosophy. But methodologists are the standard-setters and standard-keepers of "good behavior" in the social sciences. They are the makers and enforcers of professional norms. We are not referring to norms like the prohibition against sexual encounters with students or against plagiarism; these we will classify as general norms insofar as they apply to everyone, not just academics. By professional norms we mean norms that are specific to social science.

So, if good social science is our contribution to society, then the methodological norms that contribute to good social science have ethical sanction. In this respect, it may be argued, the ethics of social science extend far beyond the obligation to respect the rights of human subjects in our data-gathering efforts. They extend, in a diffuse fashion, to all the other subjects raised in this book.

The Purview of Social Science

One final point relates to the purview of social science, a theme raised initially in Chapter 1. In proposing that social science should make a positive contribution to society we are not supposing that we are the sole contributors to human advancement – or, for that matter, the sole possessors of truth. There are many ways to make a contribution and it would be vain to arrogate a greater role in human affairs than social scientists actually play, or have a right to play. Policing this line – between the appropriate and inappropriate applications of social science – is vital if social science is not to overstep its role.

In particular, a distinction must be maintained between partisan politics and social science. Of course, one hopes that social science is enlisted in partisan politics – not as a weapon to bludgeon opponents but as a means of bringing systematic evidence and reflection to bear on problems that matter. Likewise, one hopes that when social scientists engage in partisan politics (as they have every right to do) their activity is properly labeled – as partisan rather than scientific.

Noam Chomsky, a prominent linguist, served as an influential leader of the antiwar movement during the Vietnam War. However, he did not claim the mantle of social science in order to argue that his cause was just.

Naturally, it is often difficult to distinguish work that is "polemical" from work that is impartial, objective, dispassionate. After all, our motivation to study social science, as well as our choice of subjects to study, may be animated by a desire to influence political and social affairs. However, these background motivations must be separated, as much as is possible, from the conduct of inquiry.

Let us put a fine point on this. A researcher is likely to choose a topic, and identify a hypothesis, because she or he has a strong "prior": she or he believes this is the way the world works. This is well and good. Intuitions about the world must come from somewhere. However, she or he must put this hypothesis to an honest test, and must be willing to accept its refutation if that is what the evidence suggests. One's obligation to tell the truth must outweigh all other considerations, even if the results are unpalatable.

In this context, one might consider the rise and fall of academic fashions. A century ago, it was common to regard human nature and geography as wellsprings of social behavior. By mid-century, these views were regarded as passé, if not racist. Now, we find a return to these venerable explanatory foundations (purged of their racist content, one hopes).

Scholars must feel free to think and theorize freely, so long as they are also able to put their ideas to the test. This, it seems to us, is the principal ethical responsibility of social scientists.

CONCLUSIONS

In this chapter we have endeavored to cover a very large and complex subject in a synoptic fashion. We did so by dividing the subject into three areas – (a) juridical ethics, (b) the protection of human subjects, and (c) broader ethical issues. While (a) and (b) are often regarded as the sum total of professional ethics we believe that the third area deserves equal consideration when social scientists are constructing and presenting their work. Ethical considerations do not end with a stamp of approval from an IRB. Nor should the approval of an institutional review board constitute the final and authoritative judgment on the ethical nature of a piece of research – though it may, in practice, settle the matter (by allowing or preventing a study) in a particular context.

KEY TERMS

- Ethics
- Institutional Review Board
- Belmont Report
- Informed consent
- Anonymity
- Confidentiality

IV | Statistics

The previous chapters have presented a largely non-mathematical approach to methodology. This follows our belief that most methodological issues are better communicated through prose than through math, at least at introductory levels. When methodology is conflated with statistics, as it is in some textbooks, the treatment leaves many questions unaddressed. Worse, it may cause the reader to ignore fundamental problems of inference—confusing p-values with a demonstration of causality or with social relevance, for instance.

Having laid a foundation for social science methodology we turn now to a mathematical consideration of some of these same issues. Issues introduced fleetingly in the previous pages such as sampling, statistical significance, and confidence intervals will now be given a more complete treatment. Moreover, understanding the math behind a concept makes it more apprehensible, less mysterious. Additionally, we present practical tools for analyzing data, covering both descriptive statistics and inferential statistics. The purpose of this section of the book is thus to enrich your understanding of social science and to expand your toolbox of techniques.

Because statistics is hardly separate from methodology (at large) readers will note lots of overlap between this section and previous sections of the book. Even so, there is a mathematical logic to statistics and for this reason the material is best presented in a tightly sequenced manner, separate from previous sections. The reason that we present statistics last, and not first, is that we view statistics as a handmaiden of social science methodology—not the other way around. Researchers should begin with concepts, theories, and research designs and then start discussing samples and the varying utility of different statistical models.

Some might take the view that statistics is such a vast subject that it cannot be summarized in a few short chapters. We agree that this is a non-trivial task. Others may have no need for statistics at this early stage of their social science education; and thus may set aside Part IV for later. For those who read on, however, what follows is intended to serve as a step-by-step introduction to the most commonly applied statistics in the social sciences, a mere jumping-off point for further study and other works. Ultimately, understanding the techniques and topics introduced below is a prerequisite to successfully designing quantitative research in the social sciences. Thus, everybody from undergraduates taking advanced level courses that assign academic articles to graduate students desiring a refresher before engaging a dedicated applied statistics course will benefit from this quick and mostly painless introduction.

In what follows we divide the subject into seven categories: data management (Chapter 17), univariate statistics (Chapter 18), probabilities (Chapter 19), statistical inference (Chapter 20), bivariate statistics (Chapter 21), regression (Chapter 22), and causal inference (Chapter 23). We begin by noting a simple distinction between statistics and statistical inference. Statistics allow us to parsimoniously describe a host of information or data. Statistical inference is the process of inferring from a sample to a population, which has arisen out of the need to address limitations in data collection and research design, in particular time and cost. In the sections that follow we introduce the most common statistical inference tests with applications to the social sciences. Before doing so, we turn to a discussion of data management, as well as the basic statistics, concepts, and properties necessary to understand the more sophisticated analyses and hypothesis tests that follow. That is, the chapters progress by building upon each other; introducing the foundational technique necessary to conduct the more complex analyses in the later chapters. Indeed most of the statistics introduced in this book are built on a few standard mathematical tools, especially indicators of central tendency and variance. Once you have mastered these basic tools, other more complex procedures will be fairly simple to conduct and easier to understand.

Data Management

The first step toward analysis is to get your data into a format that is convenient for the sort of analysis you wish to pursue. This, in turn, probably depends on the sort of data you are collecting. Here, we shall distinguish among four data types: **qualitative**, **medium-N**, **large-N**, and **textual** (though one can have data that is a combination of these; e.g., medium-N and qualitative, large-N and textual ... etc.). Methods for handling these data types are continually invented and reinvented, so the reader may wish to consult other sources to obtain the most up-to-date information on these subjects. Our intent is to provide a useful overview, in any case, not to delve into the details.

Qualitative Data

Suppose that you are trying to integrate data drawn from a limited number of units with a diversity of evidence. The evidence may have been gathered with any of the techniques (or combination of techniques) discussed in Chapter 13. It might include text, photos, maps, and other media. The nature of the material might be variegated – a combination of what informants said and did, the researcher's own observations and theories, multi-media artifacts, locations, relevant articles from academic journals and/or popular media, feedback from colleagues, and so forth. Some of the evidence may apply across all studied units in the sample while some is specific to certain units. But one doesn't have systematic observations for a limited set of variables across all units in the sample. It may not even be clear what the variables are, what the sample is, or what the population of the study is. There may be – at least initially – no specific hypothesis but rather a general research question that awaits further refinement. In other words, the investigation may be more exploratory (to discover a theory or hypothesis) than confirmatory (to test a theory or hypothesis).

This setting exemplifies a good deal of work often described as qualitative, so we shall refer to it as **qualitative data** (as defined in Chapter 4). Because of its unstructured nature, data of this sort presents the researcher with a problem: how to collect and organize all of the material in a fruitful way, a way that allows the researcher to think through possible connections – to theorize – and also to enlist supporting evidence for the construction of a systematic argument when the process of writing has begun.

For this purpose, a number of qualitative data analysis (QDA) programs have been developed. These include ATLAS-ti, MAXqda2, and NVivo (the successor to NUD*IST). A common feature of QDA programs is the ability to cross-reference entries so that data can be assembled and reassembled in many different ways, e.g., by time, by location, by informant, by informant's social group, or by some designated theme (which must be coded by the researcher). Programs are also fully searchable, allowing the user to pull text (or some audio-visual output) from one setting to another, e.g., from the database into the text of a paper.

Like all software programs, they require some investment of time on the part of the user before they can provide efficiency gains. However, if you plan to collect a great deal of qualitative data and you have no easy way of organizing it (using simple text files), you might consider making the investment.

Sometimes, initial work with qualitative data leads to a reduction of that data – perhaps by successive recoding – into a single table or a standard dataset, as discussed in later sections of this chapter. Qualitative data can often be reconfigured as quantitative data. Of course, there is always some loss of information in any data reduction process. However, in some circumstances the advantages – the opportunity to systematically measure and test a relationship across a large number of units – outweigh the disadvantages. In any case, such a reconfiguration does not mean that the entire project shifts from a "qualitative" mode to a "quantitative" mode. The shift may be applicable to one portion of a project, as happens typically in a multi-method research design (see Chapter 10).

Medium-*N* Data

Suppose one is dealing with a small or medium number of cases and information for those cases that can be represented as variables (dimensions that are equivalent, and thus potentially measurable, for each case in the sample). One may not have sufficient information to fully code all the variables, or one can do so only preliminarily and there are question marks. The data may not be entirely numeric; it may take the form of qualitative judgments – strong/weak, present/largely present/largely absent/entirely absent, and so forth. Moreover, the precise boundaries of the population (and hence of an appropriate sample) may be open to question. In this setting, a reasonable approach is to try to represent the data one has collected in a single, unified table – sometimes called a **truth-table**.

An example, comprising 20 cases and three variables, is provided in Table 17.1. Note that this table incorporates various types of data – binary (X), textual (Z), and interval (Y). For some purposes, it may make sense to recode all variables in a binary fashion, as demonstrated in Table 17.2. And for other purposes, it may make sense to reduce this information so that cases with similar or identical codings are listed together, as part of the same "primitive" case type, as shown in Table 17.3. In this fashion we are able to collapse 20 cases into eight rows, making potential relationships easier to visualize. Because we keep track of the number of cases (N) falling into each primitive type, no information is lost.

Table 17.1 Truth-table with "raw" coding

Cases	Attributes		Y
	X	Z	
1	1	Small-medium	0
2	0	Large	5
3	1	Large	18
4	0	Small	3
5	1	Medium-large	44
6	1	Large	4
7	0	Small	6
8	1	Large	77
9	1	Large	98
10	0	Small-medium	46
11	1	Medium-large	33
12	0	Large	46
13	1	Small	68
14	0	Large	12
15	1	Medium-large	25
16	1	Small	37
17	0	Small	52
18	1	Small	51
19	1	Small-medium	11
20	0	Large	2

There are many uses for information presented in a tabular format. One use of such a table is to reveal possible causal relationships. For example, one might regard Y as the outcome and X and Z as possible causes – either independently or in combination. Truth-tables are especially useful for highlighting set-theoretic relationships, where a single variable or combination of variables has a necessary or sufficient relationship to an outcome. This is the logic of **qualitative comparative analysis** (QCA), a rather complex algorithm (actually set of related algorithms) for analyzing set-theoretic relationships in small- to medium-sized samples. Sometimes, a tabular format leads eventually to a standard dataset, as discussed in the next section.

Large-*N* Data

For evidence that can be represented as numeric data across a large number of cases a standard dataset matrix is appropriate. Here, each observation occupies a separate row (similar rows are not combined into "primitives"). There may also be short text ("string") variables – e.g., proper nouns representing persons or places

Table 17.2 Truth-table with binary coding

Cases	Attributes		
	X	Z	Y
1	1	0	0
2	0	1	0
3	1	1	0
4	0	0	0
5	1	1	0
6	1	1	0
7	0	0	0
8	1	1	1
9	1	1	1
10	0	0	0
11	1	1	0
12	0	1	0
13	1	0	1
14	0	1	0
15	1	1	0
16	1	0	0
17	0	0	1
18	1	0	1
19	1	0	0
20	0	1	0

Table 17.3 Reduced truth-table with primitive case types

Case types	N	Attributes		
		X	Z	Y
A	2	1	1	1
B	5	1	1	0
C	2	1	0	1
D	3	1	0	0
E	1	0	1	1
F	3	0	1	0
G	1	0	0	1
H	3	0	0	0
	20			

or events stored in the dataset. However, each string variable must also be represented by an accompanying numeric variable if it is to play a part in the resulting analysis.

This sort of data can generally be stored in a rectangular dataset – a two-dimensional matrix – that can be read with various software, such as R, Stata, Microsoft Excel, or simple text editors. Excel is user-friendly and able to store both numeric and string data and calculate univariate (descriptive) statistics (see Chapter 18). It is less useful for the more sophisticated statistical analyses addressed in the subsequent chapters. For this you will need a statistical package such as SPSS, Stata, SAS, or R. If you are dealing primarily with numeric data and you know you will be doing some statistical analysis (beyond univariate analysis) you may choose to enter your data directly into the statistical package. You may also start with Excel and convert at a later time (once data collection is complete). If the data is more complex, involving relationships among more than two dimensions, relational databases – for example, those based on the SQL programming language – may be required. However, this is beyond the level of complexity most researchers face in their work.

A simple two-dimensional matrix format is illustrated in Table 17.4. In the first row are the variable names. These may have to be shortened to suit the restrictions of a software program, and may need to be represented as a single word, e.g., *Country_code* rather than *Country code*. For each string variable (Country and City) there is an accompanying numeric variable (Country code and City code). The units are nested within each other – city within country.

Next, we find a time variable – measuring the year to which the data applies. Time variables might also include months, days, hours, seconds, and so forth. It depends of course upon the temporal units in which the data is collected.

If all the data refers to the same time-period, then the analysis must be **cross-sectional**, and no time variable is needed (it would have the same value for all observations). Things are slightly more complicated with **lagged** variables. In the eighth column you will see that Income/capita is lagged by one period. That is, the value entered in the first row – corresponding with the year 2005 – is actually the value for the previous year (2004). You can create complex time-dependent relationships in time-series and cross-sectional datasets simply by lagging variables at different intervals. (Sometimes, the data software will do this for you.) Note that a variable can be forward-lagged or backward-lagged.

After the time variable (Year), Table 17.4 contains a series of variables that represent the factors of theoretical interest – in this case, *Population*, *Income/capita*, and *Area*. This dataset will allow you to examine relationships among these three variables through time (at annual intervals) and across two levels (city and country).

The final column is labeled *Notes*, and is intended to store information pertaining to each observation. This might be about sources for that observation, special problems of interpretation or reliability, or whatever details one may wish to keep track of. Unfortunately, many statistical packages limit the number of characters

Table 17.4 Large-N dataset structure

1	2	3	4	5	6	7	8	9	10
Country	Country code	City	City code	Year	Population	Income / Cap	Income / Cap$_{t-1}$	Area	Notes
Austria	01	Vienna	01	2005	1632569	37900	37700	8428.1	Eurostat
Austria	01	Vienna	01	2006	1652449	39500	37900	8428.1	
Austria	01	Vienna	01	2007	1661246	40600	39500	8428.1	
Austria	01	Graz	02	2005	241298	33400	32800	3414.1	
Austria	01	Graz	02	2006	244997	34800	33400	3414.1	
Austria	01	Graz	02	2007	247624	35500	34800	3414.1	
Belgium	02	Antwerp	01	2005	457749	34900	33300	954	
Belgium	02	Antwerp	01	2006	461496	35700	34900	954	
Belgium	02	Antwerp	01	2007	466203	36800	35700	954	
Belgium	02	Ghent	02	2005	230951	30500	30200	1266	
Belgium	02	Ghent	02	2006	233120	31600	30500	1266	
Belgium	02	Ghent	02	2007	235143	33200	31600	1266	
Bulgaria	03	Sofia	01	2005	1148429	15200	13900	10679.5	Area 2010
Bulgaria	03	Sofia	01	2006	1154010	17900	15200	10679.5	Area 2010
Bulgaria	03	Sofia	01	2007	1156796	21200	17900	10679.5	Area 2010
Bulgaria	03	Plovdiv	02	2005	341873	6600	6200	5802.5	Area 2010
Bulgaria	03	Plovdiv	02	2006	343662	7100	6600	5802.5	Area 2010
Bulgaria	03	Plovdiv	02	2007	345249	7400	7100	5802.5	Area 2010

in a string variable, and thus limit the sort of notes you can take about an individual observation. Excel and Stata are more permissive. For example, if you wish to insert a note about a specific data *cell*, Excel will allow this but other statistical packages generally will not.[177]

Any piece of clarifying information that can't be inserted into a database will need to be kept somewhere – traditionally in a text file called a **codebook**, which explains what each variable means and the sources from which it is gathered. Eventually, one hopes that statistical packages will become more accommodating of meta-data, descriptions of data including its provenance, as it is quite complicated to have data in one location and explanations of that data in another.

Excel is a superb tool for data storage and management, e.g., moving variables and observations around to different locations within a spreadsheet or in related sheets, or creating new variables or observations based on those you have. However, you should be aware that this ease of manipulation also introduces a risk. Specifically, it is easy to uncouple the variables that describe a specific observation. For example, if you block all the data from column 4, and paste it down one row, it will be out of sync with the rest of the dataset. A chance error like this will likely destroy all the (real) relationships in your dataset; in their place you will find spurious (illusory) relationships. By contrast, most other statistical packages make it harder to separate variables connected with a single observation, which makes them harder to manipulate but also erects a barrier to data management errors of this sort.

Textual Data

Suppose the data of theoretical interest is textual in nature. That is, you wish to analyze a number of texts, e.g., articles drawn from newspapers, high school textbooks, novels, websites, political speeches, party platforms, constitutions, transcripts from hearings or meetings, and so forth.

If there is a modest number of texts, or just a few key texts, you may enlist the traditional approach of reading, marking up texts, and taking notes in a separate text file. The oldest continuous tradition of textual analysis, biblical exegesis, rests on the close analysis of key texts – in this case, religious texts. The tradition of in-depth analysis of key texts lives on in history and other humanities disciplines and, more selectively, in the social sciences. A close reading of texts is clearly justified in the study of constitutions or founding documents, key court decisions, key legislation, influential speeches, or influential theorists.

Suppose, however, that the number of texts that you wish to analyze is very large, e.g., thousands of speeches, newspaper articles, tweets, blogs, books, or other texts. In order to reduce this plenitude of information so that it can reveal a coherent story or pattern you will need a mechanized system of storage and retrieval, known generically as **content analysis**, or **textual analysis**. Sometimes, distinctions are drawn among these terms. However, for our purposes it is helpful to consider them as part of the same overall project: to reduce and analyze meanings contained in large-N textual data.

Early versions of text analysis relied on hand-coding. The unit of analysis might be the word, line, sentence, or paragraph, and the objective would be to code each unit along some set of parameters. Some years ago, Gerring wrote a book about party ideologies in the United States that relied, in part, on this sort of coding to differentiate party positions of the major American parties from the early nineteenth century to the present. Thus, Gerring coded the parties' positions on specific issues like tariffs and more general philosophical matters like the proper role of government in American society (Gerring 1998). Other work in this tradition has looked at the content of presidential speech (Ceaser et al. 1981), the development of American national identity (Merritt 1966), and cross-national party ideologies (Budge 2000).

Qualitative data management software such as ATLAS-ti, MAXqda2, or NVivo (reviewed above) may prove useful in assisting in the process of hand-coding, speeding up the process and accuracy with which texts can be coded and those codings stored and analyzed, and offering a handy way of retrieving the original texts for in-depth analysis or direct quotations.

The old tradition of hand-coding is now complemented by a slew of techniques that process words in an automated or semi-automated fashion. This has the advantage of incorporating a much larger (in principle, infinite) number of texts, and thus may span longer ranges of time and more contexts. It is also sometimes easier to obtain a sample that is representative of an identifiable population. And it distances (though never entirely removes) the coder from the process of coding, mitigating one source of researcher bias.

Some texts, such as those stored in text-readable format on the Internet, are already in a format suitable for automated analysis. Google has developed several online tools for this purpose. Google Trends tracks the frequency of online searches. This has been shown to be useful in predicting outcomes such as elections, flu outbreaks, and consumer behavior, as well as for measuring the salience of various issues (Granka 2013; Mellon 2013). Google Ngram Viewer counts the number of times a given word or phrase appears in the Google Books repository, a historical library of digitized books. This may be used to construct a timeline of the frequency of mentions of a keyword (e.g., "democracy"), and this in turn may be interpreted for clues about the development and salience of a concept. One may also track Twitter feeds, Facebook posts, and other social media data. Increasingly a number of political questions are being explored with data from various Web platforms.

The automated analysis of most texts requires first converting those texts into a machine-readable format, i.e., a text file. If the original is a hard copy, it may be scanned and then converted to text with optical-character-recognition (OCR) software. If the original is a PDF, it may be directly convertible into text. If it exists as part of a database like Lexis Nexis or ProQuest, it may be possible to download the texts of interest as a single batch. If the texts must be extracted from somewhere on the Web, various Web crawlers (or scrapers) may be employed. These sorts of tools generally involve some programming skill and are thus not in the purview of most social scientists, though this is likely to change as demand increases and packaged programs for data scraping become available.[178] Once texts are in a machine-readable format, one may proceed to employ various analytic techniques.[179]

Dictionary techniques compute "the rate at which key words appear in a text to classify documents into categories or to measure the extent to which documents belong to particular categories" (Grimmer and Stewart 2013). For example, one might wish to measure the "positive" or "negative" tone of various documents. Using a pre-set dictionary of words, each of which is classified as one or another, one may arrive at a summary measure, which can then be compared across texts. Much depends, evidently, on the choice of a dictionary by which texts will be analyzed.

One interesting approach to this problem derives the dictionary from texts identified as playing an especially influential or paradigmatic role. These key texts provide the reference point by which all other texts are analyzed. For example, in order to estimate ideological location one might choose several reference texts that seem archetypically "liberal/left" or "conservative/right." The frequency distribution of words in these texts may then be compared with other political texts in order to identify the latent ideology of the authors of those texts (Laver, Benoit, and Garry 2003).

Supervised learning techniques begin with old-fashioned coding by humans (either the researcher or his or her accomplices). From repeated codings, a computer program learns how to replicate the coding process, which it can then replicate for other documents. **Unsupervised techniques** rely on algorithms to sort texts into categories and to measure distances separating texts and/or piles.

It should be apparent that the results of any automated textual analysis bear close scrutiny, both for purposes of interpretation (what do the discovered patterns mean?) and validation (do they mean what the author thinks they mean?). The key point for present purposes is that we are nowhere near a situation in which artificial intelligence can replace human intelligence. Analysis by humans thus remains central to the analysis of texts produced by humans.

Examples, Data, and Software

In the statistics chapters that follow we use the same examples as in the previous sections of the book: social capital, democracy and worker-training programs. In doing so we mostly rely on hypothetical data for two reasons: (1) to make the examples as easy as possible to follow; and (2) to allow readers to work through the analyses by hand. In addition we frequently make reference to data that would allow the reader to apply these techniques to related and real inquiries. It should go without saying then that substantive inferences should not be drawn from the examples below.

Many countries have one or two standard surveys that are repeated at regular intervals to give snapshots of political, social, or economic features of that society. In the United States, the longest-running and most popular nationally representative survey of voting age Americans is the American National Election Studies (ANES).[180] Like the election years before it, in 2012 the ANES collected a host of information, including demographics, political and social behavior, as well as preferences and attitudes on politics, society, and the economy. The data allows us to explore features of social capital, like group membership, representation, political engagement, as well as potentially related factors, like identification with political parties and feelings toward political institutions and figures. An excellent source for data on comparative democracy is the Quality of Government (QoG) Institute. The QoG offers a number of datasets, including the Expert Survey of public administrators in 107 countries, the Social Policy dataset, which includes a number of social issues and conditions particularly for the OECD countries, and the Regional dataset with regional information on corruption in the EU. Perhaps most notably, they house the Standard dataset, a cross-sectional time-series with global coverage from 1946 to 2012 on various government quality measures and correlates. They have grouped their Standard dataset variables by a heuristic, which includes their "What It Is" variables, like corruption, bureaucratic quality, and democracy, and their "How To Get It" variables, pertaining to electoral rules, forms of government, federalism, legal and colonial origin, religion and social fractionalization, as well as their "What You Get" variables, such as economic and human development, international and domestic peace, environmental sustainability, gender equality, and satisfied, trusting, and confident citizens.[181]

Those interested in the worker-training examples might utilize data from LaLonde (1986) and Dehejia and Wahba (1999), which we will refer to as the LaLonde data. The LaLonde data is used to evaluate worker-training programs on earnings and includes an indicator of assignment to training programs as well as demographic variables for 313 adults. It is a sub-sample of data that includes randomized experimental data from the National Supported Work Demonstration (NSW) and non-experimental comparison groups from the Population Survey of Income Dynamics (PSID) and the Current Population Survey (CPS).[182]

You are advised to practice the techniques introduced in these chapters by hand, as well as with a dataset and statistical software such as R, SAS, SPSS, or Stata. There is no clear champion of statistical software, with each providing relative advantages. SPSS is perhaps the most user-friendly for those with little programming experience, but has traditionally been the least versatile. Stata, followed by SAS and R have steeper learning curves but include a host of more advanced features. In terms of pricing, all are proprietary and costly, apart from R which is free and open-source to boot. The tables and graphs in the statistics chapters have all been produced with R. Because different software is used across the disciplines – and even within disciplines – we do not include play-by-play introductions to any one of them. Such introductions are readily available, however, either in hard-copy or on the Web. In short, the best way to learn is to do.

CONCLUSIONS

This chapter began by addressing issues of data management. In doing so, we distinguished four types of data: qualitative, medium-N, large-N, and textual. Each involves somewhat different techniques which must be mastered if one is to work with data of that sort.

KEY TERMS

- Qualitative data
- Medium-N data
- Large-N data
- Textual data
- Truth-table
- Qualitative comparative analysis
- Lagged variables
- Codebook
- Meta-data
- Content analysis
- Textual analysis
- Dictionary techniques
- Supervised learning techniques
- Unsupervised learning techniques

18 Univariate Statistics

The purpose of this chapter is to show how we can parsimoniously describe data so that we may share our understandings of it with others. Even before calculating statistics we can begin to explore the nature of variables simply by presenting them in a particular manner. A host of both tabular and graphical presentations are available to describe data. We will touch on a few of the most helpful visualizations and then turn to univariate statistics. Univariate statistics restricts the analysis to a single variable. It typically concerns the variable's level of measurement, range of values, and the average or central tendency.

Frequency Distributions, Bar Graphs, and Histograms

We begin with the question of how to explain a lot of data with fewer numbers and fewer words. That is, ask yourself how you might quickly explain to somebody else who does not have a deep knowledge of the data the basic features of it. The answer is found in tables, graphics, and statistics. In each of these broad categories are a host of techniques for reducing the data down to a more manageable collection or visualization.

Think about how a tabular summary of data might more succinctly describe data than looking over the full dataset. **Frequency distributions** present the number of occurrences of an event of interest in a table. The data are grouped into mutually exclusive categories and summarized to show the number of occurrences in each category. The format of the table includes a title, clearly describing the concept, as well as columns referring to the values, categories, and frequency of categories. Typically, the first column lists the numeric values of a variable and the second the categories to which the values refer. The next column lists the number of units in each category, or the frequency, and the total number of observations in the margins.

Frequency distribution tables often include additional information about the distribution, including the **cumulative frequency** and **relative frequency** of the categories. The cumulative frequency shows the sum of the frequencies for the previous categories. Thus it is important in frequency distributions to arrange the categories either from top down or bottom up when they are ordered. The relative frequency is the fraction or proportion of times an outcome in a category occurs out of the total number of possible outcomes. Together this set of frequencies provides an easy-to-understand depiction of the distribution of the variable.

Consider the 5,914 person sample from the ANES 2012 dataset on respondent's identification with the political parties displayed in Figure 18.1.[183] Presenting the data in this format allows us to see how the observations are distributed for the values of this variable. We first note that there are three category responses for this variable. We see that respondents can choose Democrat, Republican, or Independent, and may also choose not to answer the question altogether, which results in missing values for this variable.[184] Out of the 5,914 individuals in the sample we see from the cumulative frequency that 5,595 answered this question. The table also makes clear that the greatest number of individuals identify as Democrats, 2,361, which, as the relative frequency conveys, is 42% of the sample.

The information in frequency distributions can also be presented in a graphical manner. **Bar graphs** plot the frequency (or percentage) of cases measured along the y-axis for each category of the variable denoted along the x-axis. Figure 18.1 presents the same party identification frequencies in Table 18.1 as a graph. While tables often provide more information, these graphs are particularly useful for quickly conveying comparisons of values of categorical variables.[185] For example, it is easy to see that Democrats make up the largest identifiers in the sample, followed by Independents and then Republicans.

Similar to bar graphs, **histograms** convey information about a variable via simple bar plots. However, the purpose of a histogram is to show the distribution, or shape, of the variable when the outcomes are continuous. That is, they are most frequently used to plot interval level data with the continuous values grouped into bins or intervals. By contrast, bar graphs are typically restricted to nominal and

Table 18.1 Frequency distribution of party identification

Values	Categories	Frequency	Cumulative Freq	Relative Freq
	Democrat	2361	2361	0.422
	Independent	1845	4206	0.330
	Republican	1389	5595	0.248
	Total	5914	5914	1

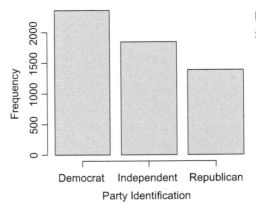

Figure 18.1 Bar graph of party identification

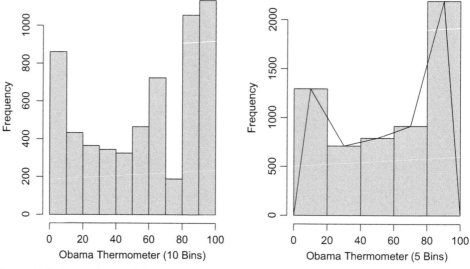

Figure 18.2 Histograms of feelings toward Obama

ordinal variables. Recall the distinctions in levels of measurement in Chapter 3 above, which will be important throughout this section of the book.

Figure 18.2 shows two histograms for the same variable of sentiment toward Obama as measured by a feeling thermometer. The feeling thermometer is a type of survey question that purports to create interval level data out of the degree of positive and negative feelings toward politicians, candidates, and institutions. This variable was collected by asking respondents to think about their feelings for Obama in terms of the degrees on a thermometer. Feeling cold about Obama suggests that you do not like him and should give him a lower score on the thermometer, somewhere between 0 and 49 degrees with lower numbers referring to colder feelings. Feeling warmly about a person translates into higher score, 51 to 100 degrees. Thus 50 degrees conveys that you feel neither warmly nor coldly toward him. Figure 18.3 is similar to the visual aid respondents on the ANES are given to help arrive at an accurate response on feeling thermometer questions.

In Figure 18.2 the histogram on the left groups the 100 possible outcome values into ten bins. The histogram on the right groups the values into five bins. By reducing the bins the general shape of the distribution becomes clearer. In the right figure, we plot a **frequency polygon** over the distribution to provide a simple line plot of its basic shape. A frequency polygon is drawn like a histogram except that the frequencies are connected by a single line rather than distinct bars. The point of both is to move us to fully considering and thus illustrating the overall shape of the variable's distribution. In the example we see that the Obama feeling thermometer appears to have two peaks with large concentrations of people feeling either very warmly or very coldly toward him, but few people feeling indifferently.

It is important to remember that while many social science variables have a single peak near the center of the distribution of scores, some have more than one

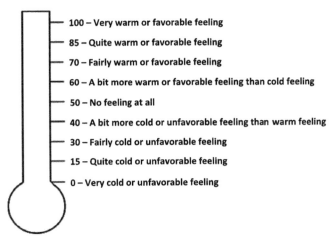

Figure 18.3 Feeling thermometer survey instrument

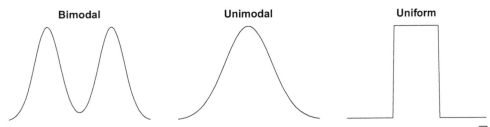

Figure 18.4 Common distribution shapes

peak. For example, oftentimes favorability attitudes about public figures have two peaks, or **bimodal**, as with the Obama feeling thermometer example. Indeed, the distribution of a variable might take on any number of different shapes, including: single-peaked or **unimodal**; or even flat, which would suggest that all the responses are the same or **uniform**. Figure 18.4 presents the general shapes of some of the most common distributions.

Coupled with the variable's level of measurement, its distribution – which can be gathered from visually inspecting a histogram, bar graph, or frequency polygon – will prove helpful in determining the statistical inference test best suited to our data. That is, hypothesis testing is not a one-size-fits-all procedure. In order to properly choose among a host of statistical inference tests we must first know our variable's level of measurement and distribution.

Central Tendency

Central tendency and **variability** give us rich descriptions of the variables of interest – presenting us with information on a variable's most typical values and dispersion. That is, similar to bar graphs and histograms, central tendency provides another useful way of parsimoniously describing data. Why "central tendency"? Because these scores are generally located at the middle of the distribution where the greatest concentration of data lies, and thus *tend toward the center*. We will focus on the three most common types: mode, median, and mean.

Mode is simply the most frequent value in a variable distribution. For example, in a distribution of all religious denominations in the United States, Protestants are the most common. The mode of this distribution is therefore Protestants. Because mode only requires the frequency of mutually exclusive categories, nominal data is sufficient to calculate the mode.

Median is the middle-most point, or fulcrum, of a sorted distribution, thus requiring at least ordinal level data. That is, it cuts the distribution – which must be ordered from high to low or low to high – into two equal parts. For data with an odd sample size the median is the case that falls exactly in the middle. The formula for the median position in an odd set of values is:

$$Median_{Odd} = \frac{(N+1)}{2} \; term.\tag{18.1}$$

But for an even sample size the median is the point above which 50% of cases fall and below which 50% of cases fall. This value is therefore midway between the two terms in the middle of the distribution and thus the median is calculated in this manner:

$$Median_{Even} = \frac{\frac{N}{2} \; term + \frac{(N)}{2+1} \; term}{2}.\tag{18.2}$$

The arithmetic **mean**, which we will note with a bar over the variable, as in $\overline{X}$ for X, is equivalent to the sum of a set of scores divided by the total number of scores in the set:

$$\overline{X} = \frac{\Sigma X}{N},\tag{18.3}$$

where Σ is a Greek letter used as the summation operator (summing the values of X). Recall, X is the raw score in the set, and N is the total number of scores in a set. Relatedly, we are often interested in knowing just how far a particular score falls from the mean. This value is what we call the deviation:

$$Deviation = X - \overline{X}.\tag{18.4}$$

Figure 18.5 shows three curved line plots for unimodal distributions with different skews. These line plots are similar to frequency polygons but rounded and without a *y*-axis to illustrate general patterns rather than specific points. Notice that when the distributions of scores are perfectly **symmetric** – that is, the same frequency of scores fall on each side of the mean so that if we folded the distribution in the middle the curves would match up – the mode, mean, and median are all the same. However, when the distribution is **skewed** – that is, comprised of a greater frequency of scores in one tail over the other – the central tendencies differ. Notice that in all cases that the mode is the highest point, or most frequent number. The median is the middlemost score and the mean is pulled by the extreme scores in the tails of the skewed distributions. Thus, when the

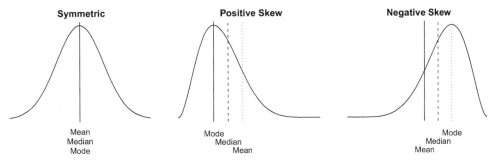

Figure 18.5 Unimodal distributions and central tendencies

distribution is symmetric we can rely on the simple arithmetic mean but in skewed distributions the median is a better indicator of central tendency.

Variance

There are two characteristics we typically use to describe a variable's tendency, or central tendency, which we addressed above, and the **variance**, which we address here. While the central tendency provides insight into the most frequently occurring values, a basic understanding of the distribution is not complete without the variance. Indeed, distributions can have the same means but look quite different due to different variances. Variance refers to the different dispersions, spread, or width in the distribution. It is thus an indicator of a distribution's variability. Consider, for example, the distributions in Figure 18.6. Each has the same mean, but different variances. Which distribution has a greater variability? And in which distribution are there more extreme scores?

The mathematical formula for the variance is straightforward. We simply want a measure that captures the distance of the observations from the central tendency, while controlling for the number of observations. Thus, we can take the sum total of deviations from the mean – and square them so they do not add up to zero – over the number of observations. We label variance s^2 and calculate it accordingly:

$$s^2 = \frac{\Sigma (X - \overline{X})^2}{N}. \tag{18.5}$$

It is often hard to make an easy interpretation of variability from variance because the formula squares the mean deviations. So we often transform the

Figure 18.6 Distributions with different variances

measure back into the original unit of analysis by taking its square root. This gives us the **standard deviation** which can be written out as a function of the variance:

$$s = \sqrt{\frac{\Sigma(X - \overline{X})^2}{N}}. \tag{18.6}$$

Thus the standard deviation gives us the average variability in a distribution, or the average deviations from the mean, and does so in the original unit. The more variability around the mean the greater the standard deviation. Accordingly, the standard deviation in the variable on the left side of Figure 18.6 is smaller than that of the variable on the right side.

Standard deviations do not only help describe our data but they also allow us to compare values in distributions with one another. We often want to know the distance of one score relative to another. When the scores come from different distributions we can use standard deviations to make accurate comparisons. For example, how does a score of 80% on a midterm exam in a political science course compare with a score of 90% on a midterm exam in a sociology course? Which grade means you did a better job on the exam? The key to answering this question is that it depends on how the students in each class performed, i.e., the distribution of scores in the class.

When comparing distributions we do not talk in raw values or scores but in standard deviations relevant to the mean. The test scores 80% and 90% mean little relative to each other. Their comparative value is relative to their own means. Thus we would like to compare them with a standardized score, and therefore we employ the standard deviation. Think about it in this manner: 80% might be one standard deviation above the mean in a political science course, while 90% might be one standard deviation below the mean in a communications course.

Example: Average State Incomes

In deciding whether to relocate to another state for a new job, individuals take into account more than just their salary. Oftentimes their considerations include thoughts about their ability to buy products relative to their neighbors in their current state and in their possible new one. We recognize that comparable goods like groceries and homes can cost more in some states and locales than others, which can offset changes in income. That is, states differ in the pricing of goods and in the income levels of their citizenries, which has led scholars to compare costs of living across states. Consider a related hypothetical example of an individual with job offers at the same salary in the neighboring states of Michigan and Ohio. In which state would an annual salary of $60,000 suggest that she is relatively better off? In order to make up her mind, she might consider the average annual incomes of individuals in each of the states. In Figure 18.7 we have graphed the distributions of income in each state. In order to answer this question she will need to compare this same salary in one state to another. She is therefore in need of a standardized unit of measurement relative to the mean of each state.

Example: Average State Incomes

Table 18.2 Calculating central tendency and variance

Values	Deviations	Squared Dev
X	$X - \overline{X}$	$(X - \overline{X})^2$
55	5	25
60	10	100
45	-5	25
45	-5	25
55	5	25
$N = 5$		
$\Sigma X = 250$		
$\overline{X} = 50$		
	$\Sigma(X - \overline{X}) = 0$	
		$\Sigma(X - \overline{X})^2 = 500$
		$s^2 = 100$
		$s = 10$

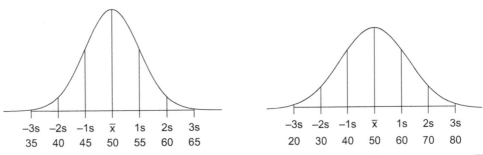

Figure 18.7 Comparing distributions with different standard deviations

Table 18.2 shows how to calculate the necessary statistics in a spreadsheet or tabular format for the Ohio sample. In this and the examples that follow we will begin by writing out the data in this format and then providing a column for each stage of the calculation. Working like this helps keep organized all the steps necessary to calculate the desired statistics.

We begin by summing the values of X, our annual incomes for individuals in thousands of dollars, which is 250. We next take the summed values of X over the number of observations, N, to arrive at the mean:

$$\overline{X} = \frac{\Sigma X}{N}$$
$$= \frac{250}{5}$$
$$= 50. \qquad (18.7)$$

With the mean, we can subtract the X value to calculate the deviation for each value of X. Next we simply square the deviations, sum over them, and divide by N to arrive at the variance:

$$s^2 = \frac{\Sigma(X - \overline{X})^2}{N}$$

$$= \frac{500}{5}$$

$$= 100. \tag{18.8}$$

Finally, we take the square root of the variance to calculate the standard deviation.

$$s = \sqrt{\frac{\Sigma(X - \overline{X})^2}{N}}$$

$$= \sqrt{100}$$

$$= 10. \tag{18.9}$$

In Ohio, we find that $\overline{X} = 50$ & $s = 10$. Thus we have also learned the raw scores that mark the distance in standard deviations for this distribution: 20, 30, 40, 60, 70, 80. Similarly, if we calculate (not shown) the parameters for a different state's distribution (e.g., Michigan) and find its central tendency and standard deviation are $\overline{X} = 50$ & $s = 5$, we also know the raw scores that mark the distance in standard deviations for it: 35, 40, 45, 55, 60, 65.

What we can see from the distributions and standard deviations is that Michigan has less variance (more scores concentrated about the mean) than Ohio. In the Michigan distribution a score of 55 is one standard deviation above the mean. In Ohio a score of 60 is one standard deviation above the mean. So a score of 60 on both implies that you are paid better in Michigan (i.e., 2 standard deviations above the mean) than in Ohio. In general, we know that a different distribution is likely to have a different mean and standard deviation. Thus we calculate the standard deviation for any distribution we are working with. We can then compare a score from one distribution with that from another.

CONCLUSIONS

Both descriptive statistics as well as tabular and graphical visualizations avail themselves to researchers in search of ways to present their data. Frequency distributions, bar graphs, and histograms are particularly common visualizations. We also explored descriptive statistics of central tendency, i.e., the mean, median, and mode. Recall that knowing which to use depends on the variable's level of measurement. Variance and standard deviation give us an idea of a variable's distribution or width. Together with the central tendency these statistics provide a rich yet parsimonious description of data.

KEY TERMS

- Frequency distribution
- Cumulative frequency
- Relative frequency
- Bar graph
- Histogram
- Frequency polygon
- Central tendencies
- Variability
- Standard deviation

The objective of this chapter is to introduce probabilities, probabilistic notation, and common probability distributions, with a focus on the **normal curve**. These concepts provide the foundation for the statistical inference in the following chapters. The first sub-section is a refresher on probabilities. Those with the requisite mathematical background may therefore wish to skip ahead to the sub-section on the normal curve.

Probabilities

Probability is how we refer to the likelihood of occurence of an event. In common parlance we use terms to describe how unusual a particular outcome is, such as "likely," "unlikely," "good chance," or "not a chance." For example: What is the chance of getting heads on the flip of a fair coin? This basic concept is the key to testing social scientific hypotheses via data analysis. For example: What chance does the candidate have of winning the election? In what follows we will refer to the mathematical probability as P. It has a direct corrolary with chance or percentage. P varies from 0.0 to 1.0, which is the equivalent of stating that a percentage can range from 0% to 100%. In the case of P then, 0 implies no chance and 1 implies certainty. More formally, the probability of an event is the number of times it occurs relative to the total number of times any event can occur:

$$P = \frac{\#events}{\#all\ possible\ outcomes}. \tag{19.1}$$

The denominator here is what we call the **sample space**, or the collection of all particular outcomes of an event. Returning to our first example then the probability of a heads in the flip of a fair coin is calculated accordingly:

$$P = \frac{heads}{heads, tails}$$
$$= \frac{1}{2} \tag{19.2}$$
$$= 0.5.$$

The traditional approach in mathematics is to start with self-evident statements and derive from those more statements from which we can prove theorems.

That is, from a few simple statements we can derive a host of useful results. The initial, self-evident statements are called axioms. There are three basic **axioms of probability**:

1 The probability of a particular event is always non-negative and real. Thus probabilities cannot be less than zero or infinite.
2 The probability of getting an event that belongs to the sample space is 1. This implies that the sample space holds everything that could possibly happen in our probability experiment and that all the probabilities must sum to one.
3 The probability of collecting a set of mutually exclusive events is the same as the sum of their probabilities. Mutually exclusive, disjoint, or independent events are those that cannot be true at the same time.

From these axioms (owed to Russian mathematician Andrey Kolmogorov) we can derive a host of useful rules for dealing with probabilities. For example, the probability of a union of disjoint events can be found by their individual probabilities. The probability of two independent events, A and B, ocurring is found by the product of their individual probabilities. This consequence is often referred to as the **multiplication rule** and notated accordingly:

$$P(A\ and\ B) = P(A) \times P(B). \tag{19.3}$$

Another important consequence of these axioms is the **sum rule**: the probability that two independent events will happen is the sum of the probabilities that the first event will happen and the second event will happen, minus the probability that both happen. If the events, A and B, are not mutually exclusive we can find the probability accordingly:

$$P(A\ or\ B) = P(A) + P(B) - P(A\ and\ B). \tag{19.4}$$

The formula works as well if they are mutually exclusive, in which case $P(A\ and\ B)$ is just zero.

Of course these are just a couple of the many important theorems that can be proved from the axioms. Thus from these statements we can logically deduct a series of propositions that will allow us to make various statements of probability. These will be especially helpful when we engage the theorems that allow us to make statistical inferences as well as when we interpret the area under the curves of **probability distributions**.

Probability Distributions

The distributions of probabilities are similar to frequency distributions, except that the former are based on theory and the latter are based on observed data. In probability distributions we specify possible values of a variable and calculate probabilities associated with each value. In frequency distributions we base proportions and percentages on observed data. In probability distributions we attach

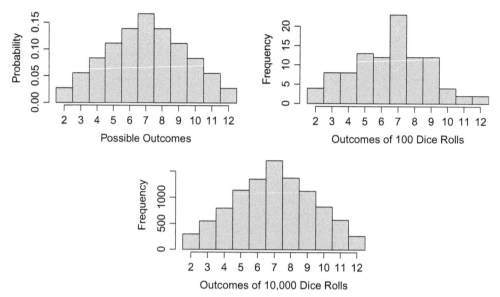

Figure 19.1 Frequency and probability outcomes: bar graphs of dice rolls

theoretical values to each value of a variable. Thus, just like percentages in frequency distributions the probability of a probability distribution gives us the likelihood of a value.

It is important to keep in mind the differences between probability and frequency distributions. Probability distributions tell us what should happen, or more precisely, the probability with which something should happen. It is the distribution in a theoretical or perfect world. Frequency distributions tell us what actually happened in the real world, or more precisely, the outcome of observed events.

Consider, for example, the act of rolling two dice multiple times and taking the sum of the two faces, as in Figure 19.1. As the frequency increases, our observed data should look more like the expected values, or the probability distribution. That is, we expect the probability of an event to measure the relative frequency of the event in the long term. Thus the more rolls we observe, the more likely it is that the frequency distribution will mirror the probability distribution. In probability theory, this theorem is called the **law of large numbers** and follows directly from our axioms of probability. The key insight is that in the long run or with large numbers of observations we can make assumptions about how patterns will play out. Of course, with most political and social phenomena we never observe the theoretical distribution. Thus we are limited in our statements about political and social behavior in a way that we are not with rolls of dice and flips of coins.

As we will discuss in the next chapter, the focal point of quantitative empirical research is drawing conclusions about the population based on a sample. In order for us to generalize our results from samples to populations we will make assumptions about the distribution of the data. We rely on probabilities to tell us how confident we can be in making this generalization. They tell us whether our findings are a result of chance or an actual relationship. When we believe that the phenomenon we are studying resembles a known process of generation, like theoretical distributions, we can use information from the distribution to generalize our findings from the sample to the population.

Before we move on to consider a particular probability distribution, the normal curve, we note that the notation we use for probability distributions is different than those we use for empirical distributions. Recall that we labeled the mean, variance, and standard deviation for a frequency distribution, $\overline{X}$, s^2, and s, respectively. Like empirical distributions, probability distributions have a mean, variance, and standard deviation. However, since we are dealing with a theoretical or known process these are not a sample mean and sample standard deviation and therefore we do not use the symbols $\overline{X}$ and s^2 to represent them. Instead, probability distributions have expected values that are derived from probability theory. We specify these values based on our understanding about the probability distribution and represent these with Greek letters. The mean is symbolized by μ (mu), the standard deviation by σ (sigma), and the variance by σ^2 (sigma squared). In addition, because knowing the full population is rare, as is naturally the case in inferential statistics, we treat the central tendencies and variance statistics of populations as theoretical or as ideals and therefore we use the Greek symbols for them as well.

The Normal Curve

The probability distributions associated with a flip of a coin and a roll of a die are "uniform" – that is, each outcome has an equal probability of occurring, so the probabilities are uniform and the distribution is flat. Recall that frequency distributions could be symmetric, skewed, or, even, have multiple peaks (see Figure 19.2). The same applies for probability distributions. Moreover, many natural phenomena give rise to a probability distribution that is not flat but follows a bell-shaped curve.

The normal curve is a theoretical distribution that captures this fequently occuring bell-shaped distribution pattern. As illustrated in Figure 19.2, the normal

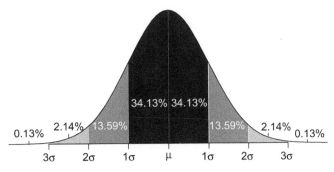

Figure 19.2 The normal curve

curve has a couple of basic characteristics or properties that make it particularly helpful to us. First, it is unimodal, having only one peak. Second, it is symmetric, or balanced around the mean, and the mean, median, and mode are identical in the normal curve. Together these properties give the normal curve its familiar bell shape.

Of course, the normal curve is a theoretical ideal and not observed. The formula for the normal curve is simply:

$$\frac{1}{\sigma\sqrt{2\pi}} \, exp^{-\frac{(x-\mu)^2}{2\sigma^2}}. \tag{19.5}$$

Thus the normal curve is a function based on a few parameters, the expected mean, μ, and standard deviation, σ, around a value, x. *Exp* is the exponential function and π a constant. Because the shape of the normal curve was derived using mathematics, it does not necessarily have a correspondence with a collection of real-world data. However, a lot of things in the real world appear to be normal. That is, distributions of a lot of variables in the real world have distributions that closely resemble the normal curve. Phenomena like height, blood pressure, intelligence, and political extremism, among others have all been shown to resemble a normal curve. In terms of political ideology, for example, this is akin to saying that among the American public we expect there to be many moderates with few radicals and few reactionaries.

When the frequency distributions for these variables closely resemble the normal probability distribution we can use what we know about the normal curve to make probabilistic statements with our actual data. As such, researchers should regularly ask themselves if the distributions of the actual data surrounding their phenomena of interest truly resemble the form of the normal curve. One example of a distribution that is not normal would be the distribution of wealth in the world, which is positively skewed with more individuals at the lower end of the wealth distribution and fewer individuals at the higher end. Those concerned that a variable is not normally distributed should at least check to see that their sample distribution as graphed with a histogram resembles a normal curve.[186]

We continue by accepting this normal assumption for some variables. Indeed, its broad application means that it has been used by researchers in many different fields. Furthermore its simple character makes it an invaluable tool for the introduction of data analysis. Indeed, many would argue that the hypothetical normal world is very similar to the real world. The law of large numbers tells us that probability distributions and frequency distributions, with the same generating process, should resemble each other when the frequency gets large enough. So if we expect that the distribution of a variable is normal in the population, we know what its frequency distribution will look like in the long run. That is, we know all the properties of what we expect it to look like from the normal distribution.

One can represent the probability of a range of outcomes in terms of area within a histogram. For probability distributions, the area between any two vertical lines represents the number of cases falling in that range. Because the normal curve is a probability distribution, we know that 100% of the cases fall below the curve in a given normal distribution. Thus the area under a curve always sums to 1. With this shape we know that the central area contains the mean and toward the tails there are increasingly fewer cases, or smaller proportions of extreme scores. Thus probability decreases as we travel away from μ.

The nature of the normal distribution is such that the same proportions of the area under the curve will always lie between the mean and some standardized score from it. That is, regardless of the μ and σ of the particular distribution the same proportion of cases will lie between μ and σ as measured by sigma units. Because the distribution is symmetric any σ distance above the mean contains the same proportion of cases as a σ distance below the mean. Thus, with μ as the point of departure, 1σ in both directions (i.e., from 1σ to -1σ) contains 68.26% of the cases, 2σ in both directions contains 95.44% and 3σ in both directions contains 99.74%.

When we are interested in calculating the difference of a raw score to the mean in the data that is not a perfect multiple of the standard deviation, we have to transform it into a standardized scale on the normal distribution. That is, we must calculate our standardized scores when the raw scores are not the 1, 2, or 3 standard deviations noted in the normal distribution graph. We call the raw score converted into a standardized score on the sigma scale a **z-score** (z).

How do we calculate a z-score? Changing a raw score to a unit of standard deviation is done by dividing the distance of the raw score from the mean by the standard deviation:

$$z = \frac{(X - \mu)}{\sigma}. \tag{19.6}$$

This process is not so different from translating feet to yards:

$$2\ yards = \frac{6\ feet}{3}. \tag{19.7}$$

However, note that σ changes depending on the distribution, but 3 feet always equals 1 yard. Thus we first need to calculate σ, or some approximation of it, to find a z-score.

Once we have calculated the z-score we utilize a table to find the exact percentage of cases within any particular interval. This book provides a z-score table in the Appendix, Table A.1. The z-score table is cumulative from the mean, such that it provides the area under the normal curve from the mean to each z-score as calculated from the formula for the normal distribution. As such, Table A.1 comprises only two columns, one for the calculated z-score and one for the area between the mean and the z-score.

Consider, for example, the top left graph in Figure 19.3. The z-score table provides us with the area of the shaded region, which ranges from μ to z. However, the table does not limit us to statements about the area in this interval. Because of the properties of the normal curve, we can also use this information to make

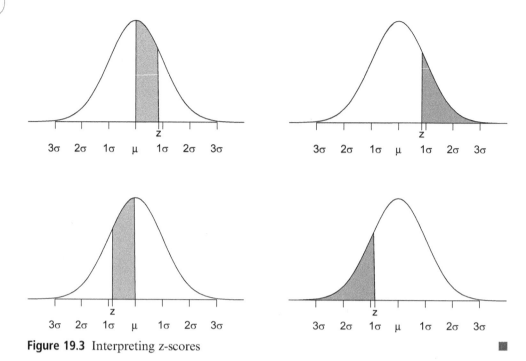

Figure 19.3 Interpreting z-scores

statements about the area under other parts of the curve that may be of substantive interest. For example, the shaded region in the top right graph in Figure 19.3 is all the area beyond z. Since we know that 50% of cases fall to the right of μ and 50% to the left, we can calculate the percentage of cases greater than z, which is indicated by the shaded region in the right graph. We do this simply by subtracting from 50% the area of the shaded region in the left graph, which is given to us in Table A.1.

Similarly, because we know the curve is symmetric, we also know that the mirror images of the areas on the left of μ are the same as the ones on the right, as shown in the bottom two graphs in Figure 19.3. That is, because of symmetry, if we think of folding the distribution in half at μ we are able to make insights about the other half of the graph as well. In particular, the area from μ to the $-z$ is the same as from μ to z, and the area from $-z$ to its tail is the same as the area from z to its tail. As such, we only need values for z for one side of μ in Table A.1 in order to make statements about the area between intervals on both sides.

Remember that z-scores are not inferential statistics. They simply allow us to assess how unusual an individual case might be, assuming a normal distribution. However, in inferential statistics we are interested in assessing samples, not individual cases. Moreover, we can rarely if ever assume a distribution the way we have above. Instead, we are usually interested in learning about μ and σ from a sample of data. As we will see, however, the properties of the normal distribution help us overcome these obstacles. For large samples, a process akin to calculating a z-score lies at the heart of our decisionmaking process, and for smaller samples, we must only add one additional consideration.

Example: Feelings about Political Institutions

Interval level data contains the most information, but is more difficult to gather in survey research, especially on opinion and behavioral report questions. However, the feeling thermometer we introduced above is one type of survey question that purports to create interval level data about some of the phenomena we care about (see Figure 18.3). Take, for example, the evaluations of two branches of government, the Supreme Court and Congress. In addition to political figures, individuals often have feelings related to entire institutions. Assuming institutional evaluations follow a normal distribution, relative differences in the variation around the mean in one branch indicate greater heterogeneity for it and greater homogeneity for the other. For example, if the σ for Congress is greater than the σ for the Supreme Court, what then do we know about the shape of the distributions relative to one another?

If we know the standard deviations and we assume that each set of data is normally distributed, we can estimate and compare the percentage of feelings toward Congress and the Supreme Court having any given range of scores. So how might the normal assumption help us in this example? Consider some hypothetical data on this topic, where for both institutions the mean is the same, $\mu = 47$, but the standard deviations are different, such that Congress has a $\sigma = 10$ and the Supreme Court has a $\sigma = 5$. Remember that σ is given in raw-score units so $\mu + 1\sigma$ to $\mu - 1\sigma$ gives us the proportion of scores in the first standardized distance range. For Congress then $\mu + 1\sigma = 57$ and $\mu - 1\sigma = 37$. We can now say that 68.26% of Congress evaluations fall between the scores of 37 and 57. Similarly, we know that $\mu + 3\sigma$ to $\mu - 3\sigma$ conveys that over 99% of the public placed Congress between 17 and 77. For the Court $\mu + 1\sigma = 52$ and $\mu - 1\sigma = 42$, which means that 68.26% of the scores fall between 42 and 52 and that over 99% fall between $\mu - 3\sigma$, 32, and $\mu + 3\sigma$, 62. In terms of the big picture, comparing the distributions allows us to say that evaluations of the Court are relatively more homogeneous.

To better understand the leverage afforded by the normal curve, we focus more specifically on the thermometer ratings of the Court. Say we want to know how many standard deviations a score of 60, feeling fairly warmly about the Court, lies from the mean. To figure this out we simply calculate our z-score:

$$z = \frac{(X - \mu)}{\sigma} \tag{19.8}$$

$$= 0.9286.$$

Thus, a raw score of 60 lies 0.93 standard deviations above the mean.

Returning to where we began, we wanted to know the probability of obtaining any raw score in a distribution. Utilizing the normal curve and corresponding z-scores we can figure this out. Checking Table A.1 for our calculated z-score we find that 32.38% of exit poll respondents rate the Court between 47 and 60 degrees.

Thus the probability is 32 in 100 that we would obtain an individual whose feelings toward the Court lie between 47 and 60 degrees.

We might also be interested in the probability of feelings toward the Court that are above a certain amount. For example, what is the probability of obtaining a thermometer rating of the Court above 60 degrees? Since the total area under the symmetric distribution is 100%, and 50% of that is above the mean, we can find the percentage of area beyond 60 by subtracting the 32.38% from the 50%:

$$50\% - 32.38\% = 17.62\%. \tag{19.9}$$

Rounding to 0.18 we can say that there is approximately an 18 in 100 chance to find a rating of 60 or higher.

The properties of the normal curve lend to even more easily calculable probabilities. Because the normal distribution is symmetric a score so many points above the mean is equivalent to a score the same amount of points below the mean in terms of the areas between the mean and each score. That is, the area under the curve to the right of one is the same as the area under the curve to the left of the other. In this example, the area between 13 above the mean and the mean is the same as 13 below the mean and the mean. A rating of 60 degrees then is the same distance from the mean, 47, as a rating of 34, so a raw score of 34 degrees implies a z-score of -0.93.

Likewise we can find probabilities for more than a single portion underneath the curve. We know now $P = 0.18$ for ratings above 60 and below 34. The probability of finding scores either less than 34 or scores greater than 60 can be arrived at by simply adding their probabilities:

$$0.176 + 0.176 = 0.352. \tag{19.10}$$

This is possible because of the sum rule for calculating the probability of disjoint events, which we introduced above. Similarly we can show that the probability of finding scores either greater than 34 or scores less than 60:

$$0.324 + 0.324 = 0.648. \tag{19.11}$$

This range of moderate evaluations is therefore found with probability of about 0.65.

CONCLUSIONS

A probability distribution provides a probability for each value of a variable. Because many phenomena we are interested in studying are believed to resemble the normal curve, we can use our knowledge of it to discover the probability of finding any raw value by translating it into a standardized score, or z-score, provided we also know some population characteristics. In the next chapter we will discuss how we can further use our knowledge of the normal curve to generalize findings from the sample to the population.

KEY TERMS

- Normal curve
- Sample space
- Axioms of probability
- Multiplication rule
- Sum rule
- Probability distribution
- Law of large numbers
- Z-score

Statistics can be more than a tool for describing data. In the social sciences we have hypotheses that move us beyond simple descriptions of populations to relationships between two or more variables. To analyze these relationships we often rely in practice on statistical inference. That is, we need to make decisions based on data collected on a small group (sample) for the larger group that we want to study (population). In Chapter 4 we introduced the concept of sampling and provided a description of the three general objectives pertaining to sampling: representativeness, size, and level of analysis. Here we move to a more focused explanation of how sampling helps researchers overcome practical limitations and what implications this has for quantitative analyses.

Sampling

As we noted earlier, when it comes to sampling, larger is generally better, the aforementioned issues aside. So why sample at all? Why not collect data on the full population? In all types of research we find the same two answers: time and money. Research occurs in the real world and collecting the ideal data is often limited by how much time and money the researcher can direct to the project. Thus every research design must take into account the practical circumstances. In doing so, researchers necessarily restrict their investigation into a sample or subset of the population that they would like to study.

In general, when we make comparisons we would like to talk about more than just the observations in the sample. We would like to talk about the larger group of interest in our research, the population. How we do this is the objective of statistical inference. More specifically, statistical inference helps researchers provide statements of confidence in our ability to generalize or infer from the sample to the population. The ability to offer an estimate of relative precision is another reason why quantitative empirical research is so useful and popular.

Consider the ANES dataset that we used for the examples in Chapter 18. How many cases or individuals do we have in our sample? Obviously, the nearly 6,000 individuals in that sample is not anywhere near the size of the full voting age population of the United States, yet we would like to use this sample of data to describe that population. In practice, we rarely study every member of the population and instead rely on a sample and statistical inference to generalize to the population.

Statistical inference depends on knowing that the people in our sample are representative of the population. If they are representative *enough* we can generalize our conclusion from the sample to the population. This inference depends on every case in the population being randomly drawn into the sample. In statistics a **random sample** means that every case in the population has an equal chance of being drawn into the sample. Thus random is not *any* chance in statistics; it has a precise definition of equal probability.

As an example, consider blindfolded draws of slips of paper from a hat. If every slip has the same shape, size, and only one name on it, then every name has the same probability of being chosen. But we would need a huge hat to do this for several thousand, let alone the millions of people in the US population. In order to perform random sampling, we typically use a random number generator or table. In either case the output is a series of numbers having no particular pattern or order. Drawing a random sample is a simple three-stage process:

1   Attain a complete list of the population.
2   Assign unique identifying numbers to each unit or member of the population.
3   Draw the members of the sample from a random number generator or a table of random numbers.

This process is our best chance to get a sample to look like a population, provided, of course, that we have no additional information about the population.

Above we saw how we can use z-scores to assess the relationship between individual observations and the population they belong to, under a specific set of assumptions about the population parameters. We now consider a more realistic scenario that is consistent with an applied research design process where we have no information about the population μ and σ. We will take a random sample of observations from the population in order to make guesses about the population. Thus, instead of looking at one observation, we now have a sample of multiple cases. Instead of just having one value, we now have two pieces of information: a sample mean, $\overline{X}$, and a sample standard deviation, s.

So why does our sample information not perfectly match the population? Because of **sampling error**. That is, because of the process of selection our sample rarely has the same mean and standard deviation as our population. This is not an error that we can fix. Moreover, it prevents us from being exact with our estimates. Thus all inference involves uncertainty.

An example of this uncertainty around our statistical inferences that should be familiar to social science students comes from election coverage. In election polling candidates' relative chances are not reported alone but along with an estimate of error based on the polling sample. For example, a candidate might be estimated to have 65% of the vote, with a margin of error of 4 percentage points. We recognize this margin of error (discussed in more detail below) as an indicator of uncertainty in our point estimate of anticipated vote choice. That is, the researcher is confident that this candidate has within 61% to 69% of the vote. How do we arrive at this range of values?

Samples and Populations

So far we have considered three types of distributions: empirical distributions of actual data (e.g., Obama's feeling thermometer scores), theoretical distributions of probabilistic processes (e.g., rolling dice), and theoretical statistical distributions (e.g., the normal curve). Now we consider the distribution of sample means as a pedagogical tool to help envision what certainty means in statistical inference. While this is a hypothetical scenario that does not represent actual research, it helps explain why we are allowed to draw conclusions about populations based on a sample. The hypothetical we are considering is as follows: We have a population from which we are repeatedly drawing samples (of any size, all the same). For each sample, we calculate the mean. We then treat each of those means, as data themselves, and assess their distribution, by calculating the mean and plotting them on a histogram. We call this distribution the **sampling distribution of the sample mean**. We can also treat the standard deviations of those samples as data and assess the distributions.

The key premise of statistical inference is that we can make generalizations from samples if the sample is representative enough of the population. We can find the extent to which our sample is representative of the population based on our understanding of the characteristics of this sampling distribution of sample means. Foremost, the sampling distribution of means approximates a normal curve. Secondly, the mean of a sampling distribution of means (the mean of means) gets closer to the true population mean as N moves toward infinity. Finally, the standard deviation of a sampling distribution of means is smaller than the standard deviation of the population.

Repeating the key characteristic, when we take repeated samples from a population the mean and standard deviation of those samples are themselves normally distributed – even if the population distribution is not. In probability theory, this is what we call the **central limit theorem**, which, like the law of large numbers, is a mathematical result of probability theory. The theorem states that the means of a series of random draws from a population distribution will be approximately normally distributed provided a sufficiently large number of draws. That is, as you increase the draws the distribution of sample means looks increasingly similar to a normal distribution.

To solidify this point, Figure 20.1 shows the results of 10 and 100 draws of means from each of three familiar distributions. Moving from the distribution in the left column to 10 mean draws in the middle column and 100 mean draws in the right column we see each of the distributions begins to converge into the normal distribution. While not shown here, it is important to remember that even for less familiar or unknown distributions – indeed for any distribution with a well-defined

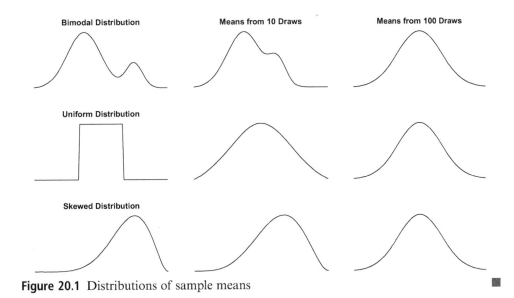

Figure 20.1 Distributions of sample means

mean and standard deviation – this theorem holds, which explains the ubiquity of the normal distribution.

With this insight we are now in a position to assess any one of our individual samples. That is, because of the characteristics of the distribution of sample means we can use what we know about the normal curve to place indicators of certainty around our estimates. Because the sampling distribution of means takes the form of the normal curve, we can say that as a score moves farther from the mean of means the probability of getting it decreases. Similarly, we know the percentage of cases falling between standard deviations and the mean.

In applied work, however, we are generally not interested in probabilities associated with a particular raw score but with samples drawn from a population. We want to make a statement about how likely our sample would be to occur, given our population mean and standard deviation. The general procedure is similar to the z-score procedure above, but, since we are assessing a sample of size N this time, we cannot simply use our population standard deviation to create z-scores. Instead we rely on the **standard error of the mean**:

$$\sigma_{\overline{X}} = \frac{\sigma}{\sqrt{N}}. \tag{20.1}$$

Note that we will often calculate (or more often be given by statistical software) **standard errors** associated with certain quantities. Generally speaking, these quantities represent our uncertainty about the estimate in question. If the ratio of our estimate to its standard error is high (e.g., the ratio of $\overline{X}$ to $\sigma_{\overline{X}}$), our guess is very precise. If the ratio is low, we hold less confidence in our estimate.

Returning to our sampling distribution of sample means now with the standard error of the mean and some population parameters (which we do not typically have in practice but are given here for pedagogical purposes), we can arrive at a z-score for the sample means distribution in the same way we arrived at a z-score for any X value above:

$$z = \frac{\overline{X} - \mu}{\sigma_{\overline{X}}}. \qquad (20.2)$$

This z-score provides us the probability of finding the mean score from the sample in the population. That is, if we then consult Table A.1 for our calculated z-score we can find the probability of randomly choosing this sample (with its particular mean and standard deviation) from a population.

Relatedly, we can also find the range of mean values within which our true population mean is likely to fall, which brings us to the concept of the **confidence interval** (CI). The confidence interval is just our estimate or statistic wrapped in some range of uncertainty. Here the estimate is the mean, but we will want to create confidence intervals for the statistics we introduce later in the book as well. The range of uncertainty around a statistic is conveyed by the **margin of error** (MOE), which expresses the amount of sampling error in our results. The larger the margin of error the less confidence we hold that our observed estimate is close to that of the population. Thus, the confidence interval is simply an estimate plus and minus the margin of error:

$$CI = \text{Statistic} \pm MOE, \qquad (20.3)$$

where the margin of error is a particular chosen value of a standardized score (e.g., z-score) multiplied by the standard error of the statistic:

$$MOE = \text{standardized score} \times \sigma_{Statistic}. \qquad (20.4)$$

Equivalently, a confidence interval is just an estimate plus and minus a standardized score times the standard error of estimate.

In the case of the mean for the normal distribution our confidence interval is calculated accordingly:

$$CI = \overline{X} \pm 1.96 \times \sigma_{\overline{X}}. \qquad (20.5)$$

The chosen value of the standardized score, 1.96, corresponds to the level of confidence we choose to hold in our estimate. That is, here we arrive at the uncertainty by adding and substracting from the estimate our standard error multiplied by a particular z-score, 1.96. But where does 1.96 come from?

Hypothesis Testing

Throughout the statistics section of the book we have asked you to consider a number of research questions and how we might answer them. In practice, however, researchers more formally put forward statements of expectation to test with their data, which we call **hypotheses** (introduced in Chapter 2). Hypothesis testing in statistics follows a specific process. We begin by offering a research hypothesis, or statement of expectation. For any hypothesis we also propose a **null hypothesis**, or opposing expectation that we will try to reject with our hypothesis test. The null hypothesis typically holds that the observed results occured by chance; i.e., sampling error. We next obtain a sample and calculate the relevant statistic. Finally, we calculate the probability of observing the statistic by chance, under the assumption that the null hypothesis is true. Based on this probability we decide whether or not to reject the null hypothesis.

The decision of whether or not to reject the null hypothesis is made easier and more consistent by accepting a conventional threshold. We refer to the **significance level** in terms of α, which equates to one less than our chosen **confidence level**:

$$\alpha = 1 - \text{confidence level.} \tag{20.6}$$

α corresponds to the area of the distribution in the tails. It is simply the probability of rejecting the null hypothesis if the null hypothesis is true. We might think of it as an expression of our chosen probability of being wrong. Thus we decide to reject the null hypothesis only when we are really confident, which means that we should choose as our threshold an α that is very small. But exactly how small is very small? The standard confidence level in the natural and social sciences is 0.95 (or 95%), which corresponds to α of 0.05 (or 5%) and a z-score of ± 1.96. The left graph in Figure 20.2 illustrates that this α means there is 2.5% in each of the tails. We call the z-scores demarcating the confidence level **critical values**, because we know that attaining a larger z-score than ± 1.96 ($z < -1.96$ or $z > 1.96$) conveys that the result is statistically significant at this confidence level. That is, statistical significance conveys that we reject the null hypothesis that the observed results occured by chance, since they are far, by conventional standards, from the null hypothesis under the assumed distribution. Thus the α value serves as a practical cutoff point at which the null hypothesis can be rejected in the context of sampling error. When rejecting the null hypothesis (at the conventional 95% level of confidence) we are conveying that there is less than a 5 in 100 chance that we have done so when we should have failed to reject it.

The interpretation of the confidence level is made clearer by reconsidering the hypothetical example of repeatedly drawing random samples and calculating the

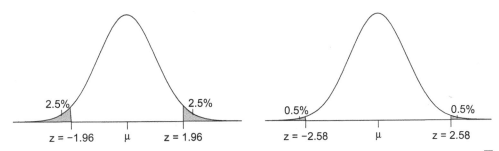

Figure 20.2 Varying alpha

mean for each one. If we were to draw 100 samples from the population, 95 of the times the confidence interval would cover the true mean. Looking under the normal curve 95% of the area falls around the mean between the z-scores of -1.96 and 1.96; the margin of error for the normal distribution follows accordingly:

$$MOE = 1.96 \times \sigma_{\overline{X}}. \tag{20.7}$$

Thus, the interval has a 95% chance of including the true value. The reason for this threshold, however, is purely conventional. We are merely accepting this significance level to make scientific work more consistent. For example, 94% also seems to be a good level of confidence, and 96% even more so. The right graph in Figure 20.2 shows a tougher test for rejecting the null hypothesis. With a 99% significance level, corresponding to z-scores of -2.58 and 2.58, there is only 0.5% in each of the tails. Why then do we choose 95%?

Importantly, 95% is just a rule of thumb. There is no statistical reason why it is most commonly used as the cutpoint. It is merely the norm in most scientific disciplines to hold estimates at this level of certainty. While it is a largely accepted matter of convention, researchers should therefore be careful in relying strictly on 95% as a cutpoint. In addition, since we have a standard choice of 95% confidence intervals, scientists have 5% chance of being wrong or $\alpha = 0.05$. That is, even though we have a random sample, samples can sometimes be very unrepresentative of the population by chance. We accept that there is always some sampling error by providing a range of confidence or certainty around each of our estimates, as with a confidence interval.

We attain statistical significance when the **p-value** for the statistic is less than α. In terms of the distribution, the p-value is the area from the z-score (or another test statistic discussed below) to the tails. It is therefore the exact probability of observing a sample statistic as or more extreme than the observed one if the null is true. Thus, if the z-score is within the tails denoted by the critical values, the p-value will be less than or equal to α, and we reject the null hypothesis. The p-value associated with the standard 95% confidence level is 0.05, so, in practice, anytime we arrive at a p-value less than or equal to 0.05 we reject the null.

There are two types of errors in statistical hypothesis testing: **Type 1** and **Type 2**. Figure 20.3 illustrates these errors in a 2×2 table. The columns refer to the two possible states of the null hypothesis in reality. The rows refer to the two possible states as perceived or measured through the statistical tests. Type 1 errors mean we rejected the null when we should have retained it. In other words the error is the rejection of the null hypothesis when in reality the null hypothesis is true, or a **false positive**. Type 2 errors mean we retained the null when we should have rejected it. This is the failure to reject the null hypothesis when in reality it is false, or a **false negative**.

It is important to remember that these concepts are intertwined in inferential statistics. In quantitative analysis – specifically, when relying on levels of significance to reject the null hypothesis – we can provide additional consideration depending on our concerns over particular errors. If we are worried about Type 1 errors, we can increase the stringency of α; e.g., move from $\alpha = 0.05$ to $\alpha = 0.01$.

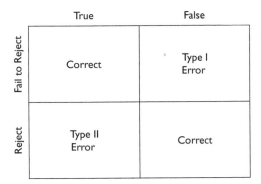

	True	False
Fail to Reject	Correct	Type I Error
Reject	Type II Error	Correct

Figure 20.3 Hypothesis test results against real state of null hypothesis ▪

The right graph in Figure 20.2 demonstrates that we have shrunk the amount of area in our tails by decreasing α. Thus the probability of getting a Type 1 error is just α. However, if we are more worried about Type 2 errors, we can increase the size of the sample so that we are more likely to reject the null hypothesis when it should be rejected. That is, failing to reject a null hypothesis is less likely by random chance if the sample is larger. The probability of getting a Type 2 error is thus directly related to our sample size.

Recall that α specifically refers to the size of the tail regions under the curve. It is the threshold value below which it is considered so small that the null hypothesis can be rejected, and is determined ahead of time by the researcher who is balancing the costs of Type 1 and Type 2 errors. In practice researchers often merely check to see if the z-score or test statistic exceeds the critical value (e.g., 1.96) associated with our chosen α (e.g., 0.95). If so we can say that the results are statistically significant at the α level. However, we need to be vigilant about the interpretation of these concepts in light of their derivation and somewhat arbitrary nature.

Estimating Population Parameters

Returning to our estimation of the population mean, we are still not in a realistic position from the perspective of practical research. In practice, we only have a sample mean and sample standard deviation. So how do we use that information to arrive at an estimate of the population mean? We begin by finding an estimate of the standard error of the mean. To do so, we simply divide our sample standard deviation, s, by the square root of N; thus the sample standard error of the mean:

$$s_{\overline{X}} = \frac{s}{\sqrt{(N)}}.$$ (20.8)

Thus in small samples this correction gives a fair estimate of the variability in the entire population. Of course, in large samples this correction is trivial and the sample means tend to be reliable estimates of the population means.

Though it brings us closer to how we use sample estimates in actual research, estimating the standard error of the mean creates a new problem: the sampling distribution of means is no longer normal due to using a random variable $s_{\overline{X}}$ in place of the population parameter $\sigma_{\overline{X}}$. The extra uncertainty in the estimated standard error makes the sampling distribution of means wider. Our distribution now has greater dispersion than a normal distribution, so we cannot use z-scores, which refer only to normal distributions. Instead, the ratio follows a **t-distribution**, where our standardized score is now:

$$t = \frac{\overline{X} - \mu}{s_{\overline{X}}}. \tag{20.9}$$

The t-distribution is, however, similar in two important ways to the normal distribution: it is symmetric and the area under the curve can be characterized by knowing the mean and standard deviation. We are still interested in stating the range in which we can be confident that the population mean falls. That is, we will need to calculate a margin of error for our estimate. However, since we are using t-ratios instead of z-scores, the appropriate cutpoints are not always 1.96. The t-ratio, unlike the z-score, depends on **degrees of freedom** (df), where

$$df = N - 1. \tag{20.10}$$

In the calculation of a statistic, the degrees of freedom is the number of values that remain variable. In other words, it is the number of observations less the number of parameters used to estimate the statistic. The greater the df, the larger the sample size, and thus the closer the t-distribution is to a normal distribution, as shown in Figure 20.4. So when the sample is large there is no difference between a z-score and t-ratio, and thus we can rely on the familiar z-score instead of the t-ratio. When the sample is small we rely on the t-ratios.

Take, for example, the sample variance for X. Because it requires the calculation of a single parameter, the mean, it has $N - 1$ degrees of freedom. The rationale is that because the sample standard deviation is smaller than the standard deviation would be when calculated from the population, we inflate the sample variance slightly with $N - 1$ in the denominator instead of N. In other words the sample mean fits the sample better than the population mean might, and so the sample standard deviation has a slight bias in that it is a smaller representative of

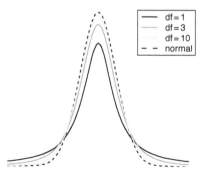

df = 1
df = 3
df = 10
normal

Figure 20.4 T-distribution at different degrees of freedom

the population standard deviation. So we make a quick correction in this by taking out a bit from the denominator. Accordingly, we arrive at less biased or, as they are frequently called, **unbiased estimates** of the population parameter:

$$s^2 = \frac{\Sigma(X - \overline{X})^2}{N - 1}. \tag{20.11}$$

Thus in small samples this correction gives a fair estimate of the variability in the entire population. Of course, in large samples the sample means tend to be reliable estimates of the population means. Like before with the normal curve, we can use a table to inform us of the area under the t-distribution. When we rely on the t-ratio table in Appendix Table A.2, we need two pieces of information, in addition to the standardized score, in order to find where our estimate sits on the distribution. First, we need the degrees of freedom and, second, we need a confidence level. As we have noted above, the margin of error depends on the sample size, but we choose the confidence level. For the mean of a small sample, then, we can get our confidence intervals from:

$$\overline{X} \pm t \times \sigma_{\overline{X}}. \tag{20.12}$$

Again, if our sample size is large enough, the t-ratio is the same as the z-score, 1.96. If the sample size is smaller, that number increases to above 2. For example, that multiplier is equal to 2.021 for a sample of 40, and 2.228 for a sample of 10. Thus the smaller the sample the more uncertainty around our estimate.

Example: Average Number of Parties in Democracies

Let's return to the concept of democracy and consider a comparative politics example. Here we would like to know about how many political parties we should expect to find in a democratic country. That is, what is the average number of parties in a democracy? We do not have the time to collect the number of parties for all democratic countries in the world and instead only collected this data for a random sample of 60 of them.

Akin to practical research, we do not know the population mean – which would answer our question – but we can use our sample to make an educated guess. We begin by calculating the sample mean, $\overline{X} = 3.75$, and the standard deviation, $s = 1.05$. Because we have a sample, we need to account for sampling error, therefore we calculate the standard error of the mean:

$$\begin{aligned} s_{\overline{X}} &= \frac{s}{\sqrt{(N)}} \\ &= \frac{1.05}{\sqrt{60}} \\ &= 0.14. \end{aligned} \tag{20.13}$$

With our degrees of freedom for the standard error of the mean, $N = 60$, we consult Appendix Table A.2 to find that for *alpha* = 0.05 our appropriate t-value is 2.0. This tells us that for a t-distribution with df = 100, 95% of the area under the curve falls between $t = -2.00$ and $t = 2.00$. Finally, we plug this into our formula for the confidence interval:

$$
\begin{aligned}
CI &= \overline{X} \pm t \times s_{\overline{X}} \\
&= 3.75 \pm (2.00 \times 0.14) \\
&= 3.75 \pm .50 \\
&= [3.47, 4.03].
\end{aligned}
\tag{20.14}
$$

We can thus say that the mean number of parties in our population is between about 3.5 and 4.

CONCLUSIONS

In statistical inference we generalize from a sample to a population by making assumptions about the true distribution of a variable. Reference to a probability distribution, like the normal curve, helps us understand how likely the results we have found in our sample are due to chance. In order to do so, we also need to ensure that we have a representative sample, which can be accomplished through random sampling, and can agree on a threshold for statistical confidence.

KEY TERMS

- Random sample
- Sampling error
- Sampling distribution of the sample mean
- Central limit theorem
- Standard error of the mean
- Standard errors
- Confidence intervals
- Margin of error
- Hypotheses
- Null hypothesis
- Significance level
- Confidence level
- Critical values
- p-value
- Type 1 error
- Type 2 error
- False positive
- False negative
- t-distribution
- Degrees of freedom
- Unbiased estimates

Bivariate Statistics

Bivariate statistics allow us to test the relationship between two variables. While simple, they provide great empirical leverage for hypotheses of association and, with the appropriate research design, causality. We next hone our ability to make controlled comparisons and introduce inference making about sample means with the difference of means test. We then proceed to correlation, which moves us beyond making a simple claim of a relationship or no relationship between two variables to a measure of both the strength and direction of the relationship.

Revisiting Levels of Measurement

In the previous chapter, we found out some important substantive information about our population means. Indeed we learned how to estimate a population mean from the information that we gain in a single sample. However, we are still not in a position to assess a hypothesis. We do not generally have expectations as simple as "the mean number of parties in a democracy is x." Our hypotheses typically suggest a relationship between an independent and dependent variable, and we have not made reference to bivariate analyses yet. We will explore a number of statistical tests for assessing hypotheses. We can divide hypothesis tests into three types based on the information they provide about the relationship between the independent and dependent variable:

1 Those that simply analyze whether or not there is a relationship between variables (e.g., Difference of Means).
2 Measures of association, which tell us the direction and strength of the relationship between two variables. (e.g., Correlation).
3 Measures of average effect, which tell us the amount of change in the dependent variable given a unit change in the independent variable (e.g., Regression).

It is important to note that knowing which test to use requires us to think not just about the question we would like to answer but also our variables' levels of measurement, their population distributions, and the sample size. In addition, all the tests discussed here demand that the data come from a random sample. In Chapter 3 we learned about levels of measurement. In quantitative analyses understanding the level of measurement is essential because it helps us decide which hypothesis test to use.

Table 21.1   Hypothesis tests guide

Independent Variable	Dependent Variable	
	Discrete	Continuous
Discrete	Chi-Square, Phi, Logit, Probit, Cramer's V	Difference of Means, ANOVA, Regression
Continuous	Logit, Probit	Regression, Correlation

Table 21.1 lists some of the common and appropriate hypothesis tests – many of which are beyond the scope of this book – by the measurement classifications of the independent and dependent variables. In the table, as is typical in the literature, we group nominal and categorical levels of measurement in the general header, **discrete**, and interval and ratio levels under **continuous** (see Table 3.4). For example, if the dependent variable is continuous and so is the independent variable, we can use regression or correlation. For discrete dependent and independent variables we might use a chi-square or phi test. And with a continuous dependent variable and a discrete indepenent variable we could use difference of means test or regression.

Cross-Tabulations

While a careful look at the frequency distribution of a single variable should be the first step in any analysis, social scientists are predominantly concerned with relationships between two or more variables, not just the distribution of a single variable. That is, the focus of research often turns to testing bivariate and multivariate hypotheses. In the case of our example above, we can easily think about relationships that might be more likely to be tested by social scientists, for example, whether particular backgrounds make individuals more likely to identify with one party or another. Even in the bivariate case, such as this, frequency distributions, appropriately structured, can provide some insight.

Returning to party identification in the 2012 ANES dataset, Table 21.2 presents two frequency distributions – one for party identification and one for gender – in a single table. The distributions for the values of party identification are noted vertically down the first column (as in a single frequency distribution) and those of gender are arranged horizontally across the first row. Thus each cell now contains information on individuals who fit in a particular category for both variables. The total values of the table (in columns and in rows) are referred to as the **marginals**.

Cross-tabulations can include raw counts as well as proportions or percentages. In the example we provide the distributions as both frequencies (counts) and percentages. When we do not have the same number of cases in each group (as above), the frequencies alone tell us little. Consider, for example, a crosstab

Table 21.2 Crosstab of partisanship by gender

	Male	Female	Row total
Democrat	1006	1355	2361
Row Percent	42.61%	57.39%	
Column Percent	37.08%	47.02%	
Total Percent	17.98%	24.22%	42.2%
Independent	999	846	1845
Row Percent	54.15%	45.85%	
Column Percent	36.82%	29.35%	
Total Percent	17.86%	15.12%	32.98%
Republican	708	681	1389
Row Percent	50.97%	49.03%	
Column Percent	26.1%	23.63%	
Total Percent	12.65%	12.17%	24.83%
Column Total	2713	2882	5595
Row Percent	48.49%	51.51%	

with equal category percentages in each cell but different frequencies. We would be tempted in this case to draw conclusions from the different frequencies. However, controlling for the sample size with percentages would show us that the different frequencies are not meaningful.

In the case of differing category sizes, we require a way to standardize frequency distributions in order to compare them. We often make use of proportions and percentages in this case. The proportion simply compares the number of cases in a given category with the total size of the distribution

$$Prop = \frac{f}{N},$$ (21.1)

where f is the frequency of observations and N is the sample size. Even more frequently, as above, we make use of percentages, which are the frequency of occurrence of a category per 100 cases,

$$Pct = 100 * \frac{f}{N}.$$ (21.2)

From Table 21.2 what can we gather about the different groups? How does party identification look for each gender? We can see, as we have above, that Democrats were the largest share of the sample at 2,361, followed by Independents. In terms of the relationship between the two variables, 1,355 of the Democrats in the survey sample were women. While Republicans appear to split fairly equally among the sexes at 708 and 681, 999 Independents were male compared to only 846 female Independents. The largest number of respondents are female Democrats at 1,355. This is the framework for cross-tabulations, or, more colloquially, **crosstabs**. Because they involve two variables and describe some aspects of the relationship between two variables crosstabs provide a basic bivariate analysis. Thus, typically, social scientific analysis begins with a crosstab.

Beyond the counts and marginals, we can get further information from our data (depending on our interests) from the row and column percents. Perhaps we want to know more about the Independent males, in which case we could look at them relative to all Independents by dividing the frequencies in each row by the number of cases in that row,

$$Pct_{Row} = 100 * \frac{f}{N_{Row}}$$
$$= 54.15\%. \tag{21.3}$$

Or we could use column percents if we wanted to know the percentage of females that are Democrat relative to the entire female sample, for example. Here we divide the frequencies in each column by the number of cases in that column,

$$Pct_{Col} = 100 * \frac{f}{N_{Col}}$$
$$= 47.02\%. \tag{21.4}$$

In all, the frequency distribution and its bivariate format, the crosstab, have the ability to provide a wealth of information. Thus, while somewhat limited – particularly in terms of multivariate considerations – it is good practice to begin any statistical analysis here.

Difference of Means

In social science we are often concerned with differences between groups. For example, do Republicans differ from Democrats with respect to how religious they are? The basic process involved in answering a question of this nature – where we are interested in the extent to which two samples resemble each other on some variable – is simple enough. First, we establish a hypothesis about the population. Second, we collect a sample. Next, we check to see how likely the sample results are given our hypotheses about the population. Finally, we reject or fail to reject the null hypothesis based on our confidence level.

When testing hypotheses, we typically talk about testing the null hypothesis. In this case, a null hypothesis says that the two samples are drawn from equivalent populations. That is, any difference between two samples is due to a chance occurrence or sampling error. In line with our notation, we symbolize it as

$$\mu_1 = \mu_2, \tag{21.5}$$

where μ_1 is the mean of the first population and μ_2 is the mean of the second population. Thus, in our example the null hypothesis would be that Republicans and Democrats are equally religious (or that there is no difference between them in terms of religiosity). Remember this does not mean that we are denying the difference in sample means, but that we are instead attributing that difference to sampling error when we retain the null hypothesis (i.e., we are unable to reject the null hypothesis).

If the null is retained our data suggests that there is no relationship between our variables. Of course, we as social scientists often want to establish relationships. The process we subscribe to begins with the presumption that relationships do not exist. That is, establishing differences between groups is often the rationale for research – even though failing to disprove the null is sometimes more informative, or more theoretically intriguing, than rejecting the null. If we reject the null, we cannot rule out the research hypothesis that a true population difference exists. In this case the two samples appear to have been taken from populations having different means. Or more precisely stated, the difference between sample means is too large to be accounted for by sampling error. We symbolize this difference in means as

$$\mu_1 \neq \mu_2. \tag{21.6}$$

In the previous chapter we saw how to construct a sampling distribution of mean scores. In order to understand whether we can expect a difference between sample means to be due to chance or a true population difference between the two groups, we now consider the construction of a **sampling distribution of differences between means**. This frequency distribution is just like those we have explored earlier, except that the frequency is based on a series of differences between sample means randomly drawn from a given population.

We want to make a probability statement about the occurrence of different scores in the sampling distribution of differences between means. In the past we have relied on known probability distributions, like the normal curve, to make probability statements. We do so again here. If we can assume that this sampling distribution of differences of means is distributed normally we can make statements of probability. Assuming normality we know the general characteristics of our distribution of differences between means.

But does it make sense to think of the sampling distribution of differences between means as a normal distribution? Instead of just taking a singular random sample, think again about what would happen if we took a series of random samples and made a distribution of differences between means. Consider, for example, the hypothetical data in Table 21.3 which occurs from repeatedly taking two samples, calculating the mean for each and then the difference between means. For the purposes of this example, assume also that we know the population mean. If the null hypothesis is correct then the two samples should look the same. Any difference between the population mean and any sample mean should be due purely to sampling error. Thus a distribution of differences between means would look approximately normal if we wanted to retain the null hypothesis. That is,

Table 21.3 Distribution of differences between means

Differences	Frequency
5	1
4	2
3	5
2	7
1	10
0	18
−1	10
−2	8
−3	5
−4	3
−5	1

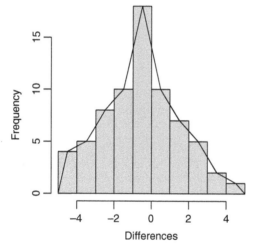

Figure 21.1 Histogram with polygon of differences between means

if there was truly no difference between means due to actual differences in the population, then the differences that do show up in the samples should look like random fluctuations about the mean with most scores close to the mean and few scores in the tail. Indeed the difference in means should overestimate and underestimate the mean in roughly equal numbers. In addition, the mean of the difference in means should be close to zero as the true central tendency of cases is to have no difference between the sample means. Figure 21.1 plots the histogram of differences overlayed with a polygon. The polygon shows that after only 70 draws from each sample we can already see a shape that somewhat resembles the normal curve, which we should expect given the central limit theorem. Moreover, the mean is zero, which suggests the samples are very similar to each other.

Again, note that we do not take many samples from a population in practice. Given what we know about the population and the normal curve, our reasoning for rejecting or retaining the null hypothesis can be constructed in terms of the score's distance to the mean – in this case the difference between means. If the difference of means that we found lies so far from the mean of differences between means for the null hypothesis (i.e., 0) that it only has a small probability of occurrence in the sampling distribution of differences between means, we reject the null. Contrarily, if the difference of means falls close to the mean of differences between means such that the probability of its occurrence in the sampling distribution of differences between means is high, we find ourselves unable to reject the null.

As we have done in the past, we need to transform our parameter of interest into a standardized unit to determine where it falls on the distribution. In this case we are dealing with sample mean differences that we need to translate into standardized units, so we calculate it accordingly:

$$z = \frac{(\overline{X}_1 - \overline{X}_2) - 0}{\sigma_{\overline{X}_1 - \overline{X}_2}}, \tag{21.7}$$

where $\overline{X}_1 - \overline{X}_2$ is the difference between the mean of the first sample and the mean of the second sample. We assume 0 for the mean of the sampling distribution of differences between means based on our null hypothesis:

$$\mu_1 - \mu_2 = 0. \tag{21.8}$$

We rarely have knowledge of the standard deviation of the distribution of mean differences; again, it is too costly to draw enough pairs of sample means from the population to calculate it. Moreover, in practical research we can rarely assume that our sample sizes or variances are equal. Not unlike our problem with the standard deviation in the sampling distribution of means then, we need an estimate for the standard deviation that combines information from both samples. That is, the variance and sample size need to be accounted for to give us an idea of how different $\overline{X}_1$ is from $\overline{X}_2$ due to sampling error alone. We therefore calculate an approximation of it from the two samples that we actually draw. We will call this our **standard error of the difference between means**:

$$s_{\overline{X}_1 - \overline{X}_2} = \sqrt{\frac{s_1^2}{N_1} + \frac{s_2^2}{N_2}}. \tag{21.9}$$

With the standard error we can rewrite the test statistic for the difference of means test in terms of how it is used in actual research:

$$t = \frac{\overline{X}_1 - \overline{X}_2}{s_{\overline{X}_1 - \overline{X}_2}}. \tag{21.10}$$

There are a few variants on the difference of means test. One common version uses the independent variable to break observations into groups over time.

A second variant involves the differences between proportions. The procedures for comparing scores between the same group tested twice (i.e., panel data) and for comparing proportions involve different assumptions and slightly different formulae than that above, where we are testing mean differences in two different populations. While we will not cover this material here, you should be aware of the difference. Also note that the formulae above can be simplifed when we can assume equal sample sizes or equal variances. We have not made those assumptions with this data, which is more common in observational data.

Parametric Models

The statistical analysis above (difference of means) as well as some of the others we introduce below (correlation and regression) assume that the distributions of the variables being assessed belong to a large collection of known parameterized families of probability distributions. A parameter is just a characteristic of a population that we can use to describe the distribution. For example, in the case of the difference of means, we rely on the normal distribution, with its familiar parameters of μ and σ. Thus, we call all tests of this nature **parametric**.

While largely beyond the scope of this book, it is important to note that there also exist **nonparametric** models. These models similarly employ a mathematical procedure for hypothesis testing, but, unlike parametric statistics, they make no assumptions about the underlying distributions of the variables. Here the model structure is not specified at the onset by assuming a known probability distribution, but, instead, determined by the data. For example, a histogram is a simple nonparametric estimate of a probability distribution. As such, the term nonparametric is not meant to imply that such models completely lack parameters but that the number and nature of the parameters are flexible and not fixed in advance. There are also **semiparametric** models that have both parametric and nonparametric components.

Generally speaking, nonparametric tests have less **statistical power** than the appropriate parametric tests (though this depends on the kind of nonparametric test), but are more robust when the assumptions underlying the parametric test are not satisfied. Power refers to the probability of rejecting the null hypothesis when it is truly false. The results of a parametric test for a sample that does not appropriately match the assumed distribution are not meaningful. In these cases we should rely on nonparametric tests.[187]

Example: Group Membership and Ideology

Let us take an example related to questions of social capital. We have a hypothesis that liberals will belong to more social groups than conservatives. That is, liberals are more likely than conservatives to be members in formal groups, like civic and social groups, professional associations, and political organizations. The null

Table 21.4 Summary statistics of group membership by ideology

Liberals	Conservatives
$N_1 = 25$	$N_2 = 37$
$\overline{X}_1 = 60$	$\overline{X}_2 = 49$
$s_1 = 8$	$s_2 = 7$

hypothesis is thus that the $\mu_{liberals} = \mu_{conservatives}$. Our research hypothesis is that $\mu_{liberals} > \mu_{conservatives}$. However, for ease of presentation, let us agree that the opposite result (conservatives are more involved) is also a matter of interest and good possibility. Thus we are simply testing whether a relationship exists between ideology and group membership. In this case, our research hypothesis is that $\mu_{liberals} \neq \mu_{conservatives}$.

Table 21.4 provides the summary statistics for the data on liberal and conservative opinions on group membership. Here, the dependent variable is a multi-item index of engagement in formal group activities ranging from 0 to 100. The independent variable is a simple liberal (1) or conservative (0) dichotomy. We are dealing with an independent variable that is nominal and a dependent variable that is continuous, which, along with the hypothesis, make it appropriate for a difference of means test.

We begin by calculating the standard error of the difference between means:

$$
\begin{aligned}
s_{\overline{X}_1 - \overline{X}_2} &= \sqrt{\frac{s_1^2}{N_1} + \frac{s_2^2}{N_2}} \\
&= \sqrt{\frac{64}{25} + \frac{49}{37}} \\
&= \sqrt{3.88} \\
&= 1.97.
\end{aligned}
\tag{21.11}
$$

If we test the hypothesis that there is a difference between liberals and conservatives on group membership we need to use a t-test to see if the samples are truly different in this case, not a z-score. Recall that z-scores are limited to situations in which we know the true population standard deviation or we have very large distributions, which is not the case in this example. Here we are estimating each σ from our s_1 and s_2, so we use t-tests.

Recall the t-ratio (this time with our new standard error):

$$
\begin{aligned}
t &= \frac{\overline{X}_1 - \overline{X}_2}{s_{x_1 - x_2}} \\
&= \frac{60 - 51}{1.97} \\
&= 4.57.
\end{aligned}
\tag{21.12}
$$

Next, we check our t-ratio with the values in Appendix A.2. In this case our degrees of freedom involve two samples, so we have:

$$\begin{aligned} df &= (N_1 - 1) + (N_2 - 1) \\ &= N_1 + N_2 - 2 \\ &= 25 + 37 - 2 \\ &= 60. \end{aligned}$$ (21.13)

For a df of 60, compare 4.57 to the critical values corresponding to the chosen α; 4.57 is larger than the critical value of 2 for the conventional $\alpha = 0.05$ as well as those for the stricter cutoffs, including $\alpha = 0.001$. We believe 0.05 is strict enough for a hypothesis of this nature (and of any nature in this book), and so we reject the null hypothesis. According to these results it is very unlikely that liberals and conservatives come from the same population with respect to their group membership activity.

In addition, we can analyze our data by appealing to confidence intervals. We have an observed difference of 9 (60 − 51), a standard error of 1.97, and degrees of freedom of 60, so we can state that the population difference of means should fall between our confidence interval. Recall, that this is simply the Observed Difference ± Critical Value × Standard Error:

$$\begin{aligned} CI &= 9 \pm 2.00 \times 1.97 \\ &= 9 \pm 3.94 \\ &= [5.06, 12.94]. \end{aligned}$$ (21.14)

Notice that this tells us that the population difference must be positive, not zero, since the range of values does not include zero. Thus, we reject the null that the population mean difference is zero. Again, we will only reject the null if zero is not included within our confidence interval.

Correlation

We began our exploration of statistical inference by generalizing differences we find in samples to differences in populations (see Chapter 20). Using data on sample differences, we described differences in populations with a particular level of certainty. In this chapter we took a similar approach to consider the difference of means on a continuous variable across groups as indicated by a nominal level variable. Finding a statistically significant relationship (rejecting the null hypothesis at a particular level of confidence) indicates that the extent of the difference in means is unlikely to be the result of sampling error.

With correlation we move from considering the relationship between an interval and nominal level variable, as with difference of means, to the relationship between two interval variables. In this context, correlation provides a measure of the strength of the relationship. Thus, **correlation** is a measure of association between two or more variables. Fortunately, correlation is conceptually straightfoward as it can be thought of as an extension of our data visualization tool, the scatter plot.

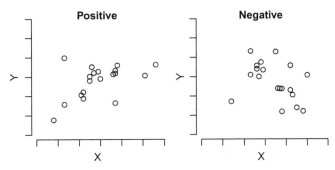

Figure 21.2 Scatter plots and direction of correlation

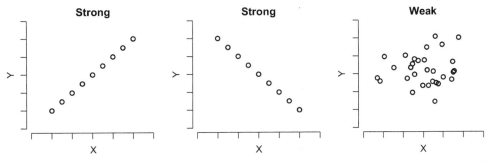

Figure 21.3 Scatter plots and strength of correlation

Visually, a scatter plot should give us a good idea whether our null hypothesis of no correlation can be rejected. Recall that in scatter plots we typically locate the X variable values along the x-axis (the horizontal base) and the Y variable values along the y-axis (the vertical base). Correlation consists of two components: strength and direction. The direction of correlation can be either negative or positive. If high scores on X correspond to low scores on Y, we have negative correlation. If high scores on X correspond to high scores on Y, we have positive correlation. In other words, if most points are in the bottom left and top right, a positive correlation is plausible, as in the left panel in Figure 21.2. If most points are in the top left and bottom right, as in the right panel, a negative correlation is plausible.

The strength of correlation can be strong or weak. If the scatter plot looks like a straight line, as in the left two panels of Figure 21.3, we are likely to have a strong correlation. If we get something that looks like a cloud of points, as in the far right panel, we have a weak correlation. Thus a correlation is strong if for a unit change in variable X, we can expect a specific change in variable Y in a particular direction (positive or negative). A correlation is weak if for a unit change in variable X, we are not sure what the change would be in variable Y. In other words, for a strong correlation we can look at X and predict the changes in Y; for a weak correlation we have a harder time doing that.

Scatter plots, however, do not allow us to make statistical inferences. Recall that statistical inference is the process of inferring from a sample to a population. In order to make statistical inferences, first we need to create a test statistic of association. The most common statistic of association between two interval level variables and the one we discuss below is **Pearson's** r. Then we need a statistical procedure for evaluating the significance of this test statistic. To reiterate, the size of Pearson's r does not by itself allow us to draw a conclusion about statistical significance. There are two separate though related analyses to conduct to arrive at statistical inference. Thus, although the formulae differ, the logic of statistical inference here is much the same as in the difference of means test above.

To understand Pearson's r, we first need to understand how we compute the **covariance** between two variables. Covariance is a measure of how much two variables change together or "covary":

$$\text{Cov} = \frac{\Sigma(X - \overline{X})(Y - \overline{Y})}{N - 1}. \tag{21.15}$$

As is evident from the formula, we use the deviations to measure change in each variable. By multiplying corresponding deviations we see that the larger the corresponding deviations the larger the covariance. Notice that covariance could be negative as well. Because we have to add the combined deviations together to get the sense of how the two variables vary together, we need to account for the fact that the sum of the combined deviations could be large due to the simple fact that the sample size is large. Thus we control for sample size and divide by $N - 1$, instead of just N, since the population mean is unknown and we are relying on the sample mean to estimate it.

While it appears that we can use the covariance as our measure of correlation, using the covariance formula may be misleading at times. What if we have a large amount of deviation in the X variable and not much deviation in the Y variable? Such will give us a large covariance. Alternatively, if we have a moderate amount of deviation in the X variable and a moderate amount of deviation in Y variable, this will give us covariance of a reasonable size. However, this does not necessarily mean that in the first case the variables correlate stronger than in the second case. All this suggests that our measure of correlation needs to adjust our covariance by the amount of deviation present in each variable. A good measure of deviation in a variable is the standard deviation. Thus we can gauge the degree of association between the two variables by dividing covariance by the product of standard deviations.

Given the logic above, we can get a particular measure of correlation simply by dividing the covariance over the combined standard deviations and simplifying. Thus, Pearson's r is:

$$r = \frac{\dfrac{\Sigma(X - \overline{X})(Y - \overline{Y})}{N - 1}}{\sqrt{\dfrac{\Sigma(X - \overline{X})^2}{N}} \times \sqrt{\dfrac{\Sigma(Y - \overline{Y})^2}{N}}} \tag{21.16}$$

$$= \frac{\Sigma(X - \overline{X})(Y - \overline{Y})}{\sqrt{\Sigma(X - \overline{X})^2 \Sigma(Y - \overline{Y})^2}}.$$

The formula for Pearson's r limits the range of values the statistic can take to falling between –1.00 and 1.00, with larger absolute values representing stronger correlations. Values of –1.00 or 1.00 represent a perfect linear relationship (i.e., you could draw a straight line and every point would fall on it). If the correlation coefficient is negative, then we have a negative correlation. If it is positive, we have a positive correlation. If the correlation is 0, we have the weakest possible correlation (no correlation, think of a cloud of points). Pearson's r therefore allows us to make statements that smaller values indicate weaker relationships. Although there is no universally accepted rule of thumb for distinguishing between strong and weak relationships, the closer to 1 or −1 the stronger, and the closer to 0 the weaker.

Note that the value of r does not tell us the slope of the best fitting line through our scatter plot, which we will discuss below with regression. An r of $|1|$ – called the **absolute value** of 1; i.e., the non-negative value of 1 – for example, does not mean that for a unit increase in one variable there is a full unit increase in another. Instead it conveys that there is no variation between the data points and the line of best fit. That is, we can have different slopes in the scatter plot with equivalent values of r.

Of course, we are typically working with samples, not populations. That is, using our sample data we would like to say whether or not the variables in the populations correlate. Here the null hypothesis refers to the situation in which the population characteristics are not correlated. Thus the null hypothesis is that $r = 0$, while our alternative hypothesis is that $r \neq 0$. It is worth explicitly restating our null hypothesis: there is no linear relationship between X and Y. Statistical theory tells us that the critical value associated with the test statistic represents the probability of finding this value of r as or more extreme than what you would get if no linear relationship actually exists. As before, we are willing to reject the null if this probability (p-value) is less than 0.05; or equivalently, if our test statistic exceeds the critical value for t.

Note that in practice one might provide a correlation coefficient as a summary statistic of the data without testing whether it is statistically different from zero. However, hypothesis testing with Pearson's r has some basic assumptions. There should be a straight line (not curvilinear) relationship between two variables. One may also detect nonlinear relationships between variables with this approach, but Pearson's r cannot be used to test these relationships, which would require a different test statistic. Second, the variables should be measured at the interval level and normally distributed, though the latter is of less importance in reasonably large samples since we can invoke the central limit theorem. Finally, random sampling is needed to allow us to generalize from the sample to the population.

In our example below we will present the relationship between two variables, issue dimensions and political parties, in terms of an independent and dependent variable. Correlation, however, does not require the specification of an independent and dependent variable. Correlation is simply a statement about association, not about causation. For instance, we might examine the correlation between two independent variables. If we control for two highly correlated independent variables at the same time, this causes statistical problems for multivariate regression. This very high correlation is called **collinearity**, and complicates estimation, which we will talk about more in the context of multiple regression.

Correlation can also be a useful tool in the operationalization process. If we want to use multiple measures to get at the same concept, there should be some correlation between the measures. This **construct validity** suggests that valid measures should be correlated with related features of the concept. On the other hand, if correlation is very high, using both measures may be redundant.

Outside of these assumptions, the general process of calculating the correlation coefficient and testing statistical significance is similar to what we did for the difference of means. We begin by calculating our means and standard deviations and plugging them into the (intuitive) formula for r. We next calculate our test statistic, t-ratio, to generalize from our sample to the population. In the case of correlation we use

$$t = \frac{r\sqrt{N-2}}{\sqrt{1-r^2}}.$$

(21.17)

To test the null we also need to state our level of confidence and calculate the degrees of freedom. In correlation with two samples the degrees of freedom is $N - 2$. As per usual, we then go to the back of the book – i.e., find the t-ratio at the appropriate confidence level and degrees of freedom in the Appendix Table A.2 – to check whether the t-ratio is larger than the critical value for t. If it is, we reject the null of no correlation. If it is not, we fail to reject the null.

In closing, it is worth repeating a familiar statistics mantra: correlation is not causation. As we noted, there are a number of reasons why we might find a correlation without ever expecting there to be a causal relationship. Even if we do expect a causal relationship, we still must have the proper temporal sequence, and rule out concerns such as antecedent variable and spurious correlation to be confident in a causal relationship.

Example: Issue Dimensions and Parties

In democratic countries are multiple issue dimensions associated with a greater number of parties? That is, should we expect more parties when there are more issue dimensions on which parties can contend for power? The concept of issue dimensions suggests that there is more than a single left/right ideological dimension to politics and instead politics can involve multiple dimensions, including socioeconomic and sociocultural issues. A straightforward hypothesis stemming from these classic questions is the expectation of a positive correlation between issue dimensions and parties.

For this exercise we have some hypothetical sample data from a population of democratic countries that provides us with the two variables necessary to test the

Example: Issue Dimensions and Parties

Table 21.5 Issue dimensions and parties data

	Issue dimensions	Parties
Switzerland	3.73	4.84
Italy	2.99	4.90
Netherlands	3.25	4.65
France	2.76	4.03
Portugal	2.32	3.43
Germany	3.24	3.43
Spain	2.11	2.76
United Kingdom	2.75	2.99
Mean	2.89	3.88

Table 21.6 Calculating r for issue dimensions and parties

	X Deviation	Y Deviation	Product	X Dev^2	Y Dev^2
Switzerland	0.84	0.96	0.81	0.71	0.92
Italy	0.1	1.02	0.10	0.01	1.04
Netherlands	0.36	0.77	0.28	0.13	0.59
France	−0.13	0.15	−0.02	0.02	0.02
Portugal	−0.57	−0.45	0.26	0.32	0.20
Germany	0.35	−0.45	−0.16	0.12	0.20
Spain	−0.78	−1.12	0.87	0.61	1.25
United Kingdom	−0.14	−0.89	0.12	0.02	0.79
Sum of products			$SP = 2.26$		
Sum of squares				$SS_X = 1.94$	$SS_Y = 5.03$

correlation, one that notes the number of issue dimensions and another the number of parties. In order to test the correlation between these two variables, we first calculate the Pearson's correlation coefficient (r) then the t-ratio to arrive at a test of statistical significance.

We begin by calculating the distances between the raw values and its mean value for each variable, which are called the X deviation and Y deviation, respectively. As shown in Table 21.6, to obtain the X deviation, we simply subtract $\overline{X}$ from the X value for that observation. We do the same for Y. Deviations can be illustrated within a scatter plot that includes a vertical line at the mean value of X and a horizontal line at the mean value of Y. Comparing Figure 21.4 to Table 21.6 we see that points or countries in the top right corner will have two positive deviations, and those in the bottom left corner will have two negative deviations. Points in the top left corner will have a positive Y deviation and negative X deviation, and those in the bottom right corner will have a negative Y deviation and positive X deviation.

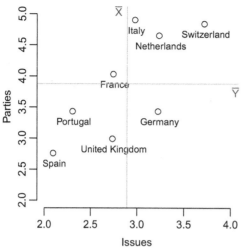

Figure 21.4 Scatter plot of parties and issues

Next, for each observation, we multiply the X deviation by the Y deviation. If this product is positive, the observation is consistent with a positive relationship; if the product is negative, this observation is consistent with a negative relationship. Then we sum these values. This is the **sum of products** (SP), the numerator of our formula for r. So far, we can note two things. The sum of products is positive, which means the relationship is positive. All but one of the individual products is positive, which means that the relationship appears to be fairly consistent. However, the scale of this output is unrelated to the values of the variables, so we cannot make a statement about the strength of association yet.

By calculating the denominator, we succeed in constraining our test statistic to the range $[-1, 1]$. We can now interpret the strength of the relationship. The denominator calculates the deviations of each variable in relation to its own mean, but without respect to the other variable. In other words, we are calculating something akin to the variance of each variable (except that we do not divide by N), which we call the **sum of squares**: SS_X for X and SS_Y for Y.

We now have all the elements we need for our formula:

$$r = \frac{SP}{\sqrt{SS_X \times SS_Y}}$$

$$= \frac{2.26}{\sqrt{1.94 \times 5.03}} \tag{21.18}$$

$$= 0.72.$$

What, then, do we make of this value of 0.72? We know there is a positive relationship between issue dimensions and number of parties, and that the relationship is quite strong. In giving a substantive interpretation of correlation, these are the two necessary elements: direction and strength.

But is it statistically significant? The same value of r may or may not be statistically significant depending on the sample size. So, answering this question is a two-step process. First, we must translate r into a t-statistic, using a formula that involves only r and N. To calculate t, we simply need our value of r and our number of observations

$$
\begin{aligned}
t &= \frac{r\sqrt{N-2}}{\sqrt{1-r^2}} \\
&= \frac{0.72\sqrt{8-2}}{\sqrt{1-0.72^2}} \\
&= \frac{1.76}{0.69} \\
&= 2.54.
\end{aligned}
\tag{21.19}
$$

Then we just need to calculate our degrees of freedom to determine the critical value. The degrees of freedom are simply:

$$
\begin{aligned}
df &= N - 2 \\
&= 6.
\end{aligned}
\tag{21.20}
$$

With six degrees of freedom, our critical value for t is 2.45. Thus, with our t-ratio of 2.54, we can reject the null.

CONCLUSIONS

Social scientists are typically interested in the relationships between two or more variables. Above we have introduced two bivariate hypothesis tests for continuous dependent variables. In quantitative analyses understanding the level of measurement is essential because it helps us decide which hypothesis test to use. The first test, difference of means, allows researchers to make comparisons of sample means. The second, correlation, moves us beyond making a simple claim of a relationship or no relationship between two variables to a measure that conveys both the strength and direction of the relationship.

KEY TERMS

- Discrete variable
- Continuous variable
- Marginals
- Cross-tabulation (crosstab)
- Sampling distribution of differences between means
- Standard error of the difference between means
- Parametric

- Nonparametric
- Semiparametric
- Statistical power
- Correlation
- Pearson's r
- Absolute value
- Collinearity
- Construct validity
- Sum of products
- Sum of squares

In this chapter we build on the concept of correlation with ordinary least squares (OLS) regression, even though the latter was invented first.[188] If we think about our scatter plot, we could draw one line through the data that best fits all of our data points. Correlation is a statement about how close the points are to the line. The objective of regression is to determine the best fitting line for the data. Using regression, we can determine the average effect of our independent variable and make predictions about cases outside our sample. We will begin with the simplest regression model, bivariate, where the dependent variable is a function of a single independent variable, before expanding to consider multivariate models with multiple independent variables.

Bivariate Regression

As social scientists we primarily want to explain why variables of interest vary and vary together. Regression allows us the ability to measure the effect of one variable on another. It tells us the effect of an independent variable on a dependent variable. Furthermore, it provides us with the degree of the effect, thereby providing more explanatory leverage than in any other technique we have discussed thus far. Not unlike correlation we can find the strength and direction of association between two variables. Here, however, we can also get at the specific nature of the relationship; i.e., how much variance in the dependent variable is "explained" by the independent variable.

In discussing correlation we implied without much specificity that one could draw a straight line that passed through the set of points in a manner that represented the overall pattern, positive or negative, steep or shallow. In addition to moving to thinking about causal relationships between independent and dependent variables (which was not required for correlation), with regression we also ask: Which linear relationship? In other words, of all the lines in Figure 22.1 that pass through the graph **centroid** – the point where $\overline{X}$ and $\overline{Y}$ intersect and marked in the figure by the intersection of the dotted lines – which fits the data the best?

Before delving into the math, it is useful to graphically illustrate the characteristics of the best fitting regression line, as in Figure 22.2. For any line, we can measure the vertical distance between the line and each observation, which is called a **residual**. Our goal is to minimize these residuals; or more specifically, the sum of squared residuals,

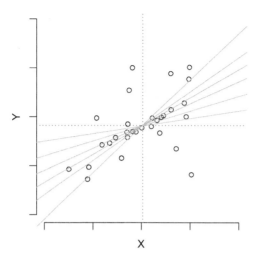

Figure 22.1 Fitting lines through a scatter plot ■

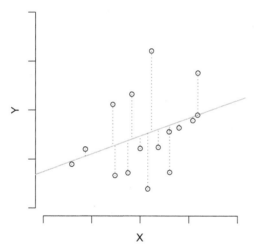

Figure 22.2 Residuals from best fitting line in a scatter plot ■

because if we did not square them our residuals would sum to zero – as you might recall from the previous chapter. The line which does so is the best fit.

Obviously, choosing possible lines by trial and error and calculating the sum of squared residuals for each line would not be very efficient. Fortunately, determining the correct line can be easily done using some of the values we calculated last time for the correlation coefficient r. We just need the sum of products and the sum of squares. In fact, the general process should be quite familiar. We will begin by summarizing the data into a single equation which states the relationship between X and Y. This equation produces two test statistics, a and b, that describe the relationship. Next we translate them into t-ratios to test the null hypothesis, at which point the rest of the procedure for checking significance is the same as the previous examples with t-ratios (e.g., correlation, difference of means test).

The regression line is based on a simple mathematical equation similar to what you used to draw a line in elementary geometry:

$$Y = a + bX + e. \tag{22.1}$$

The regression line is a statement about the relationship between X and Y in the population. The equation simply states that the predicted value of Y is the sum of three components: a, which is a constant that applies to each case; bX, which is the product of an average effect b and the specific value of the independent variable X; and e, which is a random component that varies by observation.

Generally, a is referred to as "the constant" and b "the coefficient." In order to determine the best fitting regression line, we calculate a specific numerical value for these terms. The error term, e, however, is not determined. Thus we will not calculate e, but it is important nonetheless from a statistical inference perspective. In the equation, e is merely a symbol to represent the fact that our relationship is probabilistic, not deterministic. For any given case, we would not expect our raw value of Y to equal the predicted value of $\hat{Y}$ (spoken "y-hat") because of this factor. We place a hat over Y for the predicted value to show that it is calculated from the equation and not the same as the Y variable in the data. More colloquially, we can think of the error term as collecting all the junk in the equation. It represents the random error in the stochastic model that makes our predictions less than perfect. However, for a large number of cases and on average, we would still expect the predicted value of $\hat{Y}$. Since we do not calculate the random error term, the actual regression line we calculate looks like:

$$\hat{Y} = a + bX. \tag{22.2}$$

But, again, this does not mean we can ignore the theoretical importance of e.

To elaborate with the help of Figure 22.3, a geometrically represents the y-intercept, the point where the line crosses the y-axis. Substantively, this question

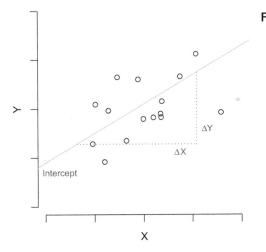

Figure 22.3 Regression line

asks about our expected value for Y when the value of the independent variable is zero ($x = 0$):

$$\hat{Y} = a + b \times 0$$
$$= a. \tag{22.3}$$

The key part of the regression equation is the bX term. The b term tells us the average effect of a unit change of X on Y. More simply stated, it tells us how much Y changes, ΔY, as X changes, ΔX. Thus, if we take our observed value of X and multiply it by our average effect b, and then add this product to the constant a, we would get our predicted value of Y, which is the regression line. Of course, the value of b also has a geometric interpretation: the slope of the regression line. Unlike our correlation coefficient, the slope is not limited in range. The value of the slope can be zero, or any positive or negative value. The one exception, of course, is that the slope cannot be infinite, as this would imply a vertical line.

In order to solve the regression equation we begin by calculating b, which is simply the sum of the products divided by the sum of squares:

$$b = \frac{SP}{SS_x}. \tag{22.4}$$

We can then solve for a:

$$a = \overline{Y} - b\overline{X}. \tag{22.5}$$

With numeric values for both a and b we can rewrite the regression equation in terms of the predicted value of Y, $\hat{Y}$. Again, we use $\hat{Y}$ instead of Y to denote that it is expected or predicted, as opposed to actual or observed. In other words, if you compute the disturbances over several trials (the differences between $\hat{Y}$ and Y) and sum them, you should get 0. At this point we can interpret the relationship between X and Y.

When interpreting a regression equation, the two most important substantive findings relate to the values of a and b. We want to relate these values to our real-world question. Foremost we note the interpretation of b. For every one unit increase in the value of X, we expect a b unit increase in the value of Y, on average. Notice this sounds very much like the mathematical interpretation of a slope, for obvious reasons.

Although we do not determine a specific value for e, we can make a statement about how much of our relationship is systematic (the bX term) and how much is random (e). This too is related to the concepts we discussed with correlation. Correlation told us about the strength of a relationship. The stronger the relationship, the less important the random component is in determining individual values of Y. The weaker the relationship, the more important the random component is in determining the values of Y. Here, when we say random we mean that the explanation is due to something outside of the equation. The e term is picking up any variance we cannot explain with our independent variable. Remember that our regression line is the one that minimizes the squared residuals. However, how small we can actually make that sum depends on the correlation. If the relationship is weak, we can only minimize that sum to a small extent. In fact, we can think about the residuals as the random component itself, for each individual observation.

Regression is flexible. Although hypothesis testing with it requires that we have an interval and normally distributed dependent variable, the independent variable can be of any level of measurement: nominal, ordinal, or interval. The regression line allows us to make a number of statements about the predicted value of Y given values of X. That is, rather than interpreting a single statistic, in regression we modify the value of X in line with our research questions to calculate substantively meaningful predictions of Y. The researcher must ask herself what value of X makes substantive sense, which does, of course, relate to the variable's level of measurement. We might be interested in what the average of an interval level independent variable explains and thus set X to $\overline{X}$. Alternatively, we might be interested in what the lowest value of X tells us about Y by setting X to its minimum value. We might even be interested in knowing what the highest levels of X predict in terms of Y, or anything in between. In sum, we choose a value or a series of values for X that make sense given the question we are asking and solve for $\hat{Y}$.

For one value of X we can make a statement that leverages the information given to us by the constant. When X is at zero, $\hat{Y}$ is a. It is important to note, however, that the interpretation of a depends on zero being a substantively meaningful value for X. For example, we would not think to ask about how many parties we would expect in a country with zero issue dimensions because all countries deal with at least some issues. Thus, though mathematically this is a fair interpretation, it does not always make substantive sense. The constant merely tells us what value of $\hat{Y}$ we should expect given that $X = 0$.

Relatedly, the regression line also allows us to make out-of-sample predictions, or extrapolations, about Y. **Extrapolation** is the process of making predictions about cases outside the range of the X variable in the sample. First, note that we do not take e into consideration when making predictions. The random component is exactly that, so we do not make predictions about it. Besides, this prediction is just an expected value. Just as we do not make statements about the constant that would not make substantive sense, we also exercise caution in making predictions beyond the sample. For example, we would not want to make predictions about countries with negative issue dimensions, which makes no sense though we could extend the regression line into the negative values of X. Nor would we want to predict Y for a hypothetical country with 250 issue dimensions, which is also substantively goofy. In sum, when making predictions, we always want to consider whether we are making extreme or nonsensical counterfactuals.

Interpolation is the process of making predictions about cases within the range of the X variable for the sample but for which no values in the sample exist. For example, if X ranged from 0 to 100 but no units in the sample had values between

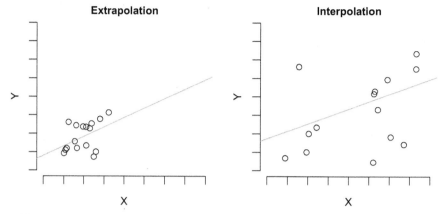

Figure 22.4 Extrapolation and interpolation

30 and 70, interpolation involves making predictions of the value of Y for Xs between 30 and 70. In general, and as should be obvious from Figure 22.4, extrapolation requires more caution than interpolation.

At this point we should be curious about the kind of leverage that regression actually provides. In the context of regression r^2 is referred to as the **coefficient of determination**. In the context of correlation, this does not give us a lot of additional information since r^2 is completely determined by the value of r. In regression, this statistic takes on a more important interpretation, particularly when we have a multivariate regression with more than one independent variable, which we discuss in the next section.

With a strong relationship, the independent variable explains more of the variance in the dependent variable. This means that the fit of the line is better; the sum of residuals is smaller, and the correlation is higher. This is where the r^2 statistic comes in. Squaring r gives us the amount of variation in Y explained by X. Thus the remainder, $1 - r^2$ is random variation, i.e., not explained by the variables in our equation.

The notion of explaining variance can be difficult to grasp. Fortunately, there is a more intuitive way of looking at this information. The r^2 statistic also belongs to a class of statistics called **proportionate reduction in error** statistics (PRE). This interpretation is mathematically equivalent to the variance explained description, but the logic is somewhat different. The power of our regression comes from its ability to make accurate predictions. Our regression allows us to make a specific prediction about the value of Y for a given observation. However, these predictions are not perfect even for our sample; there are residuals.

But, if we did not have information about the X variable, what predictions would we make about Y? The most logical answer is that we would guess the mean of Y. Recall that a central tendency gives us a good summary description of Y. So the question becomes: How much more accurate are our predictions using our regression instead of just guessing the mean of Y every time? The answer is the r^2

value. By knowing X and the resulting regression equation, we are able to reduce the amount of prediction error relative to the mean. Thus the calculated r^2 tells us how much variance in Y is accounted for by our predicted relationship $(a + bX)$.

Earlier we noted that Pearsons r has the following equation:

$$\frac{\Sigma(X - \overline{X})(Y - \overline{Y})}{\sqrt{\Sigma(X - \overline{X})^2 \Sigma(Y - \overline{Y})^2}},\tag{22.6}$$

which can be rewritten in simpler terms:

$$\frac{SP}{\sqrt{SS_X \times SS_Y}}.\tag{22.7}$$

While we could square r to get the coefficient of determination, r^2, in a regression equation, we can also derive r^2 based on our knowledge of the standard error. R^2 is a ratio of the expected or explained sum of squares to the total sum of squares. The **explained sum of squares** (ESS_Y) is the difference in the predicted and mean values of Y:

$$ESS_Y = \Sigma(\hat{Y} - \overline{Y})^2.\tag{22.8}$$

Recall that the total sum of squares for Y (SS_Y) is

$$SS_Y = \Sigma(Y - \overline{Y})^2.\tag{22.9}$$

This ratio gives us the r^2 as well:

$$r^2 = \frac{ESS_Y}{SS_Y}.\tag{22.10}$$

Similarly, we can just as easily calculate r^2 based on the residuals instead of the expected values. We take 1 less the **residual sum of squared errors** (RSS_e) over the total sum of squares. The RSS_e is the sum of the squared differences between the actual and predicted values of Y:

$$RSS_e = \Sigma(Y - \hat{Y})^2.\tag{22.11}$$

Thus r^2 can be thought of in terms of unexplained variance, since the remainder is a simple ratio of unexplained variance in the model's errors to the total variance in the data:

$$r^2 = 1 - \frac{RSS_e}{SS_Y}.\tag{22.12}$$

It should be clear now that the formulae for r^2 are equivalent:

$$r^2 = 1 - \frac{RSS_e}{SS_Y} = \frac{ESS_Y}{SS_Y}.\tag{22.13}$$

Having arrived at an understanding of how to calculate and interpret our regression equation, we next move to testing our hypothesis about the population given the sample data. That is, in practice we also need to check the statistical significance of our results, as we have done in the past (e.g., difference of means and correlation). In particular, we need to make sure that b is relevant in our relationship. But why b?

In regression our null hypotheses refer to the coefficients. The null hypothesis for the constant is that $a = 0$. If we can reject the null, we can be confident that the value of Y is greater than zero, when $X = 0$. Of course, this is likely to be substantively uninteresting.

The null hypothesis for the coefficient, b, however, is the one we typically care about. Thus in regression our null hypothesis predominantly refers to b: $b = 0$. In other words, the null holds that the independent variable has no effect on the dependent variable. Thus we focus on b because it modifies the independent variable, X. Graphically, the null hypothesis predicts a horizontal regression line, i.e., a slope of 0. If we can reject the null hypothesis, we are confident that the relationship we find in the sample between the independent variable and dependent variable exists in the population. Again, this is our major concern in hypothesis testing. The effect could be substantively large or small, but we need to test whether it is likely to exist beyond the sample.

As in the past, in order to test the null hypothesis for statistical significance we need formulae for the t-ratio and the standard error of the coefficient. The standard error of b depends on the ratio between the **mean squared errors** (MSe), which captures the average variance in Y that is unexplained by X, and a product of sample variance and size. In the bivariate case, we calculate it as such:

$$MSe = \frac{\Sigma(Y - \hat{Y})^2}{N - 2}. \tag{22.14}$$

Notice that the numerator of this equation is what we referred to above as the sum of squared errors. Thus we can abbreviate the equation for the mean squared errors,

$$MSe = \frac{RSSe}{N - 2}, \tag{22.15}$$

and calculate the standard error of b accordingly:

$$s_b = \sqrt{\frac{MSe}{s_X^2 \times N - 1}}. \tag{22.16}$$

Again, the test statistic is simply a ratio between the coefficient and its standard error:

$$t = \frac{b}{s_b}. \tag{22.17}$$

After calculating the t-ratio and standard error we proceed as usual by selecting a level of statistical significance (conventionally, $\alpha = 0.05$), noting the degrees of freedom, and checking the t-distribution table (Appendix Table A.2) for the corresponding p-value in order to decide whether or not to reject the null.[189]

Example: Education and Income

We can demonstrate regression with a simple research question: Does education lead to greater income? Perhaps part of the value of an education is that it provides skills that translate into more lucrative job opportunities. We thus hypothesize a positive relationship wherein years of post-secondary education predict annual income. The null hypothesis is that education is not related to income. We are going to use regression to solve for the predicted relationship:

$$Income = a + b \times Education + e. \tag{22.18}$$

Assume that Table 22.1 contains data from a simple random sample survey of ten adults' levels of income and education. The second and third columns contain our collected data and we use the subsequent columns to calculate our statistics. We begin by calculating the necessary statistics for use in the formulae. In the data, the mean of income, $\overline{Y} = 38.6$ and the mean of education is $\overline{X} = 2.8$. The variance for income is 142.93 and for education it is 3.29. The process for calculating the sum of squares for income, 1286.4, should be familiar by now.

Table 22.1   Calculating regression for income and education

Respondent	Income in Thousands	P – S Education	$Y - \overline{Y}$	$X - \overline{X}$	$(X - \overline{X}) \times (Y - \overline{Y})$	$(Y - \overline{Y})^2$	$(X - \overline{X})^2$
1	44	4	5.4	1.2	6.48	29.16	1.44
2	30	3	−8.6	0.2	−1.72	73.96	0.04
3	51	2	12.4	−0.8	−9.92	153.76	0.64
4	40	4	1.4	1.2	1.68	1.96	1.44
5	14	0	−24.6	−2.8	68.88	605.16	7.84
6	44	5	5.4	2.2	11.88	29.16	4.84
7	34	2	−4.6	−0.8	3.68	21.16	0.64
8	56	5	17.4	2.2	38.28	302.76	4.84
9	42	3	3.4	0.2	0.68	11.56	0.04
10	31	0	−7.6	−2.8	21.28	57.76	7.84
Sum	$\Sigma Y = 386$	$\Sigma X = 28$					
Sum of products					$SP = 141.2$		
Sum of squares						$SSy = 1286.4$	$SSx = 29.6$

Recall that our covariance can be abbreviated as $\frac{SP}{N}$, where

$$SP = \Sigma(X - \overline{X}) \times (Y - \overline{Y})$$
$$= 141.2.$$
(22.19)

With these statistics, calculating the slope of the line is trivial:

$$b = \frac{SP}{SS_X}$$

$$= \frac{141.2}{29.6}$$
(22.20)

$$= 4.77.$$

To situate the line on the x-axis we calculate the constant:

$$a = \overline{Y} - b\overline{X}$$
$$= 38.6 - 4.77 \times 2.8$$
(22.21)
$$= 25.24.$$

At this point we can interpret our regression results substantively. For instance, we might be interested in how often those of average income participate. To that end, we calculate our predicted value of Y at the mean of X:

$$\hat{Y} = a + b\overline{X}$$
$$= 25.24 + 4.77 \times 2.8$$
(22.22)
$$= 38.6.$$

Thus we expect an individual with the average amount of education to earn about $38,600. What would we expect for an individual with the highest amount of education in our sample to make?

With the regression parameters in hand we move to testing statistical significance. We will continue with the tabular format to illustrate the calculation of the sum of squared errors in Table 22.2. Our first step is to calculate the $\hat{Y}$ for each of the values of X. This allows us to draw our regression line, as in Figure 22.5.

We begin by finding the mean sum of squares:

$$MSe = \frac{RSSe}{N-2}$$

$$= \frac{\Sigma(Y - \hat{Y})^2}{(N-2)}$$
(22.23)

$$= \frac{612.84}{8}$$

$$= 76.61.$$

Example: Education and Income

Table 22.2 Calculating the sum of squared errors

Income in thousands	P – S Education	$\hat{Y}$	$Y - \hat{Y}$	$(Y - \hat{Y})^2$
44	4	44.32	−0.32	0.10
30	3	39.55	−9.55	91.20
51	2	34.78	16.22	263.09
40	4	44.32	−4.32	18.66
14	0	25.24	−11.24	126.34
44	5	49.09	−5.09	25.91
34	2	34.78	−0.78	0.61
56	5	49.09	6.91	47.75
42	3	39.55	2.45	6.00
31	0	25.24	5.76	33.18
Sum of squares				$RSSe = 612.84$

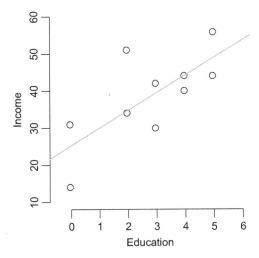

Figure 22.5 Plot regression line for education and income

With the mean sum of squares we can calculate the standard error of b:

$$s_b = \sqrt{\frac{MSe}{s_X^2 \times N - 1}}$$

$$= \sqrt{\frac{76.61}{3.29 \times 9}}$$

$$= 1.61.$$

(22.24)

Finally, we can calcuate the t-ratio,

$$t = \frac{b}{s_b}$$

$$= \frac{4.77}{1.61} \tag{22.25}$$

$$= 2.96.$$

We now check the t-ratio against the t critical value in Appendix Table A.2 for the appropriate degrees of freedom and confidence level. We find that we can reject the null hypothesis of no relationship between income and participation.

In addition, consider what this relationship means for education more generally. To what extent does education predict income? To answer this question we can calculate the coefficient of determination:

$$r^2 = 1 - \frac{RSS_e}{SS_y}$$

$$= 1 - \frac{\Sigma(Y - \hat{Y})^2}{\Sigma(Y - \overline{Y})^2} \tag{22.26}$$

$$= 1 - \frac{612.84}{1286.4}$$

$$= 1 - 0.48$$

$$= 0.52.$$

In this example, the postulated relationship explains 52% of variation in Y. In other words, 48% $(1 - r^2)$ of the variation in income is unexplained by education.

Note that we can do some rearranging of our formulae to arrive at the same answers. We begin by calculating the sample **standard error of the estimate**, SEe (also written as s_e). This can be interpreted much like a typical standard deviation, but this time in terms of the regression line. Given normally distributed errors about 68% of the observations will fall within one standard error of the line, 95% within two and and over 99% within three.

$$SEe = \sqrt{\frac{RSSe}{N - K - 1}}$$

$$= \sqrt{\frac{\Sigma(Y - \hat{Y})^2}{(N - 2)}} \tag{22.27}$$

$$= \sqrt{\frac{612.84}{8}}$$

$$= 8.75.$$

Then the standard error of b can be calculated with either the SEe or the MSE:

$$s_b = \frac{SEe}{\sqrt{SSx}}$$
$$= \frac{8.75}{\sqrt{29.6}}$$
$$= 1.61$$
$$s_b = \sqrt{\frac{MSe}{SSx}}$$
$$= \sqrt{\frac{76.61}{29.6}}$$
$$= 1.61.$$

(22.28)

Similarly, here is the way to calculate r^2 from Pearson's r:

$$r = \frac{\frac{SP}{N-1}}{s_x s_y}$$
$$= \frac{\frac{141.2}{9}}{1.81 \times 11.96}$$
$$= 0.72$$
$$r^2 = r \times r$$
$$= 0.72^2$$
$$= 0.52.$$

(22.29)

In order to present our regression results we collect these statistics into an easy-to-read table. Typically regression tables list the names of the independent variable(s) in rows of the first column with their corresponding coefficients and standard errors in one or more subsequent columns headed by the name of the dependent variable. Standard errors are presented in parentheses to distinguish them from the coefficients. Oftentimes the coefficients are followed by stars that serve as a visual heuristic denoting that the standard error is small enough to reject the corresponding null hypothesis. In Table 22.3 we have done exactly this. The star, as indicated by the note at the table, tells us what we discovered above: that the ratio of the coefficient on the education variable, 4.77, to its standard error is larger than the critical value for t at the 95% confidence level. Thus it is clear that we reject the null hypothesis of no relationship between education and income.

Multivariate Regression

In this section we provide an introduction to the multivariate version of the ordinary least squares regression model introduced above. We focus on describing

Table 22.3 Explaining income with education

	Dependent variable:
	Income
Education	4.77*
	(2.13)
Constant	25.24*
	(5.29)
N	10
R^2	0.52

Note: *p<0.05

the major intuition behind multivariate models and the interpretation of the statistics in this context, while avoiding the matrix algebra necessary to calculate the statistics in this section by hand. In addition, we note that the regression model depends on several assumptions, which can be easily violated – and often are. Therefore we also provide a discussion of the most frequent assumption violations and their potential effects on model-based inferences.

The purpose of multivariate regression is the same as in the bivariate case. We would like to estimate the effect of an independent variable on a continuous dependent variable. However, in the multivariate case we also want to **control** for and estimate the effects of other independent variables. Control in multivariate statistics is a process of parsing out the specific effect of each of two or more independent variables on a dependent variable. That is, with multivariate analysis we can "hold constant" the effects of one or more independent variables in order to get a more precise estimate of the effect of another independent variable.

Controlling for multiple independent variables is important when the researcher believes there to be a **confounding** relationship. Recall our discussion of confounders in Chapter 6. We think of a confounding variable as one that is correlated with both the independent and dependent variable. In terms of causality – a topic we return to in Chapter 23 – the concern is that change in the confounder leads to change in both the independent and dependent variables, which is not perceived by the researcher when the confounder is excluded from the model. Indeed the researcher may incorrectly infer that the independent and dependent variable are related, when in truth it is the omitted confounder that causes the variables in the model to appear to correlate. In contrast, when we include the confounder in the model with the other independent variable, we can estimate the specific effect of each independent variable on the dependent variable, thereby ensuring that our estimates are not the result of the previously omitted variable. The bias introduced from omitting a relevant variable in the linear regression model is eponymously called **omitted variable bias** and is a violation of one of the major assumptions of the regression model, which we further discuss below.

To elaborate on how multivariate regression can help us control for confounders, consider two independent variables, X_1 and X_2, and a dependent variable, Y. If X_2 is related to both X_1 and Y, in a simple bivariate model of

$$Y = a + bX_1 + e, \tag{22.30}$$

some portion of the explained variance in Y attributed to X_1 may be due to the potential confounder X_2. In regression we control for X_2 by including it in the model, which now has an additional coefficient as well:

$$Y = a + b_1 X_1 + b_2 X_2 + e. \tag{22.31}$$

Regression will estimate partial slopes for each independent variable. Thus the estimate of b_1 is the average change in Y for each unit change in X_1, controlling for X_2. And, similarly, the estimate of b_2 is the average change in Y for each unit change in X_2, controlling for X_1. We can expand the regression equation to include k independent variables:

$$Y = a + b_1 X_1 + b_2 X_2 + \ldots + b_k X_k + e. \tag{22.32}$$

Accordingly, the substantive interpretation of multivariate regression coefficients is akin to the bivariate model with the slight addition of the control, or "holding constant," terminology. That is, we would again describe the relationship between each independent variable and the dependent variable in terms of the respective slope coefficient by calculating $\hat{Y}$ for a particular value of, say, X_1, while holding X_2 constant, or at a set value. In a multivariate context it is particularly useful to look at the change in $\hat{Y}$ as a result of changing X_1 from one substantively meaningful value to another, perhaps a full unit or a standard deviation increase or decrease. Importantly, when we do so we hold X_2 constant, as well as any other independent variables in the model, to convey the specific effect of a change in one variable, X_1 in this case, on an expected change in the dependent variable, while holding constant the other independent variables in the model.

In multivariate regression the interpretation of the coefficient of determination, r^2, takes on a new meaning as well. Specifically, the proportionate reduction in error interpretation expands such that r^2 should still be thought of in terms of explained variance, but now for all independent variables in the model. The remainder, the variance in Y which is not explained by either X_1 or X_2, is the ratio of unexplained variance in the errors to the total variance; i.e., the variance in Y unexplained by all the independent variables in the model.

Assumptions

Like our other models, the linear regression model depends on a series of assumptions about the data-generating process that are required in order for us to arrive

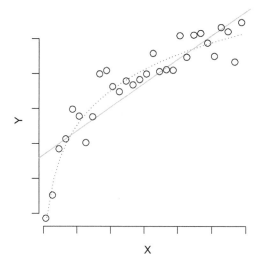

Figure 22.6 Nonlinear relationship   ■

at good estimates. These are generally called the **Gauss-Markov assumptions**. While a full description of these is beyond the basic treatment we offer in this book, we focus on the general intuition behind these assumptions and note the most common violations that can lead to problems with inference.

As should be clear by now, regression models expect that the dependent variable is a linear function of a specific set of independent variables, plus the error term. We violate the **linearity and additivity specification assumption** when we misspecify the relationships in the model. We typically do so when we try to model a relationship that is nonlinear or include the wrong set of variables in our model. We discuss each of these in turn.

In the first case, modeling a relationship that is nonlinear (Figure 22.6), recall that the regression equation solves for a line. If the expected functional form of the relationship is not linear, the regression estimates will not properly capture the relationship. We assume that the change in Y associated with a unit increase in X_1, holding all other variables constant, is the same across all values of X_1. That is, the effect of a unit increase in X_1 does not depend on the value of X_1. Violations of this nature are typically dealt with in the regression context by transforming the data. One or more variables of a nonlinear function can be mathematically transformed (e.g., taking the log or a quadratic function) so as to create a linear relationship. One can either transform the independent variables or the entire equation via the dependent variable. To make these decisions one often relies on previous work and strong theory about the expected relationships.

Furthermore, because it is an additive model we are also assuming that the change in Y from a unit X_1 is constant regardless of the values of the other independent variables in the model. We can therefore state the relationship between X_1 and Y in terms of the average expected change while holding the other variables constant.

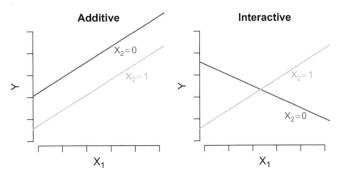

Figure 22.7 Additive and interactive relationships

Frequently in social science we would like to consider cases where the relationship between X_1 and Y is not constant, but instead depends on a third variable, say, X_2. These conditional relationships are called **interactions** and can be modeled in regression. Consider first what it would mean to have a relationship between X_1 and Y that differs depending on X_2. Most basically, we would expect different slopes for the effect of X_1 on Y depending on the value of X_2. If so, the standard posited linear and additive model is an incorrect depiction of the relationship.

For an interaction we adjust the linear regression model by making the relationship between X_1 conditional on X_2 via a multiplicative term: $X_1 \times X_2$. When we rewrite the regression line we maintain the direct, or lower order, effects and solve for the coefficient of the conditional relationship between X_1 and X_2:

$$Y = a + b_1 X_1 + b_2 X_2 + b_3 X_1 X_2 + e. \qquad (22.33)$$

Figure 22.7 shows two hypothetical graphs of relationships. The left graph shows what we should expect from the standard regression model with two lines, distinguished by their different values of X_2, of similar slopes suggesting an additive relationship. The right graph shows a clearly non-additive relationship of the effect of X_1 on Y. Conditional on X_2 the slope of the relationship between X_1 and Y differs. In this example, those with a value of 1 for X_2 have a positive relationship and those with a value of 0 have a negative relationship.

In the second case, omission of a relevant variable, the remaining coefficients will be biased. Omitting a relevant variable can either raise or lower an estimator's mean squared error, depending on the relative size of the variance reduction and the bias. Of secondary concern, the estimate of the variance will be biased upward. To understand why, recall from above our discussion of omitted variable bias and the problem of attributing explained variance when there are potential confounders.

The idea of explained variance in the multivariate context is often aided by Venn diagrams. These diagrams convey shared relationships between variables as represented by overlapping circles. Figure 22.8, for example, shows three variables, each explaining some variance of the other. In regression, for example, we would like to estimate the partial slope for the relationship between X_1 and Y. In doing so we would like to hold constant the effect of X_2 on Y. What the diagram

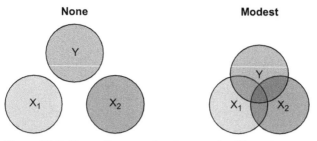
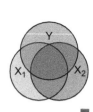

Figure 22.8 Venn diagrams by degree of collinearity

rightly suggests about multivariate regression is that in order to control for the effect of X_2 the slope coefficient for X_1 must not include the variance in Y that is explained by both X_1 and X_2, the darkest shading area in the diagram. That is, the partial slope coefficient for X_1 is the effect we get after removing the variance that is explained by both X_1 and X_2. Likewise, the partial slope coefficient for X_2 is the effect we get after removing the variance that is explained by both X_1 and X_2. Thus by including the confounder in the model we get an estimate of the effect of each variable on the dependent variable that is not tainted by the effects of the other.

We also note that the inclusion of an irrelevant variable is not helpful either. While the estimate of the explained variance remains unbiased in this case, the estimate will not be efficient. That is, we unnecessarily lose degrees of freedom as the means squared error is raised.

The second assumption we make about regression is that the **errors have an expected value of zero**. This means that on average and with enough data we get it right and the errors balance out. Related to discussion of sampling from the population, our model assumes that our estimates of the relationship will not be perfect, but that our errors will be randomly distributed around a mean value, which is correct, and thus zero. That is, to the extent we are off it is due to random error.

Our errors should also have the same variance and be uncorrelated with each other. The former assumption is referred to as **homoscedasticity**, which basically holds that the variance of each error term for each unit of observation is the same for each independent variable. Furthermore, it assumes that knowing something about the disturbance term from one observation tells us nothing about the disturbance term for another observation. Violations here are referred to as **heteroscedastic errors**, where the disturbances do not all have the same variance. The latter assumption of uncorrelated errors is referred to as **independence**, which is especially common when we have time-series or longitudinal data. Here, repeat observations create correlation between consecutive errors, which are often called **autocorrelated errors**, since the disturbances are correlated with one another.

We further assume that the independent variables are non-random and have finite variances. That is, we require that our measures of our independent variables are fixed, or reliable, such that if we were to repeat the data-gathering process from the same sample we would arrive at the same values on the independent variables.

Violations of this assumption can occur when: measuring the independent variable; autoregressing, or using a lagged value of the dependent variable as an independent variable; and in simultaneous equation estimation, or situations in which the dependent variables are determined by the simultaneous interaction of several relationships.[190]

Even more basic then the Gauss-Markov assumptions, it is also important to note that the mathematics behind the regression equation depends on a couple of key properties of the data. Foremost, the data must be **full rank matrix** for the regression estimator to work. This requires that we have at least as many if not more observations than we have independent variables. In solving equations we must have more knowns than unknowns or it is mechanically impossible to compute the estimates. In addition, there can be no exact linear relationships between the variables. These violations lead to **multicollinearity** problems, where the variables are so strongly correlated that it becomes difficult to parse out the partial effects of each.

In the presence of multicollinearity our estimates are still good; however, the variances of the estimates are quite large and unstable leading to potentially invalid predictions from particular independent variables, even though the full extent of prediction across all the variables will be correct. This is because there is not enough independent variation in a variable to precisely estimate its impact. Consider Figure 22.8. As the shared explained variance increases, it becomes more difficult to parse out the independent effects of each variable. Keep in mind that this is because the model only calculates the partial slopes. Typically, the best remedy for multicollinearity is to collect more data.

In sum, if the Gauss-Markov assumptions are met then the estimates we retrieve from our ordinary least square models are good. But what do we mean by *good*? If we change these assumptions (or they do not hold) then the regression estimator may no longer be optimal; indeed in almost all cases it will not be optimal if one of the assumptions is violated and we would want to choose a different kind of model. If it holds, then the estimator can be shown to be the **best estimator** among all the **unbiased** estimators, or all those that tell us how close our estimate is to the true parameter value (if it can be known). Usually there are several unbiased estimators and in choosing between them we like the estimator that has a sampling distribution with the smallest variance, i.e., the one that is the most **efficient**. Thus meeting the assumptions leads to the **best linear unbiased estimator** (BLUE), or an estimator that is linear and unbiased and has the minimum variance among all the linear unbiased estimators.

Example: Turnout by Region and Income

Consider the relationship between voter turnout rates in different states and the region of the country. It is not unreasonable to test this relationship as different regions of the country have had different historical experiences with the electoral system. We might suspect that those in the North, for example, with their longer

Table 22.4 Voter turnout by South and non-South regions	
	Dependent variable:
	Turnout
Region: South	−12.89*
	(1.63)
Constant	57.23*
	(0.92)
N	50
R^2	0.57

Note: *p<0.05

history of enfranchisement, to turn out to vote at greater rates. Thus our hypothesis is that state turnout is a function of region of the country (South vs. non-South). We can measure turnout simply as the percentage of those who showed up at the polls out of all those who are eligible to vote.[191] South is a dummy variable where *southern* $= 1$ and *non-southern* $= 0$. The null hypothesis is that there is no relationship between region and turnout.

Table 22.4 provides the results (from hypothetical data) of our bivariate regression model. Given what we have discussed in the sections above, we should be able to interpret every statistic in the model. Most importantly, we would look to see if we can reject the null hypothesis for our question about the relationship between region and turnout. Looking at the row for the South variable, we can interpret the average difference between two kinds of states on turnout. Notice that we do not include both the South variable as well as a non-South variable in the model. This is because the values of the singular dummy variable already represent both. We need a baseline for comparison when each dummy variable is set at 1 in order to substantively interpret the line. Thus when dummying out a single variable into its composite categories we always include $k - 1$ categories, and we interpret the coefficient as moving from baseline category to particular dummy category in the model, holding all else constant. Comparing a state in the non-South to the South (a one unit change from 0 to 1) we see that the average turnout drops by nearly 13% ($b = -12.89$) for the South. This result is statistically significant at $p < 0.05$ with a standard error of 1.63.

Of course, careful observers of modern political behavior might raise a question about the regional diversity of the United States. Perhaps the differences across it are greater than just the historical geographic divide. That is, the South non-South dichotomy may capture more than just the South's history of disenfranchising blacks. The reason for today's lower turnout in the South may be due to any number of characteristics prevalent in the South other than its history of disenfranchisement. For example, we know there is greater poverty in the South. If poverty is likely to be associated with both the independent variable, South, and

Table 22.5 Voter turnout by region and income

	Dependent variable:
	Turnout
Region: South	−10.12*
	(1.68)
Income	0.004*
	(0.001)
Constant	36.66*
	(6.02)
N	50
R^2	0.65

Note: *p<0.05

the dependent variable, turnout, how can we be sure then that poverty is not driving the low turnout rates instead of the history of disenfranchisement? To use a term we introduced above: is it possible that poverty is confounding the relationship we found in the bivariate model above?

Multivariate regression allows us to test the effect of both our original regional variable as well as the new income variable (per capita income) in the same model. By including them both as additive terms we can look at the effect of each on turnout while holding the other constant:

$$Y = a + b(South) + b(Income) + e. \tag{22.34}$$

In Table 22.5 we present the results of the multivariate regression model. Interpreting the constant we note that states in the North with a zero per capita income have an average turnout rate of only 37%. Of course no state has a zero average income so such an interpretation tells us substantively little. As before, we see a negative sign on the South coefficient. We interpret the slope of the line here to mean that in comparison to the North the southern states have about 10% lower turnout on average, holding income constant. On the contrary, the income coefficient tells us that there is a positive relationship between a state's per capita income and turnout. For a one unit increase in income we should expect a 0.004% increase in turnout. Of course, that is a very small increase given that the variable ranges several thousand points over the 50 states. We can make use of the standard deviation to provide a more substantively informative interpretation. Given a standard deviation of 614.47, we can say that a one standard deviation increase in income leads to a 2.5% increase in turnout. For both variables the relationships are significant, given the relatively small size of the standard errors. Finally, the r^2 indicates that 65% of the variance in turnout is explained by the independent variables. Note that including the income variable moves the explained variance up 15% from the bivariate model.

CONCLUSIONS

Regression is a frequently utilized tool for understanding the relationship between one or more independent variables of any level of measurement on a continuous dependent variable. It provides more explanatory leverage than any other technique we have discussed thus far by estimating the average effect of a unit change in the independent variable on the dependent variable. However, like all parametric models, regression makes various assumptions that are easily violated in practice. As such, a careful employer of regression will look to diagnose how well their model meets the assumptions before trusting their results.

KEY TERMS

- Centroid
- Residual
- Extrapolation
- Interpolation
- Coefficient of determination
- Proportionate reduction in error
- Explained sum of squares
- Residual sum of squared errors
- Mean squared errors
- Standard error of the estimate
- Control
- Confounding
- Omitted variable bias
- Gauss-Markov assumptions
- Linearity and additivity specification
- Interactions
- Errors have an expected value of zero
- Homoscedasticity
- Heteroscedastic errors
- Independence
- Autocorrelated errors
- Full rank matrix
- Multicollinearity
- Best estimator
- Unbiased estimators
- Efficient
- BLUE

23 Causal Inference

Much of social science research is concerned with causal relationships. In this chapter we explore the general framework for making causal statements using different methodological approaches. With experiments as our point of reference, we revisit regression in the context of a causal treatment variable, and then introduce a technique to evaluate the causal effect of a treatment with observational data by matching treated and control units. Before doing so we lay out the specific assumptions necessary for causality and the different motivating factors for each causal model.

Assumptions and Assignment

Why causal inference? Our statistical objective thus far has been to infer associations among variables. From these associations we can estimate probabilities of events with the statistical methods introduced above, provided that the external conditions remain the same. This allows us to answer important questions, like: What is the mean number of parties in democracies? Are turnout and geographic regions related? Are greater issue dimensions associated with greater numbers of parties? On the contrary, we need causal inference when we would like to infer probabilities under different conditions. That is, when we would like to know what would happen if something else happened. When we expect probabilities to change in response to external factors we must rely on causal analysis. Thus, causal questions ask somewhat different questions: What are the effects of worker-training programs? Does smoking cause cancer? Does viewing a campaign advertisement change vote preferences? In each case we are asking a question that posits different probabilities under different conditions: attending versus not attending a worker-training program; smoking versus not smoking; viewing versus not viewing a campaign ad.

Throughout the statistics section of this book we have identified hypothesis tests that are based on covariance between suspected cause and effect. However, the tests themselves are only covariational; that is, they are not explicitly causal. As we discussed in Chapters 21 and 22, in order to make claims of causality we need more than the evidence of covariation between cause and effect that we can attain from these statistical methods. Minimally, we also need the cause to precede the effect and to be able to eliminate plausible alternative causes. Thus, causal inference requires knowledge of the data-generating process, not just the data. When we make causal claims we must therefore rely on premises that are beyond the statistical associations we have described earlier. The information necessary for causal inference is based on assumptions that help to identify the state of relationships under different conditions. These assumptions are the focus of this section.

In order to attain meaningful causal effects we need to make a few specific assumptions about the relationship of the treatment to the units or individuals in the study. To keep the causal relationship clear, for this chapter we call our causal independent variable the **treatment** and our dependent variable the **outcome**. The treatment demarcates the different conditions under which we expect the probabilities of the outcome to differ. The **stable unit treatment value assumption** (SUTVA) assumes **non-interference**, or that for any individual i receiving the treatment does not influence the **potential outcomes** of any other individual. Here potential outcomes are conditional statements about what would be the case given some treatment, prior event, or different condition. We also need to assume a **homogeneous treatment**, or that the treatment should be the same for all individuals. Generally, SUTVA forces researchers to be precise about the research question and design. Thus it should apply to all causal inference regardless of the chosen methodological approach – e.g., matching, which we introduce below, or regression, which we discussed in the previous chapter.

Finally, we must assume **ignorability**; i.e., that the treatment is assigned independent of the outcomes. In experiments, ignorability is accounted for by random assignment, but in observational data exposure to treatment may be endogenous or contingent on an antecedent variable. A frequent violation of this assumption is one we discussed in Chapter 22 on regression, omitted variable bias. If an omitted variable causes change in the outcome variable and also affects which observations receive the treatment then there may appear to be a causal relationship between the treatment and outcome when in reality there is not.

In the statistics section of this book we have focused largely on observational data, which are common in sociology, economics, and political science, among other disciplines. We will continue to do so with the goal of adapting an observational study so that it approximates the causal leverage afforded by a randomized experiment. That is, we discuss here two frequently employed methodological techniques that adjust observational data to account for confounders with the intention of estimating causal effects, regression and **matching**. Matching allows us to estimate the causal effects with exceptionally strong control by creating quasi-experimental contrasts. Moreover it allows us to distinguish the selection process from the outcomes. To be sure, there are a number of other ways to adjust the design in line with a causal objective, including, for example, structural equation modeling, instrumental variables, regression discontinuity, difference-in-difference, and fixed effects;[192] however, we will focus on only regression and matching here.

With the objective of drawing causal inferences it is important to remember that these basic assumptions apply broadly. While less commonly used when introducing regression models, they provide the necessary additional guidance for making causal claims based on the linear regression estimates. From this perspective the difference between matching, introduced in this chapter, and linear regression, introduced in the previous chapter, is related to where and how we control for covariates in the estimate of a causal effect. While regression provides control by subtracting off the covariates from the outcome variable, matching, as we show below, is done by balancing the covariates across the treatment variable. Regression is less flexible and often less precise since it is linear and parametric. The key insight, however, is that while they go about it somewhat differently, they frequently have the same causal objective, and thus should be evaluated from the perspective of the assumptions above and the common casual framework we introduced in Chapter 2 and elaborate on in the Potential Outcomes section below.

Potential Outcomes

In order to understand how we can go about systematically inferring causal effects we need to introduce some new mathematical notation to help us focus on the **counterfactual**; i.e., how an outcome would have turned out differently if the factors that led to it were different. If we think of the treatment, T, as a cause of the outcome, Y, then we would expect Y not to have happened if T had not occurred. If Y happened regardless, then T is not the cause. To elaborate, consider that the treatment, T_i, can take on one of two states for each unit of observation, or individual, i: 1 if i receives the treatment and 0 if it does not. Thus, the effect, Δ_i, has two potential outcomes for each observation depending on exposure to T: Y_{iT} or Y_{iC}. The individual causal effect of the treatment on the outcome is therefore the difference between these two potential outcomes and denoted by the Greek letter delta:

$$\Delta_i = Y_{iT} - Y_{iC}. \tag{23.1}$$

There are a number of estimands for the potential outcomes model. We discuss two of the most frequently used here. First, the **average treatment effect** (ATE) is the expected – which is to say the long-run average, and signified with E below – difference between the potential outcomes in the population:

$$ATE = E[Y_{iT} - Y_{iC}]. \tag{23.2}$$

Second, and perhaps more usefully, the **average treatment effect on the treated** (ATT) is the expected difference between the potential outcomes in the subpopulation of those exposed to the treatment. That is, the expected difference for the ATT is conditional on the treatment, which is signified with the | sign:

$$ATT = E[Y_{iT} - Y_{iC} | T_i = 1]. \tag{23.3}$$

If we know the Y_{iT} and Y_{iC} for the same i estimating the causal effects is trivial. Consider the hypothetical data for six observations in Table 23.1. For example, we might think of the causal effect of taking aspirin for headache pain. As such, Y_{iT}

Table 23.1   Estimating treatment effects with both outcomes

i	Y_{iT}	Y_{iC}	T_i	Δ_i
1	3	1	0	2
2	8	6	0	2
3	6	3	0	3
4	7	5	1	2
5	9	7	1	2
6	9	8	1	1
Σ	42	30		
$\overline{Y}$	$E[Y_{iT}] = 7$	$E[Y_{iC}] = 5$		
ATE				$E[Y_{iT} - Y_{iC}] = 2$
ATT				$E[Y_{iT} - Y_{iC}|T_i = 1] = 1.7$

Table 23.2   Estimating treatment effects with one outcome

i	Y_{iT}	Y_{iC}	T_i	Δ_i
1	NA	1	0	?
2	NA	6	0	?
3	NA	3	0	?
4	7	NA	1	?
5	9	NA	1	?
6	9	NA	1	?

would be the degree of pain of a headache on the individual after aspirin, while Y_{iC} would be the pain of the headache on the individual without taking aspirin. The difference in pain, Δ_i, identifies the causal effect of aspirin. As such, we simply calculate the expected values for each outcome and take the difference for all of the observations to get the ATE. We do the same but just for the treated to get the ATT.

In practice the problem is that we cannot observe both potential outcomes for any single unit. That would mean observing the same individual in the treatment and control groups. In the above example, that would be akin to observing the same individual take aspirin and not take aspirin for the same headache. In practice our data looks more like Table 23.2. We only observe the respective outcomes of those who received the treatment and those who received the control. We do not have the data to estimate a causal effect directly, and therefore arriving at causal inference is like solving a missing data problem.

The potential outcomes approach, often referred to as the Neyman–Rubin model, attempts to grapple with this **fundamental problem of causal inference**. That is, how do we estimate Δ_i given that we do not observe Y_{iT} and Y_{iC} for the same i? From this perspective, the goal of causal inference is to predict the effect of each treatment state on the same unit.

Experiments attempt to solve this problem through randomization. In an experiment the researcher assigns the units of observation to one of two causal states: treatment or control. Recall that the experimental design differs from observational studies insofar as in the latter the researcher does not have the ability to control exposure to the treatment. Randomizing the treatment assignment leads to balanced control and treatment groups on average. Thus, instead of comparing the same units under each state, we compare two groups made up of similar units.

Complete randomization meets our assumption of ignorability. When the assignment is random the effect of the treatment is not contingent on observable or unobservable confounders, as any confounding characteristics should be similar across the treated and control groups. The difference in the treated and control groups should be due solely to the treatment, which allows researchers to make explicitly causal inferences through simple comparisons of the outcomes in the treatment and control group. In this case then all we need to estimate the causal effect is a difference of means test (introduced in Chapter 20), where one mean is taken from the control group and the other the treatment.

In contrast, in observational studies the causal relationship is more difficult to tease out, because the treatment assignment is often endogenous to characteristics of the units of observation. As such, in the observational context it is more difficult to meet the assumption of ignorability. The tradeoff in choosing research designs is widely recognized. Experiments offer the best control in order to measure precise treatment effects. Surveys offer generalizability given representative samples and externally valid contexts. So what then can researchers interested in making causal claims with observational data do?

Ignorability in Observational Studies

As should be clear by now, the major hurdle for observational studies is ignorability. Specifically, we would like to compare those who received the treatment to those who did not receive it but we recognize that doing so in the observational context is not as simple as comparing the treatment and control groups because the assignment was not random. When we do not have control over the assignment to treatment, as in an observational study, one or more factors may affect that assignment and confound the estimated effects.

While experiments provide a simple method for estimating causal effects, it is not always possible or wise to conduct an experiment. For instance, in a sociological study it would not be ethical to randomly fire individuals in order to study the effects of unemployment. Studies of this nature would have to rely on a sample of individuals who are already unemployed. Experimental treatments can also be unrealistic, and thus one would prefer to study similar phenomena if and when they occur in reality. Consider exposing individuals to possible electoral or political outcomes that have not yet occured. Many individuals might not believe such hypothetical situations in the context of a lab experiment making the treatment practically meaningless. For these reasons – and others, especially generalizability – researchers make use of observational data. In the observational setting the control and treatment groups are unlikely to be similar across all confounders, and indeed they may differ systematically. Even in experiments with small samples the treatment and control groups can differ greatly on various covariates by random error. To address this common issue a researcher relies on statistical modeling.

Assume for a moment that it is possible to arrive at perfectly similar observed covariates so that respondents only differed from one another in terms of whether they received the treatment or not. Such a situation meets the assumption of ignorability, assuming, of course, that there is no omitted variable bias. Conditional on the covariates we can assume ignorability and estimates of the treatment effect should be the same regardless of the chosen model.

One option then is to model the difference in potential outcomes conditional on the complete set of confounders, X. Since these covariates account for all the systematic differences between those who received the treatment and those that did not, we can identify the causal effects for observational studies conditional on the X. We can write ignorability assumptions for the ATE and ATT, respectively:

$$(Y_{iT}, Y_{iC}) \perp\!\!\!\perp T_i | X_i. \tag{23.4}$$

$$(Y_{iT}) \perp\!\!\!\perp T_i | X_i. \tag{23.5}$$

The outcomes are independent, signified with the $\perp\!\!\!\perp$ sign, from the treatment conditional on the X. Thus, provided we have conditioned on the confounder(s), we can ignore the treatment assignment process when calculating the causal effects.

While promising, this framework leads to two issues. First, selecting the correct observables for control is non-trivial. It requires one to observe the complete set of pre-treatment confounders. As such, researchers have to know which are the necessary covariates to include before they can collect them. Strong theoretical knowledge and previous works on the subject are necessary for determining the list of confounders. Second, how does one achieve similarity on one or more covariates across the treatment conditions? That is, which methods are available for ensuring comparable observations in one group with another group? In this chapter we provide two possible solutions to the dependence problem. First, we explain in the next section that regression attempts to control for the lack of independence between the treatment and outcome by subtracting off the confounding variable's effect from the treatment effect. Second, we show subsequently how matching selects on observable variables to remove the dependence.

Regression as a Causal Model

We briefly revisit the linear regression model from the potential outcomes perspective in order to show how it can be used to estimate causal effects. The goal here is to minimize the imbalance in confounding variables. As we will show below, the goal of matching is related but different, insofar as it is particularly well suited to grapple with the lack of overlap in confounders. We begin by rewriting the regression equation in terms of the treatment variable, T, as well as the now familiar intercept and error terms:

$$Y_i = a_i + b_i T_i + e_i. \tag{23.6}$$

This equation is identical to the bivariate regression equation 22.1 introduced in Chapter 22. The only difference is that instead of the general independent variable, X, we have specified the model with the treatment, T, which can take on one of two states for each unit of observation, i: 1 if i receives the treatment and 0 if it does not. Accordingly, we use the i subscript to denote the individual or unit of observation.

Were the treatment variable the only effect on the outcome variable, the b parameter would serve as an indicator of the treatment effect:

$$b_i = Y_{iT} - Y_{iC}. \tag{23.7}$$

That is, if there were no confounders, variables that affect both the treatment and the outcome, this simple bivariate regression model would meet the assumptions for causality. As such we can restate the treatment effects in terms of the average of the slope parameter, b, first for the entire population,

$$ATE = E[b_i], \tag{23.8}$$

and for just those exposed to the treatment,

$$ATT = E[b_i | T_i = 1]. \tag{23.9}$$

To see why this is so, we can further rewrite the regression equation in line with our potential outcomes notation:

$$Y_i = a_i + (Y_{iT} - Y_{iC})T_i. \tag{23.10}$$

Here we have simply replaced the b parameter with the difference in outcomes to illustrate the equivalence of the causal framework in regression. As we noted above, we never observe this difference, but instead something akin to what would have happened to the control had they received the treatment:

$$Y_i = T_i Y_{iT} + (1 - T_i) Y_{iC}. \tag{23.11}$$

Equating the a_i with Y_{iC} then we see that the causal framework can be considered in terms of a linear model with a random coefficient, where the treatment effect, b_i, is the coefficient of the treatment, T_i:

$$\begin{aligned} Y_i &= Y_{iC} + (Y_{iT} - Y_{iC})T_i \\ &= a_i + b_i T_i. \end{aligned} \tag{23.12}$$

Assuming a constant treatment effect – that the effect of the treatment is the same across all the observations – we can further reduce this equation. Because the treatment is constant we expect that the long-run average for each parameter is the population value, or that $E[b_i] = \bar{b}$ and $E[a_i] = \bar{a}$. Thus, the equation can be written in terms of constant coefficients:

$$Y_i = \bar{a} + \bar{b}T_i + e_i. \tag{23.13}$$

In this case both the ATE and ATT are provided by the average slope coefficient $\bar{b}$.

Likewise, if we are to assume random assignment, as in an experiment, these two treatment effects from the linear model are equivalent. Because treatment does not depend on the outcomes, conditioning on the treatment is useless, since the outcome is mean independent of the treatment:

$$E[Y_{iC}|T_i] = E[Y_{iC}]. \tag{23.14}$$

In the estimated regression line then the b is the ATE. Assuming the same for the treated,

$$E[Y_{iT}|T_i = 1] = E[Y_{iT}], \tag{23.15}$$

the ATE and ATT are equivalent. Moreover, the treatment effect is also the same as the difference of means between the treated and controlled in this case.

However, as mentioned above, with observational data it is unlikely that the control and treatment groups are made up of similar units on the confounding variables. Instead, systematic differences likely exist across them that complicate our abilities to make causal inferences from such simple models. In observational data, factors related to the treatment often affect treatment assignment.

The regression model attempts to solve the dependence problem by including the confounding variable(s) in the linear equation. That is, by regressing the outcome on not only the treatment variable but also the confounding variable we can estimate the causal treatment effect. Let us call the confounding variable X. By definition this variable affects both assignment to treatment as well as the outcome variable. Recall that in multivariate regression we control for X by including it in the model with its own b coefficient:

$$Y_i = a + b_1 T_i + b_2 X_i + e_i. \tag{23.16}$$

If it is the only confounder and the regression model is correctly specified then the b_1 slope parameter is an indicator of the average causal effect.

To see why this is true, recall from Chapter 22 that multivariate regression estimates partial slopes for each independent variable. Thus the estimate of b_1 is the average change in Y_i for each unit change in T_i, controlling for X_i, and vice versa. By including the confounder in a linear equation we are estimating the causal effect by subtracting off from Y and T the common dependence in X. This is because regression is equivalent to a three-step process where one first regresses Y_i on X_i and calculates the residual, which we will denote with an asterisk,

$Y_i^* = Y_i - \hat{Y}_i$. Then one regresses T_i on X_i and calculates the residual $T_i^* = T_i - \hat{T}_i$. Finally one regresses Y_i^* on T_i^*. The regression coefficient on T_i^* from the last step is simply the multivariate regression estimate b_1. In this case then, regression is no different than estimating the relationship between Y and T after their common dependence on X has been removed.[193]

This procedure generalizes to the case of multiple confounders. If all of the confounding variables are included in the model then the causal treatment effect is given by b_1. As such, a correctly specified regression model with control for the confounders provides an estimate of the treatment effect within the range of the observed data. Of course, this assumes that the confounders are all observed. As should be clear by now, unobserved confounders lead to omitted variable bias and an inaccurate treatment effect.

Matching as a Causal Model

We introduce here a statistical technique within the framework of potential outcomes as an alternative to evaluate the causal effect of a treatment with observational data by *matching* treated and control units. Similar to the previous hypothesis tests, the alloted space does not permit a full treatment of this approach. However, we provide an introduction that includes the basic assumptions, a brief summary of a number of matching methods, and a simple application. In the previous section we discussed how regression can provide causal estimates of the treatment effect. In short, regression attempts to control for the lack of independence between the treatment and outcome in observational studies by subtracting off the confounding variable's effect from the treatment's effect. In this section we offer an alternative solution to the problem of dependence. Here we show how matching selects on observable variables to remove this dependence.

The nature of many samples of observational data complicates causal inferences from regression. While we are able to control for the confounder with multivariate regression, thereby meeting the ignorability assumption, regression is less valuable as an indicator of causal effect when the distribution of the confounder is dissimilar in the treatment and control groups. Recall that the goal of regression in the causal context is to estimate what would have happened to the control had they received the treatment. When there is little balance or overlap across the treatment and control groups on the confounder – what is referred to as a lack of **common support** – the counterfactual does not exist in the data, or at least not in a large number, which puts a heavy burden on the specification of the model. On the contrary, with strong balance and overlap there is less dependence on the model specification in arriving at causal treatment effects. The goal of matching is to ensure overlap in the confounding variables.

Matching is a modeling design for observational studies that attempts to create the same kind of balance in confounders across treated and control groups that one would get in a randomized experiment. It mimics the randomization of treatment assignment in experiments by subsetting the sample in order to balance the confounder distributions in the treatment and control groups. Matching then is a process of selecting on observables. More broadly construed, it is any method that attempts to balance the treated group with control group based on a set of covariates.

Although there are many choices to make in specifying a matching design, it always follows a common procedure comprised of two parts: (a) the design or selection, and (b) the outcomes analysis. In the first part, researchers:

1 Choose some measure that will determine which units could be matched to each other based on the distance in selected covariate values.
2 Utilize a method that matches units based on the selected distance measure.
3 Evaluate the quality of the matched sample to be sure that the treated and control groups resemble each other – i.e., that there is balance across them on the covariates. Because of the number of options in both distance measures and matching methods, this is a crucial step.

In the second part, and provided there is strong balance, the researcher simply estimates the appropriate treatment effect with the matched sample, a process exactly like the statistical tests introduced in the previous chapters.[194]

The objective of matching is to match similar individuals to one another. Thus matching is a process of minimizing the distance between individuals on one or more covariates. As we noted above, the list of covariates depends on theory and insights from extant literature on the likely confounders. Given a suitable covariate or list of covariates, there are a number of ways to calculate the distance, D, between two individuals i and j. The most straightfoward is **exact matching**, wherein the distance is zero, $D_{ij} = 0$ if the covariates match, $X_i = X_j$, and infinity otherwise, $D_{ij} = \infty$. Thus individuals in the treatment group are matched to those in the control based on having the same covariate value.

Perhaps the most frequently used distance measure is the **propensity score**. In this case one or more covariates are gathered into a single value that reflects the probability of receiving the binary treatment. To calculate the propensity score, call this e, one regresses the covariates on the dichotomous treatment variable. In this case one uses a regression model with a small transformation to account for the dichotomous dependent variable (i.e., a logit or probit model), such that:

$$D_{ij} = \left| logit_{e_i} - logit_{e_j} \right|.$$

Also common in the literature are the **Mahalanobis distance**, which matches generalized distances based on covariance, and **coarsened exact matching**, which allows for matching on categorical ranges.

Having selected a distance measure, the researcher's next step is to utilize the distance measure in a matching method. Several methods avail themselves, and differ primarily in terms of the composition of the sample after matching – i.e., which, if any, units are discarded in the process – and the weights placed on them. Though we will discuss only one in detail here, there are several matching methods, including the most straightforward, **nearest neighbor**, as well as full, subclassification, and interval or weighted adjustments, which each employ different processes of weighting the sample in order to carry over the full sample of individuals into the matched sample.

Nearest neighbor works by matching individuals in the treated to those in the control group based on the smallest distance between them on one or more covariates. That is, it picks k matches of control for each treated individual. The simplest nearest neighbor matching algorithm is **greedy** insofar as it begins with an individual in the treated, looks for its closest match among the control, matches them, and then performs the same process time again with the individuals that remain. Those controls that are not matched are discarded. When matching without replacement, the order determines which controls are left to match on. Thus, the overall balance between the treated and control groups on the covariate, or the **global distance**, can be affected when matching without replacement. Recall that the goal is to ensure a strong overall balance between the two groups.

Optimal matching, however, attempts to minimize the global distance by breaking up early matches and rematching them to different individuals when it reduces the overall distance. Similarly, one has the option to match the groups with replacement, which also makes the order irrelevant. But because some of the controls are matched more than one time to individuals in the treated group the individuals in the matched sample are no longer independent. As such, those who match with replacement must account for the dependence in the matched sample in some manner, for instance, by weighting individuals according to the original sample composition.

Following the execution of the matching method, researchers have one more important step before conducting their outcomes analysis: evaluating the matched sample. That is, we need to diagnose whether or not the match worked. As with a randomly assigned experiment, we would like the control and treated groups to look virtually the same, apart from the treatment. In order to compare the outcomes between the two groups as an effect of the treatment, we require that the distributions of the one or more covariates that confound the relationship between the treatment and the outcome variable to be very similar in each group.

There are a number of ways, both graphically and numerically, to assess the balance in the original and matched samples. It is important to remember that the purpose of both is simply to alleviate concerns that the treated and control groups differ in terms of the confounding covariate. In other words, the ideal analysis would be based on a sample with identical distributions of the covariate in each group. To see why this is so, consider the distributions of a single covariate for each treatment group represented in terms of smoothed lines.[195] In Figure 23.1 the distributions of the treatment groups are illustrated by the solid lines and the distributions of the control groups by the dashed lines. On the left the sample has little overlap, or common support, which makes inference challenging due to the inability to compare like to like. That is, there are many observations in the treatment group that do not have a point of comparison in the control group,

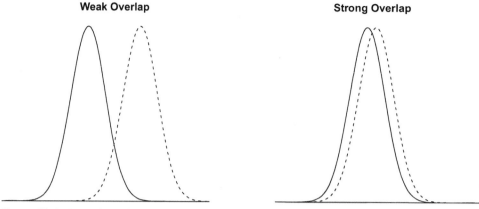

Figure 23.1 Covariate distributions for treated and control groups by overlap ■

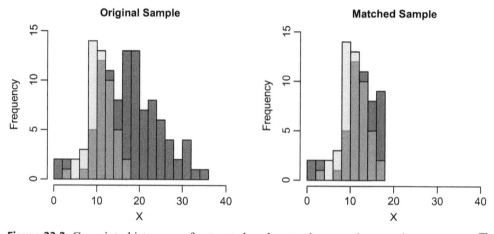

Figure 23.2 Covariate histograms for treated and control groups by sample ■

and vice versa. The lack of counterfactual observations means that in calculating the treatment effect we are forced to extrapolate beyond the support of the data. In contrast, the strong overlap on the right side allows us to compare individuals from the treated and control groups who resemble each other on the covariate, and, thus, be less concerned that the covariate is driving the treatment effect.

We learned in Chapter 18 that the histogram provides a simplified description of a variable's distribution, lending insights to the central tendency, variance, and overall shape of the variable. As such, we can use it to illustrate the intention of matching. On the left side of Figure 23.2 are two histograms for the same covariate from the original sample of data, but each from a different treatment group. The treated are in light gray and the control in dark gray. The moderately hued gray indicates the overlapping areas of the two histograms. We see that while the shapes are somewhat similar, the distribution and central tendencies are considerably different for each group. Indeed the overlap between the two is limited to a smaller set of observations in the middle of the graph. Matching should help create an appropriate comparison on this covariate by discarding the individuals in the control that are very different from the treated to create a more balanced sample. The right side of Figure 23.2 shows the same covariate broken up by treatment groups after the matching process. Here we primarily see the moderate hued bars that indicate overlap in the two distributions, which is what we would expect to see if the chosen distance measures and matching methods are successful. In short, matching should provide us with a sample comprising similar covariate distributions for each group.

More rigorous and frequently more helpful approaches to comparing the samples graphically include ensuring overlap in the distribution of propensity scores and quantile-quantile (QQ) plots, which compare the distribution for each covariate in each quantile. In addition, Rubin (2001) offers a number of numerical tests, including the standardized difference of means of the propensity score and the ratio of variances of the propensity score in each group. Regardless of which diagnostic is chosen, it is generally recommended that one conduct several balance metrics and visual inspections of the samples to ensure balance.

As we noted above, a number of distance measures and matching methods are available. Should the treated and control groups in the matched sample exhibit signs of imbalance on the covariate(s), the matched sample should be rejected and new processes for creating the sample should be tried until the researcher arrives at a balanced sample. Thus the matching process itself is contingent on arriving at a highly balanced sample. Occasionally a simple distance measure and matching method is sufficient to balance the groups. Frequently, however, more complicated procedures are necessary to arrive at balance given a host of covariates or relatively small number of treated individuals.

Once the matching methods have provided suitable balance on the covariates, the next and final step is to conduct the outcome analysis. This stage in the process is the same as the hypothesis tests we have engaged earlier in the book. That is, what makes matching different from the earlier approaches is in the distance and matching methods that make up the design stage. Once the data has been matched, or *designed*, we proceed to conduct the analyses in much the same way as before.

For example, when matching without replacement we can arrive at the marginal treatment effect by using a difference of means test.[196] In this case we are comparing the means on the outcome or dependent variable for those in the treated and control groups. If the treatment led to differences in the outcome – provided, of course that the relationship is unconfounded, which is the purpose of the matching – then we should find a significant difference in means. Alternatively, if one suspects remaining imbalance after the matching we could be especially careful and conduct a multivariate regression analysis that includes the covariates that are imbalanced. In this case the matching helps to reduce the findings dependence on the chosen statistical model by nonparametrically balancing the treated and control groups, while the researcher can still make use of a commonly used parametric test, like ordinary least squares regression, on the matched data (Ho et al. 2007). Thus, the same analyses that can be conducted on the original sample can be done with the matched sample.

Example: Worker-Training Programs

Consider some hypothetical data on the effect of job training programs inspired by the work of LaLonde (1986). Researchers and employers alike would like to know if job training results in greater long-term earnings for workers. In order to get a causal estimate of the effect of job training, researchers, in an ideal world, would randomly assign half of the workers to job training and the other half to a control group and check to see which group had greater earnings after some period of time. In reality, however, it is hard to assign job training since it involves individuals' livelihoods and they are unlikely to aquiesce to random assignment when their future may depend on it. Indeed some workers may be more likely to seek out job training than others. Perhaps those with a higher education would be more likely to believe in the benefits of training. Thus researchers may be limited to observational data on this important topic.

Table 23.3 provides earnings data on a small sample of workers, some of whom took in a job training program. We also observe the number of years of education achieved by the workers. If we can assume that education is the sole confounder, we can match individuals across the treated and control groups on this covariate and calculate the effect of job training on earnings.

Because there are no exact matches in the treated and control groups on this covariate, we are unable to use an exact pairing. Instead we begin by matching individuals that are closest to one another and discard according to the nearest neighbor method. That is, we use the nearest neighbor matching method to reduce the original sample to a matched sample that is more comparable across the treated and control groups on the education covariate. Recall that depending on the data the choice of the algorithm used for nearest neighbor matching can result in very different global distances. For example, whether we use an optimal or greedy match leads to different distances in this case:

$$
\begin{aligned}
D_{\text{Greedy}} &= |X_1 - X_4| + |X_2 - X_5| + |X_3 - X_6| \\
&= |8 - 9| + |12 - 13| + |15 - 10| \\
&= 1 + 1 + 5 \\
&= 8.
\end{aligned}
\tag{23.17}
$$

Table 23.3 Original sample worker-training data

i	Earnings (in thousands of $)	Training	Education (in years)
1	64	1	8
2	72	1	12
3	80	1	15
4	62	0	9
5	40	0	13
6	33	0	10
7	91	0	22

Example: Worker-Training Programs

$$D_{Optimal} = |X_1 - X_4| + |X_2 - X_6| + |X_3 - X_5|$$
$$= |8 - 9| + |12 - 10| + |15 - 13|$$
$$= 1 + 2 + 2$$
$$= 5. \tag{23.18}$$

The optimal match results in a smaller distance, and, as such, does a better job with the matching in this case. Importantly, however, we see that the same individuals are chosen for inclusion in the matched sample regardless of the algorithm employed in the nearest neighbor matching. We only discard the 7th observation, a control group individual whose education score is too distant from those in the treated to find a match. As such, the data that we use to run our outcomes analysis looks like Table 23.4.

With the matched sample we have completed the design stage and can move on to the outcomes analysis. That is, with the design stage complete, we move on to the outcome stage employing the same analyses we would have run on the original data but now on the matched data. For instance, it is now fairly straightforward to calculate a marginal treatment effect by comparing the earnings in the treated and control groups with a difference of means test. Recall that we begin by tallying the observations and calculating the means and standard deviations for each group, which are noted in the bottom of Table 23.4.

$$ATT = \overline{Y}_T - \overline{Y}_C$$
$$= 72 - 45 \tag{23.19}$$
$$= 27.$$

While the treatment effect appears substantively large, approximately $27,000, some of you might be wondering whether this effect is statistically significant. To

Table 23.4 Matched sample worker-training data

i	Earnings (in thousands of $)	Training	Education (in years)
1	64	1	8
2	72	1	12
3	80	1	15
4	62	0	9
5	40	0	13
6	33	0	10
$N_T = 3$			
$N_C = 3$			
	$\overline{Y}_T = 72$		
	$\overline{Y}_C = 45$		
	$s_T = 8$		
	$s_C = 15.133$		

that end, we can use what we learned in the earlier section on difference of means (Chapter 21) to test the statistical significance of the average difference between the treated and control groups. We begin by calculating the standard error of the difference between means:

$$
\begin{aligned}
s_{\overline{Y}_T - \overline{Y}_C} &= \sqrt{\frac{s_T^2}{N_T} + \frac{s_C^2}{N_C}} \\
&= \sqrt{\frac{64}{3} + \frac{229}{3}} \\
&= \sqrt{97.66} \\
&= 9.88.
\end{aligned}
\tag{23.20}
$$

With the standard error, we can calculate the t-ratio and check it against the values in Appendix Table A.2.

$$
\begin{aligned}
t &= \frac{\overline{Y}_T - \overline{Y}_C}{s_{\overline{Y}_T - \overline{Y}_C}} \\
&= \frac{72 - 45}{9.88} \\
&= 2.73.
\end{aligned}
\tag{23.21}
$$

$$
\begin{aligned}
df &= N_T + N_C - 2 \\
&= 3 + 3 - 2 \\
&= 4.
\end{aligned}
\tag{23.22}
$$

For a *df* of 4, we compare test statistic, 2.73 to the α values to find that it is smaller than the critical value for $\alpha = 0.05$ of 2.776. So for the most conventional level of significance, we fail to reject the null hypothesis. However, we note that the critical value is just a tad larger than our test statistic. Indeed, the test statistic is greater than the critical value for $\alpha = 0.1$ of 2.132, so the findings could be considered significant at a less conservative level of confidence.

As aforementioned, once we have completed the design stage we have a number of options for conducting the analyses in the outcome stage. Above we relied on a difference of means test, which allowed us to test our hypothesis in a fairly straightforward manner. However, it is important to remember that different data and research questions may lead us to use other statistical tests in the outcome stage. Even in the case of this data and hypothesis, the difference of means test was not our only option; one could have used regression, for example. If we rely on regression instead of the difference of means test for the outcome analysis, the results we obtain are presented in Table 23.5.

The results of the bivariate regression model show that a worker who receives training sees a $27,000 bump in earnings, on average, compared to a worker without training. While the coefficient is not significant at $\alpha = 0.05$, it is significant

Table 23.5 Regression with matched sample

	Dependent variable:
	Earnings
Training	27.00
	(9.88)
Constant	45.00*
	(6.99)
N	6
R^2	0.651

Note: *$p < 0.05$

at $\alpha = 0.1$. Looking at the constant we can say that the regression line crosses the y-intercept at 45, which would be the case when training is equal to zero. In other words, a worker without training should make about $45,000 a year.

Now recall the difference of means results and notice that the coefficient for training in the regression model is the same as the difference of means between the control and treatment groups. Their t-ratios are also the same (prove this). Finally, note that the intercept is the same as the mean earnings for the control group. These shared findings illustrate the equivalence of the difference of means and regression in this context. A difference of means test across two groups is the same as a regression with a dummy variable, since regression simply plots a line through the mean of each group. Thus the null hypothesis of equal means for a difference of means test is equivalent to the null hypothesis of a flat line for a dummy variable regression. Indeed the difference of means test and regression are really just two cases of the same general linear model that is explored in more advanced texts.

CONCLUSIONS

Both regression and matching offer methods of getting the control we desire from experiments in the observational setting that typically provides more generalizable data. In the context of potential outcomes inference, often called the Neyman–Rubin causal model, we showed how regression and matching each enables causal statements under specific circumstances and strict assumptions. In the former we attempt to minimize imbalance in confounders while in the latter we deal with their lack of overlap.

KEY TERMS

- Treatment
- Outcome
- Stable unit treatment value assumption
- Non-interference
- Potential outcomes
- Homogeneous treatment
- Ignorability
- Matching
- Counterfactual
- Average treatment effect
- Average treatment effect on the treated
- Fundamental problem of causal inference
- Common support
- Exact matching
- Propensity score
- Mahalanobis distance matching
- Coarsened exact matching
- Nearest neighbor
- Greedy algorithm
- Global distance
- Optimal matching

Appendix

Normal Curve

	Table A1	Proportions of area under the normal curve						

z	Area Between Mean and z	z	Area Between Mean and z	z	Area Between Mean and z	z	Area Between Mean and z
0.00	0.0000	0.40	0.1554	0.80	0.2881	1.20	0.3849
0.01	0.0040	0.41	0.1591	0.81	0.2910	1.21	0.3869
0.02	0.0080	0.42	0.1628	0.82	0.2939	1.22	0.3888
0.03	0.0120	0.43	0.1664	0.83	0.2967	1.23	0.3907
0.04	0.0160	0.44	0.1700	0.84	0.2995	1.24	0.3925
0.05	0.0199	0.45	0.1736	0.85	0.3023	1.25	0.3944
0.06	0.0239	0.46	0.1772	0.86	0.3051	1.26	0.3962
0.07	0.0279	0.47	0.1808	0.87	0.3078	1.27	0.3980
0.08	0.0319	0.48	0.1844	0.88	0.3106	1.28	0.3997
0.09	0.0359	0.49	0.1879	0.89	0.3133	1.29	0.4015
0.10	0.0398	0.50	0.1915	0.90	0.3159	1.30	0.4032
0.11	0.0438	0.51	0.1950	0.91	0.3186	1.31	0.4049
0.12	0.0478	0.52	0.1985	0.92	0.3212	1.32	0.4066
0.13	0.0517	0.53	0.2019	0.93	0.3238	1.33	0.4082
0.14	0.0557	0.54	0.2054	0.94	0.3264	1.34	0.4099
0.15	0.0596	0.55	0.2088	0.95	0.3289	1.35	0.4115
0.16	0.0636	0.56	0.2123	0.96	0.3315	1.36	0.4131
0.17	0.0675	0.57	0.2157	0.97	0.3340	1.37	0.4147
0.18	0.0714	0.58	0.2190	0.98	0.3365	1.38	0.4162
0.19	0.0753	0.59	0.2224	0.99	0.3389	1.39	0.4177
0.20	0.0793	0.60	0.2257	1.00	0.3413	1.40	0.4192
0.21	0.0832	0.61	0.2391	1.01	0.3438	1.41	0.4207
0.22	0.0871	0.62	0.2324	1.02	0.3461	1.42	0.4222
0.23	0.0910	0.63	0.2357	1.03	0.3485	1.43	0.4236
0.24	0.0948	0.64	0.2389	1.04	0.3508	1.44	0.4251
0.25	0.0987	0.65	0.2422	1.05	0.3531	1.45	0.4265
0.26	0.1026	0.66	0.2454	1.06	0.3554	1.46	0.4279
0.27	0.1064	0.67	0.2486	1.07	0.3577	1.47	0.4292

Table A1 (cont.)

z	Area Between Mean and z	z	Area Between Mean and z	z	Area Between Mean and z	z	Area Between Mean and z
0.28	0.1103	0.68	0.2517	1.08	0.3599	1.48	0.4306
0.29	0.1141	0.69	0.2549	1.09	0.3621	1.49	0.4319
0.30	0.1179	0.70	0.2580	1.10	0.3643	1.50	0.4332
0.31	0.1217	0.71	0.2611	1.11	0.3665	1.51	0.4345
0.32	0.1255	0.72	0.2642	1.12	0.3686	1.52	0.4357
0.33	0.1293	0.73	0.2673	1.13	0.3708	1.53	0.4370
0.34	0.1331	0.74	0.2704	1.14	0.3729	1.54	0.4382
0.35	0.1368	0.75	0.2734	1.15	0.3749	1.55	0.4394
0.36	0.1406	0.76	0.2764	1.16	0.3770	1.56	0.4406
0.37	0.1443	0.77	0.2794	1.17	0.3790	1.57	0.4418
0.38	0.1480	0.78	0.2823	1.18	0.3810	1.58	0.4429
0.39	0.1517	0.79	0.2852	1.19	0.3830	1.59	0.4441
0.60	0.4452	2.04	0.4793	2.48	0.4934	2.92	0.4982
0.61	0.4463	2.05	0.4798	2.49	0.4936	2.93	0.4983
0.62	0.4474	2.06	0.4803	2.50	0.4938	2.94	0.4984
0.63	0.4484	2.07	0.4808	2.51	0.4940	2.95	0.4984
0.64	0.4495	2.08	0.4812	2.52	0.4941	2.96	0.4985
0.65	0.4505	2.09	0.4817	2.53	0.4943	2.97	0.4985
0.66	0.4515	2.10	0.4821	2.54	0.4945	2.98	0.4986
0.67	0.4525	2.11	0.4826	2.55	0.4946	2.99	0.4986
0.68	0.4535	2.12	0.4830	2.56	0.4948	3.00	0.4987
0.69	0.4545	2.13	0.4834	2.57	0.4949	3.01	0.4987
0.70	0.4554	2.14	0.4838	2.58	0.4951	3.02	0.4987
0.71	0.4564	2.15	0.4842	2.59	0.4952	3.03	0.4988
0.72	0.4573	2.16	0.4846	2.60	0.4953	3.04	0.4988
0.73	0.4582	2.17	0.4850	2.61	0.4955	3.05	0.4989
0.74	0.4591	2.18	0.4854	2.62	0.4956	3.06	0.4989
0.75	0.4599	2.19	0.4857	2.63	0.4957	3.07	0.4989
0.76	0.4608	2.20	0.4861	2.64	0.4959	3.08	0.4990
0.77	0.4616	2.21	0.4864	2.65	0.4960	3.09	0.4990
0.78	0.4625	2.22	0.4868	2.66	0.4961	3.10	0.4990
0.79	0.4633	2.23	0.4871	2.67	0.4962	3.11	0.4991
0.80	0.4641	2.24	0.4875	2.68	0.4963	3.12	0.4991
0.81	0.4649	2.25	0.4878	2.69	0.4964	3.13	0.4991
0.82	0.4656	2.26	0.4881	2.70	0.4965	3.14	0.4992
0.83	0.4664	2.27	0.4884	2.71	0.4966	3.15	0.4992
0.84	0.4671	2.28	0.4887	2.72	0.4967	3.16	0.4992
0.85	0.4678	2.29	0.4890	2.73	0.4968	3.17	0.4992
0.86	0.4686	2.30	0.4893	2.74	0.4969	3.18	0.4993

Table A1 (cont.)

z	Area Between Mean and z	z	Area Between Mean and z	z	Area Between Mean and z	z	Area Between Mean and z
0.87	0.4693	2.31	0.4896	2.75	0.4970	3.19	0.4993
0.88	0.4699	2.32	0.4898	2.76	0.4971	3.20	0.4993
0.89	0.4706	2.33	0.4901	2.77	0.4972	3.21	0.4993
0.90	0.4713	2.34	0.4904	2.78	0.4973	3.22	0.4994
0.91	0.4719	2.35	0.4906	2.79	0.4974	3.23	0.4994
0.92	0.4726	2.36	0.4909	2.80	0.4974	3.24	0.4994
0.93	0.4732	2.37	0.4911	2.81	0.4975	3.25	0.4994
0.94	0.4738	2.38	0.4913	2.82	0.4976	3.30	0.4995
0.95	0.4744	2.39	0.4916	2.83	0.4977	3.35	0.4996
0.96	0.4750	2.40	0.4918	2.84	0.4977	3.40	0.4997
0.97	0.4756	2.41	0.4920	2.85	0.4978	3.45	0.4997
0.98	0.4761	2.42	0.4922	2.86	0.4979	3.50	0.4998
0.99	0.4767	2.43	0.4925	2.87	0.4979	3.60	0.4998
0.00	0.4772	2.44	0.4927	2.88	0.4980	3.70	0.4999
0.01	0.4778	2.45	0.4929	2.89	0.4981	3.80	0.4999
0.02	0.4783	2.46	0.4931	2.90	0.4981	3.90	0.49995
0.03	0.4788	2.47	0.4932	2.91	0.4982	4.00	0.49997

T-Distribution

Table A2 Critical values of the T-distribution

df	α					
	0.50	0.20	0.10	0.05	0.02	0.01
	1.000	3.078	6.314	12.706	31.821	63.657
	0.816	1.886	2.920	4.303	6.965	9.925
	0.765	1.638	2.353	3.182	4.541	5.841
	0.741	1.533	2.132	2.776	3.747	4.604
	0.727	1.476	2.015	2.571	3.365	4.032
	0.718	1.440	1.943	2.447	3.143	3.707
	0.711	1.415	1.895	2.365	2.998	3.499
	0.706	1.397	1.860	2.306	2.896	3.355
	0.703	1.383	1.833	2.282	2.821	3.250
	0.700	1.372	1.812	2.228	2.764	3.169
	0.697	1.363	1.796	2.201	2.718	3.106
	0.695	1.356	1.782	2.179	2.681	3.055

Table A2 *(cont.)*

df	0.50	0.20	0.10	0.05	0.02	0.01
	0.694	1.350	1.771	2.160	2.650	3.012
	0.692	1.345	1.761	2.145	2.624	2.977
	0.691	1.341	1.753	2.131	2.602	2.947
	0.690	1.337	1.746	2.120	2.583	2.921
	0.689	1.333	1.740	2.110	2.567	2.898
	0.688	1.330	1.734	2.101	2.552	2.878
	0.688	1.328	1.729	2.093	2.539	2.861
	0.687	1.325	1.725	2.086	2.528	2.845
	0.686	1.323	1.721	2.080	2.518	2.831
	0.686	1.321	1.717	2.074	2.508	2.819
	0.685	1.319	1.714	2.069	2.500	2.807
	0.685	1.318	1.711	2.064	2.492	2.797
	0.684	1.316	1.708	2.060	2.485	2.787
	0.684	1.315	1.706	2.056	2.479	2.779
	0.684	1.314	1.703	2.052	2.473	2.771
	0.683	1.313	1.701	2.048	2.467	2.763
	0.683	1.311	1.699	2.045	2.462	2.756
	0.683	1.310	1.697	2.042	2.457	2.750
	0.681	1.303	1.684	2.021	2.423	2.704
	0.679	1.296	1.671	2.000	2.390	2.660
	0.677	1.289	1.658	1.980	2.358	2.617
∞	0.674	1.282	1.645	1.960	2.326	2.576

Notes

1 Some disciplines begin methodological training early, and others delay this training until a substantive grounding in the subject has been conveyed. This means that the reader's first substantial encounter with methods may occur during the course of an undergraduate, master's, or PhD program.

2 Philosophy of science is one such topic. This is not because we view it as unimportant. It is, rather, because we find it too important, and too complicated, to reduce to a concise format. The topic quickly becomes unwieldy in the context of an introductory text. Moreover, the abstract arguments generated by philosophers are often difficult to integrate in a meaningful way with the more prosaic tasks of applied social science methodology. Thus, we leave philosophy of science aside (see suggested readings at the end of Chapter 1).

3 Federal Bureau of Investigation, Uniform Crime Reporting Statistics, downloaded February 17, 2013: www.ucrdatatool.gov/Search/Crime/State/RunCrimeTrendsInOneVar.cfm

4 Latzer (2016).

5 UNODC (2011).

6 Our perspective echoes the perspective of an influential book edited by Henry Brady and David Collier (2004), subtitled *Diverse Tools, Shared Standards*.

7 This episode can be accessed via YouTube.

8 Lieberson and Horwich (2008).

9 Putnam (2001).

10 Putman (2004).

11 Paxton (1999).

12 Putnam (1993).

13 Woolcock (1998).

14 Knack and Keefer (1997).

15 Berman (1997).

16 Freedom House employs two indices, "Political Rights" and "Civil Liberties" (sometimes they are employed in tandem, sometimes singly) each of which extends back to 1972 and covers most sovereign and semi-sovereign nations (see www.freedomhouse.org). Polity IV (Marshall and Jaggers 2007) also provides two aggregate indices, "Democracy" and "Autocracy," usually used in tandem (by subtracting one from the other), which provides the Polity 2 variable. Coverage extends back to 1800 for most sovereign countries with populations greater than 500,000 (www.cidcm.umd.edu/inscr/polity).

17 Cheibub, Ghandi, and Vreeland (2010).

18 Cheibub, Gandhi, and Vreeland (2010: 69).

19 Huntington (1991).
20 Doorenspleet (2000); Paxton (2000).
21 Doorenspleet (2000).
22 Kurzman (1998).
23 Coppedge (2012).
24 Carbone (2009).
25 Brown, Lynn-Jones, and Miller (1996).
26 Schattschneider (1960); Verba, Schlozman, and Brady (1995).
27 Putnam (2001).
28 Jackson (2010).
29 Hartz (1955); Tocqueville (1945).
30 Patterson (1982).
31 In a later study, Hartz (1964) develops a "fragment" thesis to explain political cultures in settler societies such as the United States, Canada, Australia, and South Africa.
32 Confusingly, three words are often used semi-synonymously: typology, classification, and taxonomy. In my adopted usage, "taxonomy" refers to a specific kind of typology.
33 Weber (1918/1958).
34 Finer (1997).
35 Hirschman (1970).
36 Esping-Andersen (1990).
37 Doorenspleet (2000); Huntington (1991).
38 Sundquist (1983).
39 For discussion, see Cochran (1948); Zelizer (2002).
40 Dahl (1971: 7). Another example of a matrix typology is Aristotle's ancient typology of regime-types (Lehnert 2007: 65). Here, the number of rulers (one, a few, or many) is cross-tabulated with the rulers' goals (self-interest or the greater good) to produce six categories: tyranny, oligarchy, democracy, monarchy, aristocracy, and polity. Additional examples of matrix typologies related to the concept of democracy can be found in Almond and Verba (1963/1989: 16); Weyland (1995).
41 As a second example, one might consider Reynolds and Reilly's (2005: 28) taxonomy of electoral systems. The still-classic example of a taxonomy is the Linnaean system of biological classification (Linsley and Usinger 1959).
42 Goldstone et al. (2010).
43 We do not mean to imply that all wrong theories can be decisively falsified; this goal of Popper's seems unrealistic.
44 Alvarez et al. (1996).
45 Levitsky and Way (2002).
46 Marshall and Jaggers (2007).
47 Coppedge and Gerring (2011).
48 The twin desiderata of coherence and differentiation correspond to "lumping and splitting" operations in social classification (Zerubavel 1996) and to "similarity and difference" judgments in cognitive linguistics (Tversky and Gati 1978).
49 Sartori (1984).

50 Collier and Mahon (1993); Sartori (1970).

51 Source: Coppedge, Gerring, Lindberg, Teorell et al. (2015).

52 Weber (1905/1949: 90). See also Burger (1976). In citing Weber, we do not claim to be using the concept of an ideal-type in precisely the way that Weber envisioned.

53 Drawn from Munck (2009: 45).

54 Alvarez et al. (1996).

55 Munck (2009: 45).

56 Goertz (2006); Ragin (1987).

57 Vanhanen (2000).

58 While Coppedge, Alvarez, and Maldonado (2008) employ principal components analysis, other recent studies have enlisted Bayesian techniques (Pemstein, Meserve, and Melton 2010; Treier and Jackman 2008).

59 Dahl (1971).

60 We do not mean to imply that these terms are identical, merely that they are overlapping.

61 For further discussion, see Gerring (2017b).

62 Stackhouse (2002).

63 Griffin (2002).

64 Hogan (1993).

65 Allison (2002).

66 Hume (1888).

67 Pearl (2000: 345). See also Woodward (2005).

68 A broader definition, including whatever individuals define as worthwhile, becomes so diffuse as to lose its explanatory power or merges into a preference-based analysis, as discussed at the end of the chapter.

69 E.g., Acemoglu and Robinson (2012); Beard (1913); Becker (1976).

70 Scheper-Hughes (1992).

71 Harris (1974).

72 Diamond (1992).

73 Alesina, Giuliano, and Nunn (2013).

74 Derthick (1979).

75 Holland (1986); Rubin (1975; 2008: 812).

76 *Webster's Unabridged Dictionary* (New York: Random House, 2006).

77 Kuznets (1955).

78 Strictly speaking, a single observation cannot be causally comparable to another because a single observation does not register variation between X and Y. Causal comparability is the attribute of a set of observations, sometimes understood as a case or unit.

79 A maximal understanding of causal comparability (sometimes expressed as *unithomogeneity*) is that units should evidence *identical* responses of Y to a given value of X across units. The latter ideal is rarely, if ever, realized in the world of social science, and perhaps not even in the world of natural science. However, the minimal definition seems too minimal. After all, non-comparabilities are always somewhat problematic – at the very least, they introduce problems of noise (random error). They also may hide heterogeneous causal effects within the chosen sample (where different units respond differently to the same treatment). Thus,

we shall regard this goal as a matter of degrees. Greater causal comparability in a sample of observations is desirable, even if perfect comparability is rarely (if ever) accomplished.

80 Gillespie (1991).

81 Rubin (1991) reviews four approaches.

82 But see Kirschenman and Neckerman (1991).

83 E.g., Kenney and Wissoker (1994); Neumark et al. (1996). For an overview of this genre of field experiment see Pager (2007).

84 For other criticisms of the audit technique see Heckman and Siegelman (1993) and discussion in Pager (2007).

85 Bertrand and Mullainathan (2004).

86 E.g., Gerring and Thacker (2004).

87 Olken (2007: 203) explains: "I assembled a team of engineers and surveyors who, after the projects were completed, dug core samples in each road to estimate the quantity of materials used, surveyed local suppliers to estimate prices, and interviewed villagers to determine the wages paid on the project. From these data, I construct an independent estimate of the amount each project actually cost to build and then compare this estimate with what the village reported it spent on the project on a line-item by line-item basis. The difference between what the village claimed the road cost to build and what the engineers estimated it actually cost to build is the key measure of messing expenditures" – i.e., the measure of corruption.

88 Jamieson (1996).

89 Mendelberg (1997). See also Mendelberg (2001).

90 Additional issues pertaining to internal and external validity are discussed in a subsequent study by Huber and Lapinski (2006). See also the colloquy between Huber/Lapinski and Mendelberg in *Perspectives on Politics* 6.1 (March 2008) and Hutchings and Jardina (2009).

91 Beckwith and Cowell-Meyers (2007); Mansbridge (1999); Paxton and Hughes (2007: ch. 7), Reingold (2008).

92 Dollar, Fisman, and Gatti (2001).

93 Chattapadhyay and Duflo (2004: 1410).

94 Chattapadhyay and Duflo (2004: 1411).

95 Paluck (2010).

96 For a compilation of experimental studies on turnout see the Get Out The Vote (GOTV) website maintained by Yale University's Institute for Social and Policy Studies (http://research.yale.edu/GOTV/).

97 Another approach to causal inference is through the mechanism (M) that connects X with Y. However, this "front-door" approach remains unusual. For further discussion see Glynn and Gerring (2013); Morgan and Winship (2007); Pearl (2009).

98 Posner (2004: 529–30).

99 Hamilton (1994).

100 Goldin and Rouse (2000).

101 England et al. (1988).

102 Those who are interested in the DD estimator will find a short discussion in Gerring (2012: 280–83).

103 Reiss (2007: 138).

104 For further discussion of the Card and Krueger (1994) study, see Neumark and Wascher (2000); Reiss (2007: 138–40).

105 Berk and Rauma (1983).

106 Acemoglu, Johnson, and Robinson (2001).

107 Murray (2006).

108 McArthur and Sachs (2001).

109 See Gerring (2017a).

110 A longer list of strategies is presented in Gerring (2017a).

111 Gerry Munck, personal communication (2015).

112 Ragin (2000: 35). See also Ragin (1987).

113 An alternative estimation strategy – the "frontdoor" approach – focuses on the path from X to Y through M, i.e., an indirect approach to causal inference. However, this approach remains quite rare in the social sciences and will not concern us here.

114 Hyde (2007: 48).

115 The preceding paragraphs draw on suggestions from Evan Lieberman (personal communication, 2009).

116 Diamond (1992).

117 Myrdal (1944).

118 The foregoing list builds on Johnson and Reynolds (2009: 187).

119 Most of these approaches are reviewed in Coppedge (2012).

120 www.unified-democracy-scores.org/

121 Quoted in King, Keohane, and Verba (1994: 129).

122 Snyder (2007).

123 Mills (1959: 202).

124 Kaplan (1964: 86), paraphrasing Charles Sanders Peirce.

125 Finlay and Gough (2003); Krieger (1991); Mills (1959); Snyder (2007).

126 Mills (1959: 196).

127 Gadamer (1975) refers to this as a fusion of horizons – us and theirs (the actors we are attempting to understand).

128 Gerring and Yesnowitz (2006); Shapiro (2005); Smith (2003).

129 Firebaugh (2008: ch. 1).

130 Collier (1995); Schmitter (1974).

131 Root-Bernstein (1989: 408).

132 Root-Bernstein (1989: 408).

133 Koestler (1964: 119–20).

134 Koestler (1964: 169).

135 Koestler (1964: 210).

136 Quoted in Robinson (1954: 6).

137 Gadamer (1975).

138 Quoted in Root-Bernstein (1989: 409).

139 Mills (1959: 196).

140 Mills (1959: 214).

141 Kuhn (1962/1970); Lakatos (1978); Laudan (1977).

142 Ragin (1992).

143 Gerring et al. (2011).

144 Linsley and Usinger (1959).

145 Root-Bernstein (1989: 413).

146 Typically, either surveys or unobtrusive measures are used to measure pre-treatment covariates and outcomes of interest in an experiment. Surveys may even be used as the experimental intervention (the split-sample survey or survey experiment). There is usually a post-experiment interview in which the researcher debriefs the subject and attempts to understand his or her subjective experience. In field experiments it is common to apply ethnographic methods to the community under study.

147 Groves and Fultz (1985); Hatchett and Schuman (1975).

148 Barath and Cannell (1976).

149 A particular problem with the agree/disagree Likert scale is that some respondents may be more inclined to agree than to disagree. A study conducted some years ago found this bias to be strongest among less educated respondents (Schuman and Presser 1981: 233; cited in Converse and Presser 1986: 39).

150 Peeters et al. (2010); Warner (1965). Experiments employed to measure the concept of trust are reviewed in Nannestad (2008).

151 Kane, Craig, and Wald (2004); Sniderman and Carmines (1997).

152 Sniderman et al. (1991).

153 Jennings and Niemi (1981); Levy and Brink (2005); Vaillant (2012).

154 Johnson (2002: 110)

155 Wade (1982). See also Smith (2007).

156 Gray et al. (2007: 164).

157 Conover et al. (1991).

158 Posner (2004).

159 Geertz (1973).

160 Pachirat (2011).

161 Frank et al. (1993).

162 Bertrand and Mullainathan (2004).

163 It should be noted that Fisman and Miguel's (2007) primary purpose in this study is to assess a causal question – whether norms or sanctions are more important in influencing corrupt behavior. However, the strength of that causal assessment rests largely on the strength of the measurement instrument.

164 Poole and Rosenthal (1991).

165 Dills and Miron (2004).

166 Bourgin and Henriot (1924).

167 Davenport and Ball (2002: 428).

168 Davenport and Ball (2002: 446).

169 Davenport and Ball (2002: 446).

170 Bowman, Lehoucq, and Mahoney (2005).

171 Forster (1927: ch. 5).

172 "The economist who wants to influence actual policy choices must in the final resort convince ordinary people, not only his confreres among the economic scientists," notes Gunnar Myrdal (1970: 450–51).

173 Williams and Bizup (2014: 186).

174 This statement is adapted from a document entitled "Use of Source Materials," Pomona College Department of Government, Claremont, CA.

175 See http://quoteinvestigator.com/2010/07/14/luck/.

176 There are additional "finger rules"; but, to our knowledge, they are infrequently employed. See www.utn.uu.se/best/aboutbest/fingerrules.html.

177 This also means if you convert Excel into another statistical package you will lose these notes.

178 E.g., Jackman (2006).

179 Our presentation builds on a recent review by Grimmer and Stewart (2013).

180 The ANES data and further information about it can be found at www.electionstudies.org. Note that weighting the data is required for a representative cross-section. In order to keep our examples simple, we generally present hypothetical data that is assumed to come from a simple random sample (see Chapter 20) and therefore does not require weighting to ensure generalizability. For a thorough discussion of survey weighting see Lohr (2009).

181 Jan Teorell, Nicholas Charron, Stefan Dahlberg, Stefan Holmberg, Bo Rothstein, Petrus Sundin, and Richard Svensson (2013). "The Quality of Government Dataset," version 20 Dec. 2013. University of Gothenburg: The Quality of Government Institute, www.qog .pol.gu.se.

182 The full LaLonde dataset and additional information on it is available at www.columbia.edu/~rd247/nswdata.html. See also Ho et al. (2007).

183 Refer to Chapter 4 for an introduction to the concept of samples and Chapter 20 for the statistical implications of sampling.

184 Respondents can also offer alternative responses from the major three, which we consider to be missing values in Table 18.1 for presentation purposes.

185 Refer to Chapter 3 for a discussion of categorical scales and Chapter 14 for a general introduction to levels of measurement.

186 In addition, a number of tests beyond the scope of this book avail themselves to test normality, including the Shapiro/Wilk and Pearson chi-squared tests.

187 The Resources section in this chapter provides a number of works on nonparametric models.

188 While Legendre (1805) and Gauss (1809) developed the method of least squares in the early nineteenth century it was not until the end of the century that Pearson (1895) introduced the correlation coefficient based on related work from Galton (1877). Of course, the application of ordinary least squares to statistics is primarily owed to later work in the 1920s by Fisher.

189 Though the topic is beyond this text, we could also test the null hypothesis of no slope – i.e., a flat line – using an F-statistic, as is common in analysis of variance.

190 For a more detailed and still non-technical explanation of the situations in which these violation assumptions occur see Kennedy (2003).

191 The social sciences frequently model state turnout percentages with ordinary least squares regression. However, there are some reasons to be careful when modeling a percentage or proportion dependent variable with ordinary least squares. Foremost, the regression models can provide nonsensical predictions below 0 and above 100. Second, the shape of

the relationship may be sigmoidal when there are extreme values, thus not meeting the linear assumption. In this particular hypothetical example our dependent variable values all fall near the center of the distribution (between 40% and 70%), thus we can truly model a linear relationship and we are unlikely to get predicted values much beyond 0 or 100. An alternative and appropriate though more complicated approach in this case would be to model the percentage as a censored continous variable with a tobit model (Long 1997).

192 Readers desiring an introduction to these other methods should consult the relevant pieces listed in the Resources section at the end of this chapter.

193 Our approach and notation here follows Morgan and Winship (2007: 137).

194 See Stuart (2010) for an excellent introduction to each stage of the matching process.

195 Our treatment here follows Gelman and Hill (2007: ch. 10).

196 When matching with replacement, weights should be used in the analysis in proportion to the frequency of times the control was used for each match.

References

Acemoglu, Daron, Simon Johnson, and James A. Robinson. 2001. "Colonial Origins of Comparative Development: An Empirical Investigation." *American Economic Review* 91.5: 1369–1401.

Acemoglu, Daron, Simon Johnson, James A. Robinson, and Pierre Yared. 2008. "Income and Democracy." *American Economic Review* 98: 808–42.

Acemoglu, Daron and James A. Robinson. 2012. *Why Nations Fail: Origins of Power, Poverty and Prosperity*. New York: Crown Publishers.

Alesina, Alberto, Paola Giuliano, and Nathan Nunn. 2013. "On the Origins of Gender Roles: Women and the Plough." *Quarterly Journal of Economics* 128.2: 469–530.

Allison, Paul D. 2002. *Missing Data*. Thousand Oaks, CA: Sage.

Almond, Gabriel A. 1956. "Comparative Political Systems." *Journal of Politics* 18: 391–409.

Almond, Gabriel A. and Sidney Verba. 1963/1989. *The Civic Culture: Political Attitudes and Democracy in Five Nations*. Newbury Park, CA: Sage.

Alvarez, Mike, José Antonio Cheibub, Fernando Limongi, and Adam Przeworski. 1996. "Classifying Political Regimes." *Studies in Comparative International Development* 31.2: 3–36.

Barath, Arpad and Charles F. Cannell. 1976. "Effect of Interviewer's Voice Intonation." *Public Opinion Quarterly* 40.3: 370–73.

Barro, Robert J. 1999. "Determinants of Democracy." *Journal of Political Economy* 107.6: 158–83.

Beard, Charles. 1913. *An Economic Interpretation of the Constitution of the United States*. New York: Free Press.

Becker, Gary S. 1976. *The Economic Approach to Human Behavior*. University of Chicago Press.

Beckwith, Karen and Kimberly Cowell-Meyers. 2007. "Sheer Numbers: Critical Representation Thresholds and Women's Political Representation." *Perspectives on Politics* 5.3: 553–65.

Belsey, David A., Edwin Kuh, and Roy E. Welsch. 2004. *Regression Diagnostics: Identifying Influential Data and Sources of Collinearity*. New York: John Wiley.

Bentley, Arthur. 1908/1967. *The Process of Government*. Cambridge, MA: Harvard University Press.

Berk, Richard A. and David Rauma. 1983. "Capitalizing on Nonrandom Assignment to Treatments: A Regression-Discontinuity Evaluation of a Crime-Control Program." *Journal of the American Statistical Association* 78.381: 21–27.

Berman, Sheri. 1997. "Civil Society and the Collapse of the Weimar Republic." *World Politics* 49.3: 401–29.

Bertrand, Marianne and Sendhil Mullainathan. 2004. "Are Emily and

Greg More Employable Than Lakisha and Jamal? A Field Experiment on Labor Market Discrimination." *American Economic Review* 94.4: 991–1013.

Best, Amy L. 2000. *Prom Night: Youth, Schools, and Popular Culture.* New York: Routledge.

Boix, Carles, Michael Miller, and Sebastian Rosato. 2013. "A Complete Dataset of Political Regimes, 1800–2007." *Comparative Political Studies* 46: 1523–54.

Boix, Carles and Susan C. Stokes. 2003. "Endogenous Democratization." *World Politics* 55.4: 517–49.

Bourgin, G. and G. Henriot. 1924. *Procès-Verbaux de La Commune de 1871: Édition Critique.* Paris: E. Leroux.

Bowman, Kirk, Fabrice Lehoucq, and James Mahoney. 2005. "Measuring Political Democracy: Case Expertise, Data Adequacy, and Central America." *Comparative Political Studies* 38.8: 939–70.

Brady, Henry E. and David Collier (eds.). 2004. *Rethinking Social Inquiry: Diverse Tools, Shared Standards.* Lanham, MD: Rowman & Littlefield.

Braumoeller, Bear F. 2003. "Causal Complexity and the Study of Politics." *Political Analysis* 11.3: 209–33.

Brown, Michael E., Sean M. Lynn-Jones, and Steven E. Miller (eds.). 1996. *Debating the Democratic Peace.* Cambridge, MA: MIT Press.

Browne, Angela. 1987. *When Battered Women Kill.* New York: Free Press.

Buchbinder, Susan and Eric Vittinghoff. 1999. "HIV-Infected Long-Term Nonprogressors: Epidemiology, Mechanisms of Delayed Progression, and Clinical and Research Implications." *Microbes and Infection* 1.13: 1113–20.

Budge, Ian. 2000. "Expert Judgments of Party Policy Positions: Uses and Limitations in Political Research." *European Journal of Political Research* 37.1: 103–13.

Burger, Thomas. 1976. *Max Weber's Theory of Concept Formation: History, Laws, and Ideal Types.* Durham, NC: Duke University Press.

Carbone, Giovanni. 2009. "The Consequences of Democratization." *Journal of Democracy* 20.2: 123–37.

Card, David and Alan B. Krueger. 1994. "Minimum Wages and Employment: A Case Study of the Fast-Food Industry in New Jersey and Pennsylvania." *American Economic Review* 84.4: 772–93.

Ceaser, James W., Glen E. Thurow, Jeffrey Tulis, and Joseph M. Bessette. 1981. "The Rise of the Rhetorical Presidency." *Presidential Studies Quarterly* 11.2: 158–71.

Chattopadhyay, Raghabendra and Esther Duflo. 2004. "Women as Policy Makers: Evidence from a Randomized Policy Experiment in India." *Econometrica* 72.5: 1409–43.

Cheibub, José Antonio, Jennifer Gandhi, and James Raymond Vreeland. 2010. "Democracy and Dictatorship Revisited." *Public Choice* 143.1–2: 67–101.

Cochran, Thomas C. 1948. "The 'Presidential Synthesis' in American History." *American Historical Review* 53.4: 748–59.

Collier, David. 1995. "Trajectory of a Concept: 'Corporatism' in the Study of Latin American Politics," in Peter Smith (ed.), *Latin America in Comparative Perspective.* Boulder, CO: Westview, 135–62.

Collier, David and James E. Mahon, Jr. 1993. "Conceptual 'Stretching' Revisited: Adapting Categories in Comparative Analysis." *American Political Science Review* 87.4: 845–55.

Collier, David and James Mahoney. 1996. "Insights and Pitfalls: Selection Bias in Qualitative Research." *World Politics* 49.1: 56–91.

Colomer, Josep M. 1991. "Transitions by Agreement: Modeling the Spanish Way." *American Political Science Review* 85: 1283–1302.

Conover, Pamela Johnston, Ivor M. Crewe, and Donald D. Searing. 1991. "The Nature of Citizenship in the United States and Great Britain: Empirical Comments on Theoretical Themes." *Journal of Politics* 53.3: 800–32.

Converse, Jean M. and Stanley Presser. 1986. *Survey Questions: Handcrafting the Standardized Questionnaire*. Thousand Oaks, CA: Sage.

Coppedge, Michael. 2012. *Approaching Democracy: Research Methods in Comparative Politics*. Cambridge University Press.

Coppedge, Michael, Angel Alvarez, and Claudia Maldonado. 2008. "Two Persistent Dimensions of Democracy: Contestation and Inclusiveness." *Journal of Politics* 70.3: 632–47.

Coppedge, Michael and John Gerring. 2011. "Conceptualizing and Measuring Democracy: A New Approach." *Perspectives on Politics* 9.2: 247–67.

Coppedge, Michael, John Gerring, Staffan I. Lindberg, Jan Teorell, David Altman, Michael Bernhard, M. Steven Fish, Adam Glynn, Allen Hicken, Carl Henrik Knutsen, Kelly McMann, Daniel Pemstein, Megan Reif, Svend-Erik Skaaning, Jeffrey Staton, Eitan Tzelgov, and Yi-ting Wang. 2015. "Varieties of Democracy: Methodology v4." Varieties of Democracy (V-Dem) Project.

Dahl, Robert A. 1971. *Polyarchy: Participation and Opposition*. New Haven, CT: Yale University Press.

Darity, William A. and Patrick L. Mason. 1998. "Evidence on Discrimination in Employment: Codes of Color, Codes of Gender." *Journal of Economic Perspectives* 12.2: 63–90.

Davenport, Christian and Patrick Ball. 2002. "Views to a Kill: Exploring the Implications of Source Selection in the Case of Guatemalan State Terror, 1977–1995." *Journal of Conflict Resolution* 46.3: 427–50.

David, Paul. 1985. "Clio and the Economics of QWERTY." *American Economic Review* 75: 332–37.

Dehejia, Rajeev H. and Sadek Wahba. 1999. "Causal Effects in Non-Experimental Studies: Reevaluating the Evaluation of Training Programs." *Journal of the American Statistical Association* 94.448: 1053–62.

Derthick, Martha. 1979. *Policymaking for Social Security*. Washington, DC: Brookings Institution Press.

Deyo, Frederic (ed.). 1987. *The Political Economy of the New Asian Industrialism*. Ithaca, NY: Cornell University Press.

Diamond, Jared. 1992. *Guns, Germs, and Steel*. New York: W. W. Norton.

Dills, Angela K. and Jeffrey A. Miron. 2004. "Alcohol Prohibition and Cirrhosis." *American Law and Economics Review* 6.2: 285–318.

Dion, Douglas. 1998. "Evidence and Inference in the Comparative Case Study." *Comparative Politics* 30.2: 127–45.

Dollar, David, Raymond Fisman, and Roberta Gatti. 2001. "Are Women Really the 'Fairer' Sex? Corruption and Women in Government." *Journal of Economic Behavior & Organization* 46.4: 423–29.

Doorenspleet, Renske. 2000. "Reassessing the Three Waves of Democratization." *World Politics* 52.3: 384–406.

Eichengreen, Barry. 1992. *Golden Fetters: The Gold Standard and the Great Depression, 1919–1939.* Oxford University Press.

Elman, Colin. 2003. "Lessons from Lakatos," in Colin Elman and Miriam Fendius Elman (eds.), *Progress in International Relations Theory: Appraising the Field.* Cambridge, MA: MIT Press.

2005. "Explanatory Typologies in Qualitative Studies of International Politics." *International Organization* 59.2: 293–326.

England, Paula, George Farkas, Barbara Stanek Kilbourne, and Thomas Dou. 1988. "Explaining Occupational Sex Segregation and Wages: Findings from a Model with Fixed Effects." *American Sociological Review* 53.4: 544–58.

Epstein, David L., Robert Bates, Jack Goldstone, Ida Kristensen, and Sharyn O'Halloran. 2006. "Democratic Transitions." *American Journal of Political Science* 50.3: 551–69.

Ertman, Thomas. 1997. *Birth of the Leviathan: Building States and Regimes in Medieval and Early Modern Europe.* Cambridge University Press.

Esping-Andersen, Gosta. 1990. *Three Worlds of Welfare Capitalism.* Princeton University Press.

Fenno, Richard F., Jr. 1978. *Home Style: House Members in Their Districts.* Boston, MA: Little, Brown.

1986. "Observation, Context, and Sequence in the Study of Politics." *American Political Science Review* 80.1: 3–15.

1990. *Watching Politicians: Essays on Participant Observation.* Berkeley: IGS Press.

Ferwerda, Jeremy and Nicholas Miller. 2014. "Political Devolution and Resistance to Foreign Rule: A Natural Experiment." *American Political Science Review* 108.3: 642–60.

Finer, Samuel E. 1997. *The History of Government.* Cambridge University Press.

Finlay, Linda and Brendan Gough (eds.). 2003. *Reflexivity: A Practical Guide for Researchers in Health and Social Sciences.* Oxford: Blackwell.

Firebaugh, Glenn. 2008. *Seven Rules for Social Research.* Cambridge, MA: Harvard University Press.

Fisman, Raymond and Edward Miguel. 2007. "Corruption, Norms, and Legal Enforcement: Evidence from Diplomatic Parking Tickets." *Journal of Political Economy* 115.6: 1020–48.

Forster, E. M. 1927. *Aspects of the Novel.* New York: Harcourt, Brace & World.

Frank, Robert, Thomas Gilovich, and Dennis Regan. 1993. "Does Studying Economics Inhibit Cooperation?" *Journal of Economic Perspectives* 7.2: 159–71.

Freedom House. 2007. "Methodology." *Freedom in the World 2007.* www.freedomhouse.org/template.cfm?page=351&ana_page=333&year=2007.

Friedman, Milton and Anna J. Schwartz. 1963. *A Monetary History of the United States, 1867–1960.* Princeton University Press.

Gadamer, Hans-Georg. 1975. *Truth and Method.* New York: Seabury Press.

Geddes, Barbara. 1990. "How the Cases You Choose Affect the Answers You Get: Selection Bias in Comparative Politics," in James A. Stimson (ed.), *Political Analysis, Vol. 2.* Ann Arbor, MI: University of Michigan Press, 131–50.

2003. *Paradigms and Sand Castles: Theory Building and Research Design in Comparative Politics.* Ann Arbor, MI: University of Michigan Press.

Geertz, Clifford. 1973. *The Interpretation of Cultures*. New York: Basic Books.
   1980. *Negara: The Theatre State in Bali*. Princeton University Press.

Gelman, Andrew and Jennifer Hill. 2007. *Data Analysis Using Regression and Multilevel/Hierarchical Models*. Cambridge University Press.

George, Alexander L. and Andrew Bennett. 2005. *Case Studies and Theory Development*. Cambridge, MA: MIT Press.

George, Alexander L. and Richard Smoke. 1974. *Deterrence in American Foreign Policy: Theory and Practice*. New York: Columbia University Press.

Gerring, John. 1998. *Party Ideologies in America, 1828–1996*. Cambridge University Press.
   2007. *Case Study Research: Principles and Practices*. Cambridge University Press.
   2012. *Social Science Methodology: A Unified Framework*, 2nd edn. Cambridge University Press.
   2017a. *Case Study Research: Principles and Practices*, 2nd edn. Cambridge University Press.
   2017b. "Qualitative Methods." *Annual Review of Political Science* 20 (May/June).

Gerring, John and Lee Cojocaru. 2016. "Case-Selection: A Diversity of Goals and Methods." *Sociological Methods and Research* (forthcoming).

Gerring, John and Strom C. Thacker. 2004. "Political Institutions and Corruption: The Role of Unitarism and Parliamentarism." *British Journal of Political Science* 34.2: 295–330.

Gerring, John and Joshua Yesnowitz. 2006. "A Normative Turn in Political Science?" *Polity* 38.1: 101–33.

Gerring, John, Daniel Ziblatt, Johan Van Gorp, and Julián Arévalo. 2011. "An Institutional Theory of Direct and Indirect Rule." *World Politics* 63.3: 377–433.

Gillespie, Richard. 1991. *Manufacturing Knowledge: A History of the Hawthorne Experiments*. Cambridge University Press.

Glynn, Adam and John Gerring. 2013. "Strategies of Research Design with Confounding: A Graphical Description." Unpublished Manuscript, Department of Political Science, Emory University.

Goertz, Gary. 2006. *Social Science Concepts*. Princeton University Press.

Goertz, Gary and Harvey Starr (eds.). 2003. *Necessary Conditions: Theory, Methodology, and Applications*. Lanham, MD: Rowman & Littlefield.

Goggin, Malcolm L. 1986. "The 'Too Few Cases/Too Many Variables' Problem in Implementation Research." *Western Political Quarterly* 39.2: 328–47.

Goldberg, Ellis, Erik Wibbels, and Eric Mvukiyehe. 2008. "Lessons from Strange Cases: Democracy, Development, and the Resource Curse in the U.S. States." *Comparative Political Studies* 41: 477–514.

Goldin, Claudia and Cecilia Rouse. 2000. "Orchestrating Impartiality: The Impact of 'Blind' Auditions on Female Musicians." *American Economic Review* 90.4: 715–41.

Goldstone, Jack A., Robert H. Bates, David L. Epstein, Ted Robert Gurr, Michael B. Lustik, Monty G. Marshall, Jay Ulfelder, and Mark Woodward. 2010. "A Global Model for Forecasting Political Instability." *American Journal of Political Science* 54.1: 190–208.

Granka, Laura. 2013. "Using Online Search Traffic to Predict US Presidential Elections." *PS: Political Science & Politics* 46.2: 271–79.

Gray, Paul S., John B. Williamson, David A. Karp, and John R. Dalphin. 2007. *The Research Imagination: An Introduction to Qualitative and Quantitative Methods.* Cambridge University Press.

Griffin, Deborah H. 2002. "Measuring Survey Nonresponse by Race and Ethnicity." Washington, DC: United States Bureau of the Census.

Grimmer, Justin and Brandon M. Stewart. 2013. "Text as Data: The Promise and Pitfalls of Automatic Content Analysis Methods for Political Texts." *Political Analysis* 21.3: 267–97.

Groves, Robert M. and Nancy H. Fultz. 1985. "Gender Effects Among Telephone Interviewers in a Survey of Economic Attitudes." *Sociological Methods & Research* 14.1: 31–52.

Hamilton, James D. 1994. *Time Series Analysis.* Princeton University Press.

Harris, Marvin. 1974. *Cows, Pigs, Wars & Witches: The Riddles of Culture.* New York: Random House.

Hartz, Louis. 1955. *The Liberal Tradition in America.* New York: Harcourt, Brace & World.

1964. *The Founding of New Societies: Studies in the History of the United States, Latin America, South Africa, Canada, and Australia.* New York: Harcourt, Brace & World.

Hatchett, Shirley and Howard Schuman. 1975. "White Respondents and Race-of-Interviewer Effects." *Public Opinion Quarterly* 39.4: 523–28.

Haynes, Barton F., Giuseppe Pantaleo, and Anthony S. Fauci. 1996. "Toward an Understanding of the Correlates of Protective Immunity to HIV Infection." *Science* 271.5247: 324–28.

Heckman, James J. and Peter Siegelman. 1993. "The Urban Institute Audit Studies: Their Methods," in Michael Fix and Raymond Struyk (eds.), *Clear and Convincing Evidence: Measurement of Discrimination in America.* Washington, DC: Brookings Institution Press, 187–258.

Hirschman, Albert O. 1970. *Exit, Voice, and Loyalty: Responses to Decline in Firms, Organizations, and States.* Cambridge, MA: Harvard University Press.

Ho, Daniel E., Kosuke Imai, Gary King, and Elizabeth A. Stuart. 2007. "Matching as Nonparametric Preprocessing for Reducing Model Dependence in Parametric Causal Inference." *Political Analysis* 15.3: 199–236.

Hogan, H. 1993. "The 1990 Post Enumeration Survey: Operations and Results." *Journal of the American Statistical Association* 88: 1047–60.

Holland, Paul W. 1986. "Statistics and Causal Inference." *Journal of the American Statistical Association* 81.396: 945–60.

Howson, Colin and Peter Urbach. 1989. *Scientific Reasoning: The Bayesian Approach.* La Salle, IL: Open Court.

Hsieh, Chang-Tai and Christina D. Romer. 2001. "Was the Federal Reserve Fettered? Devaluation Expectations in the 1932 Monetary Expansion." National Bureau of Economic Research Working Paper. www.nber.org/papers/w8113.

Huber, Gregory A. and John S. Lapinski. 2006. "The 'Race Card' Revisited: Assessing Racial Priming in Policy Contests." *American Journal of Political Science* 50.2: 421–40.

2008. "Testing the Implicit–Explicit Model of Racialized Political Communication." *Perspectives on Politics* 6.1: 125–34.

Hume, David. 1888. *Treatise of Human Nature.* Oxford University Press.

Humphreys, Macartan. 2005. "Natural Resources, Conflict, and Conflict Resolution: Uncovering the

Mechanisms." *Journal of Conflict Resolution* 49.4: 508–37.

Huntington, Samuel P. 1991. *The Third Wave: Democratization in the Late Twentieth Century*. Norman, OK: University of Oklahoma Press.

Hutchings, Vincent L. and Ashley E. Jardina. 2009. "Experiments on Racial Priming in Political Campaigns." *Annual Review of Political Science* 12: 397–402.

Hyde, Susan D. 2007. "The Observer Effect in International Politics: Evidence from a Natural Experiment." *World Politics* 60.1: 37–63.

Jackman, Robert W. 1985. "Cross-National Statistical Research and the Study of Comparative Politics." *American Journal of Political Science* 29.1: 161–82.

Jackman, Simon. 2006. "Data from Web into R." *The Political Methodologist* 14.2: 11–16.

Jackson, Matthew O. 2010. *Social and Economic Networks*. Princeton University Press.

Jamieson, Kathleen Hall. 1996. *Packaging the Presidency: A History and Criticism of Presidential Campaign Advertising*, 3rd edn. Oxford University Press.

Jenicek, Milos. 2001. *Clinical Case Reporting in Evidence-Based Medicine*. Oxford University Press.

Jennings, M. Kent and Richard G. Niemi. 1981. *Generations and Politics: A Panel Study of Young Adults and Their Parents*. Princeton University Press.

Johnson, Janet Buttolph and H. T. Reynolds. 2009. *Political Science Research Methods*, 6th edn. Washington, DC: CQ Press.

Johnson, John M. 2002. "In-Depth Interviewing," in Jaber F. Gubrium and James E. Holstein (eds.), *The Handbook of Interview Research*. Thousand Oaks, CA: Sage, 103–20.

Kane, James G., Stephen C. Craig, and Kenneth D. Wald. 2004. "Religion and Presidential Politics in Florida: A List Experiment." *Social Science Quarterly* 85.2: 281–93.

Kaplan, Abraham. 1964. *The Conduct of Inquiry: Methodology for Behavioral Science*. San Francisco, CA: Chandler Publishing.

Kaufman, Herbert. 1960. *The Forest Ranger: A Study in Administrative Behavior*. Baltimore, MD: Johns Hopkins University Press.

Keith, Bruce E., David B. Magleby, Candice J. Nelson, Elizabeth Orr, Mark C. Westlye, and Raymond E. Wolfinger. 1992. *The Myth of the Independent Voter*. Berkeley, CA: University of California Press.

Kennedy, Peter. 2003. *A Guide to Econometrics*. Cambridge, MA: MIT Press.

Kenney, Genevieve M. and Douglas A. Wissoker. 1994. "An Analysis of the Correlates of Discrimination Facing Young Hispanic Job-Seekers." *American Economic Review* 84.3: 674–83.

Khong, Yuen Foong. 1992. *Analogies at War: Korea, Munich, Dien Bien Phu, and the Vietnam Decisions of 1965*. Princeton University Press.

King, Gary, Robert O. Keohane, and Sidney Verba. 1994. *Designing Social Inquiry: Scientific Inference in Qualitative Research*. Princeton University Press.

Kirschenman, Kathryn M. and Joleen Neckerman. 1991. "'We'd Love to Hire Them, But . . .': The Meaning of Race for Employers," in Christopher Jencks and Paul E. Peterson (eds.), *The Urban Underclass*. Washington, DC: Brookings Institution Press, 203–34.

Knack, Stephen and Philip Keefer. 1997. "Does Social Capital Have an Economic Payoff?" *Quarterly Journal of Economics* 112: 1251–88.

Kocher, Matthew and Nuno Monteiro. 2015. "What's in a Line? Natural Experiments and the Line of Demarcation in WWII Occupied France." Unpublished manuscript, Department of Political Science, Yale University.

Koestler, Arthur. 1964. *The Act of Creation*. New York: Macmillan.

Krieger, Susan. 1991. *Social Science and the Self: Personal Essays on an Art Form*. New Brunswick, NJ: Rutgers University Press.

Kuhn, Thomas S. 1962/1970. *The Structure of Scientific Revolutions*. University of Chicago Press.

Kurzman, Charles. 1998. "Waves of Democratization." *Studies in Comparative Development* 33.1: 42–64.

Kuznets, Simon. 1955. "Economic Growth and Income Inequality." *American Economic Review* 45: 1–28.

Lakatos, Imre. 1978. *The Methodology of Scientific Research Programmes*. Cambridge University Press.

LaLonde, Robert J. 1986. "Evaluating the Econometric Evaluations of Training Programs with Experimental Data." *American Economic Review* 76.4: 604–20.

Latzer, Barry. 2016. *The Rise and Fall of Violent Crime in America*. New York: Encounter Books.

Laudan, Larry. 1977. *Progress and Its Problems: Toward a Theory of Scientific Growth*. Berkeley, CA: University of California Press.

Laver, Michael, Kenneth Benoit, and John Garry. 2003. "Extracting Policy Positions from Political Texts Using Words as Data." *American Political Science Review* 97.2: 311–31.

Lazarsfeld, Paul F. and Allen H. Barton. 1951. "Qualitative Measurement in the Social Sciences: Classification, Typologies, and Indices," in Daniel Lerner and Harold D. Lasswell (eds.), *The Policy Sciences*. Stanford University Press, 155–92.

Lehnert, Matthias. 2007. "Typologies in Social Inquiry," in Thomas Gschwend and Frank Schimmelfennig (eds.), *Research Design in Political Science: How to Practice What They Preach*. Basingstoke: Palgrave Macmillan, 62–82.

Leidner, Robin. 1993. *Fast Food, Fast Talk: Service Work and the Routinization of Everyday Life*. Berkeley, CA: University of California Press.

Levitsky, Steven and Lucan A. Way. 2002. "The Rise of Competitive Authoritarianism." *Journal of Democracy* 13.2: 51–65.

Levy, Daniel and Susan Brink. 2005. *A Change of Heart: How the Framingham Heart Study Helped Unravel the Mysteries of Cardiovascular Disease*. New York: Knopf.

Levy, Jack S. 2002. "Qualitative Methods in International Relations," in Frank P. Harvey and Michael Brecher (eds.), *Evaluating Methodology in International Studies*. Ann Arbor, MI: University of Michigan Press, 432–54.

Lieberson, Stanley and Joel Horwich. 2008. "Implication Analysis: A Pragmatic Proposal for Linking Theory and Data in the Social Sciences." *Sociological Methodology* 38.1: 1–50.

Lijphart, Arend. 1968. "Typologies of Democratic Systems." *Comparative Political Studies* 1.1: 3–44.

Linsley, E. G. and R. L. Usinger. 1959. "Linnaeus and the Development of the International Code of Zoological Nomenclature." *Systematic Biology* 8.1: 39–47.

Linz, Juan J. 1978. "From Great Hopes to Civil War: The Breakdown of Democracy in Spain," in Juan J. Linz and Alfred Stepan, *The Breakdown of Democratic Regimes: Europe*. Baltimore, MD: Johns Hopkins University Press, 142–216.

Linz, Juan J. and Alfred Stepan (eds.). 1978. *The Breakdown of Democratic Regimes: Europe*. Baltimore, MD: Johns Hopkins University Press.

1996. *Problems of Democratic Transition and Consolidation: Southern Europe, South America, and Post-Communist Europe*. Baltimore, MD: Johns Hopkins University Press.

Lipset, Seymour Martin. 1959. "Some Social Requisites of Democracy: Economic Development and Political Legitimacy." *American Political Science Review* 53.1: 69–105.

1960/1963. *Political Man: The Social Bases of Politics*. Garden City, NY: Anchor Books.

Lipset, Seymour Martin, Martin A. Trow, and James S. Coleman. 1956. *Union Democracy: The Internal Politics of the International Typographical Union*. New York: Free Press.

Lohr, Sharon. 2009. *Sampling: Design and Analysis*. Boston, MA: Cengage Learning.

Long, J. Scott. 1997. *Regression Models for Categorical and Limited Dependent Variables*. Thousand Oaks, CA: Sage.

Lutfey, Karen and Jeremy Freese. 2005. "Toward Some Fundamentals of Fundamental Causality: Socioeconomic Status and Health in the Routine Clinic Visit for Diabetes." *American Journal of Sociology* 110.5: 1326–72.

Lynd, Robert Staughton and Helen Merrell Lynd. 1929/1956. *Middletown: A Study in American Culture*. New York: Harcourt, Brace & World.

Mansbridge, Jane. 1999. "Should Blacks Represent Blacks and Women Represent Women? A Contingent 'Yes.'" *Journal of Politics* 61.3: 628–57.

Mansfield, Edward D. and Jack Snyder. 2005. *Electing to Fight: Why Emerging Democracies Go To War*. Cambridge, MA: MIT Press.

Marshall, Monty G. and Keith Jaggers. 2007. *Polity IV Project: Political Regime Characteristics and Transitions, 1800–2006*. www.systemicpeace.org/inscr/p4manualv2006.pdf.

McArthur, John W. and Jeffrey D. Sachs. 2001. "Institutions and Geography: Comment on Acemoglu, Johnson and Robinson (2000)." National Bureau of Economic Research Working Paper. www.nber.org/papers/w8114.

Mellon, Jonathan. 2013. "Where and When Can We Use Google Trends to Measure Issue Salience?" *PS: Political Science & Politics* 46.2: 280–90.

Mendelberg, Tali. 1997. "Executing Hortons: Racial Crime in the 1988 Presidential Campaign." *Public Opinion Quarterly* 61.1: 134–57.

2001. *The Race Card: Campaign Strategy, Implicit Messages, and the Norm of Equality*. Princeton University Press.

2008a. "Racial Priming Revived." *Perspectives on Politics* 6.1: 109–23.

2008b. "Racial Priming: Issues in Research Design and Interpretation." *Perspectives on Politics* 6.1: 135–40.

Merritt, Richard L. 1966. "The Emergence of American Nationalism: A Quantitative Approach." *American Quarterly* 11: 319–35.

Mills, C. Wright. 1959. *The Sociological Imagination*. Oxford University Press.

Miron, Jeffrey A. 1994. "Empirical Methodology in Macroeconomics Explaining the Success of Friedman and Schwartz's 'A Monetary History of the

United States, 1867–1960.'" *Journal of Monetary Economics* 34.1: 17–25.

Monroe, Kristen Renwick. 1996. *The Heart of Altruism: Perceptions of a Common Humanity*. Princeton University Press.

Morgan, Stephen L. and Christopher Winship. 2007. *Counterfactuals and Causal Inference: Methods and Principles for Social Research*. Cambridge University Press.

Munck, Gerardo L. 2004. "Tools for Qualitative Research," in Henry E. Brady and David Collier (eds.), *Rethinking Social Inquiry: Diverse Tools, Shared Standards*. Lanham, MD: Rowman & Littlefield, 105–21.

2009. *Measuring Democracy: A Bridge between Scholarship and Politics*. Baltimore, MD: Johns Hopkins University Press.

Murray, Michael P. 2006. "Avoiding Invalid Instruments and Coping with Weak Instruments." *Journal of Economic Perspectives* 20.4: 111–32.

Myrdal, Gunnar. 1944. *An American Dilemma: The Negro Problem and Modern Democracy*. New York: Harper & Brothers.

1970. *The Challenge of World Poverty: A World Anti-Poverty Program in Outline*. New York: Pantheon.

Nannestad, Peter. 2008. "What Have We Learned About Generalized Trust, If Anything?" *Annual Review of Political Science* 11: 413–36.

Neumark, David, Roy J. Bank, and Kyle D. Van Nort. 1996. "Sex Discrimination in Restaurant Hiring: An Audit Study." *Quarterly Journal of Economics* 111.3: 915–41.

Neumark, David and William Wascher. 2000. "Minimum Wages and Employment: A Case Study of the Fast-Food Industry in New Jersey and Pennsylvania:

Comment." *American Economic Review* 90.5: 1362–96.

Neyman, Jerzy and Karolina Iwaszkiewicz. 1935. "Statistical Problems in Agricultural Experimentation." *Supplement to the Journal of the Royal Statistical Society* 2.2: 107–80.

O'Donnell, Guillermo and Philippe Schmitter. 1986. *Transitions from Authoritarian Rule: Tentative Conclusions about Uncertain Democracies*. Baltimore, MD: Johns Hopkins University Press.

Olken, Benjamin A. 2007. "Monitoring Corruption: Evidence from a Field Experiment in Indonesia." *Journal of Political Economy* 115.2: 200–49.

Pachirat, Timothy. 2011. *Every Twelve Seconds: Industrialized Slaughter and the Politics of Sight*. New Haven, CT: Yale University Press.

Pager, Devah. 2007. "The Use of Field Experiments for Studies of Employment Discrimination: Contributions, Critiques, and Directions for the Future." *Annals of the American Academy of Political and Social Science* 609.1: 104–33.

Paluck, Elizabeth Levy. 2010. "The Promising Integration of Qualitative Methods and Field Experiments." *Annals of the American Academy of Political and Social Science* 628.1: 59–71.

Patterson, Orlando. 1982. *Slavery and Social Death: A Comparative Study*. Cambridge, MA: Harvard University Press.

Paxton, Pamela. 1999. "Is Social Capital Declining in the United States? A Multiple Indicator Assessment." *American Journal of Sociology* 105.1: 88–127.

2000. "Women's Suffrage in the Measurement of Democracy: Problems of Operationalization." *Studies in Comparative International Development* 35.3: 92–111.

Paxton, Pamela and Melanie Hughes. 2007. *Women, Politics, and Power*. Thousand Oaks, CA: Pine Forge Press.

Pearl, Judea. 2000. *Causality: Models, Reasoning, and Inference*. Cambridge University Press.

2009. "Causal Inference in Statistics: An Overview." *Statistics Surveys* 3: 96–146.

Peeters, Carel F. W., Gerty J. L. M. Lensvelt-Mulders, and Karin Lasthuizen. 2010. "A Note on a Simple and Practical Randomized Response Framework for Eliciting Sensitive Dichotomous and Quantitative Information." *Sociological Methods & Research* 39.2: 283–96.

Pemstein, Daniel, Stephen A. Meserve, and James Melton. 2010. "Democratic Compromise: A Latent Variable Analysis of Ten Measures of Regime Type." *Political Analysis* 18.4: 426–49.

Poole, Keith T. and Howard Rosenthal. 1991. "Patterns of Congressional Voting." *American Journal of Political Science* 35.1: 228–78.

Popper, Karl. 1934/1968. *The Logic of Scientific Discovery*. New York: Harper & Row.

1963. *Conjectures and Refutations*. London: Routledge & Kegan Paul.

Posner, Daniel N. 2004. "The Political Salience of Cultural Difference: Why Chewas and Tumbukas are Allies in Zambia and Adversaries in Malawi." *American Political Science Review* 98.4: 529–46.

Pressman, Jeffrey L. and Aaron Wildavsky. 1973. *Implementation*. Berkeley, CA: University of California Press.

Przeworski, Adam and Fernando Limongi. 1997. "Modernization: Theories and Facts." *World Politics* 49: 155–83.

Putnam, Robert D. 1993. *Making Democracy Work: Civic Traditions in Modern Italy*. Princeton University Press.

2001. *Bowling Alone: The Collapse and Revival of American Community*. New York: Touchstone.

(ed.). 2004. *Democracies in Flux: The Evolution of Social Capital in Contemporary Society*. Oxford University Press.

Ragin, Charles C. 1987. *The Comparative Method: Moving beyond Qualitative and Quantitative Strategies*. Berkeley, CA: University of California Press.

1992. "'Casing' and the Process of Social Inquiry," in Charles C. Ragin and Howard S. Becker (eds.), *What Is a Case? Exploring the Foundations of Social Inquiry*. Cambridge University Press, 217–26.

2000. *Fuzzy-Set Social Science*. University of Chicago Press.

Reilly, Benjamin. 2000–2001. "Democracy, Ethnic Fragmentation, and Internal Conflict: Confused Theories, Faulty Data, and the 'Crucial Case' of Papua New Guinea." *International Security* 25.3: 162–85.

Reingold, Beth. 2008. "Women as Officeholders: Linking Descriptive and Substantive Representation," in Christina Wolbrecht, Karen Beckwith, and Lisa Baldez (eds.), *Political Women and American Democracy*. Cambridge University Press, 128–47.

Reiss, Julian. 2007. *Error in Economics: Towards a More Evidence-Based Methodology*. London: Routledge.

Reynolds, Andrew and Ben Reilly. 2005. *Electoral System Design: The New International IDEA Handbook*. Stockholm: International Institute for Democracy.

Robinson, Richard. 1954. *Definition*. Oxford: Clarendon Press.

Rogowski, Ronald. 1995. "The Role of Theory and Anomaly in Social-Scientific Inference." *American Political Science Review* 89.2: 467–70.

Root-Bernstein, Robert. 1989. *Discovering: Inventing and Solving Problems at the Frontiers of Scientific Knowledge.* Cambridge, MA: Harvard University Press.

Rosenbaum, Paul R. and Jeffrey H. Silber. 2001. "Matching and Thick Description in an Observational Study of Mortality after Surgery." *Biostatistics* 2: 217–32.

Ross, Michael L. 2001. "Does Oil Hinder Democracy?" *World Politics* 53.3: 325–61.

2014. "What Have We Learned about the Resource Curse?" Unpublished paper, Department of Political Science, UCLA.

Rubin, Donald B. 1974. "Estimating Causal Effects of Treatments in Randomized and Nonrandomized Studies." *Journal of Educational Psychology* 66.5: 688–701.

1975. "Bayesian Inference for Causality: The Importance of Randomization," in *Proceedings of the Social Statistics Section of the American Statistical Association*, 233–9.

1991. "Practical Implications of Modes of Statistical Inference for Causal Effects and the Critical Role of the Assignment Mechanism." *Biometrics* 47.4: 1213–34.

2001. "Using Propensity Scores to Help Design Observational Studies: Application to the Tobacco Litigation." *Health Services and Outcomes Research Methodology* 2.3–4: 169–88.

2008. "For Objective Causal Inference, Design Trumps Analysis." *Annals of Applied Statistics* 2.3: 808–40.

Sagan, Scott. 1995. *The Limits of Safety: Organizations, Accidents, and Nuclear Weapons.* Princeton University Press.

Sartori, Giovanni. 1970. "Concept Misformation in Comparative Politics." *American Political Science Review* 64.4: 1033–53.

1984. "Guidelines for Concept Analysis," in *Social Science Concepts: A Systematic Analysis.* Beverly Hills, CA: Sage, 15–48.

Schattschneider, E. E. 1960. *The Semi-Sovereign People.* New York: Holt, Rinehart, and Winston.

Scheper-Hughes, Nancy. 1992. *Death Without Weeping: The Violence of Everyday Life in Brazil.* Berkeley, CA: University of California Press.

Schmitter, Philippe C. 1974. "Still the Century of Corporatism?" *Review of Politics* 36.1: 85–131.

Schneider, Carsten Q. and Claudius Wagemann. 2012. *Set-Theoretic Methods for the Social Sciences: A Guide to Qualitative Comparative Analysis.* Cambridge University Press.

Schuman, Howard and Stanley Presser. 1981. *Questions and Answers in Attitude Surveys: Experiments on Question Form, Working, and Context.* New York: Academic Press.

Sekhon, Jasjeet. 2004. "Quality Meets Quantity: Case Studies, Conditional Probability and Counterfactuals." *Perspectives on Politics* 2.2: 281–93.

Sengupta, Somini. 2005. "Where Maoists Still Matter." *New York Times Magazine*, October 30, 1–7.

Shafer, Michael D. 1988. *Deadly Paradigms: The Failure of U.S. Counterinsurgency Policy.* Princeton University Press.

Shapiro, Ian. 2005. *The Flight from Reality in the Human Sciences.* Princeton University Press.

Skocpol, Theda. 1979. *States and Revolutions: A Comparative Analysis of France, Russia, and China.* Cambridge University Press.

Smith, Daniel Jordan. 2007. *A Culture of Corruption: Everyday Deception and Popular Discontent in Nigeria*. Princeton University Press.

Smith, Rogers M. 2003. "Reconnecting Political Theory to Empirical Inquiry, or a Return to the Cave?" in Edward D. Mansfield and Richard Sisson (eds.), *The Evolution of Political Knowledge: Theory and Inquiry in American Politics*. Columbus, OH: Ohio State University Press, 60–88.

Sniderman, Paul M. and Edward G. Carmines. 1997. *Reaching Beyond Race*. Cambridge, MA: Harvard University Press.

Sniderman, Paul M., Thomas Piazza, Philip E. Tetlock, and Ann Kendrick. 1991. "The New Racism." *American Journal of Political Science* 35.2: 423–47.

Snyder, Richard. 2007. "The Human Dimension of Comparative Research," in Gerardo L. Munck and Richard Snyder (eds.), *Passion, Craft and Method in Comparative Politics*. Baltimore, MD: Johns Hopkins University Press, 1–32.

Splawa-Neyman, Jerzy, D. M. Dabrowska, and T. P. Speed. 1990. "On the Application of Probability Theory to Agricultural Experiments. Essay on Principles. Section 9." *Statistical Science* 5.4: 465–72.

Stackhouse, H. F. and J. B. Treat. 2002. "Census 2000 Response and Return Rates: National and State by Form Type." DSSD Census 2000 Procedures and Operations Memorandum Series L-10, February 12.

Stuart, Elizabeth A. 2010. "Matching Methods for Causal Inference: A Review and a Look Forward." *Statistical Science* 25.1: 1–21.

Sundquist, James L. 1983. *Dynamics of the Party System: Alignment and Realignment of Political Parties in the United States*. Washington, DC: Brookings Institution Press.

Swank, Duane. 2002. *Global Capital, Political Institutions, and Policy Change in Developed Welfare States*. Cambridge University Press.

Tocqueville, Alexis de. 1945. *Democracy in America*. New York: Knopf.

Treier, Shawn and Simon Jackman. 2008. "Democracy as a Latent Variable." *American Journal of Political Science* 52.1: 201–17.

Truman, David B. 1951. *The Governmental Process*. New York: Knopf.

Tsai, Lily. 2007. *Accountability without Democracy: How Solidary Groups Provide Public Goods in Rural China*. Cambridge University Press.

Tsui, Kevin K. 2011. "More Oil, Less Democracy: Evidence from Worldwide Crude Oil Discoveries." *The Economic Journal* 121.551: 89–115.

Tversky, Amos and Itamar Gati. 1978. "Studies of Similarity," in Eleanor Lloyd and B. B. Lloyd (eds.), *Cognition and Categorization*. Hillsdale, NJ: Lawrence Erlbaum, 79–98.

UNODC. 2011. *2011 Global Study on Homicide: Trends, Context, Data*. New York: United Nations Office on Drugs and Crime.

Vaillant, George E. 2012. *Triumphs of Experience: The Men of the Harvard Grant Study*. Cambridge, MA: Harvard University Press.

Van Evera, Stephen. 1997. *Guide to Methods for Students of Political Science*. Ithaca, NY: Cornell University Press.

Vanhanen, Tatu. 2000. "A New Dataset for Measuring Democracy, 1810–1998." *Journal of Peace Research* 37: 251–65.

Verba, Sidney, Kay Lehman Schlozman, and Henry E. Brady. 1995. *Voice and*

Equality: Civic Voluntarism in American Life. Cambridge, MA: Harvard University Press.

Wade, Robert. 1982. "The System of Administrative and Political Corruption: Canal Irrigation in South India." *Journal of Development Studies* 18.3: 287–328.

Warner, Stanley L. 1965. "Randomized Response: A Survey Technique for Eliminating Evasive Answer Bias." *Journal of the American Statistical Association* 60.309: 63–69.

Weaver, R. Kent and Bert A. Rockman (eds.). 1993. *Do Institutions Matter? Government Capabilities in the United States and Abroad*. Washington, DC: Brookings Institution Press.

Weber, Max. 1905/1949. *The Methodology of the Social Sciences*. New York: Free Press.

1918/1958. "Politics as a Vocation," in *From Max Weber: Essays in Sociology*, ed. Hans Gerth and C. Wright Mills. Oxford University Press, 77–156.

Weyland, Kurt Gerhard. 1995. "Latin America's Four Political Models." *Journal of Democracy* 6.4: 125–39.

Williams, Joseph M. and Joseph Bizup. 2014. *Style: Lessons in Clarity and Grace*, 11th edn. New York: Pearson.

Wilson, James Q. 1992. *Political Organizations*. Princeton University Press.

Woodward, James. 2005. *Making Things Happen: A Theory of Causal Explanation*. Oxford University Press.

Woolcock, Michael. 1998. "Social Capital and Economic Development: Toward a Theoretical Synthesis and Policy Framework." *Theory and Society* 27.2: 151–208.

Yin, Robert K. 2004. *Case Study Anthology*. Thousand Oaks, CA: Sage.

Zelizer, Julian E. 2002. "Beyond the Presidential Synthesis: Reordering Political Time," in Jean-Christophe Agnew and Roy Rosenzweig (eds.), *A Companion to Post-1945 America*. Oxford: Blackwell, 345–70.

Zerubavel, Eviatar. 1996. "Lumping and Splitting: Notes on Social Classification." *Sociological Forum* 11.3: 421–33.

Author Index

Page numbers *in italics* are endnote references.

Subject Index

Page numbers in **bold** refer to definitions.

Subject Index